6/2000

SIXTH EDITION

Creative Management

in Recreation, Parks, and Leisure Services

Richard G. Kraus

Temple University, Philadelphia, Pennsylvania

Joseph E. Curtis

Boston   Burr Ridge, IL   Dubuque, IA   Madison, WI   New York   San Francisco   St. Louis
Bangkok   Bogotá   Caracas   Lisbon   London   Madrid
Mexico City   Milan   New Delhi   Seoul   Singapore   Sydney   Taipei   Toronto

McGraw-Hill Higher Education

A Division of The **McGraw-Hill** *Companies*

CREATIVE MANAGEMENT IN RECREATION, PARKS, AND LEISURE SERVICES, SIXTH EDITION

This book is printed on acid-free paper.

1 2 3 4 5 6 7 8 9 0 QPF/QPF 9 0 9 8 7 6 5 4 3 2 1 0 9

ISBN 0–07–230031–0

Vice president and editorial director: *Kevin T. Kane*
Executive editor: *Vicki Malinee*
Senior development editor: *Melissa Martin*
Senior marketing manage: *Pamela S. Cooper*
Senior project manage: *Kay J. Brimeyer*
Production supervisor: *Sandy Ludovissy*
Design manager: *Stuart D. Paterson*
Senior photo research coordinator: *Lori Hancock*
Supplement coordinator: *Stacy A. Patch*
Compositor: *GAC/Indianapolis*
Typeface: *10/12 Palatino*
Printer: *Quebecor Printing Book Group/Fairfield, PA*

Cover/interior designer: *Elise Lansdon*
Cover images: Polar bear—*Tony Stone Images*, ranger with family—*FPG International*, executive—*The Stock Market*

Library of Congress Cataloging-in-Publication Data

Kraus, Richard G.
    Creative management in recreation, parks, and leisure services /
Richard G. Kraus, Joseph E. Curtis. — 6th ed.
       p.   cm.
    Includes bibliographical references and indexes.
    ISBN 0–07–230031–0
      1. Recreation—Management. 2. Parks—Management. 3. Leisure industry—Management. 4. Recreation—United States—Management. 5. Recreation—Canada—Management. 6. Parks—United States—Management. 7. Parks —Canada—Management. 8. Leisure industry—United States—Management. 9. Leisure industry—Canada—Management. I. Curtis, Joseph E., 1922–   . II. Title.

GV181.5 .K62 2000
790' .06'9—dc21

99–047190
CIP

www.mhhe.com

About the Authors

Richard G. Kraus, M.A., Ed.D.

Dr. Kraus is primarily known as an educator, having taught at the University of Utah and Cortland College, New York, and headed recreation and leisure-service curricula at Teachers College, Columbia University, Lehman College of the City University of New York, and Temple University. He has written over 40 textbooks and monographs, including several widely used texts in recreation fundamentals, program planning and leadership, and therapeutic recreation. Dr. Kraus has served as a consultant to many agencies, including the Job Corps, the Office of Economic Opportunity, the YWCA, and numerous colleges and public agencies. He has done planning studies for the cities of Pittsburgh and Philadelphia and has carried out national studies on urban recreation and parks. Dr. Kraus has received the Distinguished Fellow Award of the Society of Parks and Recreation Educators, was selected the Jay B. Nash Scholar of the American Association for Leisure and Recreation, and was given the National Literary Award of the National Recreation and Park Association. Following his retirement from Temple University as professor and department chairperson, he continued to teach there as an adjunct faculty member and to write professionally.

Joseph E. Curtis, M.A.

During his 38 years of parks and recreation and leadership, Mr. Curtis headed major leisure-service departments in Boston, White Plains, New York, Oceanside, New York, and Baltimore County. Most recently, he was Commissioner of Human Services, including Parks and Recreation, for the City of New Rochelle, New York. He is the author of three texts and numerous articles. Mr. Curtis has served as president of the American Park and Recreation Society, as well as president of state societies in Massachusetts, New York, and Maryland. He has taught recreation management at Columbia University, New York University, Northeastern University, the University of New Hampshire, City University of New York, Massachusetts Institute of Technology, and Harvard University. He has received 65 awards and honors, including the Healthy America Fitness Award, and is a Distinguished Fellow of the American Park and Recreation Society. He has served as a special consultant to government departments, corporations, and a number of major American and Canadian cities. He was a member of the President's Council on Physical Fitness and Sports, and served on a number of committees of the American Academy for Park and Recreation Administration.

Brief Contents

Contents

8. ## Public and Community Relations: Growing Use of Partnerships　　237

Preface

This is the sixth edition of a management textbook that has been used in many college and university recreation, parks, and leisure-studies departments throughout the United States and Canada over the past three decades. Particularly in the 1990s, major changes have occurred both in the overall society and in the leisure-service field itself, which are reflected in this new text. Its purpose, therefore, is to provide a realistic and practical set of guidelines that will equip students for the challenges that will face them in the twenty-first century.

Once concerned almost exclusively with local public recreation and park agencies, today the leisure-service field embraces such other major systems as nonprofit youth-serving organizations, commercial recreation businesses, therapeutic recreation services, armed forces, campus programs, and other sponsors. Thousands of men and women enter such fields as sports management, travel and tourism, or fitness programming each year. To facilitate their career development and as a matter of professional awareness, students in this field should become fully aware of management practices in these areas of leisure-service specialization.

Similarly, for many years, most recreation and park agencies served chiefly white, middle-class families within a traditional model of service consisting primarily of sports, games, outdoor pursuits, and other hobbies or social programs. Today, both the United States and Canada have become increasingly multicultural—with varied racial and ethnic populations—constituting a "mosaic" society. The needs and interests of girls and women, persons with disabilities and the elderly, and those with nontraditional families or alternative lifestyles, all constitute an immensely varied audience for leisure services.

At the same time, recreation, parks, and leisure-service programs today embrace a much greater range of activities and services, including many designed to achieve important personal or community benefits, such as at-risk youth programs, environmental needs, substance abuse, or family-enrichment activities.

Fiscal cutbacks in the 1970s and 1980s led to the widespread acceptance of an entrepreneurial, marketing-based thrust in many public and nonprofit leisure-service organizations. Today, many recreation, parks, and leisure-service agencies rely on sophisticated fiscal strategies, including expanded fees and charges, partnership arrangements, target marketing, and similar methods to achieve a higher level of self-sufficiency and provide attractive programs and facilities.

At the same time, the traditional social-service role of many community recreation departments continues to represent a high priority for leisure-service managers. Increasingly, in an era in which many leisure-service pursuits—such as alcohol or drug abuse, obsessive gambling, or exploitative and commercialized sexual activity—represent serious threats to personal well-being, constructive recreation programming has become increasingly recognized as an important health-related service. Thus, in the late 1990s, benefits-based management strategies, which emphasize the need to achieve and document the positive outcomes of organized recreation service, became widely accepted.

OTHER IMPORTANT TRENDS

Throughout its history, the recreation and parks movement has been closely linked to conservation-minded causes. Today, many leisure-service organizations promote ecologically sound outdoor recreation programs, or work with citizens' groups in joint efforts to overcome past pollution or resist further environmental degradation.

In urban settings as well, recreation serves as a means of strengthening community-development programs, reviving decayed waterfronts or industrial areas, and making cities livable for residents and attracting visitors who help to build the economic base of cities.

Numerous other trends today influence the work of leisure-service managers. In today's "information age," electronic data processing through the use of computers, E-mail, fax machines, and the Internet provide both new technologies for the management of recreation agencies and new leisure opportunities for participants.

Synergetic partnerships among public, private, commercial, and other types of organizations have become a major force in the ongoing operation of many leisure-service agencies, yielding funding, volunteer workers, and a fuller base of community support for their programs.

Finally, many management thrusts that appeared initially in the business world or in government agencies, such as the emphasis on total quality programming and customer satisfaction, the use of benchmarking, or the current reliance on strategic planning and reengineering of organizations, have all had a profound effect on leisure-service managers.

CHANGES IN THIS TEXT

All of these trends have influenced the preparation of this new text, which has been heavily revised to meet the changing needs and career goals of tomorrow's leisure-service professionals. The book has been systematically updated, reflecting current issues and practices reported in research journals, professional publications, the popular press, and recent management textbooks. It contains hundreds of examples of current management practices, drawn from a wide variety of organizations of every type throughout the United States and Canada.

While it is not possible to list all such sources here, a number of the outstanding public recreation and park agencies that contributed materials include the following: in the United States, such cities or counties as San Mateo and Long Beach, California; Phoenix, Arizona; Arlington, Texas; and Westchester County, New York. In Canada, excellent materials in the form of reports, planning studies, or manuals were gathered from cities such as Vancouver, British Columbia; Edmonton, Alberta; and North York, Ontario.

Leading nonprofit organizations represented in the text include both Boy Scouts and Girl Scouts; YMCA and YWCA; Boys and Girls Clubs; the Police Athletic League; Little League Baseball; and Woodswomen, Inc. Therapeutic and special recreation agencies include San Francisco's RCH Inc.; the South East Consortium in New York; and Special Olympics. Armed forces Morale, Welfare and Recreation programs reflect both national practices and services at Florida's Orlando Naval Training Center. Much campus recreation material was taken from information supplied by the Southern Illinois University in Carbondale, and commercial recreation practices drew upon the successful Dollywood theme park in Tennessee.

With its heavy reliance on such agencies, representing the cutting edge in leisure-service management practices, the book constitutes clear-cut guidelines for the field today and tomorrow and might well be subtitled "Profiles in Success." Throughout, its effort is to go beyond simply reporting traditional, bureaucratic practices in such areas as fiscal or personnel operations, and instead to provide a vivid, living picture of how recreation, park, and leisure-service agencies achieve success and overcome challenges today. With this in mind, it seeks to be as realistic and practical as possible in equipping leisure-service students for the career specializations they will be entering.

Pedagogical Features

Based on the suggestions of reviewers of the fifth edition and professors who have used the book, this edition's overall length has been reduced and the number of chapters cut from sixteen to eleven. Within this tighter structure, the effort has been to provide both breadth and depth, in the sense of covering the major areas of responsibility of leisure-service managers, but also presenting numerous examples of actual practices in each area.

Each chapter includes opening quotations, introductions, listings of objectives based on Curriculum Accreditation standards, chapter summaries, suggested discussion questions or class assignments and projects, and references.

Eight chapters include a total of twenty-four case studies for class analysis, dealing with the realistic kinds of problems facing managers today. While fictional in that they do not describe actual agencies or individuals, the case studies are based on real experiences and issues.

ACKNOWLEDGMENTS

The authors owe a debt of gratitude to the many leisure-service organizations or professionals who provided materials used in this book. In addition, we acknowledge the contributions of numerous recreation, park, and leisure-studies educators who influenced our thinking or were directly quoted in the text. They include: Lawrence Allen, James Busser, Deborah Bialeschki, John Crompton, Dan Dustin, Susan and Christopher Edginton, Geoffrey Godbey, Thomas Goodale, Karla Henderson, Lynn Jamieson, Debra Jordan, James Murphy, J. Robert Rossman, Ruth Russell, and H. Douglas Sessoms. Special mention must be made of James Kozlowski, whose research on legal issues and recreation is extensively reported in Chapter 9.

Finally, thanks must be given to reviewers of the fifth edition and the draft of this edition: Nick DiGrino, Western Illinois University; Gerald Maas, Arizona State University; Matthew Pantera, Springfield College; and Craig Ross, Indiana University.

Also thank you to the editors at McGraw-Hill who assisted in its production: Vicki Malinee, Executive editor; Melissa J. Martin, Developmental Editor; and Kay J. Brimeyer, Senior Project Manager.

Richard Kraus

Joseph Curtis

Managers in the Leisure-Service System

Park and recreation agencies are increasingly being called upon to create strategies that positively affect the lifestyle behavior patterns of the citizens who live, work, and play in their communities. Crime reduction, youth development, tourism revenue, subsidized food programs, environmental stewardship, community harmony, ADA coordination [for persons with disabilities] and a host of specifically important issues have become the strategic focus of communities nationwide, and our profession has often been asked to step up to the plate and take a leadership role.[1]

No job is more vital to our society than that of the manager. It is the manager who determines whether our social institutions serve us well or whether they squander our talents and resources. It is time to strip away the folklore about managerial work, and time to study it realistically so that we can begin the difficult task of making significant improvements in its performance.[2]

INTRODUCTION

Recreation, parks, and leisure services have become important social institutions in contemporary North America. Each year, hundreds of millions of people engage in a host of rewarding leisure experiences offered by government agencies, nonprofit organizations, commercial businesses, and other program sponsors. Several hundred billion dollars are spent each year on leisure pursuits in the United States and Canada, and social and behavioral scientists have documented the value of recreation involvement for participants young and old.

Critical to the success of all recreation, parks, and leisure services are managers. These individuals—superintendents, directors, division heads, supervisors, program specialists, and other key staff members—coordinate and direct all agency operations. Their task is to develop mission statements, identify goals, plan, organize, and carry out programs and develop and maintain facilities. In such functions as personnel management, fiscal operations, and public and community relations, they provide essential leadership for the entire recreation, park, and leisure-service enterprise.

This text seeks to provide readers with a detailed and realistic understanding of leisure-service management today. Chapter by chapter, it is designed to achieve the basic understandings and professional competencies identified as essential in the Baccalaureate Degree Accreditation Standards of the Council on Accreditation of the National Recreation and Park Association (NRPA) and the American Association for Leisure and Recreation (AALR).[3] For example, this chapter addresses the following understandings and competencies identified in the Accreditation Standards:

> Knowledge of social systems and community organization (7.03).
>
> Understanding of the psychological, sociological, and physiological significance of play, recreation, and leisure from an historical perspective of all populations and settings (8.02).
>
> Understanding of the technological, economic, and political significance of play, recreation, and leisure in contemporary society (8.03).
>
> Understanding of and ability to use diverse community, institutional, natural, and human-service resources to promote and enhance the leisure experience (8.11).
>
> Understanding of the roles and interrelationships of diverse leisure-service delivery systems, including such specialties as the therapeutic recreation and the business enterprise systems (8.12).

O B J E C T I V E S

At the conclusion of this chapter, readers should be familiar with the following concepts, management functions, and societal trends:

1. The meaning and importance of recreation, parks, and leisure services, both as forms of personal participation and as social institutions.
2. The purpose and functions of eight major types of leisure-service agencies, such as governmental, nonprofit, commercial, or therapeutic organizations, or those involved in such leisure-service functions as sports management or travel and tourism.
3. An understanding of leisure services as a system, involving its scope and diversity, linkage with other social services, and both competitive and cooperative interaction among different types of agencies.
4. The essential meaning of management, and the major roles played by managers within the recreation, park, and leisure-service field.
5. Several important social, economic, demographic, and spiritual trends that influence leisure participation today, with their implications for the management of leisure-service organizations.

The term *management* may be understood from two perspectives. First, it is often defined as a *professional role* or *job level* that involves a significant degree of responsibility for policy development, planning, coordinating, and supervising the work of other employees or staff members. Such titles as "superintendent," "center director," "program coordinator," "activity specialist," or "district supervisor" are all examples of management positions.

Second, management may be understood as a *dynamic process,* in which these individuals play a key leadership role in motivating and encouraging all employees to accomplish mutually agreed upon goals and objectives. In terms of its overall responsibilities, management has been defined as:

> . . . the process of acquiring and combining human, financial, and physical resources to attain the organization's primary goal of producing a product or service desired by some segment of society. This process is essential to the functioning of all organizations—profit and nonprofit; essential resources must be acquired and combined in some way to produce an output.[4]

Management is a process or function that is common to all human organizations and institutions. Large hospitals, public-service agencies, the armed forces, educational systems, and businesses of every type are only a few of the settings in which it must operate. Whenever people join together to accomplish specific goals, the management process is at work. Although much of the impetus for developing professional management approaches has come from private industry, it would be false to assume that the only place management skills are needed is in profit-making enterprises. Instead, whenever two or more people become involved in cooperative efforts, the process of management comes into play.

THE CONTEXT OF LEISURE-SERVICE MANAGEMENT

Before describing the specific functions of recreation, park, and leisure-service managers in detail, it is helpful to examine the context in which leisure-service directors carry out their work. Therefore, this chapter begins with a brief discussion of three terms that are commonly linked to agency operations: *recreation, parks,* and *leisure services.*

Meaning of Recreation

Recreation has traditionally been defined as a form of human activity, carried on voluntarily in one's free time, usually pleasurable, and without extrinsic or other practical purposes. Recently, scholars have concluded that recreation is not so much a form of pleasure-seeking activity as it is an emotionally transforming activity designed to meet important personal needs and motivations. These might include the need for personal achievement, creative self-discovery, social involvement, relaxation and stress reduction, or mental and physical fitness.

Beyond these values, recreation has become an important social and economic institution in the United States and Canada. It is provided by many government agencies on local, state or provincial, and federal levels, and by nonprofit community organizations, commercial businesses, and other specialized types of sponsors.

Meaning of Parks

Parks are usually defined as outdoor areas provided chiefly by government to serve varied purposes, such as wilderness or heritage preservation or the provision of such nature-centered pursuits as backpacking, camping, hunting, fishing, boating, or skiing.

Initially, parks were established in the United States and Canada during the nineteenth century as a separate branch of government and professional responsibility. During the mid-twentieth century, they merged with the growing field of recreation management in joint recreation and park agencies, and in combined departments of college and university professional preparation. They involve important environmental and economic concerns, and are linked to the dramatic growth of the travel and tourism industry.

Meaning of Leisure Services

The term *leisure* has traditionally referred to time free from obligated tasks, such as work or work-connected activity, or personal maintenance functions. It has also had the connotation of wealth and social class, in that the nobility and rich industrialists or landowners in European society tended to have the great bulk of free time—while peasants or laborers had little leisure.

Today, leisure is viewed more broadly as the possession of all classes, and as both the opportunity for free choice in a wide range of creative and social involvements and as a key element in the cultural life of a nation. While leisure services include recreation as a primary thrust, they also involve such diverse elements as popular and elite forms of entertainment, community-service activities, religious expression, continuing education, and a host of related social services.

UNDERSTANDING THE LEISURE-SERVICE SYSTEM

Collectively, recreation, parks, and leisure-service programs must be viewed as a vital part of daily life and overall community well-being. As later chapters will show in detail, these programs contribute significantly to critical personal and social goals. A recent report by the Parks and Recreation Federation of Ontario, Canada, concluded that the benefits of community recreation fell under four major headings: *personal, social, economic,* and *environmental.* The report presented research findings that documented the outcomes of organized recreation and park services in the following areas: building strong communities; promoting ethnic and cultural harmony; strengthening family life; assisting persons with disabilities and the socially or economically disadvantaged; contributing to economic growth and stability; offering services for latchkey children and assisting at-risk youth; and promoting environmental well-being and ecological values.[5]

Although some authors have divided the leisure-service system into two major categories, "public" and "private," this is an oversimplification. Instead, eight different types of organizations sponsor recreation, park, and leisure services today.

1. Public recreation and park departments

These are formally structured government agencies with a mandate to provide socially constructive and ecologically sound programs and facilities to the public. On the federal level, such agencies as the National Park Service or the Forest Service in the United States, or Parks Canada in that nation, own and operate millions of acres of forest land, lakes, reservoirs, beaches, historic monuments, and other scenic properties that are used for recreation. This function includes the direct operation of such parks and recreation sites, the preservation of wildlife and fisheries, the promotion of tourism and travel as an economic asset, assistance to local communities in providing needed social programs, promotion of physical fitness and sports, and other aid to health and human services, education, and housing.

Throughout the United States and in fifteen Canadian provinces, varied state and provincial departments operate extensive networks of parks, historic monuments, lakes and reservoirs, scenic sites, and other settings for outdoor recreation. In Canada particularly, provincial agencies focus on promoting pride in ethnic heritage, encouraging sound values in youth sports, ensuring gender equity for girls and women in recreation, supporting programs for at-risk youth, and similar social priorities.

Closer to home, local government recreation and park departments are directly responsible for providing organized programs and varied facilities that meet leisure needs. These departments may be part of municipal (city, town, or village) governments, or may be structured as county or special district operations, covering larger geographical areas.

In addition to recreation and park departments, many communities have libraries, museums, social agencies, schools, or community colleges that also provide leisure programs. Cooperation among various community agencies, including police, youth boards, and housing and welfare departments, also assist many local government recreation programs.

2. Nonprofit community organizations

A second major category of recreation sponsorship consists of community organizations that operate under the leadership of private citizens on a nonprofit basis. Often called "voluntary" agencies, they tend to rely heavily on volunteers for direct program leadership, but are managed by professional paid staff members. Also, while they are classified as nonprofit, they often charge substantial fees for membership or participation in order to support their overall operation.

The most common example of such groups consists of national youth-serving organizations like the Boys and Girls Clubs of America, the Young Women's Christian Association, Camp Fire, or the Police Athletic League. Many such organizations are tremendous in scale. For example, in the mid- to late-1990s, a total of 964 YMCAs operated 1,233 branches, units, and camps with a combined operating budget of $2.3 billion. The Girl Scouts of the United States has approximately 3.5 million members, including 2.6 million girls on five program levels, and over 800,000 adult members, including volunteer leaders, board members, and paid professional employees.

The programs of such youth-serving organizations include both educational, character-building, and civic activities and many recreational pursuits, including sports, camping, arts and crafts, and social programs. Voluntary nonprofit agencies may either be independent, with their own boards, or be part of national or regional federations. Many are affiliated with religious denominations, while others are completely nonsectarian.

Special-Interest Organizations.   Another category of nonprofit leisure-service agencies includes groups that promote a particular type of recreational activity or that serve a special population. Thousands of such organizations provide instruction, sponsor competition, and organize local units and promotional activities in such sports as golf, tennis, archery, or softball. For example, Little League baseball serves millions of children and youth on eight membership levels in eighty-three countries around the world.

Other nonprofit groups promote ecological concerns or serve the needs of persons with disabilities.

3. Commercial recreation

While government and nonprofit agencies represent key elements in leisure-service programming and are generally viewed as the heart of the recreation profession, the greatest bulk of leisure involvement in the United States and Canada today is in response to commercial recreation offerings.

Commercial recreation businesses, operated for profit, are composed of such elements as: resorts and travel agencies, private campgrounds, health and fitness spas, professional sports teams and stadiums, cruise ships and tour agencies, theme parks and water play parks, bowling centers, skating rinks, dance studios, and privately operated camps of many types. In a broad sense, other forms of entertainment and hospitality, including movies, theater, television, and popular music companies, are also part of the commercial recreation spectrum.[6]

While many small, independent, or mom-and-pop ventures exist within the overall for-profit recreation field, the trend has been for huge, multibillion-dollar conglomerates to assume control of varied commercial recreation enterprises. These powerful groups own newspapers and magazines, television and radio networks, toy and video game companies, sports teams and stadiums, theme parks, and numerous other businesses that dominate the recreational lives of Americans and Canadians of all ages. The scope of such ventures and their economic impact is shown in Table 1.1, which reports the estimated public spending on recreation in recent years.

4. Private membership organizations

Such groups are chiefly of two types: (1) closed-membership clubs that serve a few specific sports interests, such as golf or tennis, along with social programs and hospitality services; and (2) groups based primarily on one's residential

TABLE 1.1 Personal Consumption Expenditures: 1985 to 1995

(In billions of dollars, except percent. Represents market value of leisure goods and services purchased by individuals and nonprofit institutions.)

Type of Product or Service	1985	1990	1995
Total recreation expenditures	116.3	281.6	401.7
Percent of total personal consumption	6.6	7.3	8.2
Books and maps	6.6	16.5	20.9
Magazines, newspapers, and sheet music	12.0	21.5	25.6
Nondurable toys and sport supplies	14.6	31.6	42.7
Wheel goods, sports, and photographic equipment	15.6	29.8	43.8
Video and audio products, computer equipment, and musical instruments	19.9	53.8	88.3
Radio and television repair	2.5	4.2	5.1
Flowers, seeds, and potted plants	4.7	11.1	14.2
Admissions to specified spectator amusements	6.7	15.1	19.9
Motion picture theaters	2.6	5.2	5.6
Legitimate theaters and opera, and entertainments of nonprofit institutions	1.8	5.6	9.0
Spectator sports	2.3	4.4	5.3
Clubs and fraternal organizations	3.1	8.9	12.9
Commercial participant amusements	9.1	23.0	37.0
Pari-mutuel net receipts	2.3	3.4	3.3
Other (includes net receipts of lotteries, pet and pet care, cable TV, sport and recreation camps, videocassette rental, etc.)	19.4	62.6	88.2

Source: Statistical Abstract of the United States (U.S. Department of Commerce, 1997). p. 252.
It should be noted that this table does not include many other forms of leisure spending, including major areas of gambling, use of alcohol, varied forms of sports participation, tourism and travel, etc. Other estimates of total spending on recreation run as high as a trillion dollars annually.

status, such as retirement communities or condominium or vacation-home developments.

In the past, the first type of organization, which includes country clubs, yacht clubs, or golf or tennis clubs, tended to be extremely exclusive in racial or religious terms, while limiting membership to upper-middle class or wealthy individuals and families. Today, social and legal pressures have forced many private sports or social clubs to remove such discriminatory bars to membership.

The second type of private-membership recreation program has become an increasingly popular aspect of home ownership. With the steady increase in the number of older persons in American and Canadian society, retirement villages have been established, usually in Sun Belt states, that serve millions of elderly residents with varied hobby, sports, fitness, and social programs. Similarly, a growing number of real estate developments have appealed to potential home-owners by offering a host of security and maintenance services, along with private-membership leisure opportunities such as swimming pools, golf courses and tennis centers, fitness programs, and club houses.

5. Campus recreation

A fifth specialized form of organized leisure service in the United States and Canada today consists of campus recreation, offered in colleges and universities for students, staff, and faculty, and in some limited cases, community residents.

Campus recreation generally takes two forms: (1) intramural and club sports and outdoor recreation activities that are usually administered by an institution's athletic department or affiliated with its health, physical education, and recreation program; and (2) a broader program that includes college union or dormitory-based social activities, concerts, publications, cultural activities, fraternities, and sororities that is usually administered by a dean or office of student life with input from student leaders. While these two functions are usually separate, occasionally the college or university administrative unit responsible for recreational sports management—a term that is increasingly being used—may also supervise other social or cultural activities.

In many cases, student recreation organizations are given responsibility for organizing and conducting complex student union and other social and recreational activities. For example, at San Diego State University in California, the Associated Students Organization sponsors a broad range of films, concerts, recreational and athletic programs, and other activities. This multimillion-dollar organization, funded by annual student fees, operates the Aztec Center, the university's student union building. In addition, it runs a successful travel service, intramurals and sports clubs, leisure-skills classes, lectures, movies, an open-air theater, a large aquatics center, a campus radio station, a child-care center, a general store, legal services, a campus information booth, and many other services and leisure activities under the direction of the Recreation Activities Board.

6. Employee recreation programs

Thousands of businesses today, including manufacturing, airlines, health care, banking, insurance, and other types of companies, provide recreation and related services for their employees. In the mid-1980s, a survey conducted by the National Employee Services and Recreation Association showed the range and variety of such programs (Table 1.2). Today, company recreation directors sponsor sports, hobby, social, and other leisure activities, along with chartered vacation travel, discount shopping services, child care, and other special services.

The strongest thrust in employee recreation programs today is in the area of health and fitness programming. In addition to providing facilities and skilled leadership in fitness centers, many companies also assist their employees with substance abuse, stress management, weight reduction, and similar wellness-enhancing services. Often, company recreation directors play an important role in promoting employee service-award programs, community relations activities, and other aspects of the business's public relations operation.

7. Armed Forces recreation

Since World War I, when Special Services Divisions were established in the U.S. military forces to sustain favorable morale, reduce AWOL (absent without leave) rates, and curb venereal disease, recreation has been recognized as an important support service in the armed forces. Today, each branch of the military sponsors varied recreation activities as part of the overall Morale, Welfare and Recreation (MWR) program that is directed by the Office for Manpower, Reserve Affairs and Logistics of the U.S. Department of Defense. Lankford and

DeGraaf point out that armed forces recreation serves more than 2.1 million military personnel on active service, more than 2.7 million family members ranging from infants to retirees, and more than 1.4 million National Guard members—serving more participants and spending more on programming than any other federal, state, or local recreation operation.[7]

MWR programs include an extensive range of sports, fitness, social, creative, and outdoor recreation, along with entertainment, travel, hobby, and other leisure pursuits. Health and fitness have become a key thrust of armed forces recreation, with the Air Force, for example, installing Health and Wellness Centers (HAWC) on each base, with diversified equipment and well-qualified fitness specialists.

Over the past several years, a number of major U.S. military bases have been closed down or have cut back sharply in their funding, and armed forces recreation has had to reduce its programming in these areas to place greater reliance on self-generated revenues for support. However, as later chapters will show, military recreation continues to represent an innovative and sophisticated approach to leisure-service management.

8. Therapeutic recreation service

A final important area of recreation sponsorship today consists of therapeutic recreation services, defined as the purposeful use of recreational activity in the care, treatment, and rehabilitation of persons with disabilities, including dependent aging persons, through directed programs. As it has developed over the past several decades, therapeutic recreation takes two forms: (1) *clinical treatment*, which involves carefully designed therapy intended to overcome or minimize the effects of disability, leisure education, and recreational participation to promote independent living capability; and (2) so-called *special recreation*,

TABLE 1.2 Elements of Company Services and Recreation Programs

Physical Programs	% Response	Service Programs	% Response
Softball	64.5	Discount service/tickets	73.5
Bowling	57.8	United Way drive	63.4
Golf	48.4	Blood drives	59.2
Basketball	42.9	Award/recognition program	58.9
Volleyball	35.5	Discount service/products	54.4
Tennis	30.3	First aid/CPR training	50.2
Fitness program	30.0	Employee assistance program	28.6
Social/Cultural Programs		Facilities Operated	
Picnics	64.5	Ball diamond	19.9
Christmas parties	60.0	Fitness facility	18.8
Dinner/theater outings	28.6	Basketball court	16.0
Travel program	24.0	Activities field	15.3
Adult education (non-job-related)	20.9	Activities building	13.2
Drama/theater	19.2	Employee park	9.4
		Fitness trail	9.4

Source: Employee Services Management (December/January 1984–1985).

which is provided in a community setting with integrated participation with nondisabled persons to the fullest extent possible.

Today, therapeutic recreation is no longer restricted to hospitals and other long-term residential facilities, as it was initially intended to be.

To illustrate, the Therapeutic Recreation Section of the California Park and Recreation Society stresses that services are provided in varied residential, clinical, and community settings:

Activity centers	Nursing homes
Adult day care centers	Recreation and park departments
Camps	Rehabilitation centers
Children's hospitals	Residential facilities
Community recreation agencies	Senior citizen centers
Community special population agencies	State hospitals and developmental centers
Independent living centers	Veterans' hospitals
Long-term care facilities	Wellness-oriented settings[8]
Mental health centers	

Increasingly, the major types of recreation sponsors have become aware of the need to serve persons with disabilities. YM and YWCAs, Scouts, Boys and Girls Clubs, and numerous other youth-service agencies either sponsor separate programs for children and youth with physical or mental impairments, or integrate them with others within a "mainstreaming" and "normalization" framework. Many colleges offer special programs for students with disabilities, including adapted instruction in outdoor recreation skills and sports. Organizations like the Special Olympics and the National Wheelchair Athletic Association have developed local instructional and competitive programs that lead to national and even international games, with participation by thousands of athletes with disabilities. Consequently, therapeutic recreation has become a highly professionalized branch of the overall leisure-service field, with major national, state, and provincial societies, and hundreds of specialized degree programs in universities.

OTHER ELEMENTS IN THE LEISURE-SERVICE SYSTEM

In addition to the eight types of agencies just described, the leisure-service field may be understood in terms of such major recreational "interest clusters" as sports or travel and tourism. Each such field represents a major form of public leisure involvement, and is sponsored by public, nonprofit, campus, armed forces, and commercial recreation agencies today.

Sport Management

With the immense growth of interest in amateur and professional sports in the United States and Canada, this field has moved rapidly from its initial linkage with physical education administration. Today, it involves planning, programming, marketing, and fiscal management of sports leagues, facilities, merchandising operations, and other businesses in a host of settings: community leagues, school and college competitive programs, the operation of professional teams and stadiums, and even the manufacture and sale of sports equipment and memorabilia as multibillion-dollar industries. Sports-management professionals must possess skills in communications and public relations, accounting, personnel management, contract development, and other legal skills applicable to the sports setting. The emergence of this field, both as an independent career area and as a subset of the leisure-service field, testifies to the popularity of sport in North America.

In economic terms, if all elements of the sport industry were combined, Bonnie Parkhouse points out that sport in the early 1990s represented a $61.1 billion-a-year business:

> . . . making it the twenty-second largest industry in the United States. When compared with other industrial giants, sport is bigger than the automobile, petroleum, lumber, and air transportation sectors of the U.S. economy [with estimates that early in the next century] the gross national sports product will have increased to $121.1 billion.[9]

As a consequence of this growth, interest in sport management as a career field has grown rapidly. In 1990, a survey conducted by the National Association for Sport and Physical Education revealed that 181 sport-management curricula had been established in colleges and universities.

Travel and Tourism

As a second example of recreational interest clusters that are served by many types of agencies, travel and tourism offers a broad spectrum of experiences and professional services. The motivations for pleasure travel are several—to visit friends and family, to revitalize or enrich one's life, to relax in a break from work routine, to be in a more pleasant climate or interesting setting, or to engage in sightseeing, adventure, or educational or cultural experiences.

To satisfy such varied deviations, the following four elements are essential: (1) *destination*, such as famous parks, cities, resort areas, or historical sites; (2) *means of travel*, ranging from car, plane, or boat, to horseback or bicycling; (3) *events and entertainment*, such as major sports events, festivals and fairs, or theme parks or gambling casinos; and (4) *hospitality*, in the form of hotels, motels, restaurants and taverns, rental condominiums, or gift and equipment shops to serve tourist or traveler needs.

Serving these four functions provides a huge bulk of employment within an industry that was estimated in the early 1990s as involving an annual expenditure of approximately $560 billion in the United States alone. International travel in the late 1990s (U.S. citizens abroad, or foreign travelers in the United States) totaled $125.2 billion annually.[10]

With tourism representing a major source of revenue for many cities, states, and regions, concerted efforts are made to encourage pleasure travel by sponsoring appealing events or facilities or providing other amenities. Often, public departments of commerce or recreation, parks, and cultural affairs will cooperate with theme park managers and other commercial recreation managers to offer jointly sponsored programs and services. Beyond this, company recreation programs often offer discount travel tours for their employees, and military MWR managers also promote guided tours and outings.

CHARACTERISTICS OF THE LEISURE-SERVICE SYSTEM

What are the key characteristics of recreation, park, and leisure-service agencies when seen as a "system"? The term itself refers to an assembly or network of different units or parts that share a significant degree of interdependence. Jubenville and Twight, in discussing the outdoor recreation management model, call these parts "subsystems" that can react as a total organism under given situations. They continue:

> The "organism" or system exists because of demands for its products or services from elements of its environment, and it produces outputs of products or services which it exchanges with the environment in return for social support . . . .
> Each of the recreation management system's subsystems specializes in different technical aspects of the output production process . . . . If one subsystem or phase of a subsystem is altered, then the whole system is affected; therefore the boundary of a system is flexible to meet both external and internal changes. . . . For example, for a given input such as a new law or a budget cut, we may reasonably forecast its effects over the entire system.[11]

The overall leisure-service system is composed of the eight categories of recreation, park, and leisure-service agencies described earlier, along with such interest clusters of sponsors as those in the sport-management or travel and tourism fields. In turn, each of these elements has its own varied subsystems, with varying missions and program emphases.

Recreation, park, and leisure-service organizations may range from those staffed by one or two professionals in small community agencies or hospital-based recreation units, to thousands of employees in huge businesses or non-profit federations. The goals and program services of these organizations may vary widely from enriching the lives of participants to protecting the natural environment, combating juvenile delinquency, or simply making a profit. Therefore, the leisure-service field must be understood as a diverse assembly of different types of organizations that function relatively independently, with little coordination among its units. With different kinds of administrative controls and subject to unpredictable market forces, the field itself is marked both by duplication and gaps in providing leisure opportunities to the public.

Competition among Leisure-Service Agencies

In seeking a market for its products and services, each type of recreation program sponsor must compete against other leisure-service providers. Often, as new forms of recreational participation become popular, they influence or displace other program sponsors. For example, when television became popular in the

United States and Canada, it dealt a shattering blow to motion-picture attendance. Similarly, when legalized casino gambling was established in Atlantic City, New Jersey, pari-mutuel horse-track betting throughout the East fell off sharply, and other resort areas or nightlife entertainment settings were affected. Also, when Disney and other theme park chains became successful with their approach to family-oriented tourism, other more traditional amusement parks could no longer compete successfully.

Within each subset of the overall leisure-service field, there is an intense struggle to attract participants. As commercial health and fitness spas, YMCAs and YWCAs, colleges and universities, and public departments all established fitness complexes as a result of the wave of public interest in adult wellness, they soon found themselves competing for paid members. In several cases, lawsuits or legislative efforts were launched in the 1990s by commercial health spa chains or organizations to deny nonprofit organizations their tax-exempt status, on the grounds that they provide services essentially similar to those of profit-oriented businesses. For example, in 1996 the International Health, Racquet and Sportsclub Association (IHRSA) initiated a public-awareness campaign against nonprofit organizations operating fitness centers, arguing that:

> . . . government agencies like park and recreation departments, as well as non-profits like the YMCA, colleges and hospitals, have no business operating commercial fitness clubs. Calling it "unfair competition," IHRSA says tax-exempt clubs enjoy financial advantages that suffocate taxpaying clubs, and dissuade new taxpaying clubs from entering the field.[12]

At another level, competition exists within each subsystem of the overall leisure-service system, such as the outdoor recreation field. Here, different groups of enthusiasts are often pitted against each other because of their competing interests or value systems. For example, powerboat operators are often in conflict with canoers or kayakers, and lakeside residents or campers often object to users of small personal watercraft. Cross-country skiers seek limits on snowmobiling, while wildlife enthusiasts urge controls or bans on varied forms of hunting. Within the diversified sports fields, apart from the obvious competition among teams in organized amateur or professional leagues, each of the major sports competes strenuously against the others for public interest, attendance, and television revenues.

Cooperation in the Leisure-Service System

At the same time, there was a a growing trend toward developing varied forms of interagency partnerships during the 1990s. This trend was especially evident in the field of outdoor recreation and park management. Vaske, Donnelly, and LaPage wrote that growing economic pressures and conflicting user demands resulted in major park systems being confronted by new demands for privatization, the transfer of federal lands to state ownership, or even "declassification" of publicly owned parks:

> The parks profession, not unfamiliar to such pressures in the past, has taken the lead in experimenting with more efficient ways of delivering its services to the public. Unwilling to see parks and natural areas closed . . . during periods

of budget austerity, managers have for years been building an impressive catalogue of partnerships with public and private entities. Today, these partnerships represent not only significant cost savings to taxpayers but have greatly expanded the quality of public services.[13]

Today, cooperation among different types of leisure-service organizations takes many forms:

Universities cosponsoring summer youth camps and day camps with branches of the armed forces, or establishing summer sports camps for at-risk and inner-city youth with federal fiscal support.

County and special-district recreation and park agencies providing employee fitness and other recreation programs under contracts with local corporations.

Banks, insurance companies, and other financial institutions sponsoring or providing financial support for road races, civic festivals, or other charitable events in cooperation with local government.

Varied civic groups, businesses, and foundations taking responsibility for park maintenance or environmental clean-up and recovery efforts.

City and state governments cooperating with sports team owners to finance new stadium or arena construction.

Such examples of collaboration in the leisure-service field illustrate the degree to which interagency cooperation has become an important strategy and serve to provide a degree of unity within the overall system.

Many leisure-service agencies of different types are brought together in the quest for funding support. In government or foundation grants programs, partnerships are encouraged, with drug prevention and intervention programs, family service units, and nonprofit organizations such as YM and YWCAs, Boys and Girls Clubs, or Police Athletic Leagues undertaking specially funded, cosponsored social-service projects. In inner-city neighborhoods especially, "turf" issues take second place to the need to provide critical programming for needy residents.

Role of Professional Societies

In many cases, professional recreation and park societies or councils of social agencies serve to promote partnership efforts. In Canada, for example, the Saskatchewan Provincial Park and Recreation Association maintains an extensive directory of all leisure-related groups and promotes cooperative planning and action among them. Active members of this association include: Boys and Girls Clubs; hosteling organizations; the Canadian Red Cross Society; Girl Guides; urban park and conservation agencies; Air Cadets; the Navy League and Army Cadet league; senior citizens groups; mental health programs; the Indian Sport, Culture and Recreation Association; the 4-H Club Council; and numerous outdoor recreation organizations. These groups, together with twenty-three Regional Recreation Associations, promote extensive provincial recreation programs, aided by Saskatchewan lotteries, which has contributed over $30 million a year of lottery income to volunteer groups in every part of the province.

On the county level in the United States, Pete Soderberg, Director of Monterey County Parks in California, shows how the parks system collaborates with a host of public, business, and special-interest organizations, serving as the hub within a "Wheel of Service" that yields significant social and economic benefits to residents throughout the county. (Fig. 1.1).

FIGURE 1.1 Monterey County Parks "Wheel of Service."

Source: California Park and Recreation Society *Phoenix Project Handbook,* 1995.

Increasingly, the overall leisure-service field has become characterized as an industry, with professional societies, educational institutions, and publications using this term, and referring to those served—or potential participants—as "customers." This trend stemmed from the field's widespread adoption of an entrepreneurial stance and acceptance of marketing practices taken from the current literature on business management during the 1970s and 1980s. Increasingly, thousands of cultural, educational, health-care, and other types of recreation providers adopted entrepreneurial marketing approaches at this time. With the goals of broadening their base of participation and obtaining higher levels of self-generated revenues through fees and charges, many such leisure-service agencies diversified their programs, offering a greater variety of recreational clubs, classes, and specialized hobby interests, often in impressive new facilities. They employed such strategies as target marketing and sophisticated advertising and promotional methods, and varied their scheduling and pricing approaches to meet different participant needs and capabilities. Emphasis was placed on benchmarking as a means of monitoring agency performance, and on achieving a high level of participant satisfaction within a framework of "total quality management." Within different branches of the overall recreation field, the term *leisure industry* was widely accepted, and patrons of agency programs were referred to as "customers."

"Corporate" Identity of Parks Ontario

As a single vivid example of this trend, it was reported in 1996 that Parks Ontario, the Canadian provincial agency operating a major network of parks and outdoor recreation resources, was "going corporate."

> . . . [T]he department is now called Ontario Parks, a new entrepreneurial venture of the provincial government. Ontario Parks will operate like a business as an organization within the Ministry of Natural Resources through a newly appointed board of directors. A special purpose account will be developed for retaining and managing park revenue . . . .
>
> One of the business objectives of Ontario Parks is to involve the private sector in program delivery, from service contracts to parks contracting to partnerships [with] new opportunities for service contracts for road and ground maintenance, garbage disposal, janitorial services and snow removal [saving the parks system substantial sums].[14]

Implications of the Entrepreneurial Trend

While the dramatic shift toward marketing-based philosophies and strategies was a logical one in terms of gaining needed fiscal support and community respect, the idea of regarding the entire leisure-service field as an industry raised serious questions. Certainly, many public, nonprofit, and other organizations were able to improve their services, diversify their offerings, and operate more successfully by adopting business-based methods. At the same time, it is difficult to regard the provision of municipal playgrounds or parks as an "industrial" function. By the same token, it is difficult to regard families on public assistance, dependent elderly persons, at-risk youth in urban ghettoes, or physically or mentally disabled persons without fiscal resources as "customers" in any true sense.

The point then is that while major sectors of the recreation, park, and leisure-service field can legitimately be considered part of a complex, umbrella-like industry and can best be carried on using modern marketing principles and methods, the overall field *must* also be recognized as a vital cog in the network of essential community human-service organizations.

Linked to this principle, it is desirable to limit the use of the term *customers* to describe only patrons of commercial establishments. For others, particularly public and nonprofit organizations, a better term would be *stakeholder,* which refers to all individuals involved in or affected by leisure-service agency operations (see page 44).

*RESPONSIBILITIES OF
LEISURE-SERVICE MANAGERS*

We now turn to the functions of recreation, park, and leisure-service managers within nine major areas of responsibility. These are briefly described in the following pages and more fully analyzed in later chapters.

1. Providing philosophical leadership
Agency managers play a key role in defining or reformulating their organization's statement of overall purpose, as well as its specific goals and objectives, which may change over time in response to shifting environmental conditions. In part, this is done through planning efforts that develop short- and long-term goals. It may also be done as a continuous process as the manager makes decisions or takes action that reflects his or her organization's essential mission and philosophy of service. The manager serves as a visionary and spiritual leader or role model, in striving to help all staff members understand and accept the agency's value system and adhere to it at all levels of programming or community involvement.

2. Organizational structure
Linked to the first function, managers have the task of reviewing and continuing to develop or improve the organizational structure of their agencies, as well as their relationship with supervisory boards, commissions, or other advisory groups. In addition to overseeing the performance of each administrative unit within the agency structure, managers must also encourage the coordination and cooperative action of different units or personnel on various levels, through special project teams or task forces.

3. Program service
Planning and implementing successful programs that serve participants with absorbing, constructive leisure opportunities and that fulfill the organization's overall mission is a critical part of the recreation, park, and leisure-service manager's responsibility. Managers should be significantly involved in planning

program activities and services, to ensure that they cover a diversified range of recreational areas, that they are appropriately distributed in a geographical sense or in terms of age-level needs, and that they represent the highest possible quality of personal leisure experience.

4. Facilities planning, construction, and maintenance

This represents a critical function of most leisure-service managers, with the exception of those groups that do not possess or operate their own facilities, such as major youth organizations that use borrowed or rented structures, or therapeutic recreation programs in hospitals or rehabilitation centers that have limited areas or special facilities of their own.

Certainly, in most other types of recreation, park and leisure-service organizations, the successful operation of facilities is a critical element in the agency's success. Managers are therefore responsible for conducting planning or feasibility studies, spearheading property-acquisition efforts, overseeing facility design and construction processes, and maintaining facilities to ensure safe and enjoyable participation at all times.

5. Fiscal administration

Recreation, park, and leisure-service agencies, like all public, private, or commercial organizations, require money to pay employees, buy and maintain equipment, pay utility bills, and conduct every aspect of their year-round operation. Fiscal functions include the formulation of money-related policies and procedures; the planning, presentation, and execution of budgets; maintaining effective accounting and auditing controls; and maximizing the organization's fund-raising capabilities. To achieve a higher level of financial efficiency, managers are expected today to stress cost-benefit analysis, differentiated pricing policies, privatization and subcontracting of agency functions, and demanding productivity standards as part of this total approach.

6. Human resource management

Recreation, park, and leisure services is a highly labor-intensive field. Unlike many industries in which automated equipment turns out the product, or other business or service fields that rely heavily on a small corps of managers and technicians, recreation requires many leaders, program specialists, center directors, maintenance workers, and other support personnel to deliver services effectively. The recruitment, hiring, training, and ongoing supervision of personnel are important management responsibilities.

Today, organizations of every kind have been influenced by the human resource approach, which stresses a flexible, creative, and participatory approach to assigning and supervising team members. Counseling, job enrichment and rotation, shared decision making, delegation of authority, and the fuller use of part-time, seasonal, and volunteer leadership are an integral part of this management function.

7. Public and community relations

As a field of public service that must constantly seek to attract members of the community at large to take part in and to support its programs and services, recreation, parks, and leisure services must make intensive use of carefully designed public relations messages. These take the form of printed materials (brochures, advertisements, newsletters, and reports), information transmitted through the mass media (newspapers, magazines, radio, and television), and varied events, open houses, or other programs designed to promote the leisure service's agenda. As an extension of the public relations process, varied forms of community-relations activities involve two-way communication through advisory committees and neighborhood or district councils, community hearings or forums, focus groups, and similar efforts.

When community relations efforts include special projects designed to improve neighborhood life, such as environmental clean-up or antidrug coalitions, residents learn to work together for civic betterment; recreation often plays an important role in this process.

8. Legal functions and risk management

Leisure-service managers must operate—as administrators, planners, and program heads in other types of agencies do—within a framework of law as outlined in enabling or controlling legislation or court decisions. Such laws govern their fiscal and revenue-gathering operations, their hiring and firing of personnel, their acquiring and managing of facilities, occupational health and safety issues, leasing and concession agreements, and most important, the need to maintain effective risk-management procedures to avoid accidents and potentially crippling liability suits for negligence. Leisure-service managers, particularly those with responsibility for strenuous or risky outdoor recreation and sports activities, must be acutely aware of safety guidelines and the need for sound emergency and follow-up procedures. Linked to this concern, the prevention of vandalism and crowd control or other law-enforcement functions also represent high-priority tasks for leisure-service managers.

While sound legal counsel is essential in all areas of agency management that have the potential for lawsuits or claims of illegal practice, managers themselves should be thoroughly familiar with general legal principles governing their agency operations.

9. Evaluation, research, and information management

Evaluation, meaning the systematic measurement of the effectiveness or overall quality of leisure-service programs, is a final important responsibility of managers. This may take the form of annual, periodic, or ongoing monitoring or reporting of programs and their outcomes by participants and staff members to determine whether goals are being achieved. It may also involve agency-wide examinations of all elements of the organization's operation, making use of professionally approved standards of practice as part of accreditation, certification, or planning studies. When evaluation is carried out in a rigorous way, making use of objective and reliable data-gathering methods, sound sampling procedures, and similar controls, it is often considered to be a significant form of research.

Linked to the evaluation process, the comprehensive gathering of performance data about all elements of an agency's operation is an important management responsibility. This is usually done through computerized recording and analysis of such elements as program enrollments and revenues, staff assignments and personnel actions, facility needs and scheduling, and similar items. Efficient management and processing of such information is essential as a means of monitoring agency performance, evaluating its outcomes, making sound planning decisions, and projecting future needs and priorities.

INTEGRATION OF MANAGEMENT FUNCTIONS

The nine areas of management responsibility that have just been described are presented separately in the chapters that follow since they represent distinct functional areas. However, in actual practice, *they are closely interrelated.*

Programs represent a key purpose of all leisure-service agencies, but it would be impossible to present them without staff members to plan and direct them, facilities to house them, or money to pay for them. People would not take part in program activities without publicity, and legal advice and comprehensive risk-management procedures help to protect agencies against possible lawsuits. Thus, although they are examined as distinct functional areas in this text, the integration of functions is emphasized within each chapter.

Beyond this, it should also be made clear that leisure-service management is no longer a simple matter of recreation agencies providing "fun-oriented" programs and facilities. Instead, many organizations that do *not* have recreation as a primary responsibility—such as the military forces, hospitals, libraries, housing boards, or museums—often sponsor or assist leisure-service programs as a secondary function that contributes to their overall mission.

At the same time, many recreation and park departments or other leisure-service organizations provide numerous activities that are *not* recreation as such. Typically, employee-service programs that sponsor sports, social, and cultural leisure activities also offer health and fitness classes or clubs, substance abuse and stress-management workshops, and similar kinds of health-related or life-enrichment activities. YMCAs and YWCAs in particular combine recreational and other educational, cultural, and social-service functions that serve millions of youth and adults.

Clearly then, recreation management involves a wide variety of responsibilities and is carried on in a host of public, nonprofit, private, and commercial settings. As such, managers must be keenly aware of social, economic, and other cultural changes that affect the leisure services and that pose both challenges and opportunities for them, now and in the years to come. We live in an era of sudden and dramatic change, and leisure-service agencies should be proactive in anticipating the shifts in national and community life that affect their work and in responding effectively to them.

CHANGES AFFECTING LEISURE SERVICES

What are some of the most obvious developments in contemporary society that affected recreation, park, and leisure-service organizations during the 1990s and that are likely to continue in the early decades of the twenty-first century? In demographic terms, the increased birthrate noted in the last decades of the twentieth century resulted in a wave of young children entering the schools, creating demand for improved daycare and latchkey services, as well as diversified facilities and programming for this age group. At the other end of the age spectrum, steady growth in the number of elderly persons will create greater need for improved senior citizen centers and other social services, as well as improved recreation programming in long-term care facilities.

The continuing high divorce rate and increase in the number of children born to unmarried parents has resulted in a greater number of single-parent families who represent a high priority—along with *all* families—for appropriate recreation programs.

The impact of the Americans with Disabilities Act will continue to promote awareness of the need to provide enriching and mainstreaming recreational experiences for persons with disabilities, in both the United States and Canada.

The remarkable expansion of non-Caucasian populations, in which African-, Hispanic-, and Asian-American residents now represent a majority in a growing number of central cities, will have major implications for multicultural programming and employment policies.

Similarly, the women's drive for equity in modern society has resulted in a dramatic increase of participation by girls and women in sports, outdoor recreation, and other leisure pursuits, as well as concern about improved career opportunities for females in parks, recreation, and leisure services.

The emergence of a growing class of extremely wealthy persons who have withdrawn from the use of public facilities to a marked degree, or who live in affluent suburbs or "edge" cities, shows a marked contrast with the lives of socially and economically disadvantaged persons in inner-city ghettoes—often with barren recreation facilities and programs. This problem became increasingly apparent in the last years of the twentieth century, and is likely to continue in the decades ahead.

From an environmental point of view, the struggle among lumbering, mining, grazing, or oil-drilling business interests and environmental activities and public-interest societies for fuller use of wilderness areas in the United States and Canada represents a key economic issue. Western residents and legislators in the United States and Canada often support fuller business access to natural areas, while environmentalists argue that outdoor recreation and "ecotourism" also provide jobs on a continuing basis, without destroying the environment.

Historically, recreation, play, and leisure were often thought of in religious or spiritual terms. More recently, numerous authors have argued that they offer the opportunity for humanistic and holistic experiences that enrich the quality of human life and improve societal relationships. However, it is evident that many leisure elements today—such as popular movies, television, video games, or rap and rock music—depict violence, sexual exploitation, and other tawdry aspects of human behavior. Some critics argue that these aspects of popular Western culture are in part responsible for the wave of youth violence, drug abuse, or sexual permissiveness or irresponsibility that is found in society today.

Linked to this trend is the way we commonly regard recreation and leisure—not so much as healthy and wholesome, character-building experiences as simply commodities to be bought and sold. Every type of recreation that families once engaged in, creating their own forms of play, has been transformed—with high-pressure advertising and promotion—into business opportunity. Even gambling, which was once regarded as immoral and prohibited by law in most communities, is today accepted as economically desirable and even packaged as an attractive feature of many vacation destinations for family groups.[15]

Still other economic and social trends will affect the changing employment patterns of many men and women. Some individuals will hold home-based jobs using new technologies, while others will be forced by continuing company downsizing policies to hold two jobs, resulting in reduced leisure time and greater work stress.

IMPLICATIONS FOR
LEISURE-SERVICE MANAGERS

The above trends and issues comprise the framework in which leisure-service managers will work in the years ahead. As Chapter 11 shows in greater detail, these trends and issues will offer both challenges and opportunities for recreation agencies of all types.

They make it crystally clear that successful managers must have a sound philosophy of service, based both on the important roles that recreation, parks, and leisure play in community life and on the economic and political realities and pressures that professionals face in directing this aspect of community life.

Their philosophy of service should include the need for managers to serve as positive advocates for leisure in community life. Through their programming, public relations, and community development activities, leisure-service managers should seek to educate residents or organization members with respect to the importance of recreation, and the social and personal values that stem from creative, constructive play.

Throughout the chapters that follow, which deal with the basic concepts underlying management practices and the nine major areas of functional responsibilities in leisure-service organizations, the "why" and "how" of effective management will be made clear.

SUMMARY

Recreation, parks, and leisure services today are composed of a broad spectrum of community organizations with varied goals and objectives. These range from the simple delivery of pleasurable leisure activities to environmental protection, combating social problems, or providing important health-related services.

Managers play a key role in all such organizations. They provide leadership and coordination in such functions as determining missions, goals, and objectives; planning; organizing and implementing recreation programs and facilities development; and fiscal management. They serve as role models and decision makers, and help to determine priorities, policies, and procedures.

This chapter describes each of the major types of leisure-service agencies and the nine separate areas of management responsibility, while stressing that all of these elements should be closely integrated in actual practice. It concludes with a summary of several important social trends, environmental issues, and demographic shifts that will have important implications for leisure-service managers in the years ahead.

QUESTIONS FOR CLASS DISCUSSION OR ESSAY EXAMINATIONS

1. What are the major differences between voluntary nonprofit agencies and government departments providing recreation facilities and programs? Compare goals and objectives, funding, individuals or groups served, and major program elements.
2. Define *commercial recreation agencies* and indicate several of the types of leisure programs or services provided by such businesses. Select one major area of commercial recreation, such as travel and tourism or outdoor recreation, and describe trends in this field, the variety of services offered, and possible problems or issues connected to it.
3. Discuss what you see as the key roles of leisure-service managers today. How do they vary according to different types of recreation agencies, such as public, nonprofit, armed forces, therapeutic, or other types of sponsors?
4. Examine recreation, parks, and leisure services as a system, giving examples of both competition and cooperation in the interaction among different agencies. In your view, should the field be regarded primarily as an industry, a human- or social-service discipline, or with another type of identity or image?

REFERENCES

1. Murphy, James, Niepoth, E. William, Jamieson, Lynn, and Williams, John: *Leisure Systems: Critical Concepts and Applications,* Champaign, Ill., 1991, Sagamore Publishing, p. 318.
2. Lippitt, Gordon L.: *Organization Renewal: A Holistic Approach to Organization Development,* Englewood Cliffs, N.J., 1982, Prentice-Hall, p. 19.
3. *Standards and Evaluative Criteria for Baccalaureate Programs in Recreation, Park Resources and Leisure Services,* National Recreation and Park Association, Council on Accreditation, Ashburn, Va., July 1992.
4. Sullivan, James V.: *Management of Health and Fitness Programs,* Springfield, Ill., 1990, Charles C. Thomas.
5. *Benefits Catalogue, 2nd ed.,* Gloucester, Ontario, Can., 1997, Canadian Parks/Recreation Association.
6. Crossley, John, and Jamieson, Lynn: *Introduction to Commercial and Entrepreneurial Recreation,* Champaign, Ill., 1997, Sagamore Publishing, p. 11.
7. Lankford, Sam, and DeGraaf, Don: "Strengths, Weaknesses, Opportunities and Threats in Morale, Welfare and Recreation Organizations: Challenges of the 1990s," *Journal of Park and Recreation Administration* 10 (1), 1992, pp. 31–32.
8. *Promoting Wellness Through Leisure,* Brochure of Therapeutic Recreation Section, California Park and Recreation Society, Sacramento, Calif., 1997.
9. Parkhouse, Bonnie: *The Management of Sport: Its Foundations and Application,* St. Louis, Mo., 1996, National Association for Sport and Physical Education, and C. V. Mosby, pp. 3–4.
10. Crossley and Jamieson, *op. cit.,* pp. 17–18. See also *Statistical Abstract of the United States,* 1997, p. 266.

11. Jubenville, Alan, and Twight, Ben: *Outdoor Recreation Management: Theory and Application*, State College, Pa., 1993, Venture Publishing, p. 13.

12. "Tax Fight Heats Up South of Border," *Parks and Recreation Canada*, May/June 1996, p. 26.

13. Vaske, Jerry, Donnelly, Maureen, and LaPage, W. F.: "Partnerships for the 21st Century: A Return to Democracy," *Journal of Park and Recreation Administration*, Winter 1995, p. 1.

14. "Ontario Parks Goes Corporate," *Parks and Recreation Canada*, May/June 1996, p. 26.

15. Bragg, Rick, "Las Vegas Is Booming after City Reinvention," *New York Times*, May 4, 1997, p. 22.

TWO

Management as a Professional Discipline

In response [to environmental challenges] we have experimented with various approaches to help bring about change. In the late 1980s, it was Total Quality Management, followed by empowerment, which took place against a backdrop of downsizing and cost-cutting. More recently, we have seen an enthusiasm for Business Process Re-engineering . . . which began to set a new tone for change. It came from the perspective that it was no use just fiddling and fixing; it was necessary to step back and take a much longer, more thoughtful[1] look at the underlying business processes within an enterprise.

Management control is effectively applied in the private sector, and today many types of not-for-profit organizations also utilize some of its elements. Management control is a motivational process, involving formal and informal procedures, communication, performance reviews, and planning; it seeks to motivate members of an organization to take actions that are in its best interests. Thus, management control attempts to achieve congruence between the personal goals of individuals, the goals of their departments, and the goals of the entire organization. It is a dynamic process recognizing the ever-changing goals of organizations and individuals.[2]

INTRODUCTION

Management represents a key element in the successful operation of recreation, park, and leisure-service organizations. While it has been studied as a professional discipline chiefly within business and industrial settings, it also is an important function in government, social service, health and educational institutions, and other major systems in American and Canadian society.

For this reason, management has become a focus of organized research and publication. Hundreds of colleges and universities offer specialized degree programs in management theory and practice, and several major professional societies develop management standards and guidelines that influence professional practice.

This chapter begins by defining management as a generic process found in many different kinds of organizations. It then summarizes the development of management theory during the twentieth century and concludes by describing a number of currently popular management concepts and strategic approaches.

The following foundational understandings and professional competencies designated as essential in the Baccalaureate Degree Accreditation Standards of the NRPA/AALR Council on Accreditation are addressed in this chapter:

Knowledge of political and economic systems (7.02).

Knowledge of social systems and community organization (7.03).

Knowledge of people in their group relationships, including awareness of interests, attitudes, personal goals, and values as they affect human interaction (7.08).

Understanding of the concepts of organizational behavior, accountability, interpersonal relations, and decision-making strategies (8.29).

Understanding of and the ability to apply personnel management techniques, including job analysis, recruitment, selection, training, motivation, career development, and evaluation of staff and volunteers (8.30).

O B J E C T I V E S

At the conclusion of this chapter, readers should be familiar with the following concepts and trends in management theory and practice:

1. The meaning of management, as differentiated from administration, and its primary functions.
2. Classical management theory, also known as "scientific management" or the "machine-model," with such subconcepts as division of labor and job specialization, span of control, the scalar principle, and unity of command.
3. Linked to classical management theory, principles of organizational structure, involving departmentalization, horizontal and vertical differentiation, staff and line functions, and other bureaucratic structures.
4. The "human relations" era, including findings of the Hawthorne studies, McGregor's Theory X and Theory Y, and new analyses of job motivation, authority, power, and delegation.
5. Communication as a focus of management theory, linked to problem-solving and participative decision-making processes.
6. Application of "systems management" processes and management science approaches in business and government settings.
7. Influence of Japanese management theory, including the use of "quality circles," in American organizations.

8. More recent management approaches, including "total quality management" with strong customer emphasis; the use of benchmarking; strategic management; and reengineering emphases.

MEANING OF MANAGEMENT

Management is an integral part of all organizations and reaches into all aspects of ongoing operations. It is more than just a set of job titles, or the title assigned to a company executive or department commissioner. In a sense, it is like the nerve center of an individual, or the steering mechanism, accelerator, and brake of an automobile, in that it serves to drive the entire enterprise.

Initially, the term most widely used in referring to the highest level of power or control in organizations was *administration.* Typically, books on public recreation administration identified such functions as organizing, staffing, directing, or coordinating as the primary responsibilities of business or government executives with such titles as "president," "superintendent," "director," or "chief executive officer." The term implied that such individuals were chiefly responsible for all policy making within important areas of agency operations.

Following World War II, however, it was recognized that many organizational functions, such as planning, budgeting, supervising, evaluating, and reporting, were carried out not on the highest levels of organizational control, but on lower levels of staff operations.

Gradually, emphasis shifted from the work of top executives or company directors to so-called middle-management personnel who shared supervisory, decision-making, and planning responsibilities, or who headed service divisions or authority based on geographical location. Today, the most popular term that is used to describe the overall process of directing organizations—including several levels of authority and power—is management.

As a single example, in a recent newspaper listing of health-care job openings, the following titles appear: "Manager, Pediatric Service," "Case Manager, Acute Care Specialty," "Reimbursement Manager," or "Human Resources Manager." In terms of actual job titles, within the recreation, park, and leisure-service field, such terms as "director," "superintendent," "commissioner," "division head," or "district supervisor" may all be used to identify individuals who are essentially managers. They hold responsibility, not only for decision making or policy setting, but for carrying on the day-by-day operations of organizations and institutions in modern society. This is illustrated in Figure 2.1, which shows how the title of "manager" is used both at the executive level and at the level of those responsible for several specialized operations in a large, present-day municipal recreation and park department.

DEVELOPMENT OF MANAGEMENT THEORY

Management has frequently been described as an "art," in the sense that it is dependent on the use of human sensitivity, intelligence, and creativity—with no single formula for success. However, management has also been

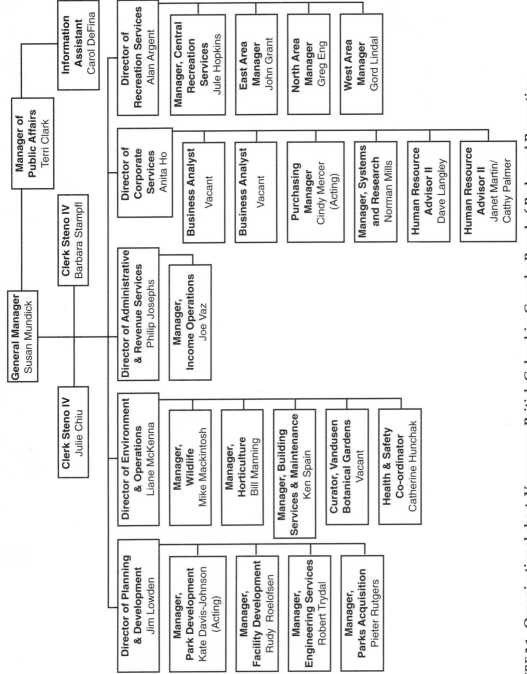

FIGURE 2.1. Organizational chart: Vancouver, British Columbia, Canada, Board of Parks and Recreation.

28

considered a science, in that systematic research and experimentation have developed a number of widely accepted theories or principles of successful organizational leadership. Such theories have dealt with both the structure and ongoing operation of businesses or human-service agencies, and with the effective management of personnel, fiscal resources, and other critical elements.

In an effort to develop a sound rationale for business organizations at the height of the Industrial Revolution, a number of business authorities and social scientists began to propose principles of effective management practice. The first approach, which came to be known as "classical management theory," or the "machine-model," was developed during the late nineteenth and early twentieth centuries.

CLASSICAL MANAGEMENT THEORY

While many authorities contributed to the development of classical management theory, three pioneers were chiefly responsible for its influence: Max Weber, Frederick Taylor, and Henri Fayol.

Max Weber and Bureaucracy

Max Weber was a German sociologist who analyzed varied forms of societal structures, including the military forces. He developed what was called a "rational-legal" model of bureaucracy that contrasted with more traditional concepts of control. In Weber's view, employees of large operating systems tended to be highly individualistic and unpredictable in their behavior.

To control this factor and to ensure efficient performance, Weber argued for a depersonalized approach to organizational structure and operation that came to be known as the bureaucratic model. In this model, there would be precisely defined and enforced employee roles, functions, and processes, with strict regulation to enforce conformity and eliminate dysfunctional job performance.

Frederick Taylor's Machine-Model

Frederick Taylor was an American engineer and steel company executive who studied varied forms of production scientifically and created what came to be known as the "machine-model" of industrial organizations. Taylor believed that most factories and other business concerns were hampered by hostility and a continuing conflict between company owners and administrators and employees, with many assembly-line workers deliberately resisting efforts to speed production.

Convinced that many job assignments were poorly designed and inefficient, he carried out "time-and-motion" studies to determine the most efficient and streamlined ways of accomplishing different tasks.

Fayol's Fourteen Principles

The third important contributor to classical management theory was Henri Fayol, a successful French industrialist. Fayol believed that five administrative functions were important in all kinds of organizations: planning, organizing, commanding, coordinating, and controlling. He published a text on administration that was widely distributed throughout the industrial world, and that presented fourteen key principles (Fig. 2.2).

PRINCIPLES OF ORGANIZATION THEORY

It was agreed that the functions or operational tasks of any institution or enterprise should be clearly identified and assigned to specific organizational divisions or units. Exact procedures for carrying out each function should be precisely defined, with standards for correct performance that are enforced consistently by supervisors.

FIGURE 2.2. Fayol's fourteen principles.
Modified from Fayol, H.: *General and Industrial Management*, London, 1949, Pitman & Sons, Ltd.

1. *Division of work.* Work assignments should be highly specialized and concentrated on narrower functions, in order to produce more and better work with the same time and effort.
2. *Authority and responsibility.* Authority is the right to give orders and to demand obedience and responsibility.
3. *Discipline.* Discipline implies respect for the agreements between the company and its employees, and is essential for the smooth operation of the organization. Without it, enterprises cannot prosper, and it must be enforced if necessary by judiciously applied sanctions.
4. *Unity of command.* An employee should receive orders from one superior only.
5. *Unity of direction.* There should be one plan and one head for each group of activities having the same objectives.
6. *Subordination of individual interest to general interest.* The interests of any employee or group of employees should not prevail over those of the company or overall organization.
7. *Remuneration of personnel.* Personnel compensation should be fair and satisfactory both to employees and to the organization, to maintain the loyalty and support of employees.
8. *Centralization.* Centralized management authority is a natural consequence of organizing, although the appropriate degree of centralization will vary according to the particular organization.
9. *Scalar chain.* The scalar chain is the chain of superior-subordinate relationships, ranging from the highest authority to the lowest rank of employees.
10. *Order.* The organization should provide an orderly place for each individual; a place for everyone and everyone in his place.
11. *Equity.* Equity, consisting of balanced fairness and a sense of justice, is found throughout the organization.
12. *Stability of tenure of personnel.* Time is needed for the employee to adapt to his work and perform efficiently. Since high turnover increases inefficiency, a mediocre manager who stays is preferable to a highly competent manager who comes and goes.
13. *Initiative.* At all organizational levels, employee initiative is augmented by zeal and energy.
14. *Esprit de corps.* Teamwork marked by the harmonious interpersonal relationship of employees provides strength to the organization.

Within all organizations, the assignment of authority is legitimated, with superiors having the right to command others, and subordinates the obligation to obey their orders, provided that the orders do not infringe on personnel policies, labor union contracts, or other formal policies or regulations. The scalar principle established authority at the top of the organization, with each successive level having authority over the levels below it. Administrative power flows vertically down the chain of command, with each employee directly responsible to only one supervisor above him or her.

"Span of control" refers to the number of subordinates who report to one superior or supervisor. In beginning classical management theory, it was held that this should not be more than six. Later, the principle emerged that at higher levels in the organization, a manager can effectively supervise four to eight employees; at lower levels, from eight to fifteen. It was recognized that the optimum span of control was also affected by job complexity, physical location (the geographical "spread" of employees), and the extent to which work operations could be standardized.

Linked to the principle of task specialization, employees are grouped into manageable units or departments. Each such unit is headed by a supervisor who then reports to a manager or supervisor at a higher level within the administrative hierarchy. Typical departmental functions might consist of such tasks as finance, marketing, or manufacturing.

Other Organizational Concepts and Approaches

As classical management theory became firmly established, a number of additional concepts emerged, involving different approaches to departmentalization.

Vertical/Horizontal Contrasts

This principle is concerned with the number of levels within the organization's ladder of authority, or hierarchy. Because information and decision making must flow through a number of levels, or layers, a highly vertical, narrow structure with many levels may prove cumbersome and inefficient.

On the other hand, a horizontal, broad structure may make it easier for information to flow from top to bottom, or vice versa, but may make it difficult for managers to supervise a large number of department or unit heads who are under their command.

Centralization/Decentralization

A centralized organization is one in which authority and decision making reside narrowly within a small group of individuals in a tightly structured control or policy-making group or board. In contrast, a decentralized structure is one in which different department managers have a greater degree of authority to direct their own functional units or programs.

Use of Organization Charts

In classically managed organizations, it became customary to develop organization charts that visually depicted the major departments and functional units of the business or other institution. Typically, they took the shape of a pyramid (narrow above, wider below), showing both the vertical chain of command with power flowing from top to bottom, and the horizontal departmentalization showing the division of functions into separate units. Accompanying this organizational chart, there might be separate, detailed charts of each of the functional units, giving the titles and often the names of individuals in specific positions on each level.

It became customary to designate units or specific employees in organization charts as "staff" or "line." Staff employees were usually attached to central management in such roles as planning, consulting, or research, while line employees actually manufactured a product or provided other specific services or functions for customers.

Formal and Informal Systems

Formal organization structures and roles are defined in printed policy statements, personnel handbooks, production procedures, and similar documents or training plans. Such formal, established rules and relationships tended to make it difficult for individual employees to take independent action or show initiative or creativity on the job.

However, it was also recognized that individuals or groups of employees may bypass the formal system. Murphy and his coauthors describe the informal system as consisting of cliques, clubs, or other groupings of employees who have common concerns who, by ignoring excessively restrictive policies, may bring greater efficiency or productivity to the organization—or, by defying the formal structure, may promote conflict and disharmony.[3] Particularly in large, complex enterprises, such groups and informal working arrangements often act as a subtext to the official structure—with or without top management's knowledge or approval.

HUMAN RELATIONS MANAGEMENT ERA

Classical management theory was widely accepted and put into practice in the early decades of the twentieth century in business and industry, government, the armed forces, and numerous other types of institutions. It lent itself to highly organized, efficient operations, particularly in manufacturing concerns, where work operations could be sharply defined and standards of performance applied.

However, after World War I, during the 1920s and 1930s, a number of factors combined to encourage what came to be called the human relations era in management theory and practice. Critics pointed out that if organizations existed in an unchanging, stable environment, rigidly structured management policies and procedures could serve company goals effectively. However, businesses and other social institutions were rarely in a fixed setting. Instead, they were constantly subject to changing factors and influences: financial ups and downs, legal and regulatory controls, customer or client needs, shifting suppliers, and similar unpredictable elements. The kinds of rigid, tightly controlled decision-making and supervisory practices that bureaucracy encouraged did not give organizations the flexibility to respond quickly and creatively to changing environmental conditions.

Increasingly, it was recognized that bureaucratic management failed to consider the human factor in organizations. Workers were too often regarded as cogs in a machine, with arbitrary, "speed-up" production standards, poor working conditions, and little attention paid to factors of job satisfaction, group process, or individual motivation.

Gradually, a new wave of attention was given to such concerns, spearheaded by social scientists who conducted field research in the growing discipline of social psychology. They challenged the view that monetary pay represented adequate compensation for employees, and instead focused on the impact of different styles of management and supervision on employee motivation and job productivity.

Hawthorne Experiments

For example, a leading set of experiments was conducted at the Hawthorne Branch of the Western Electric Company in Cicero, Illinois, in the late 1920s. It was found that changes in work hours, lighting, rest periods, and similar elements markedly improved productivity and reduced absenteeism at the plant. However, the key factor was not the specific changes in job conditions as much as the impact on workers of having their needs considered. The Hawthorne studies concluded also that employees tended to form groups that developed their own codes of on-the-job behavior, and that they were able to apply group sanctions such as social ostracism or ridicule that pressured other workers to comply with informal group norms.[4]

A number of other studies during the 1930s examined the impact of different leadership styles—authoritarian, democratic, and laissez-faire (permissive)—on group behavior in work and other social settings. Still other studies explored situational variables affecting leadership effectiveness and group productivity. They found that when employees were given the feeling of being important, and not being "bossed" arbitrarily, their motivation and job performance responded positively. The physical conditions of the work setting were not as important as its emotional climate.

Studies of Employee Motivation

A number of social scientists explored issues of personality in relation to work and other areas of human achievement.

McGregor's Theory X and Theory Y

Douglas McGregor presented two contrasting views that depicted traditional and contemporary views of work attitudes. Theory X, which was linked to classical, bureaucratic management approaches, held that most workers had an inherent dislike of work and would avoid it if possible. Therefore, the workers had to be controlled, directed, and threatened with punishment, to make them perform satisfactorily. Theory Y, instead, held that for many people, work could be truly satisfying and enjoyable, and that if they were given the opportunity to exercise creative self-direction and work toward goals that they saw as truly challenging, they would not only accept, but seek, responsibility.

McGregor argued that conventional organization theory was unrealistic in its simplistic principles when applied to the complex relations and roles of employees in present-day business or government operations. He concluded that a higher level of open communications, mutual trust, and support, and sensitive management of human differences was essential for success, rather than formal authority and rigid operational rules.[5]

Maslow's Human Needs Hierarchy

In an influential analysis of human motivations that affected work behavior, psychologist Abraham Maslow identified five groups of human needs, which he placed in rank order of importance. Beginning with the most basic needs, these were:

Physiological, including food, water, shelter and other survival-connected needs;

Safety and security, consisting of freedom from environmental threats;

Social and affiliation needs, including needs for friendship, love, and acceptance by others;

Esteem consisting of a sense of accomplishment and competence, and recognition by others; and

Self-actualization, meaning the degree to which an individual reaches his or her fullest growth and human potential.[6]

Maslow's needs hierarchy held essentially that people are motivated by a number of different kinds of needs and that, if these needs are met in a significant way in the work environment, workers will perform more effectively on the job.

Herzberg's Hygiene and Motivator Factors

Frederick Herzberg identified two sets of factors that influenced work behavior. The first set, which he called hygiene factors, dealt with such job elements as working conditions, pay, fringe benefits, or other aspects of the work environment. He concluded that if these were unsatisfactory, the worker's motivation and job performance would be low. At best, if these factors were satisfactory, they would bring employees only to a neutral level of motivation and performance.

In contrast, Herzberg described such elements as the opportunity for taking responsibility, creative achievement, or advancement on the job as motivator factors, which helped workers become highly motivated and committed to the organization's success.[7] A number of other behavioral scientists conducted research on personality factors affecting work performance. Their findings, chiefly during the 1950s and 1960s, did much to counter the repressive style of personnel supervision that had been widely used as part of the bureaucratic management approach.

Today, the human factor in organizations is more fully acknowledged, and employees are regarded as valuable resources, rather than as cogs in a machine. Chapter 7 describes participative approaches to human resource management that stemmed from these developments.

With a growing trend toward the use of participative management styles in which employers encouraged workers to share in decision-making and other organizational processes, fuller attention was focused on such issues as authority, power, and delegation.

Researchers in the human relations movement defined *authority* as legitimate power, possessed by the individual who holds a particular post within the organization's chain of command. Authority usually comes about through appointment, election, or some other form of promotion based on successful performance or other criteria for advancement.

Power, defined as the ability to make decisions or issue orders to other employees within an organization, is usually attached to one's authority or position level. However, it may also represent the ability to influence or direct others *without* formal authority, based on one's expertise, experience, strategic skills, or other personal leadership traits.

Delegation refers to entrusting a degree of one's authority and responsibility for a particular agency function to another employee—usually at a subordinate level. Both the individual who delegates the responsibility and the employee who accepts the task are then held accountable for its successful accomplishment.

The delegation of broader work responsibilities is regarded as an important means, not only of having tasks accomplished, but as a useful method of upgrading the skills and career potential of staff members. It strengthens their sense of commitment to the organization, serves as a reward for good job performance, and thus promotes a positive job climate and contributes to employee motivation.

At the same time, many managers hesitate to delegate job responsibilities for a variety of reasons. They may lack confidence in the capability of subordinate employees, or may fear that the subordinate's success will "outshine" their own performance. Often, managers may argue that lower-level employees lack the experience or skill to accept delegated responsibilities and carry them out successfully.

Despite such reservations, delegation of management authority has proven to be a significant element in creating highly motivated and efficient workforces. It plays an important part in such organizational processes as shared decision making and conflict resolution, and in the "quality circle" approach, which became popular in the 1980s.

Decision-Making as Management Responsibility

A key function of successful managers involves making decisions. These may have to do with the hiring or firing of personnel, the development of new products or services, the initiation of a new public relations campaign, or a host of other areas in which managers must make choices between alternative courses of action. The manager's job is essentially to make wise decisions and then to implement them successfully.

Agency decisions that managers must make fall into several categories: (1) those that are fairly routine and that are covered by organizational policies or regulations; (2) those that are new or in which the problem to be solved does not fit under existing procedural controls; (3) those that involve minor consequences for the organization and that can be made with little risk; and (4) those that have major implications and that require careful analysis and soundly based decisions.

In general, routine decisions on problems or issues that appear frequently can be made by lower-level personnel on the basis of existing policies. Those that are of greater weight, or in which the stakes are critical and the outcomes uncertain, are normally the responsibility of higher level managers. Often, decisions are reached incrementally, in that a series of small decisions are made over a period of time, leading to a final major decision or policy statement.

Decision making, conflict resolution, and problem solving became important concerns for management researchers during the human relations era because of the growing emphasis on democratic, participative management approaches. A basic model showing the steps that are usually found in decision-making processes is shown in Figure 2.3, and a fuller presentation of problem-solving methods is given on pages 225–227. Many schools of business management typically make extensive use of the case study approach to problem solving and decision making. Therefore, several chapters in this text give examples of case studies in recreation, parks, and leisure studies that lend themselves to individual or team analysis as a course assignment.

THE COMMUNICATION PROCESS

During the 1960s and 1970s, emphasis was given to the study of the communication process, which was seen as a vital part of effective manager-employee relationships. *Communication* may be defined as the process of formulating, transmitting, and receiving messages in varied forms: verbal, written, or other symbolic forms. It is carried out in a host of settings (through memorandums, in meetings, personal conferences, news releases, and reports) and with a variety of purposes (to train personnel or counsel them, to reward or punish employees, to inspire them, to present relevant facts, or to influence a course of action).

Some researchers have estimated that managers spend between 50 percent and 90 percent of their work time communicating within each major organizational function, such as planning, controlling, directing, or organizing. Because of its importance, communication has been carefully analyzed by researchers and represents an independent area of study in many higher education curricula.

Elements and Stages in Communication

The component parts of communication include the following four elements: (1) the *sender,* who creates and transmits the message; (2) the *message* itself, which must be transformed into language or other symbols appropriate for sending; (3) the *medium* or *channel* through which the message is transmitted, such as the telephone, fax machine, or office memorandum; and (4) the *receiver,* who receives and interprets the message. The sequence in which these elements come into play is shown in a five-stage model, as seen in Figure 2.4.

Beyond the need to ensure that communication is made as clear and explicit as possible and appropriate to its purpose, it was recognized that messages are

FIGURE 2.3. Problem-solving/decision-making sequence.
Adapted from Jubenville, Alan and Wright, Ben: *Outdoor Recreation Management: Theory and Application*, State College, Pa., 1993, Venture Publishing, p. 53.

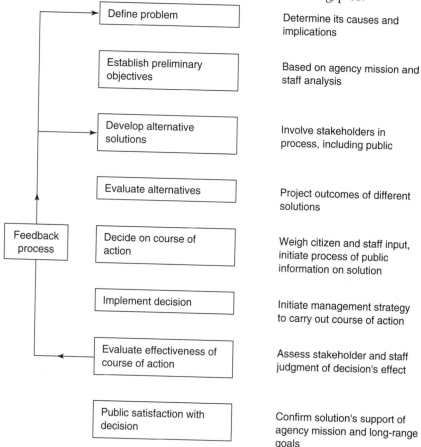

Define problem	Determine its causes and implications
Establish preliminary objectives	Based on agency mission and staff analysis
Develop alternative solutions	Involve stakeholders in process, including public
Evaluate alternatives	Project outcomes of different solutions
Decide on course of action	Weigh citizen and staff input, initiate process of public information on solution
Implement decision	Initiate management strategy to carry out course of action
Evaluate effectiveness of course of action	Assess stakeholder and staff judgment of decision's effect
Public satisfaction with decision	Confirm solution's support of agency mission and long-range goals

Feedback process

sent and received within a framework of psychological and emotional over-tones. They may contain elements of information or advice, praise and support, blame or threat, or other content that may have effects not intended by the sender. Thus, in the era of human relations management that sought to be sensitive to the needs of employees in order to free them to perform at their highest potential, it was essential that both the goals and the language of communication be carefully thought out and effectively delivered.

NEW APPROACHES TO DEPARTMENTAL STRUCTURES

Linked to such efforts to develop more flexible staff relationships, the rigid approach to departmental structures found in bureaucracies also came under fire. The principles of having sharply specialized functions, with each employee responsible to the individual above himself or herself within the chain of command, and with little provision made for joint planning or cooperative action between different departments, made it difficult for organizations to respond creatively to new challenges or opportunities.

Typically, if an employee had an idea for an innovative service or form of production that would require the input or cooperation of those in another department, he or she would have to submit the suggestion to a supervisor who might move it laboriously up the chain of command within his or her department. Ultimately, when the suggestion reached an appropriate level for approval, it would require consideration by successive levels of employees within the other department—with the likelihood of excessive delay or rejection at any point.

This situation, at a time when competition and the need to be as productive as possible had heightened dramatically, made many management authorities question the formal structure of departments that was part of the classical management approach. Many organizations began to experiment with new kinds of work structures, including "matrix" and "linking-pin" methods.

Matrix Approach

Under this approach, employees continue to be assigned to their regular departments or work units, but are also assigned to temporary or regular work with members of other departments on planning teams or other special projects. With the formal walls that separated them arbitrarily broken down, and with less need to submit to several levels of authority or decision making, employees with varying skills and outlooks were able to share their resources creatively, with improved information processing.

Linking-Pin Approach

In a variation of the matrix structure, individuals are designated as "linking-pins" in an organization and are given the assignment of working with project

FIGURE 2.4. Stages of the communication process.

Stage Number	Stage	Explanation
1	Formulation of message	Determining what the communicator wants to say and what its impact or effect should be
2	Encoding information	Translating information into language or symbols for effective communication; need for clarity, nonthreatening, and constructive impact
3	Transmitting	Using appropriate channel (speech, conversation, telephone call, memorandum, newsletter, etc.), plus method of delivery (style and efficiency of presentation)
4	Reception	Ensuring that those receiving the message are in a situation where they can be reached accurately and where they will be attentive to it
5	Decoding	Checking that all elements in the message are clearly understood by follow-up questions, discussions, or monitoring methods

groups both above and below their own levels of authority. The purpose of this approach is to improve integration within the overall agency structure, by facilitating communication and decision making among individuals with different perspectives, skills, and job responsibilities.

INFLUENCE OF THE QUALITY CIRCLE APPROACH

In the 1970s and 1980s, a new influence on management theory and practice appeared as Japan became a leading world competitor as a producer of automobiles and motorcycles, cameras and electronic equipment, and other major manufactured products. Once a second-rate, imitative, and generally scorned industrial nation, Japan was now recognized for its effective management approaches and business success.

A key element in Japan's economy recovery was the adoption of the quality circle approach. This involved having groups of employees, usually ranging in size from five to ten, meet regularly within each work unit. Led by a team foreperson or other senior employee, they are taught group communication and decision-making skills, and become involved in evaluating their work unit's performance and problem-solving tasks. Robert Cole writes that, while intended to improve methods of production as a primary purpose, the quality circle approach also

> . . . focuses on the self-development of workers. This includes: development of leadership abilities of foremen and workers, skill development among workers, identification of natural leaders with supervisory potential, improvement of worker morale and motivation, and the stimulation of teamwork within work groups.[8]

Beyond the quality circle emphasis, Japanese workers were routinely involved in several other work groups, each with a different task, with frequent socialization among employees on different job levels. Emphasis on developing stronger product standards resulted in all employees throughout the business hierarchy being given training in quality control, rather than having it be the limited responsibility of a few engineers or quality-control supervisors.

While the quality circle approach as such was not fully adopted by a great number of Western businesses or institutions, the general principles found in Japanese management practices had a strong impact on North American business leaders. In particular, the emphasis on quality control resulted in a major new thrust toward total quality management and "benchmarking" in the late 1980s and 1990s (see pages 44–45).

MANAGEMENT SCIENCE: USE OF THE SYSTEMS THEORY

At the same time that human relations research influenced management practice, a second, sharply different approach also gained prominence in the post–World War II period. This involved a so-called operations management thrust, which applied scientific principles of analysis and systems theory to organizational planning and production. In contrast with the humanistic emphasis of the human relations approach, this management science model had the following thrusts:

1. It emphasized the need for planning and decision making on every level to rely on factual data, analyzed through mathematical techniques, making use of computer processing;
2. It made extensive use of theoretical or abstract models, which tended to express production, marketing, or other organizational processes in diagrammatical form; and
3. It relied heavily on systems theory in examining the interaction among elements in an organization, or between the organization and its surrounding environment.

Meaning of System

The term *system* generally refers to an assembly or network of different units or parts that have a significant degree of interaction. There are varied types of systems, including: (1) *natural systems*, existing in nature, as contrasted with *human-created* systems (such as business or government); (2) *physical systems*, involving tangible elements, compared to *abstract systems*, such as goal statements or philosophical ideas; and (3) *open systems*, where there is significant interaction between a system and its environment, contrasted with *closed systems*, which are walled off from outside influences.

The basic elements of a systems approach are *input, process, output, equilibrium*, and *feedback*, as shown in Figure 2.5. A sixth element might include *control*, which involves the use of feedback to provide timely knowledge of the system's operational success and permits those operating the system to modify it in constructive ways at any point.

Jubenville and Twight point out that the systems approach may be used to better understand any organization's total operation. In the field of outdoor recreation, for example, they point out that many separate subsystems may be integrated to form a single complex management system, with a clear picture of the interrelationships between subsystems internally and the social environment externally. However, they caution:

> . . . we must also keep in mind that this is an open system where external factors are continually affecting the internal operations and changing the program composition of the system. For example, a highly publicized injury in one park or zone can affect how the total system responds to hazard management in the future.[9]

In terms of practical applications, systems theory suggests that, in order to make intelligent plans or carry out the basic functions of management, it is necessary to develop accurate models of all elements within the overall system of a given agency and the societal, governmental, or economic forces that affect them. Different courses of action or responses to changing environment conditions may then be tested as they interact with each other.

FIGURE 2.5. Key elements of systems.

INPUT

Input is the generating function or initiating force that starts a system (such as the continuation of a previous system or process or the decision to initiate a new program), along with the human and material resources that are fed into the process.

PROCESS

Process refers to the ongoing action of the system, which is carried out to achieve stated objectives. It includes both internally generated efforts and interaction with environmental forces.

OUTPUT

Output is the result, or what actually happens, in the transformation of the input during the process. It typically includes specific products, information, services, or ways in which clients or participants themselves are transformed or satisfied within the system.

Since systems theory emphasizes the influences of all subsystems and external forces on a given organization or process, models are often constructed to demonstrate these relationships. Two key aspects of such models are equilibrium and feedback.

EQUILIBRIUM

The concept of equilibrium implies that most human or natural processes tend to achieve a state of relative balance or steadiness. This centers around a fixed point or level of balance, which is the normal state. When external forces are brought to bear on the system, modifications occur. If the system is a highly stable one, the forces needed to create change must be powerful. If it is unstable or precarious, even small outside forces may affect the equilibrium.

FEEDBACK

The concept of feedback refers to the process through which diagnostic information is gathered about the effects of various inputs or influences on the system. It also describes the reactions of the environment to the process that is in effect or to its products. In highly automated systems, feedback may be used as a self-regulating device to control the rate or volume of production, as in the simple example of a home-heating thermostat, or as a way to provide flow of information used in modifying a model or actual on-the-job performance. Feedback provides organizations with critical information regarding the effects of actions they have taken. Therefore, they must be able to respond promptly and effectively to such messages — as in the case of a business organization that conducts marketing research about the public's reaction to its new products and services.

To carry this out, models may be developed that simplify the agency's processes by reducing the variables to manageable numbers, presenting them in abstract form, and identifying the probable outcomes of different courses of action. Often this is done through computer programs, which enable managers to test the predictable effects of different variables or inputs without having to actually carry out projects in real life. While this is most feasible in management tasks that can be reduced to statistically or physically controllable elements—

such as construction problems or the income-related effect of different pricing decisions—it can also be used to analyze the feasibility of decisions involving human behavior and social interactions.

Use of Network Models

During the 1960s and 1970s, network models were used extensively to track the planning and implementation of varied governmental or business projects.

Program Evaluation Review Techniques (PERT)

This planning system outlines starting and completion times for each task or event in an overall project, and plots them diagramatically to show how individual tasks are dependent on earlier ones being carried out successfully. Using mathematical and computer analysis, estimates may be made of a project's probable time requirements (PERT-TIME) and financial costs (PERT-COST). In addition to providing useful guidance at the initial stages of any project, the critical path method (CPM), which outlines the flow sequence of needed activities, is also valuable in monitoring the progress, day by day, of work teams. Thus, it illustrates the feedback and control mechanisms used in systems management.

Program-Planning Budgeting Systems (PPBS)

This model was developed in the 1960s by the U.S. Department of Defense. It made use of computer-based systems for organizing information of all sorts into a single, integrated management plan, with special emphasis on budget factors. While it was applied primarily within the military forces, it was useful also in other large-scale government or business operations, requiring a precise identification of the organization's goals and objectives, the projected benefits and estimated costs of a given venture, alternative ways of achieving the desired outcomes, and major assumptions and uncertainties connected with the project.

MANAGEMENT TRENDS IN THE 1980S AND 1990S

In general, both the human relations and systems-based approaches to management lost impetus during the 1980s, a decade marked by economic uncertainty with intermittent waves of recession and prosperity, and by dramatic shifts in the ownership of huge corporations through mergers and hostile takeovers. During this time, business competition became more intense, and public and nonprofit organizations found it necessary to adopt more entrepreneurial identities to assure fiscal support and public involvement.

Emphasis on Total Quality Management

The quality assurance approach, in which the company guarantees the quality of its product or service to customers, had its origins in the early twentieth century machine-model urged by Frederick Taylor. In industries that had accepted Taylor's principles of task segmentation and precise definition of each manufacturing function, it became customary to assign quality inspectors to the end of each production line. Their task was to approve products for shipping, based on approved specifications, and to reject them or return them for reworking. Thus, quality assurance was an internal organization function.

However, in the search for "total quality management," a slogan that became popular in the late 1980s, business heads recognized that too often the needs and wishes of customers were ignored or slighted. In part, the immense success of Japanese automobile manufacturers in the 1960s and 1970s was due to the widespread belief of American consumers that Detroit-built cars were poorly constructed and had numerous defects, while Japanese vehicles had a higher level of quality and long-term dependability.

Through the 1990s, the management literature stressed the critical need to meet and surpass customer expectations throughout the business world. Numerous critics argued that all consumers could tell horror stories—of banks that treat their long-time depositors as strangers, of credit-card companies that can't get address changes right, or airlines that totally mangle reservation requests. In the effort to overcome such problems, managers began to demand honest evaluations of the way their organizations were being run, and the way customers were being served. To achieve the highest possible level of quality, it became necessary to continually diagnose and improve performance. Rather than disregard or "brush off" customer complaints, quality assurance authorities argued that they should be welcomed. Oren Harari writes:

> Most companies treat customer complaints either as dreaded plagues that they avoid dealing with at all cost or as necessary "evils" in doing business, worthy of a brief span of reluctant, patronizing attention.[10]

Emphasis on "Customer-Defined Value"

Instead, Harari urges, companies would be wiser to view customer complaints as a source of strategic opportunity, treating complainers with the same dignity and respect given to their own high-priced analysts or consultants. In the effort to achieve the maximum degree of quality and customer satisfaction, Bert Spector suggests the following strategies:

1. The need to refocus the organization on customer-defined value (i.e., what *they* regard as important);
2. To demand responsiveness from all levels of the organization, from top executives to front-line employees;
3. Enable front-line employees to meet and exceed customer expectations;
4. Create and maintain cross-organization teamwork, to achieve maximum quality and achieve customer satisfaction;
5. Continuously diagnose and improve value-serving performance; and
6. Allow employee discretion within a well-defined set of parameters or guidelines.[11]

Use of Benchmarking

A strategic approach that became widely popular at this time was benchmarking, defined as the continuous process of measuring products, services, and practices against an organization's strongest competitors, or those recognized as industry leaders. The basic point of benchmarking is the pursuit of excellence, in order to achieve competitive advantage. It has also been defined as the search for industry-best practices that lead to superior performance, through the use of standards that serve as reference points through which any product or service can be judged.

Robert Camp suggests a model of the steps involved in the benchmarking process (Figure 2.6). It makes clear that benchmarking is not an abstract idea, but must be a proactive endeavor that results in the change of organizational practices in order to achieve superior performance.

Identification of Stakeholders

Moving beyond the concept of simply satisfying customers, benchmarking also focuses on serving many different constituents, referred to as stakeholders. As Chapter 1 points out, the notion of stakeholders is that many different individuals have a stake in the success of businesses or other types of organizations. These might include company owners or shareholders, employees, those directly served by the organization, or others affected by its operation.

For example, Liebfried and McNair write about the stakeholder perspective:

> . . . the company is serving many different constituents at all times. Benchmarking succeeds best when everyone's interests are understood and considered in the chosen solutions. Placing customers ahead of employee interests may seem to be a formula for success, but the employees are the ones who will make the customer happy, not the "organization." Conversely, placing employees above owner interests can also lead to downstream problems, resulting in the withdrawal of the capital essential for supporting the organization's activities.[12]

Stakeholders in the Leisure-Service Field

While benchmarking and considering the needs of stakeholders may appear to be chiefly concerned with the needs of commercial businesses, they may also be applied readily to agencies in the recreation, park, and leisure-service field. For example, Caneday and Kuzmic present a model of different groups of stakeholders in the operation of a national forest in the Ouachita Mountains, in southeastern Oklahoma and southwestern Arkansas. They write:

> The stakeholders of a national forest can be viewed as individuals and groups of people arranged in concentric circles, radiating from the resource base. [Understanding their needs] becomes important to the U.S. Forest Service as they manage the resource for the varying interests represented by the public.[13]

In this case, the Ouachita Mountain stakeholders include: (1) an innermost circle of on-site visitors or users of the national forest; (2) private landowners, business managers, timber companies, and other interest groups on the fringe of the

FIGURE 2.6. Steps in the benchmarking process.
Adapted from Camp, Robert: *Benchmarking: The Search for Industry Best Practices that Lead to Superior Performance*, Milwaukee, Wis., 1995, Quality Press, p. 17.

Planning

Identify what is to be benchmarked: agency performance

Identify comparable organizations

Determine data collection methods and collect benchmarking data

Analysis

Determine current performance gap in agency

Project desired future performance levels

Decision making

Communicate benchmark findings and gain approval/agreement

Establish functional goals and strategic plan

Develop action plans

Action

Implement specific actions and monitor progress

Recalibrate benchmarks as needed or revise strategies

Maturity

Practices fully integrated into agency operations

national forest, many of whom serve forest users directly; and (3) people at a distance from the forest, such as outdoor recreation enthusiasts who may occasionally visit the area, environmentalists or advocates for wilderness preservation, or others with an interest in the forest's uses.

ENTREPRENEURSHIP AND CREATIVE CHANGE

As Chapter 1 points out, during the 1980s many recreation and park agencies, along with other leisure-service providers, moved strongly in the direction of a marketing, commercially influenced management orientation. In so doing, they adopted an entrepreneurial stance. Entrepreneurs are generally defined as business-minded individuals who are creative and innovative, who take risks, and who seek out new and unconventional ways of delivering services or finding new markets. Leisure-service authors and educators urged practitioners at this time to get away from formal staff and patron relationships, fixed organization charts and personnel assignments, and traditional approaches to developing and delivering programs.

David Gray, for example, urged that in an era of growing social problems and challenges to leisure-service organizations, new management approaches were necessary:

> Entrepreneurial organizations support reasonable risk taking, learn from failure, and reward success. . . . They realize that change creates opportunity and maintain an environmental scan to assess where [it] exists. . . . They tolerate ambiguity, encourage intuitive path-findings. They plan by working backward from a preferred future.[14]

In the business world, the rate of change and the challenges it posed for company executives accelerated even more rapidly in the 1990s. It was an era in which: (1) new legislation opened formerly restricted markets, allowing new competition from abroad; (2) customers became increasingly sophisticated in their purchasing behavior, and more knowledgeable about the service they could expect; (3) the new global marketplace created an even greater freedom for many nations and companies; and (4) social, cultural, demographic, and political changes were accompanied by new forms of information technology, growing at a relentless pace.

Linked to these factors, the creation of huge new conglomerates in fields related to public leisure, the leveraged takeover and buyouts of many companies, and the dramatic downsizing of company workforces all underlined the need for managers to develop the capability for creative change. Increasingly during the years just before the turn of the twenty-first century, management experts argued that organizations of all types had the following pressing needs.

1. Organizational processes must be designed and redefined, then piloted, tested, and adapted to different geographical and cultural markets.
2. Staff members must be trained in new ways of working, both in terms of production or service methods and in terms of their relationships with customers or others served.
3. Organizations must be reshaped, both in terms of basic beliefs, values, and goals, and often in terms of their structure, including job roles and departments or service units.
4. Reward systems for employees need to be improved, with new career advancement plans created, along with more effective personnel evaluation procedures.[15]

Within the business world, major changes were occurring, such as the widespread downsizing of many companies that terminated tens of thousands of employees, and the increased reliance on outsourcing, contracting of work projects, or the use of detached, temporary employees. Many of the changes affected elements of the leisure-service field, both profit- and non-profit-oriented. Bainbridge writes:

> . . . what we once took for granted can no longer be assumed. Computer corporations merge with publishing houses and film companies in the race to capitalize on the convergence between multiple media. Entrepreneurial start-ups take on mighty established players and win. Football clubs become quoted companies on the stock market, making more profit from merchandising than from spectators. Hospitals struggle with the principles of market forces [and the trend toward managed care]. Customers demand service in hours, not days; they are no longer prepared to accept poor quality goods or shoddy service.[16]

In the leisure-service field, the social, economic, and spiritual trends described in Chapter 1 created a new set of challenges for recreation and park managers. In response to these conditions, the key thrust in the 1990s moved in the direction of strategy management.

Strategy Management

This may be defined as a total process of evaluating an organization's internal and external environments, its current operations, and its prospects for the future—both short- and long-range. It makes use of an intensive planning effort at all levels of an organization, and results in the selection of strategies for change that may include new goals and priorities, programming or production tactics, marketing ventures, and organizational restructuring.

Smith, Bucklin Associates conclude:

> A strategic plan does not provide a detailed chronology of action; that is a function of an "operational" or "business" plan. Rather, a strategic plan broadly maps the activities the organization should pursue to maintain its desired character and identity. It is a tool to guide decision-making by the organization's leaders on issues which are fundamental to the organization [in] responding to a changing environment.[17]

Some management authorities stress that management strategy has its roots in warfare, as competition becomes more and more fierce and survival more problematic. Dobson and Starkey write that companies and armies have much in common:

> They both, for example, pursue strategies of deterrence, offence, defence and alliance. One can think of a well-developed business strategy in terms of probing opponents' weaknesses; forcing opponents to stretch their resources; overwhelming selected markets or market segments; establishing a leadership position of dominance in certain markets, etc.[18]

Still other writers stress that strategic planning may involve a high level of cooperative, rather than competitive, action. John Bryson, for example, points out that public agencies and nonprofit organizations make extensive use of strategic planning, particularly as their top administrators share their knowledge, needs, and resources. He writes:

Certainly this is true of public agencies, local governments, and nonprofit organizations that deliver "public" services. When most of the key decision makers are insiders, it will likely be easier to get people together to decide important matters, reconcile differences, and coordinate implementation activities.[19]

Emphasis on Reengineering

Finally, in the last years of the 1990s, emphasis in management theory focused on the need for organizations of all types to transform themselves radically when necessary to achieve success in the decades ahead.

The term that has been widely applied to such needed restructuring, both of the organization's culture and values, and of its actual physical units, chain of command, decision-making processes, and ongoing tactics, is *reengineering*. It involves such elements as team building, leadership, and crossing departmental boundaries.

Alceste Pappas argues that strategic transformation in nonprofit organizations must preserve the important values of care, service, and community benefit that have traditionally motivated this field. These values, however, must be embedded in the context of constant change and self-examination. He writes:

> Reengineering involves the fundamental redesign of a nonprofit's organizational structure, processes, service delivery mechanism, and technology. In our experience, such basic self-analysis cannot be done in a vacuum, nor can it be expected to yield sustained improvement in efficiency and service levels without an organization-wide or long term perspective [and on a blueprint created by] a deliberate strategic planning process.[20]

A number of examples of such strategic planning and of successful reengineering efforts in recreation, park, and leisure-service organizations are presented in later chapters of this text. They make it clear that, although the bulk of management analysis and theory building over the years has focused on business and industry, the same principles apply in the leisure-service field. This will be illustrated in Chapter 3, which deals with the role of agency managers with respect to determining organizational missions, goals, and objectives, and developing structures to facilitate these purposes. After that, such leisure-related functions as program and facility operations and fiscal and personnel management will be considered, with illustrations of effective practices drawn from numerous organizations throughout the United States and Canada.

SUMMARY

Management is a process found in every type of agency and organization in contemporary society. In addition to executive personnel, it is carried on by many supervisory employees, program, or division directors and similar middle-management individuals, who have significant planning, policy-making, and related functions.

Over the past century, a number of different schools of thought have dominated management practice. During the classical period of management development, in the early 1900s, emphasis was placed on a bureaucratic approach with clearly defined organization charts, lines of authority, and job responsibilities and methods. There was little opportunity for individuals to demonstrate personal initiative or creativity within this framework.

This was succeeded in the post–World War II decades by the so-called human relations era of management philosophy, which stressed the need to consider the social aspects of the job setting. At this time, studies of employee motivation, communication skills, shared decision making and delegation of authority were all part of a popular participative management approach. During the same period, a management science model of management that stressed systems-based planning and network models that made extensive use of computer analysis also was widely adopted.

In the late 1980s and 1990s, primary emphasis was given to total quality management and promoting customer-defined value, making use of benchmarking and similar methods of promoting product or service quality. At century's end, the strongest thrust in generic management thinking involves the use of new forms of management strategy, and the reengineering or transformation of organizational structures and processes.

QUESTIONS FOR CLASS DISCUSSION OR ESSAY EXAMINATIONS

1. Summarize the major principles underlying the classical school of management theory that were developed by Taylor, Weber, and Fayol, including such elements as the division of labor and task specialization, the scalar principle, or span of control. What factors made these principles useful for their times and industrial settings, and why did they become less useful in the modern era?
2. Why did the human relations and industrial humanism approaches gain acceptance in management practices? What were some of their key principles, and how might they apply in a recreation, park, or leisure-service agency?
3. Explain some of the later concepts presented in this chapter, including the focus on customer satisfaction, benchmarking, management strategy, and reengineering. How could these be applied in a higher education setting, such as degree programs in leisure-service management?
4. As a form of individual or small-group task, students may be asked to do a sample study of a community leisure-service agency, in terms of its organization, chain of command, task specialization, policy development, and strategic planning.

REFERENCES

1. Bainbridge, Colin: *Designing for Change: A Practical Guide to Business Transformation,* New York, 1996, John Wiley & Sons, p. viii.
2. Ramanathan, Kavasseri, and Hegstad, Larry: *Readings in Management Control in Nonprofit Organizations,* New York, 1982, John Wiley & Sons, p. v.

3. Murphy, James, Niepoth, E. William, Jamieson, Lynn, and Williams, John: *Leisure Systems: Critical Concepts and Applications*, Champaign, Ill., 1991, Sagamore Publishing, p. 292.

4. Mayo, E.: *The Human Problems of an Industrial Civilization*, New York, 1933, Macmillan Co.

5. McGregor, Douglas, in Bennis, Warren, and McGregor, Caroline (eds.): *The Professional Manager*, New York, 1967, McGraw-Hill Book Co.

6. Maslow, Abraham: *Motivation and Personality*, New York, 1954, Harper and Row.

7. See discussion of Herzberg in Mescon, Michal, Albert, Michael, and Khodouri, Franklin: *Management: Individual and Organizational Effectiveness*, New York, 1981, Harper and Row.

8. Cole, Robert, in Fischer, Frank, and Sirianni, Carmen (eds.): *Critical Studies in Organization and Bureaucracy*, Philadelphia, Pa., 1984, Temple University Press, p. 423.

9. Jubenville, Alan, and Twight, Ben: *Outdoor Recreation Management: Theory and Application*, State College, Pa., 1993, Venture Publishing, p. 15.

10. Harari, Oren: "Thank Heaven for Complainers," *Management Review*, March 1997, p. 25.

11. Spector, Bert: *Taking Charge and Letting Go: A Breakthrough Strategy for Creating and Managing the Horizontal Company*, New York, 1995, Free Press, pp. 18–28.

12. Liebfried, Kathleen, and McNair, C. J.: *Benchmarking: A Tool for Continuous Improvement*, New York, 1992, Harper Business, p. 8.

13. Caneday, Lowell, and Kuzmic, Tom: "Managing the Diverse Interests of Stakeholders," *Parks and Recreation*, September 1997, p. 199.

14. Gray, David: "Managing Our Way to a Preferred Future," *Parks and Recreation*, May 1984, p. 48.

15. Salmon, Robert: *The Future of Management*, Oxford, Eng., 1996, Blackwell Business, pp. 5–7.

16. Bainbridge, *op.cit.*, p. 3.

17. Smith, Bucklin Associates: *The Complete Guide to Nonprofit Management*, New York, 1994, John Wiley & Sons, p. 3.

18. Dobson, Paul, and Starkey, Ken: *The Strategic Management Blueprint*, Oxford, Eng., 1993, Blackwell, Business, p. 2.

19. Bryson, John: *Strategic Planning for Public and Nonprofit Organizations*, San Francisco, 1995, Jossey-Bass Publishers, p. 5.

20. Pappas, Alceste: *Reengineering Your Nonprofit Organization: A Guide to Strategic Transformation*, New York, 1996, John Wiley & Sons, p. 13.

Three

Key Management Roles in Leisure-Service Agencies

The City of Ottawa will foster an environment which promotes creativity, access to, and the pursuit of excellence in cultural experiences; and the preservation and enhancement of Ottawa's dynamic and diverse local cultural identity. The Mission Statement establishes the cultural mandate for the City of Ottawa. It is a statement of intent which defines the City's role and responsibilities, and its relationship with other partners involved in the area of local cultural development.[1]

With 691 affiliated Boys and Girls Clubs of America, B&GCA comprises the nation's largest network of local youth organizations addressing the developmental needs of disadvantaged children. Each local Club organization is autonomous and usually incorporated. Clubs maintain a board of directors, conduct fundraising efforts and implement sound management policies.

There are service centers located in each of B&GCA's five regions. The headquarters operation in Atlanta supports the work of the regional service centers with program research and development, staff recruitment and training, marketing support and building consultation.[2]

INTRODUCTION

We move now to an examination of the central roles of managers in recreation, park, and leisure-service organizations. Essentially, their function is to provide inspiration and direction to all other individuals within their agency structures. Subject to the approval of boards, commissions, or other supervising or advisory groups, they offer creative leadership in defining agency mission statements, goals, and objectives. They improve and maintain their organizations' operating systems and procedures, and initiate and carry out planning studies.

Throughout, leisure-service managers serve both as professional role models and philosophical leaders in promoting effective recreation programming, and as pragmatic, business-minded directors in helping their organizations recognize and deal with challenges and opportunities. Striking a balance between creative innovation and hard-headed fiscal reality, their key contribution is to ensure the highest possible level of agency performance.

The following understandings and competencies designated as essential by the NRPA/AALR Council on Accreditation are addressed in this chapter:

Understanding of and ability to use diverse community, institutional, natural, and human service resources to promote and enhance the leisure experience (8.11).

Ability to promote, advocate, interpret, and articulate the concerns of leisure service systems for all populations and services (8.14).

Understanding of principles and procedures for planning leisure services, resources, areas, and facilities (8.23).

Understanding of the management role, including organizational behavior and relationships, politics of organizations, strategic planning, policy development and implementation (7A.02).

O B J E C T I V E S

At the conclusion of this chapter, readers should be familiar with the following areas of management responsibility:

1. Management functions in developing and maintaining organizational structures and operational policies and procedures.
2. The nature of agency mission statements in several types of leisure-service organizations, linked to the development of short- and long-term goals and objectives.
3. The manager's role in the planning process, including traditional facility planning studies, more comprehensive master planning, and more sharply focused project planning.
4. Policy making, with examples of typical operational policies in leisure-service organizations influenced by benefits-based management principles.

GENERIC MANAGEMENT ROLES

As Chapter 1 points out, management experts have traditionally identified several specific functions that all managers are normally expected to fulfill. These include such tasks as organizing, staffing, planning, budgeting, directing, supervising, and evaluating the work of their agencies. These are generic roles, in the sense that they are commonly found in all types of organizations and institutions.

Obviously specific management responsibilities vary in different types of agencies. In health and fitness programs, for example, James Sullivan points out that managers must develop program content, establish safety precautions and emergency medical policies, purchase supplies and fitness equipment, conduct in-service training for all instructional personnel, and carry out other specific tasks.[3]

Herb Appenzeller lists over twenty specific responsibilities of athletic directors within the overall sports-management field. These include supervising the coaching staff and teams, checking on the eligibility of athletes and maintaining their records, working with booster clubs and the athletic advisory council, supervising the sports information director, and working cooperatively with coaches in scheduling their sports events and coordinating travel and facility arrangements.[4]

Within every other specialized type of leisure-service organization, the specific tasks of agency directors or program supervisors will vary greatly. Nonetheless, in all settings, the core management functions are similar. The first of these to be considered in this chapter involves the manager's role in developing, maintaining, and improving the organization's actual structure.

LEGAL BASIS OF LEISURE-SERVICE ORGANIZATIONS

How do recreation, park, and other types of leisure-service organizations come into being? What is the legal basis for their existence, and how does this influence the forms they take and the functions they carry out?

First, it should be understood that different types of recreation providers have widely varying origins. For example, a therapeutic recreation program may simply be developed as a unit of adjunctive service within a larger hospital department or division of medical or rehabilitative service. It may also be established as an independent, nonprofit organization serving disabled persons generally or those with a particular disability. It may also represent a partnership among different public, nonprofit, and health-care organizations.

A campus recreation program is usually initiated as a function of a college or university department of student life, or an intramural sports program sponsored by a physical education department or athletic office. In many such situations, recreation is essentially a service provided within a larger organization and does not require a formal legal process to be established.

In some cases, as in the armed forces' Morale, Welfare and Recreation programs, the agency's administrative structure and policy-making powers may be rooted in several different national offices. For example, in the Department of the Navy (DON), the Assistant Secretary of the Navy for Manpower and Reserve Affairs provides broad policy guidance on programming, while the Assistant Secretary for Financial Management has responsibility for MWR financial practices. In addition:

> The Chief of Naval Operations (CNO) and the Commandant of the Marine Corps (CMC) are responsible for detailed policy and coordination of MWR programs within their respective services. Further, within the Navy, the Chief of Naval Personnel acts as an agent for the CNO and the Commander, Naval Supply Systems Command has been assigned technical management responsibility for the Navy Exchange System. . . .[5]

Within this complex administrative system, the actual planning and operation of Morale, Welfare and Recreation programs on individual Navy bases or on shipboard are subject to the direct control of the commanders of those units. However, all activities operate under financial and budget policies and general guidance controlling personnel, program elements, and other management functions that are established on a national basis.

LOCAL PUBLIC RECREATION AND PARK AGENCIES

Within the overall leisure-service system, local public recreation and park departments are usually assigned the role of providing leisure facilities and programs to meet community needs. Such agencies, sponsored by township, county, municipal, or other forms of local government, must normally function within a framework of state legislation. Under the American system of government, states have the authority to regulate governmental programs and various areas of human activity within their territories, except as limited by the federal Constitution or their own constitutions. This regulatory power is commonly known as "police power" and provides authorization to enact laws necessary for the health, safety, morals, and general welfare of the citizens of each state.

In the early days of the recreation and park movement, as local governments began to assume the responsibility for operating recreation programs and facilities, they often did so on the basis of the police powers granted to them by their states. Providing local government the right to frame and enforce reasonable measures for the protection of health, life, property, and morals, these were used to justify a broad range of governmental functions intended to serve the common good.

As recreation became a more widely recognized form of government responsibility, the following types of legislation were developed.

Special Recreation and Park Laws

One approach to state legislation supporting local recreation and park agencies was the *special law*. These laws, many of which are operative today, were passed by state legislatures and empowered cities or towns to sponsor recreation and park facilities and programs. They usually dealt with specific types of facilities (such as auditoriums, community buildings, stadiums, swimming pools, or golf courses) and provided legal authorization for taxing, floating bonds, or otherwise funding such ventures.

Regulatory Laws

A second type of state legislation affecting recreation was the *regulatory law*. These are laws that seek to control, license, censor, or supervise recreation programs to protect the public health, safety, and general well-being. They usually apply not only to governmental agencies but also to voluntary, commercial, private, educational, and other organizations.

Enabling Laws

The major type of state legislation affecting recreation and parks is the *enabling law*. This type of state law empowers local branches of government to acquire, develop, and maintain recreation and park areas and facilities and to operate programs under leadership. It usually specifies the types of local governmental units that may operate such programs as well as their specific permissible functions, including fiscal practices, cosponsorship activities, and other operational processes. State enabling laws usually stipulate whether a recreation and park board or commission must be established to oversee the local public leisure-service agency and, if so, the manner of its appointment, the number of members, and its powers and responsibilities.

State law is usually *permissive* rather than *mandatory* in this area; it permits local communities to establish recreation and park programs, but it does not compel them to do so. In some cases, enabling provisions may be found as part of the state education code, in which local school districts are authorized to sponsor community education and recreation programs and tax specifically for such purposes.

Special District Laws

In some states, special enabling legislation has passed that permits two or more municipalities or other political subdivisions to establish joint park or recreation programs. This is normally done by setting up independent districts that function in this area of government alone. Such laws may include provisions giving special districts the right to impose taxes on residents within their borders as well as the power to acquire, develop, and maintain recreation areas and facilities, sponsor programs, and employ personnel.

Home Rule Legislation

Many states encourage a high level of local self-determination by permitting municipalities and counties to develop their own charters for home rule. If provision for recreation and parks is not made in the original charter, it may be added in the form of an amendment that provides general authority for this function, to be followed by more specific ordinances outlining the responsibilities and powers of government in this area.

Varying Sponsorship Arrangements

Recreation and park agencies sponsored by local government have several different kinds of sponsorship arrangements. These include: (1) separate recreation departments operating under their own boards or commissions or reporting directly to mayors or city managers; (2) separate park departments similarly structured; (3) school-sponsored programs, often linked to adult education activities; (4) combined recreation and park departments; or (5) other municipal or county agencies, such as youth boards, housing authorities, welfare departments, or police, which may operate or assist leisure-service programs.

A growing trend in local recreation and park operations has been for two or more units of local government to join forces in carrying out specific service functions. Such intercommunity partnerships grew rapidly in the 1980s as a result of shrinking federal funding and the need to share resources. County governments, in particular, have increasingly taken on responsibility for health and law-enforcement services, under contracts with local municipalities. In numerous other cases, regional councils or clusters of local government units have undertaken joint projects under different types of coordinating mechanisms.

Commercial Recreation Businesses

For-profit recreation enterprises fall into three categories of ownership and management control: (1) *sole proprietorship,* in which one individual owns the business fully and is in total charge of its operation; (2) *partnerships,* in which two or more persons own and operate a business with shared financial responsibilities and management functions; and (3) *corporations,* which are legal entities with all the rights and powers of individuals. Corporations represent only 20 percent of all types of businesses, but they carry on about 80 percent of the total dollar volume of annual sales. They are typically owned by shareholders (either publicly or privately), who are represented by a board of directors who oversee the corporation's overall goals and policies and hire the management team that puts these into action.

Of the three types of ownership, sole proprietorship is the most common form of business sponsorship. Although this arrangement may give the leisure-service entrepreneur flexibility in that he or she has complete decision-making power over the operation, it lacks certain advantages of partnerships. Bullaro and Edginton write:

> A partner may provide capital, technical competence or managerial skill that complements the work of another person. For example, a partner may be a person who provides capital to help develop a business, or a partner may be a person who has a great deal of technical competence in a particular leisure area (i.e., outdoor recreation, aquatics, children's play, or dance) . . . [but] may not possess the managerial skills necessary to form and profitably operate a business venture.[6]

Particularly for more extensive operations, the corporation is often the preferred type of legal structure for recreation businesses. As a legal entity, it has an unlimited life, and the death or retirement of its principal members or officers does not terminate it.

Nonprofit Youth-Serving or Recreation Organizations

Voluntary nonprofit leisure-service organizations are usually established on a legal basis to gain charitable tax-exempt status to carry out their programs with a degree of public recreation and stability. For example, such organizations as the YMCA and YWCA, Boy Scouts and Girl Scouts, Police Athletic League, or Little League, are typically chartered and approved as nonprofit agencies—in some cases through formal recognition by Congress and in others by registration under state laws governing such bodies.

Numerous nonprofit organizations operate under policy guidelines established by national offices and boards. In addition, local or district units typically have their own trustees or boards of directors who assist in fund-raising and recruiting other forms of political or social support.

Boys and Girls Clubs

Typical of such groups, Boys and Girls Clubs of America publishes a constitution, set of bylaws and procedural guidelines to assist local chapters in developing their own clubs. An individual club may be structured as a corporation, association, or administrative committee, although the national organization generally recommends that it be incorporated under existing state law. This arrangement ensures that a large group of representative citizens will be closely associated with the organization and have responsibility for its development. The overall membership elects a board of directors, who directly oversee club operations.

Girl Scouts of the U.S.A.

This youth organization has a more tightly structured governance system. Founded through Congressional charter, the Girl Scouts have a constitution identifying three major levels of administrative control: national council, national board of directors, and local Girl Scout councils.

The membership of the national council is constituted by the members of the Girl Scout corporation, who are elected delegates from local councils (up to 2,000), members of the national board of directors, and other elected persons. The council serves as the coordinating head of the Girl Scout movement in the United States. More specific powers are assigned to the national board of directors. This body has the responsibility for establishing requirements for membership, local council charters, standards, and other major operating procedures. Finally, local Girl Scout councils directly administer and supervise programs implemented in individual troops based on the goals and policies that have been established by the national council.

Employee Recreation Units

Recreation programs are often established as a secondary function within the ongoing operation of a larger institution or organization. For example, employee recreational programs within a large corporation might function as a service unit within an overall division of human resource management, and be linked to other employee social-service or benefits functions. Since fitness programs have become an increasingly important emphasis in employee-service units, these might be linked administratively to health-service or medical functions.

In some cases, recreation may be established in the form of a separate employee association, attached to the company and using its facilities but operating under its own financing and leadership. In other cases, the corporation or other organization may maintain full control over the recreation and related employee services, although it may rely on income from vending machines, company stores, or similar sources for funding support.

TYPES OF ORGANIZATIONAL STRUCTURES

In all types of leisure-service organizations, one of the primary responsibilities of managers is to establish and maintain effective structures that facilitate progress toward achieving desired goals and objectives.

As Chapter 2 points out, this involves developing an overall system of divisions, departments, or other operating units designed to carry out specified tasks. There are two elements within this system: (1) the formal structure, which arranges the various parts of the system, including all employees on appropriate levels of authority in a chain of command and with assigned work functions; and (2) the informal set of working relationships that involve planning, decision making, and other forms of cooperative action within and among different operating units.

The formal structure is usually made explicit within an organization chart that identifies departments, their functions, the reporting relationships of all personnel members, and various special subgroups within larger agency divisions. Departments are usually based both on the assignment of specialized functions, and on geographical location or responsibility.

The most common type of structure involves a *centralized approach*, in which the various units of an organization respond to their own directors or division heads, who in turn are responsible to upper-level centralized agency executives. Major areas of management functions, such as finance, personnel, or marketing, are usually directed by central organization offices.

In contrast, a *self-contained unit* structure is one in which all functions needed to provide a given service are combined within a relatively autonomous department or division. An example might be a large state park system, in which each individual park has its own maintenance teams, personnel department, budget office, and similar elements. This is often called a decentralized structure, since it operates in relative freedom from centralized, bureaucratic control.

Some large organizations may have a *hybrid* structure, in which some functional departments operate within a central office or headquarters, whereas others are decentralized in self-contained units. Still others make use of a *matrix* structure, in which both functional and self-contained approaches operate simultaneously. In such a system (see p. 38), personnel may be responsible both to managers within self-contained service-delivery units and also to system-wide managers who are responsible for specific functions, such as program, maintenance, planning, or finance.

EXAMPLES OF LEISURE-SERVICE ORGANIZATIONS

Examples of several different types of recreation, park, and leisure-service organizations follow, beginning with the organization charts of public recreation and park departments.

This organization chart illustrates the chain of command, with the Parks and Recreation director at the top level of authority, although she must report to the city council and city manager, and must also work closely with a Park and Recreation Commission, a Youth Advisory Council, and a Senior Commission (Figure 3.1).

At the next level of authority, there are four divisions of responsibility, involving Parks and Landscape Resources and Maintenance, Landscape Architect, Golf Services, and Community Services, which includes responsibility for several areas of recreation programming. The third level designates approximately sixty-five so-called merit employees, who are chiefly line personnel carrying out programming and maintenance functions.

FIGURE 3.1. Department of Parks and Recreation, City of San Mateo, California.

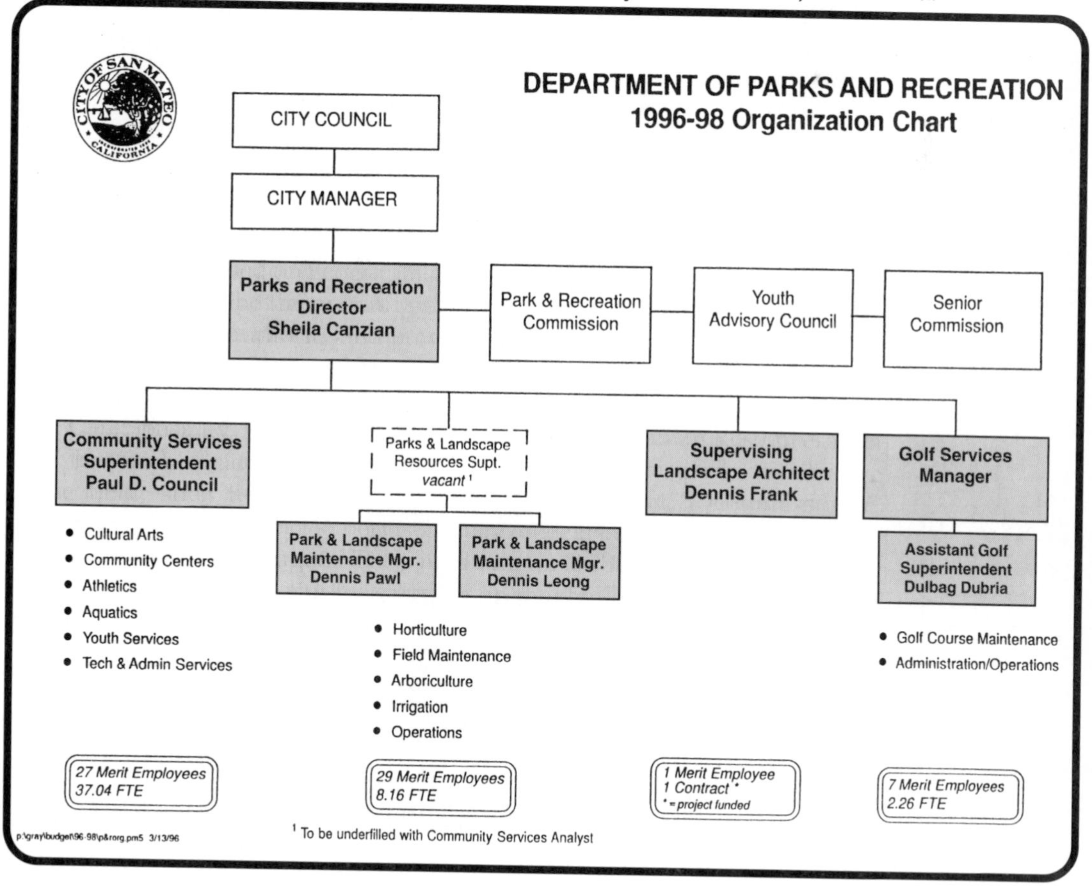

National Nonprofit Organization: YMCA

Figure 3.2 illustrates the structure of a major national nonprofit organization, the Young Men's Christian Association (YMCA). Like many other youth-serving or social-service organization that provide recreation as an important form of service, the YMCA operates with a national board and executive director, and with several departments that establish national policy, provide resource services to local YMCA branches across the country, conduct research and planning, legal support and financial direction, and other forms of technical aid. The Program Group, for example:

> . . . develops and supports local YMCA program activities. It creates manuals and materials for sale from the Program Store. It also directs the network that trains and certifies instructors in major program areas. It tracks trends, discovers models and innovations, provides quality guidelines, identifies key issues, and conducts national program events.[7]

As an example of how local units exist within the framework of a larger national federation or governing body, a single YMCA, the Peninsula Family YMCA in San Mateo, California, is part of the YMCA of San Francisco, an incorporated nonprofit organization with thirteen branches in a four-county area. Other community YMCAs may be totally separate or independent agencies, but all report participation statistics and financial data to the national board, and all adhere to its policies and make use of its services.

FIGURE 3.2. Organization chart: National YMCA.

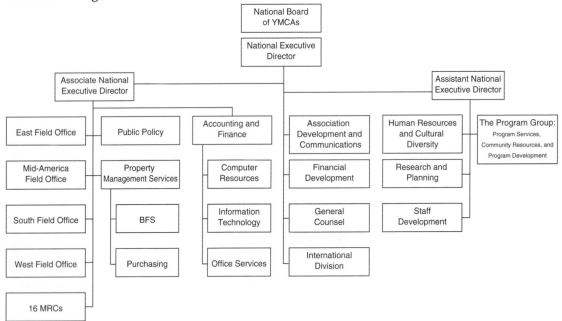

As an example of a large, complex military recreation organization, Figure 3.3 presents the organization chart of the Memphis, Tennessee, Naval Air Station as it was structured in the early 1990s.

Operating under the Department of Defense's Morale, Welfare and Recreation (MWR) administrative structure, and with guidance by several councils and advisory groups, the organization contains four functional divisions. Three of these, administrative services, equipment management, and finance, provide general support. The fourth is responsible for direct program services, with four units: (1) the athletic division, with fitness, sport, and aquatic emphases; (2) the

FIGURE 3.3. Military recreation: Naval air station MWR structure, Memphis, Tennessee.

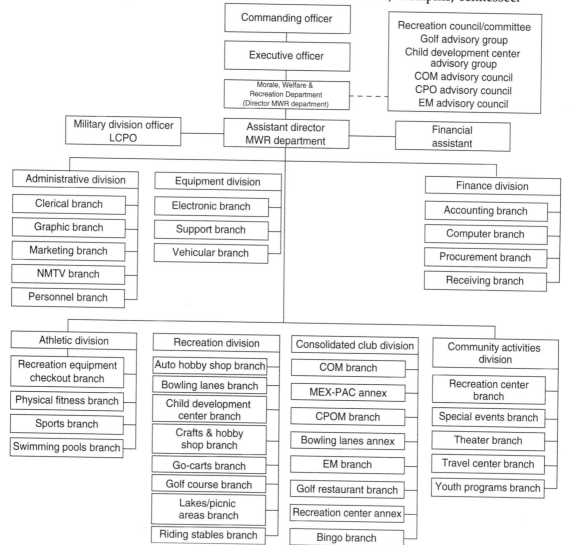

recreation division, which includes varied cultural, hobby, and social activities; (3) the community activities division, focusing on off-base and youth-centered programs; and (4) the consolidated club division, including an enlisted club branch (EM), a commissioned officers club branch (COM), and a chief petty officers branch (CPOM), which organizes such special programs as bowling, golf, and bingo.

The effort throughout the 1990s has been to tighten and integrate varied armed forces programs and fiscal operations into a "single-fund" structures, with unified and carefully controlled revenue-source elements, rather than numerous semi-independent operations with different procedures and controls. In addition, with a continuing reduction in the number of bases and available funding support, many such programs have been downsized or eliminated.

Commercial Recreation: Disney World

As a leading example of for-profit recreation businesses, Disney World and Epcot Center in Lake Buena Vista, Florida, has a structure that is too complicated to depict in a single organization chart. It may be briefly described as including both internal functional divisions and external subsidiary companies. These include the following operational units:

1. *Finance:* handles the business side of the operation: financial planning, budgets, income and expenditures statistics, etc.;
2. *Food:* responsible for food outlets, restaurants, and special sales;
3. *General services:* provides essential services such as wardrobe, safety, warehousing, and staff development and training;
4. *Administration:* coordinates, plans, and directs entire Disney operation;
5. *Employee relations:* hiring, personnel records, job assignment, compensation, benefits, and other employee relations;
6. *Entertainment:* produces all special live shows and schedules entertainment groups;
7. *Facilities:* responsible for maintaining and operating facilities with safety, efficiency and cleanliness;
8. *Operations:* supervises guest relations, security, and fire prevention; operates actual program attractions and rides;
9. *Marketing:* communications and promotional unit that coordinates various industry and business group trips and events; researches consumer interest and target-group needs;
10. *Merchandising:* designs and sells souvenirs and other specialty merchandise in Disney World; and
11. *Hotels:* operates major resort hotels for visitors.

Among the subsidiary companies are units responsible for such functions as construction, engineering, land development and master planning, insurance, advertising and outside merchandising, gift shops, and electric, gas, water, incinerator, and sewage systems.

The examples of leisure-service agency structures that have just been cited represent formal patterns of organization. They are usually accompanied by standardized operating procedures, directives, and policies designed to encourage order, predictability, and stable and consistent performance of personnel.

At the same time, it has been pointed out that often overly rigid organizational structures may constrict an agency's ability to respond promptly and creatively to sudden challenges or opportunities. Therefore, all organizations tend to develop informal structures or processes through which the formal lines of communication or segregated policy-making and decision-making powers may be bypassed.

Matrix Approaches

As Chapter 2 points out, one way of breaking down the barriers to organizational efficiency that are often found in rigid structures is through the matrix approach. Individuals may continue to function within their regular department but also be assigned to another agency project on a short- or long-term basis. Thus, they report to two managers, one in their functional department and one in the special project unit.

To illustrate how an organization may develop a structure that is deliberately designed to facilitate such interactive processes, Figure 3.4 shows the structure of a voluntary agency known as Shared Outdoor Adventure Recreation (SOAR) in Portland, Oregon. SOAR's mission is to promote and sponsor challenging outdoor adventure programs for disabled individuals. As a non-profit community organization, it must work with many civic groups and individuals, coordinating their efforts in joint projects. In such a situation, a formal agency structure with rigid lines of authority would probably be self-defeating.

Instead, SOAR has developed a flexible plan in which various committees, volunteers, and staff members work together with shared or overlapping functions. These shared areas, in which the circles of committee responsibility overlap, show very clearly how the matrix approach may be applied in linking various agency functions. Although the SOAR structure might not be readily applicable to larger or more formal or bureaucratic organizations, it shows how the informal approach to management may be used for maximum productivity.

Business Units and Special Projects Teams

Within their overall structures, many leisure-service organizations develop a system of separate units or work teams designed to carry out specific functions with a degree of independence and the ability to draw together different resources of the organization.

FIGURE 3.4. Organization of Shared Outdoor Adventure Recreation (SOAR), Portland, Oregon.

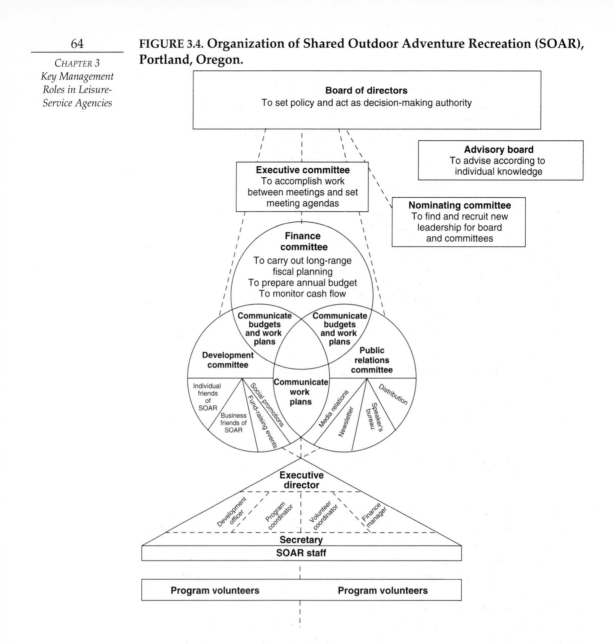

For example, the senior executives of the Arlington, Texas, Department of Parks and Recreation comprise a Management Council, with each member of this group being responsible for a service unit of the organization. In turn, each unit prepares a business plan that addresses key service issues, strengths, opportunities and threats, and alternative strategic approaches. Plans are updated, with employee participation, in January of each year, and cover a period of five years. In turn, plans are presented to the Park and Recreation Advisory Board, a group of eleven citizens appointed by the Arlington city council, to provide direct citizen interface with the department's management.

In Arlington, it is believed that this separate business unit structure allows managers a high degree of freedom and responsibility in maintaining effective operations, with a direct line of accountability between each unit manager and the results of his or her team's operation. Much problem solving is done within units, with all staff members and those served taking part in systematic program evaluation.

Similarly, in the same department, for special community events, temporary organizations or project teams are established, with staff members assigned from different work units to each individual project. Employees often assist as volunteers, apart from their regular work assignments. A program specialist is assigned responsibility for the event on a one-time basis.

FORMULATING AGENCY MISSIONS AND GOALS STATEMENTS

We now turn to a second core area of management responsibility—helping the leisure-service agency define its essential mission, goals, and objectives.

A leisure-service agency's philosophy, as defined in mission statements, serves as a compass or rudder. It provides direction to the organization, by helping managers identify program needs, fiscal priorities, or appropriate short- and long-term goals. As a field of service that has significant impact on the lives of people young and old, and that contributes to community well-being, recreation, parks, and leisure services must adhere to a set of constructive and carefully thought out values and purposes.

In part, such values are usually derived from a broad philosophical view that justifies all agencies in the field. For example, Dustin, McAvoy, and Schultz describe the democratic purpose of public parks and recreation programs:

> There is a symbolic significance to public recreation areas that transcends their everyday meaning. In a nation committed to equality of conditions, public parks and playgrounds serve an equalizing function. Regardless of one's station in life, one has the right of access to these resources. They are both the poor person's and the rich person's property.[8]

Other authorities have identified a broad range of social, personal, and economic benefits achieved by organized recreation and park agencies. Increasingly, emphasis has been placed on recreation's role as a health-related field of service. A number of authorities have pointed out, for example, that reconceptualizing the idea of health as a matter of total wellness means that communities must place greater emphasis on making facilities and leadership available for varied forms of physical activities and fitness-producing leisure pursuits.

Role of Mission Statements

Beyond such broad statements of purpose, many leisure-service organizations formulate specific mission statements that summarize their own values and purposes. Florence Heffron describes the role of such statements:

A mission is an organization's function in society—the products it produces and the services it provides. . . . [T]he mission and the substantive goals derived from it provide a rationale for organization design and structure.

Missions are extremely important to public organizations. . . . They provide a sense of legitimacy, direction, and purpose, and serve as criteria for performance evaluation for the overall organization and for individual employees. . . . Official goals are the general purposes of the organization as described in the charter (legal mandate) or public statements by key officials. . . .[9]

Typically, mission statements are revised from time to time and are published not only in charters, constitutions, or bylaws, but in departmental brochures, annual reports, leadership manuals, and other agency documents. It is the manager's responsibility to ensure that mission statements are periodically reviewed and, when appropriate—as in master planning studies that indicate new priorities or purposes—revised.

In some cases, mission statements represent rather idealistic and philosophical values and beliefs. In others, they express concrete statements of purpose (i.e., the benefits that the organization seeks to achieve for the community or for its membership). In still others, they combine both elements of values and purposes. Several examples of specific organizational mission statements follow.

Public Park and Recreation Departments

The public Park and Recreation Department in San Mateo, California, states that its primary mission is to facilitate leisure experiences for the citizens of San Mateo by:

Providing safe, well maintained and attractive parks, open space and community center facilities;

Offering and facilitating a wide array of leisure opportunities for all age groups that enhance the physical, intellectual, social and cultural growth and development of our citizenry;

Ensuring reasonable access to all programs and facilities by bridging physical and economic gaps that impede participation; and

Preserving and protecting the City's natural resources including its urban forest, public open spaces, pedestrian and bicycle trails and landscaped medians and islands.[10]

Frequently, public departments will develop separate mission statements for specific areas of their overall programs that have a distinct set of social purposes. For example, the Phoenix, Arizona, Department of Parks, Recreation and Library has developed a mission statement for its City Streets/At-Risk Youth Division that includes the overall purpose of providing a variety of:

. . . quality recreation, education, cultural and leisure activities that will assist in the development of life-enhancing skills for the future adult population of the metropolitan Phoenix area. The Department shall provide a well-rounded selection of activities, opportunities and services in a safe, non-threatening environment for the diverse youth population.

The role of the Department is to: (1) advocate for programs and services specifically addressing youth; (2) monitor and evaluate existing programs; (3) conduct liaison activities between the Department, community, businesses, and schools; (4) provide appropriate and safe programs; (5) promote greater awareness of existing programs; (6) provide information and referral network between service agencies, the community, and the parks; and (7) address issues for youth at risk.[11]

In many cases, civic organizations that collaborate with public departments will define their missions in such specialized areas of service. For example, the Center for the Arts, a nonprofit organization with thousands of participants and members, which operates an outstanding facility in a public park in Vero Beach, Florida, states:

The Center for the Arts is an educational institution providing opportunity for the cultural enrichment of the public through:

Exhibition of the highest accomplishments of all cultures in the visual arts, with an emphasis on American art and Florida artists in particular;

Explorations in the humanities through programs of lectures and seminars by eminent scholars and cultural leaders and offerings in the musical, cinematic, and dramatic arts by recognized artists and producers;

Professional studio and classroom instruction in the arts for students of all ages;

The collection, preservation, and presentation of important art with emphasis on American art and Florida artists in particular.[12]

In carrying out this mission, the Center for the Arts receives support from various sources, including membership fees, earned income from events and classes, contributions by individuals and corporations, and grants from foundations and government agencies concerned with cultural development.

Nonprofit Agency Mission: YWCA

Many nonprofit organizations define their purposes in broad, idealistic terms that are then translated into concrete social-action or human-service programs in local communities. For example, the national Young Women's Christian Association (YWCA) states:

The YWCA works for the empowerment of women through advocacy on public issues that affect and concern women and the lives they touch. Men can join as associate members with all membership benefits except voting rights. The YWCA's goals encompass the struggle for peace, justice, freedom and dignity for all people and the elimination of racism wherever it exists. . . .[13]

To achieve such purposes, local YWCAs typically offer numerous recreational, social, and educational programs designed to serve women and girls in areas related to home and family life, civic and community roles, or career development. Numerous YWCAs sponsor conferences, workshops, or other services dealing with domestic violence, job counseling, single-parent roles and day-care options, juvenile justice programs, and similar needs.

Special Recreation Mission: RCH Inc.

The overall goals of therapeutic recreation service are generally considered to embrace three elements: therapy, leisure education, and the opportunity for positive forms of leisure participation. In community-based settings, sponsors of special recreation services for persons with disabilities often strive to promote mainstreaming and normalization in a wide range of leisure pursuits, along with other needed social services.

RCH Inc., an outstanding organization serving persons with disability in the San Francisco region, describes its mission as follows:

> Our programs are designed with the goals of stimulating the development of self-esteem, social interaction, leisure skills and interests, health and physical fitness, and creative expression.
>
> It is our belief that men, women and children with disabilities are entitled to participate in community-based programs, and that they have a fundamental right to inclusion in every aspect of community life. Our Mission embodies the following objectives:
>
> - to provide programs in recreation and leisure, vocational rehabilitation and supported employment, adult development, children's services, and respite care services for individuals of all ages who have all types of disabilities;
> - to promote the development of the recreation and social skills appropriate and necessary for successful participation in community life;
> - to promote the development of vocational training skills needed for successful community-based employment;
> - to create and provide programs designed to give people with disabilities the opportunity to live and work safely in the least restrictive environment;
> - to educate the community by serving as advocates for the rights of persons with disabilities, and by training professionals in methods to meet the community's changing needs.[14]

DEVELOPMENT OF AGENCY GOALS

Mission statements usually serve as the basis for more specific and policy-oriented goals that agency managers formulate or that are developed as part of planning studies.

Goals reflect the underlying philosophy of an organization, but are also influenced by such factors as: (1) the legal mandate that empowers a public, non-profit, or other agency to function; (2) the wishes of community residents, organization members, or other stakeholders or target populations; (3) political and social factors within a community; (4) such practical factors as available funding and physical resources; and (5) the input of boards, commissions, or advisory groups, along with the shared views of staff members on different levels.

While the recommendations of national organizations or professional societies may help to shape agency goals in terms of desirable societal needs, leisure-service agency managers are often chiefly responsive to needs related to their organization's continuing support.

In a study of urban recreation and park directors in the United States, Edginton and Neal found that these municipal leisure-service managers gave the highest priority to securing fees and charges, receiving adequate tax-based support, and maintaining a high level of political and public status—with relatively little emphasis on social-service needs or other philosophical values.[15]

TYPES OF GOALS: OPERATIONAL AND OUTCOME-DIRECTED

Goals generally represent the agency's effort to translate its mission into concrete accomplishments during a given period of time ahead. They tend to fall into two categories: *operational* and *outcome-directed*.

Operational goals involve an organization's continuing effort to make effective decisions, use its resources efficiently, adapt to changing circumstances, gain community support, recruit and supervise productive staff members, or develop partnerships with other leisure-service groups.

In contrast, outcome-directed goals represent the positive results that an organization seeks to accomplish through its programming efforts. These might involve improving health and fitness of its participants, reducing juvenile delinquency, strengthening neighborhood or family unity, or improving racial or interethnic relations.

Operational goals are often referred to as *internal,* since they involve an agency's effort to improve its internal operation, while outcome-directed goals are often considered to be *external* in that they are concerned with the organization's contribution to participants or to community life.

Meaning of Objectives

Often, organizational goals and objectives are presented together, as in Figure 3.5, which includes examples of both elements. However, they differ in that goals are usually considered to be broad statements of purpose within a fairly long-range perspective, while objectives are short-range and more sharply focused. Graham and Klar write:

> Objectives which are specific, measurable, and expected to be attained within a predetermined time period give clear direction to the leisure-service practitioner. . . . Programs cannot be said to be successful according to any type of objective criteria *unless* objectives are specified, evaluated, and attained.[16]

Objectives tend to deal with specific elements of *program implementation* or *actions to be taken,* such as:

1. To initiate a multiservice program of recreation, counseling, educational tutoring, and vocational guidance for at-risk youth in three inner-city districts.
2. To mobilize volunteer efforts to carry out cleanup, tree planting, and other environmental activities in three park or riverside locations.

They may also deal with *measurable behavior change,* such as the following:

FIGURE 3.5. Statement of the Naval Training Center (NTC), Orlando, Florida, Morale, Welfare and Recreation Unit, 1997.

GOALS AND OBJECTIVES

CARING

Enhance Morale, Welfare and Recreation through personalized services, creative programs and excellent facilities.

- *Improve and personalize customer services throughout NTC Orlando.*
- *Improve or establish creative programs by anticipating community needs.*
- *Ensure viable programs incorporate current and projected community needs.*

COOPERATING

Foster mutually beneficial and harmonious relationships among commands, agencies, sailors, employees, families, neighbors and local community.

- *Improve and maximize the communication process.*
- *Broaden information management system.*
- *Expand and enrich programs and events that draw NTC Orlando community together.*
- *Expand and cultivate command relations.*

LEADING/MANAGING

Create an environment in which standards are clearly identified, enabling each individual and department to achieve fullest potential.

- *Enforce high standards of appearance throughout NTC Orlando MWR*
- *Expect and reward individual initiative, mutual trust and department excellence.*
- *Provide a safe, secure and healthy environment.*

TRAINING

Maximize training and educational opportunities consistent with the MWR Mission.

- *Enhance job performance and career development opportunities through training.*
- *Minimize distractions essential to civilian training.*
- *Promote individual and family health and fitness.*

3. Developmentally disabled young adults learning specific independent-living skills, such as personal care, shopping, using public transportation, cooking and cleaning, or attending sports or social events.
4. Significant reduction in such behaviors as school dropout or absenteeism, gang violence, vandalism, teenage pregnancy, or similar problems in target populations of at-risk youth.

Planning represents a third important area of management responsibility and is used in every element of agency operations, from determining goals and objectives to programming and facility development. It is generally considered to be the initial stage of determining agency needs, resources, and goals, and of evolving a set of recommendations or scheme of action to be carried out.

The most common application of planning in recreation, parks, and leisure-services in the past involved developing so-called master plans for individual communities or regions. Typically, such planning studies examined the present physical resources—open space, parks, playgrounds, swimming pools, sports facilities, centers, and other facilities—within the region under study. They also compared these resources to nationally established standards or facility guidelines, developed population and economic projections, identified possible sites for future acquisition or development, and recommended plans for immediate and long-range resource development.

Today, planning takes many forms. One approach involves land-use planning, which is part of comprehensive regional studies including such other elements as industry, transportation, and housing. In some communities, planning focuses on all elements of an agency's operation, as part of total community master planning. For example, Arlington, Texas, carries out a comprehensive study that is required by municipal ordinance to be updated every four years.

> The update involves extensive citizen interaction, public hearings, and adoption by the [Arlington] Planning Commission and City Council.
> Plan development for parks and recreation is carried out by the Assistant Director of Parks and Recreation. Meetings are held with staff, advisory committees, and public groups to review the current plan and assumptions. All baseline data used for planning are updated through the City Planning Department.
> The plan details existing conditions and trends, major service issues, analysis of the issues, and strategies for service. Park and Recreation issues are reported under a park section and a natural resources section.[17]

After adoption of the plan, each Arlington city department must file a five-year implementation plan related to strategic issues with the city council, and annual budget proposals must take into account this implementation plan. The updated plan provides a basis for approving capital improvements, including land acquisition, new facilities, and facility renovation.

Key operational factors that are stressed in this process include *safety and risk management,* with each department unit developing a formal safety plan; *customer satisfaction,* with specific standards of performance for all customer contact personnel; and guidelines for *quality facilities, programs, and services,* which help to guide overall agency operation throughout the year.

Summing up, *planning* can be defined as a deliberate, carefully designed, and usually collaborative effort to improve the operations of a leisure-service system in dealing creatively with change. It may be broad or narrow in scope, and may focus on the entire agency's performance, or on a single operational area, such as fiscal management, programming, or community relations. Frequently, it contributes to policy development designed to meet changing community needs or environmental conditions.

While many leisure-service organizations carry out planning studies as an in-house function, there is growing use of professional planning firms that serve as consultants in designing, carrying out, and reporting study findings.

FORMULATING AGENCY POLICIES

A final management function that is closely related to agency missions, goals, objectives, and planning involves the development of operational policies. Policies are official guidelines that agencies create to govern varied practices or processes in a consistent, approved way. Unlike goals and objectives, which may be regularly reviewed and revised, or strategic planning which may need to respond quickly to emergency situations or crisis, policies tend to be carefully framed, based on an organization's governing principles, and to remain in place over a substantial period of time.

Essentially, policies give direction to a leisure-service agency's operation. They are usually derived from several sources: (1) recommendations from the professional literature, or from policy statements by professional societies; (2) the shared views of department staff members, advisory commissions or boards, and other interested parties; (3) the bylaws, charter, or other legal statements or governing documents that control an organization's operation; and (4) input from community groups, participants, advocacy organizations, or expert consultants.

Formal Policy Manuals

Most government agencies and many nonprofit, armed forces, and other types of leisure-service organizations establish formal policy manuals or handbooks in printed form. These are normally distributed to all personnel in the form of bulletins or listings or approved practices in a number of key management areas. They are used in the orientation of new personnel, in in-service training, and as part of ongoing program supervision. Their value is that they provide a clear-cut basis for action, and outline the procedures which are to be followed in most areas of agency operations.

Typically, managers keep records of policies by entering them into policy books or manuals when they are changed or adopted; manuals may be organized in bound loose-leaf forms, with numbering systems according to category of management function. In the case of municipal recreation and park departments, McChesney and Tappley suggest that each policy be listed on a separate page, along with the legal authority (law, ordinance, or resolution of governing agency), and the date of its adoption. In their system, policies are presented under seven headings, and on three levels of specificity, as follows:

1000	Administration
2000	Community relations
3000	Finances
4000	Personnel
5000	Participants
6000	Program
7000	Maintenance

In each category, a second level of entries would begin with the appropriate number prefix. In the case of Personnel, for example:

4000	Personnel
4100	Personnel organization chart
4200	Employment
4300	Duties and qualifications
4400	Rules of conduct
4500	In-service training
4600	Travel
4700	Compensation and related benefits

In the same category, a third level would spell out such procedural subheadings as: 4710, Salary classifications and guidelines; 4720, Time reports and paychecks; 4730, Insurance.[18]

This approach to developing formal policy manuals or handbooks reflects the classical management approach, with its emphasis on fixed practices within a clearly defined range of operational functions. While it represents a useful tool in handling routine tasks or procedures, it does not deal with a host of other, more difficult or controversial issues that may confront management. These may involve such matters as: (1) eligibility for membership or participation in agency programs; (2) linkage of agency with religious groups, or religious content in programming; (3) access to program and special services for persons with disabilities; (4) guidelines for preventing sexual harassment; (5) acceptance of gifts by staff members; (6) partnerships or program cosponsorships with other community groups; (7) services for or employment of individuals, based on racial/ethnic or gender-related concerns; (8) political involvement by staff members; or (9) use of the agency's name in advertising or other commercial connections.

If such issues are relatively minor in importance, managers may determine appropriate policies in consultation with other supervisors or staff members. If the issues are more complex or controversial, they may require discussion with and approval from governing boards, administrators, or other officials.

Examples of Policies: Campus Recreation

Each type of leisure-service organization is likely to have policy manuals that apply to its special purposes, participants, and program operations. For example, within the category of campus recreation, the Office of Intramural and Recreational Sports at Southern Illinois University in Carbondale publishes a Policies and Procedures Manual that outlines the organization's philosophy and presents rules related to eligibility for participation; student recreation center fees; use of facilities for specific activities; and participation by outside groups, including political events or concessions policies.

Major sections of this campus recreation manual deal with safety regulations designed to control participant behavior and prevent accidents. Similarly, numerous rules govern varied types of sports competition, including intramural, club, and other activities, with respect to eligibility for participation, permitted and prohibited behaviors, and similar elements, along with penalties for unsafe or unacceptable forms of play.

Policy Making in Other Organizations

An example of the use of policies in national youth-serving organizations is found in the Girl Scouts of the U.S.A., which formulates policies that govern the operation of local programs. To illustrate, the National Board of Directors of the Girl Scouts has developed a list of twenty-two policies that each local or regional council must agree to enforce in its application for a Girl Scout charter.

These policies are intended to uphold the values of the Girl Scout movement and protect it against exploitation or misuse. They deal with such subjects as admission qualifications for membership; the selection of adult members and boards of directors; religion in the Girl Scout movement; health and safety; political and legislative activity; restricted use of membership and mailing lists; fund-raising methods; and permissions for commercial endorsements or use of Girl Scouting.

Private, employee, and armed forces organizations customarily develop their own policies—with respect to both broad, mission-related goals and action-oriented operational guidelines. Therapeutic agencies, such as recreation programs in hospitals or other treatment settings, are increasingly adopting program guidelines that reflect the recommendations of national professional societies or meet the standards of accrediting agencies.

Commercial recreation businesses are particularly sensitive to public opinion and the expressed views of influential citizens' groups in determining their policies. For example, recreational events are often used as part of public relations campaigns by major manufacturers of beer, soft drinks, and automobiles and other companies that appeal to a youth market. In the spring of 1989, public attention was focused on several major companies that were sponsoring games, rock concerts, wet T-shirt contests, and other events for hundreds of thousands of college students on spring break along Florida beaches. When it was pointed out that these programs were in poor taste, perpetuated sexual stereotypes, and were particularly insulting to women—

including advertisements placed in college newspapers that described "sure-fire ways to scam babes"—the companies involved quickly reviewed and changed their promotional policies.

While policy statements or manuals should *not* be viewed as vague or easily ignored verbiage, rather than explicit outlines of appropriate operational procedures, at the same time certain situations may call for flexible interpretation or enforcement. This may occur particularly when public recreation and park managers must respond to political demands, emergency situations, or other sudden pressures.

INFLUENCE OF THE BENEFITS-BASED MANAGEMENT APPROACH

The strongest single thrust today, in terms of the manager's role in defining agency missions, goals, and objectives, and in formulating appropriate organizational structures and policies, is the benefits-based management (BBM) approach.

As described by Lawrence Allen and associates at the National Recreation and Park Congress in Salt Lake City, Utah, in 1997, benefits-based management argues that recreation services must be recognized as an integral component of preventative, developmental, and rehabilitative services in community life. It is not enough to amass statistics about amounts of participation in community programs or the use of an organization's facilities. Instead, leisure-service agencies or program units *must* focus on achieving positive outcomes for participants and the community at large.[19]

Benefits-based management involves four major components: (1) clear goal identification, (2) the structuring of program content to directly address goals, (3) an efficient and systematic monitoring and evaluation process to document the impact of agency programs and services, and (4) a comprehensive public relations approach to communicating the agency's successes to its various publics and policy makers.

Particularly in an era when every form of public or nonprofit community service must demonstrate its value if it is to continue to receive fiscal support, benefits-based management represents an invaluable approach to every aspect of managerial responsibility. Along with the entrepreneurial, marketing model of service, it must have significant input to program and facility planning, budget making, and human resource development and supervision—as illustrated in the chapters that follow.

SUMMARY

While many of the specific functions of leisure-service managers vary according to the nature of their agencies, all managers tend to share certain common or generic responsibilities, including the following four areas;

1. Developing a sound legal basis and organizational structure, and maintaining effective relations with governing bodies or higher authorities that control fiscal and other policy-related decisions;
2. Reviewing and refining their organizations' philosophical position and mission statement, and guiding the ongoing statement of long-term goals and short-term objectives;
3. Providing leadership in planning efforts, including both resource-based or open-space and facility planning and master planning, which links recreation, parks, and leisure services with other municipal and social-service functions; and
4. Formulating agency policies to reinforce the organization's mission and goals and respond to changing social and environmental conditions.

Throughout the chapter, examples are given of these functions as they are carried out or appear in several different types of leisure-service organizations, such as public, nonprofit, employee, therapeutic, and armed forces recreation units. Other management functions, in areas such as fiscal operations, human resource management, or programming, are examined in the chapters that follow.

SUGGESTED CLASS ASSIGNMENTS

1. As an individual or small-group project, visit selected community leisure-service organizations, gather information and then report to the class on: (a) the agency's legal basis or the steps through which it was established; (b) its organizational structure, including its board, commission, advisory council, or other supervising body, and its major functional divisions; and (c) its allocation of work and policy-making responsibilities and lines of authority.
2. In small teams, select hypothetical recreation, park, or leisure-service organizations, describing their missions, goals, and objectives, and examples of planning studies that might be carried out, and their recommendations.
3. In a class brainstorming session (see page 226), students may be asked to identify and explore several controversial issues or problem situations, in such areas as sports management (with such issues as recruitment or academic standards violations), staff or participants' diversity (with possible issues involving race, gender or sexual orientation), or similar problems. Then form small groups and discuss these issues, arriving at recommendations for administrative action. If appropriate, propose formal policies to deal with such problem situations in the future. The problems themselves might be drawn from the past experiences of class members, from the professional literature, or might be suggested by the course instructor.

Chapters 3 through 10 include case studies of typical problem situations in recreation, park, and leisure-service management. They may simply be read and then discussed in class informally. They may also be used in the following ways.

1. They may be assigned to small teams of two or three students each, to research, and then to present *alternative solutions* or more *formal recommendations* to deal with a problem situation.
2. *Role-playing,* or *sociodrama approaches,* may be used, with individual students playing the part of the major protagonists in the case studies in an informal dramatic presentation before the class. This would be followed by a class discussion of the implications of the case and possible solutions.
3. The class might identify two sharply opposed solutions to a problem, with students then assigned to argue the two sides within a time-limited *debate format.*

Case Study 3.1 *A Policy Issue: Gambling for Seniors— Permissible or Prohibited?*

YOU ARE KATHY GRANDOLFI, director of a large multiservice senior center that meets daily in the parish hall of a church in your community. Among your various program activities, which include both human service and recreational opportunities, you regularly hold bingo sessions, which are used for fund-raising purposes. You also schedule occasional "casino" nights, in which gambling games are played for small stakes. Both of these programs are popular with many participants.

The center council recommends that you plan a charter bus trip to Las Vegas over a spring weekend. Since you are in a nearby southwestern location, this would be a trip of reasonable length. You are making the arrangements, when suddenly the minister of the church and several elders call you in for a meeting. They want to discuss the gambling aspect of your program. Although they have not previously objected to the bingo games or casino nights, they now have two concerns. Should gambling be a prominent part of a senior center program that meets in a church, and, if members of the senior center go to Las Vegas, will some of them lose more money than they can afford?

You are at the point of negotiating a new three-year lease for your center with the church's governing board, and the gambling issue is on everybody's mind. The minister, Harold Porter, asks you to begin by giving your point of view with regard to the appropriateness of gambling as a senior center activity.

QUESTIONS FOR CLASS DISCUSSION AND ANALYSIS

1. Define the basic goals of your senior center and then indicate the kinds of policies that might flow from these with respect to gambling as part of the program.
2. You find yourself in a somewhat hostile, even adversary, relationship with the church minister and board. The gambling issue threatens to damage your formerly close and friendly relationship. How could this have been avoided or made less confrontational?
3. As the senior center director, what course of action would you recommend to deal with this situation?

Case Study 3.2   *Member of the Board:*
A Conflict in Authority

YOU ARE ELLIOT SIMON, a member of the board of trustees of a Young Men's—
Young women's Hebrew Association (YM-YWHA) in your community, and you
have many ideas about program activities that would be successful. However, you
find that the center director, Harry Goldfarb, tends to be slow in accepting or acting on your suggestions. While you like Harry, you do not feel that he is creative
or aggressive enough in promoting Y programs.

Therefore, you have developed a practice of initiating contacts with the different program specialists or division heads in the YM-YWHA and giving them advice regarding new program activities or events. Since you are friendly with many
business people in the community, you have also been able to get them to make
contributions or provide volunteer services to assist these programs. Although you
have bypassed Harry Goldfarb in taking these steps, you feel that it has been justified because it has helped make the Y's program more successful.

At a monthly meeting of the board, Harry accuses you of going beyond your
prerogatives and making his position as agency director untenable. Either you
stop your direct contacts with members of his staff and work through him, he says,
or he will consider resigning. As it happens, he has the offer of a business position
that is tempting. How do you respond?

QUESTIONS FOR CLASS DISCUSSION AND ANALYSIS

1. *How valid are Harry's charges? Do
   you feel that you have done anything
   wrong in bypassing Harry? After
   all, you had nothing to gain and
   only had the Y's interests at heart.*
2. *Regarding your relationship with
   other staff members, what kinds of
   policies could have prevented this
   crisis from developing?*
3. *Is there any way in which you could
   have provided creative input to the
   program other than the approach
   you used?*
4. *What principles presented in this
   chapter apply to this conflict
   situation?*

4. Students might use *brainstorming* to develop a range of possible solutions to the
   problem, before narrowing them down to one or two "best" courses of action.

Note: The case-study method is widely used in many management courses,
schools, or textbooks as a means of simulating actual field situations. In studying
a case, it is important not only to deal with the outward symptoms of a given problem, but to understand and attack its underlying causes. See also discussions of
problem solving, decision making and crisis management, on pages 36 and 225.

YOU ARE PERRY MALONE, assistant dean in charge of campus recreation programs at Mifflin State College and director of the college's student union. You are responsible for campus social programs, entertainment events, clubs, and publications, along with counseling the dormitory residents.

A separate recreational sports program is managed by Mifflin's athletic director, Bill Gomez. This program includes intramurals, sports clubs, and outdoor recreation trips. You have gotten along fairly well with the recreational sports program in the past. However, friction has begun to develop between the two programs. For example, twice during the last year, there were major conflicts when both the student union and the recreational sports program scheduled large-scale events on the same weekend. Attendance suffered, and students complained that they could not attend both events. Beyond this, there are now bad feelings with respect to the interchange of facilities. In the past, you were able to use the gyms for dances, and the sports programs used your facilities for award ceremonies and banquets. However, lately it has been difficult to cooperate with Bill Gomez. He has indicated that next year his schedule might not permit him to let your department use the regular gyms for social events.

You recognize that the real problem is in the arbitrary division of the campus recreation program into two separate units. However, no one seems willing to give up any authority, and the result is confusion and inefficiency.

QUESTIONS FOR CLASS DISCUSSION AND ANALYSIS

1. Would it be a good idea for you to deny Bill Gomez the use of your facilities in retaliation for his reluctance to let you use the gyms for your programs?

2. From a program planning point of view, how could you combine your efforts, even if you continue to be administratively separate?

3. On the issue of program scheduling, would there be a simple way to avoid overlap or conflict? What is the real issue here?

4. As a group assignment, could you construct a preferred model of leisure-service delivery for the campus?

REFERENCES

1. "A Cultural Policy for City of Ottawa," *Planning Report*, Ottawa, Ontario, Can., 1989.
2. *Annual Report: National/Local Partnerships*, Boys and Girls Clubs of America, 1997.
3. Sullivan, James V.: *Management of Health and Fitness Programs*, Springfield, Ill., 1990, Charles C. Thomas, p. 19.
4. Appenzeller, Herb: *Managing Sports and Risk Management Strategies*, Durham, N.C., 1993, Carolina Academic Press, pp. 9–10.
5. *Program Management and Classification*, Bureau of Naval Personnel, Morale, Welfare and Recreation Manual, 1994, vol. 7, pp. 5–171.
6. Bullaro, John, and Edginton, Christopher: *Commercial Leisure Services: Managing for Profit, Service and Personal Satisfaction*, New York, 1986, Macmillan Co., p. 106.
7. *The YMCA Movement: Leadership, Services and Organization*, Chicago, 1994, Young Men's Christian Association.
8. Dustin, Daniel, McAvoy, Leo, and Schultz, John: *Stewards of Access: Custodians of Choice*, Champaign, Ill., 1995, Sagamore Publishing, p. 6.
9. Florence Heffron, cited in Jubenville, Alan, and Twight, Ben: *Outdoor Recreation Management*, State College, Pa., 1993, Venture Publishing, p. 1.
10. *Goals, Structure and Services*, San Mateo, Calif., Department of Parks and Recreation, 1997.
11. *City Streets/At-Risk Youth Division 1994 Update*, Phoenix, Ariz., Department of Parks, Recreation and Library, 1994.
12. *Annual Report*, Center for the Arts, Vero Beach, Fla., 1997.
13. *Membership in the YWCA*, New York, 1995, Young Women's Christian Association Program Brochure.
14. *RCH, Inc. 40th Anniversary Report*, San Francisco, Calif., 1992.
15. Edginton, Christopher, and Neal, Larry: "Ordering Organizational Goals," *California Parks and Recreation*, June/July 1982, p. 12.
16. Graham, Peter, and Klar, Lawrence: *Planning and Delivering Leisure Services*, Dubuque, Iowa, 1979, Wm. C. Brown, p. 25.
17. *Texas Quality Award Report*, Arlington, Tex., Parks and Recreation Department, 1997, p. 14.
18. McChesney, James, and Tappley, Richard: *Administrative Policy Manual*, Arlington, Va., 1966, National Recreation and Park Association, Management Aids Bulletin, no. 61, p. 5.
19. Allen, Lawrence, Harwell, Rick, Stevens, Bonnie, and Paisley, Karen: "Benefits-Based Programming," Presentation at 1997 NRPA Congress, Salt Lake City, Utah.

Four

Leisure-Service Program Development

From the recreational aspect, we [Employee Relations Department, M. D. Anderson Cancer Center, Houston, Texas] offer team and individual sports such as volleyball, softball, golf, swimming, tennis, jogging and aerobic programs. We recruit our employees for community events such as the Houston/Tenneco Marathon and the University of Texas Health Science Center Sportathon. We sponsor health fairs. . . .

We promote cultural events in Houston throughout the workplace with the Council for the Visual and Performing Arts. We maintain seasonal special events, such as our Employee Christmas Dinner, Christmas decorating contest, National Hospital Week, Savings Bond Drive, United Way, etc. We also manage our recreation facilities—two lighted tennis courts, a lighted quarter mile jogging track, swimming pool, volleyball courts, exercise room, picnic grounds and employee lounge. We handle discount programs for employees dealing with sporting and cultural events and various coupon books. We are also in charge of the monthly Outstanding Employee Award program.[1]

INTRODUCTION

Programming represents a key responsibility of recreation, parks, and leisure-service managers since it—along with the provision of facilities—is the vehicle through which agency missions, goals, and objectives are achieved.

All other management functions, including developing organizational structures, fiscal operations, staffing, public relations and risk-management tasks, are designed chiefly to ensure that successful programming realizes its goal of providing participants with enjoyable and healthful recreational involvement.

This chapter examines the total process of recreation program planning and implementation. Following a brief discussion of the meaning of programming, it identifies and describes ten major areas of recreation activities and related services. It examines the philosophical basis for programming centered about the specific missions of sponsoring agencies, and outlines the process of activity planning, scheduling, registration, and public relations.

The following understandings and competencies listed as essential in the Baccalaureate Degree standards of the NRPA/AALR Council on Accreditation are addressed in this chapter:

Knowledge of the responsibility of the leisure service profession to make available opportunities for leisure experiences for all populations, including those with special needs and disabilities (8.13).

Knowledge of the role and content of leisure programs and services (8.15).

Ability to organize and conduct leisure programs and services in a variety of settings (8.16).

Understanding of procedures and techniques for assessment of leisure needs (8.21).

Understanding of and ability to utilize programmatically a breadth of diverse activity content area (9C.01).

Ability to conceptualize, develop and implement recreation programs for various populations, marshaling diverse community and human service resources (9C.03).

Ability to apply the concepts of mainstreaming, integration and normalization in all programming (9D.10).

O B J E C T I V E S

At the conclusion of this chapter, readers should be familiar with the following concepts and processes:

1. The meaning and relevance of programming as an important management function in recreation, parks, and leisure services.
2. Ten major categories of recreation program activities and related service areas.
3. The process of developing and implementing programs, including needs assessment, environmental scans, registering, scheduling, publicizing, pricing, and staffing activities and events.
4. The most commonly found formats through which leisure-service activities are presented.
5. Examples of successful programs designed to meet varied participant and community needs, including services for special populations and operational policies.

Numerous authors have suggested different definitions of *recreation programming*. J. Robert Rossman, for example, suggests that its primary purpose is to manipulate and create environments to provide participants with the leisure experiences they seek.[2] Ford and Blanchard stress the need to see programming from the sponsoring agency's perspective:

> Program is defined as the practical implementation of the sponsoring agency's goals and objectives.... In reality, the program is everything—planned and unplanned—that affects the participants.[3]

Simply stated, the term *programming* refers to the planning and presentation of organized and purposeful leisure experiences, designed systematically to achieve desired and socially positive individual and group outcomes. It has three components:

1. The *direct delivery* of organized or supervised activities, such as sports leagues, special-interest groups, day camps, classes, clubs, outings, or special events carried out in a scheduled way under supervision or leadership;
2. The *design, construction,* and *maintenance* of facilities for recreational involvement that is largely self-directed, such as the use of golf courses, tennis courts, beaches, picnic grounds, or hiking trails, in which there may be a degree of supervision (such as in swimming pools) but little formal leadership; and
3. The *facilitation* or *coordination* of leisure-service activities in the community at large, through assistance or partnership arrangements in funding, staffing, scheduling, sharing of facilities, joint sponsorship, advocacy, or other cooperative efforts.

PROGRAM DEVELOPMENT SEQUENCE

The recreation programming cycle is often discussed in terms of an annual plan—in which varied activities or services are planned in advance in a fully coordinated, carefully scheduled way, and then carried out throughout the year.

While this is true in general terms, programs are often developed with varying time frames or operational schedules. Some activities are carried on only during specific seasons, or for shorter periods of weeks or months. Special events may occur only once during the year, and special circumstances or opportunities may lead to spontaneous, short-notice scheduling of activities.

Nonetheless, most programs do follow a series of seven important steps. These are briefly outlined as follows, and described in fuller detail throughout the chapter.

1. *Establish agency mission.* As Chapter 3 points out, it is necessary for each recreation, park, and leisure-service organization to identify its basic mission or philosophical base in order to provide direction for all program planning.

2. *Assess needs, interests, and resources.* The second important stage in the program-planning cycle involves systematically assessing the leisure needs of present or potential participants, community residents, or organization members.

 Linked to this is the examination of both internal and external environments—meaning the agency's fiscal, physical, and human resources, as well as the availability of recreational programs sponsored by other, competitive community organizations.

3. *Identify program goals and objectives.* Based on the information that has been gathered, the third step is to identify a concrete set of goals and objectives for the program. These include both *outcome goals* and objectives that the program should reach for participants, and *operational goals* and objectives that govern the policies, procedures, and decisions that guide ongoing program activities.

4. *Select appropriate activities, services, and events.* A key stage in the programming cycle involves the selection of activities, services, and events to be sponsored throughout the year, or at specific times. These may include program elements that are familiar and widely popular, as well as new, innovative or experimental elements.

5. *Develop detailed program plan.* This step involves the following: (1) determining the precise program elements to be offered, along with a designation of their formats (see pages 104–105), locations, time schedules, populations to be served, and charges, if any; (2) an overall time frame, which outlines when such tasks as publicity, registration, program implementation, and reporting or evaluation, are to be carried out; (3) the assignment of leaders, program specialists, or other staff members to specific locations or activities; and (4) fiscal breakdowns, which outline specific budgets for program activities—both in terms of expenditures by the agency and expected revenues from fees, rentals, or other charges.

6. *Implementation.* This is the service-delivery stage of the programming cycle, including the actual steps of publicizing activities and events, registering participants or groups, conducting activities, supervising them according to approved policies and procedures, and dealing with problem situations or making program changes as the need occurs.

7. *Program evaluation.* The final step in programming involves the objective and systematic evaluation of each activity, service, or event. How effectively was it carried on, in terms of attendance or participant satisfaction? Although evaluation is usually described as happening at *the end* of program activities, it should also be carried on *throughout* the public's participation, so that problems may be corrected or service delivery modified in a timely way.

NEEDS ASSESSMENT AND ENVIRONMENTAL SCANS

Since the role of developing agency mission statements has already been discussed in Chapter 3, we now turn to the tasks of determining participant needs and interests, and conducting environmental scans.

Briefly defined, needs represent the physical, emotional, social, intellectual, or other drives or other urges that individuals may have that can be met through leisure activities. Often, we tend to think of recreation or play as intended solely to provide fun or pleasure. The reality, however, is that leisure activities may be carried out to meet a wide range of needs—for excitement and challenge, companionship and friendship, health and fitness, sense of personal accomplishment, providing service for others, or intellectual stimulation.

How are such needs to be identified? In part, they may be determined arbitrarily—through a set of general principles having to do with the developmental stages of individuals throughout the life span. In addition to the age of participants, other factors to be considered might include their educational background, physical or mental health and possible degree of disability, socioeconomic status, and similar elements.

Needs and Interests

Clearly, since recreation involves the voluntary choices of participants, it is essential that all program activities and services be keyed to the actual wishes or desires of community residents or organization members, and that they are perceived as potentially enjoyable or valuable in other ways.

Varied methods can be used to assess participant needs and interests, including the use of focus groups, individual interviews, or suggestion boxes. One direct and accurate way of gathering information systematically involves the use of questionnaires—either written or administered in individual or group settings.

Use of Survey Instruments

Customarily, such questionnaires would deal with the preferences of potential participants for specific activities, as shown in Figure 4.1a, and with the choices with respect to time and location of program offerings, as shown in Figure 4.1b. They may be administered directly to members of an organization, those already involved in program activities, or to a sampling of community residents, and provide a basis for determining what program elements might find a receptive audience—as well as other guidelines for their effective presentation.

Environmental Scans

A second important basis for selecting program activities and services consists of two types of *environmental scans*, internal and external.

Internal scans involve a systematic examination of the agency's *current* and *recent programming activities* and *resources*. It is essential to review ongoing operation of all sports leagues, clubs, classes, playground, and center activities or

FIGURE 4.1a. Section of an interest survey form. Surveys of this type might present a very broad range of possible program elements, or might focus on a small number that program planners are considering for sponsorship.

Please indicate your interest in the following recreation activities, by checking the appropriate boxes.

Activities or Programs	Very High	High	Moderate	Little Interest
Volleyball club	( )	( )	( )	( )
Cooking lessons	( )	( )	( )	( )
Softball league	( )	( )	( )	( )
Scuba diving class	( )	( )	( )	( )
Adult singles group	( )	( )	( )	( )

FIGURE 4.1b. Section of a survey form, to determine preferred details of participation. *Note:* **Instead of listing so many possible times, the choice might be narrowed down to two or three times that would fit the agency's schedule or facilities.**

Frequency   How often do you expect to participate in this activity? Check one box.

Daily (in season) ( )   Once a month ( )
Several times a week ( )   Occasionally during year ( )
Several times a month ( )

Preferred Times   Please indicate your first, second, and third choice of times for participation:

	Early Morning	Later Morning	Lunchtime	Early Afternoon	Later Afternoon	Evening
Monday	( )	( )	( )	( )	( )	( )
Tuesday	( )	( )	( )	( )	( )	( )
Wednesday	( )	( )	( )	( )	( )	( )
Thursday	( )	( )	( )	( )	( )	( )
Friday	( )	( )	( )	( )	( )	( )
Saturday	( )	( )	( )	( )	( )	( )
Sunday	( )	( )	( )	( )	( )	( )

Location   Please indicate your first choice of a preferred location for participation in this activity. Check one box.

Barker Center ( )   Hamilton Center ( )
Gonzalez School ( )   Carver Park ( )

special events to determine how successful they have been. Have they justified themselves in terms of attendance? Have participants indicated their satisfaction with them in formal or informal evaluation reports?

A second aspect of internal scans consists of *reviewing* the *agency's resources,* in terms of staffing capability, available areas and facilities for different types of programs, and fiscal picture. Some program elements require relatively little support of this kind, while others demand a high level of expert leadership or specialized facilities. Some may yield substantial revenues in fees and charges, while others need to be totally subsidized.

External scans examine the agency's environment. What are the special needs of the community for program opportunities? What recreational services are being provided by other, competing organizations? What gaps in service suggest a high priority, while others would create unnecessary duplication of leisure activities? Figure 4.1c shows how one agency takes all of these factors into account, in determining whether classes or other program elements should be scheduled.

Target Marketing

Needs and interests surveys and environmental scans may also focus on specific population groups and their special recreational priorities. Such studies gain information about age groups, household income groups, family structures, gender factors, and similar demographic elements, often broken down by area of residence.

Mapping the characteristics of community residents based on such factors is helpful in identifying *target markets.* In one section of a community, in the case of a public recreation and park department, there may be a considerable number of at-risk youth and the need for relevant social-service programming. In other areas, there may be many elderly persons, young couples, or single individuals with high income levels who would welcome certain other types of programs.

DETERMINING PROGRAM GOALS

Based on all the information that has been gathered, agency program planners should be ready to develop or revise short- and long-term goals as a basis for selecting activities that will best serve the organization's mission *and* meet community and target group needs.

In many cases, recreation programs will have been successful and should be continued. However, given the rate of social change and other factors that influence family life and leisure needs, every program planner must be alert to new needs and priorities. Creative managers welcome such situations, seeing them not as threats or crises, but rather as the opportunity to break new ground and respond in an innovative way.

To do this, clearly stated goals and objectives should be established both for the overall agency program, and for specific areas of the community or population groups that are to be served. This may mean introducing or expanding different activity areas or services, and cutting back on others. It may also mean providing activities within different formats, such as instruction, competition, or special events.

FIGURE 4.1c. Example of form developed by Dept. of Leisure Services, Sunnyvale, California, in rating appropriateness of different classes or other activities for agency sponsorship, including market demand, potential for cosponsorship, and other factors.

CLASS BEING RATED _____ TOTAL SCORE _____

* RATING FOR POTENTIAL PARTNERSHIP _____

** Rating Scale 1 - 10
   (1) Indicates Lowest Demand/Recommendation for the Class,
   (10) Indicates Highest Demand/Recommendation for the Class.

	Rate	WT	Score
Competition: Similar activities already being offered by private business other nearby agencies. High competition = low score Low competition = high score	8	x 1.0 =	8
Profitability Revenue _____ Expenses _____	7	x 1.0 =	7
Expense/Participant ratio	6	x 1.0 =	6
Availability and Capacity of Facility	9	x 1.0 =	9
Trends in Market Interest growing/declining	10	x 1.0 =	10
Current Demand Interest in this type of activity	5	x 2.0 =	10
Staff Time Acceptable amount of staff time required	2	x 1.0 =	2
Political or Special Factors Special population needs or any other factor that would supercede the other scores.	10	x 2.0 =	20
TOTAL SCORE			72

A score 80 or above, or (10) under Political or Special Factor, suggests an activity should be offered.
**Scores to be based on responses to Activity Market Surveys conducted. (attached).

*If, based on Market Survey, there is a potential for Partnership for this activity, complete the Activity Rating Form again, factoring the partnership concept into your responses.

Comments:_____
_____
_____

There are essentially ten widely found, popular categories of recreation activities and services that different types of leisure-service agencies offer.

1. Sports, Games and Fitness Programs

This broad area represents the most popular single category of recreational participation today, in terms of active involvement. Sports in particular—defined as participant or spectator activities, involving physical skills and competition, carried on under both formal rules and within a framework of appropriate behavior or fair play—may be engaged in informally, through free play in a school yard or college gymnasium (Fig. 4.2), or formally in organized youth or adult league play.

Active sports are usually classified as either *team, individual,* or *dual* sports. Examples of popular team sports include: baseball, softball, ice or field hockey, basketball, football, and their variants. Individual or dual sports include golf, tennis, fencing, boxing, bowling, and archery. While they usually involve one-against-one or two-against-two competition, they may also be part of team events. Thus, while a girl may compete as an individual in a sprint event, she may also be part of relay events or team competition against other schools or organizations.

Administrative Values

Sports have many administrative advantages for community or other leisure-service organizations. They are immensely popular and usually attract great numbers of participants or spectators. They are linked to the development and maintenance of physical health, and have traditionally been seen as promoting such desirable personal values as discipline, loyalty, teamwork, fair play, and good citizenship, although they may be given the wrong emphases.

The other activities included under this heading, *games* and *fitness,* share some common elements with sports. Games like kickball, dodgeball, or other active playground contests include the factors of physical competition, team play, and rules that govern play.

Fitness activities may overlap with sports in that such activities as running, racquetball, or swimming are often part of organized health and fitness programming. However, in such settings, they are engaged in primarily for their cardiovascular health benefits, rather than for competitive reasons. In many situations, such as employee-service programs, fitness activities have become a major emphasis for health and job-productivity reasons. Even in such settings, however, the degree to which fitness activities can be presented within a recreational or social framework will influence their popularity and holding power for participants.

2. Outdoor Recreation Activities

A second major category of leisure pursuits that is widely sponsored by varied types of recreation sponsors involves outdoor recreation and related environmental activities. Essentially, these are defined as forms of play that are closely

FIGURE 4.2. Example of campus sports programming: Southern Illinois University.

WHAT THE OFFICE OF INTRAMURAL-RECREATIONAL SPORTS HAS TO OFFER:

WELCOME

The Office of Intramural-Recreational Sports welcomes all students, university-affiliated persons, and their families to visit our facilities and participate in any of these programs. We welcome your comments and suggestions. Please call **(618) 536-5531**. We would like to hear from you.

STUDENT RECREATION CENTER

Aerobics Room
Alumni Lounge
Boxing Room
Carpeted, suspended
   jogging track
28' Climbing Wall
Dry Heat Saunas
Equipment Checkout
Fitness Forum
Free Weight Room
Indoor Tennis Court
Inverted Climbing Roof
Martial Arts Room
6-Multi-Sport Courts
  *6 Basketball Courts
  *6 Volleyball Courts
  *16 Badminton Courts
  *1 Team Handball Court
Olympic-Size Pool
14 Racquetball Courts
2 Squash Courts
200 Meter Track
Towel Service
& MUCH MORE!!!

SATELLITE FACILITIES

Grand Avenue Playfields:
  Flag Football
  Sand Volleyball
  Soccer
  Softball

Pulliam Hall:
  Swimming Pool

SIUC Arena Playfields:
  Flag Football
  Softball
  Ultimate Frisbee

SIUC School of Law:
  Basketball Courts
  Tennis Courts
  Volleyball Courts

Southern Hills
  Tennis Courts

University Tennis &
  Racquetball Courts

Wall Street Courts:
  Roller Hockey
  Tennis

Sport Club Fields:
  Rugby
  Ultimate Frisbee

Check out our web site at:
http://www.siu.edu/~oirs/index.html

SPORT CLUBS
453-1376

Aikido
Badminton
Bike Racing
Bowling
Boxing
Canoe & Kayak
Cricket
Equestrian
Footbag
Judo
Karate
Kung Fu
Lacrosse
Martial Arts
Outdoor Adventure
Racquetball
Roller Hockey
Rugby (Men's)
Rugby (Women's)
Sailing
SIU Sky Dogs
Soccer (Men's)
Soccer (Women's)
Triathlon
Ultimate Frisbee
Volleyball
Water Polo
Water Skiing
Weight Lifting
Wrestling

INSTRUCTIONAL PROGRAMS
453-1272

Aerobics
Dancing:
  African
  Ballet
  Middle Eastern
  Modern
Karate
Meditation
Racquetball
Swimming
Tai Chi
Tennis
Therapeutic Massage
Yoga

INTRAMURAL SPORTS
453-1273

Basketball
Bike Race
Flag Football
Floor Hockey
Golf
Racquetball
Soccer
Softball
Squash
Table Tennis
Tennis
2 Person Canoe Race
Volleyball
Wallyball
Innertube Water Polo

If you have any questions about any of these programs or activities, please call 536-5531.
OR stop by the Information Center.
(Located on the upper level of the Student Recreation Center)

Outdoor recreation often centers around participants' interest in animals and nature. Visitors enjoy getting close to wild creatures at Silver Springs, FL, theme parks. Some public park systems have established fenced areas, as in Sarasota, FL, Paw Park, where residents can let their dogs, large and small, run free.

linked to or dependent on the natural environment. Examples include: backpacking, bird-watching, gardening, hunting, hiking, ice skating, orienteering, skiing, or surfing.

While some such activities may be carried on within a competitive format, such as fishing contests or winter sports events that include ski jumping or luge racing, customarily outdoor recreation is engaged in as an end in itself. Often they involve family participation such as vacation camping, and may be enjoyed by people of all ages. Increasingly organized outdoor recreation has been made available for participants with disabilities.

Administrative Values

Like sports, outdoor recreation activities are extremely popular. Obviously, they tend to be offered primarily by public agencies, such as federal or state park departments, which have extensive tracts of forest or wilderness lands, or beaches, lakes, and similar areas.

However, many local agencies sponsor instructional classes in outdoor recreation skills, such as riflery or gardening. In some cases, public recreation and park departments may present activities linked to regional climates or traditional customs. For example, the city of Dartmouth, Nova Scotia, sponsors canoe and kayaking instruction, horseback riding, making maple syrup, coastline and wetlands hiking events, maritime folklore programs, and similar events. Other Canadian cities, because of their northern climate, give heavy emphasis to winter sports such as ice skating, ice fishing, hockey, curling, snowshoeing, or tobogganing.

Use of the outdoors should be based on careful environmental policies that do not harm natural surrounding or wildlife through overuse or the impact of off-road vehicles. Many public and nonprofit leisure-service organizations teach outdoor skills with a strong emphasis on sound ecological values, and often engage in environmental clean-up programs (see Fig. 4.3).

To illustrate the range of possible outdoor recreation pursuits, the Edmonton, Alberta, Canada, recreation and park department has a three-thousand-acre Capital City Recreation Park along a river valley, used by nearly 100 different special-interest groups for activities ranging from hot-air ballooning and hang gliding to orienteering and cross-country skiing. The wide variety of outdoor recreation programs that may be sponsored by nonprofit organizations in this field is shown in Figure 4.4.

3. Aquatic Recreation

Swimming and other types of water-based leisure activity might be classified as either sport or outdoor recreation, since they clearly are linked to both categories of play.

However, since they represent such a widely found area of activity and since they share a common, unique environment—the water—they often are classified as a separate program category. Many public recreation and park departments, for example, have separate divisions of beaches and pools, operate marinas, and have extensive swimming instruction or boating programs. Aquatic activities include: boating (canoeing, powerboating or sailing); fishing; scuba diving; swimming and life-saving classes; water polo; and swimming competition.

Administrative Values

Surveys have shown that swimming and related water-based activities are among the most popular leisure pursuits among participants of all ages and backgrounds.

Swimming in particular satisfies a variety of personal needs and motivations. It is an ideal form of exercise and maintaining physical fitness. It can be a competitive activity or simply a pleasant outing experience shared by entire

FIGURE 4.3. Environmental Education and Service Program for teenagers: Westchester County, N.Y., Department of Parks, Recreation and Conservation.

C.I.T. (Conservationists in Training) Program
For students entering grades 7, 8 and 9

Make a difference!
Learn While Improving the Environment

The staff is made up of environmental educators who are experienced and enthusiastic. The program is specifically designed for students entering grades 7, 8 and 9 in September 1997.

Activities:

Bridge Building ▲ Hiking ▲Trail Maintenance ▲ Overnight Camp-outs
Survival Skills ▲ Rock Climbing Techniques ▲ Stream Walks
Increase Self-Esteem ▲ Leadership Skills ▲ Team Spirit

Two-Week Sessions

Session 1 • July 7 - 11 &14 - 18
Session 2 • July 21 - 25 & 28 - August 1
Session 3 • August 4 - 8 & August 11 - 15

Each session is Monday through Friday, 10 a.m. to 4 p.m.
Bring a picnic lunch - $450 per session

For more information, call (914) 242-6327

Trailside Nature Museum
Ward Pound Ridge Reservation
Cross River, New York

FIGURE 4.4. Trip programs sponsored by Woodswomen, Inc., Minneapolis, Minn. *Note:* Activities are designed for women and in some cases their children. Other activities include leadership development, horseback riding, skiing and snowshoeing, and adventure trips to countries around the world.

1998 WOODSWOMEN TRIPS AT A GLANCE

	Trip	Dates	Level	Location	Price
Backpacking & Mountaineering	St. Croix Spring Hike	May 8-10	S/WJ	WI	$195
	Desert Slickrock Backpack	May 10-16	WJ	UT	$785
	Rocky Mountain Backpack- NEW	June 21-25	WJ	CO	$475
	Mountaineering & Glacier Travel	July 10-16	HA	WA	$825
	Olympic National Park	July 26-Aug 1	WJ	WA	$825
	Mt. Rainier Backpack	Aug 3-9	WJ	WA	$785
	Isle Royale Backpack	Aug 16-22	WJ	MI	$785
	North Shore Hike	Sept 17-20	S/WJ	MN	$225
	Grand Canyon Backpack	Sept 20-26	HA	AZ	$785
Bicycling	New Zealand Bicycle Tour	Feb 14-Mar 1	ET	New Z	$2975
	Learn to Bicycle Tour	June 5-7	S/WJ	WI	$225
	Cycling in Ireland	Aug 2-16	ET	Ireland	$2450
	Mountain Biking in Utah- NEW	September 27-30	WJ	UT	$595
Canoeing & Kayaking	Namekagon River Odyssey	May 15-17	S/WJ	WI	$195
	Whitewater School	May 22-24	S/WJ	WI	$235
	St. Croix Canoe Day	June 24 or July 7	S	MN	$39
	BWCA Northern Lakes Loop	July 5-11	WJ	MN	$675
	BWCA Lakes, Rivers & Pictographs	July 12-18	HA	MN	$675
	BWCA Rainbow Island Retreat	July 19-25	ET	MN	$795
	Apostle Islands Voyage- NEW	July 24-27	WJ	MN	$475
	Kenai Fjords Sea Kayak	July 25-30	WJ	AK	$1310
	BWCA Northern Lakes/Special	July 26-Aug 1	WJ	MN	$675
	BWCA Canadian Wilds	Aug 2-15	HA	MN	$1050
	BWCA Autumn Canoe Trip	Sept 6-12	WJ	MN	$675
Dogsledding	Dogsledding in the Northland	Dec 28 -Jan 1, Jan 28-Feb 1, or Feb 4-8	ET	MN	$695
Hiking	Navajo Land Trek- NEW	May 23-28	WJ	AZ	$945
	Discovering Newfoundland- NEW	July 4-11	ET	Canada	$1495
	Walking in the Swiss Alps	July 29-Aug 8	ET	Switz	$2350
	Hiking in Denali Park	Aug 1-7 or Aug 9-15	WJ	AK	$995
	Trekking in the Himalayas	Oct 14-Nov 1	WJ	Nepal	$2595
Horseback Riding	Horseback Riding in Wisconsin	June 12-15 or Aug 14-17	WJ	WI	$395
Leadership Development	Integrated Leadership- NEW	Jan 17-18	L	CO	$195
	Joshua Tree Leadership	Apr 2-9	WJ/L	CA	$860
	Integrated Leadership	Apr 18-19 or Nov 7-8	L	MN	$195

families or social groups. It is a key element in camping and day camp programming, and is often presented in a sequence of instructional classes ranging from beginner to advanced skills.

Apart from simple swimming, aquatic activities also include a range of other appealing or innovative outdoor recreation possibilities, such as parasailing or waterskiing. When used with elderly participants or those with disabilities, aerobic water exercises can readily be adapted to special class needs.

Water-based play. (top) pool play in Silver Springs, FL; (middle) White water rafting in the Poconos; (bottom) backyard pool.

4. Arts, Crafts, and Related Hobby Activities

Another popular area of leisure activities includes creative or aesthetic forms of expression. These include varied art activities, which produce objects that are essentially decorative and without practical purpose. Obvious examples include:

drawing and sketching	oil or watercolor painting
sculpture or carving	silk screen or woodblock printing
other graphic activities, such as etching or lithography	

Craft pursuits are generally regarded as more practical or functional, although it is now recognized that they too may have important aesthetic or design values. Typical examples of crafts activities include:

leather working	macrame
weaving or knitting	metalcraft
photography	ceramics or pottery

Other hobbies that involve craft-like skills include varied types of model building (planes, ships, or train layouts), clothing design or construction, flower arrangement, collections, or nature-study activities that involve creating visual displays.

Administrative Values

Arts, crafts, and related hobbies have a wide range of appeal to different age groups and may be offered on every level of skill. They require little physical output, in contrast to sports or most outdoor pursuits, and may readily be used with groups with severe physical or mental limitations.

Creative activities may be offered in different formats, including such simple playground pursuits as finger painting or clay modeling, or advanced studio classes requiring special equipment, such as looms or kilns. They promote personal growth and aesthetic appreciation, and may lend themselves to seasonal or annual shows and exhibitions of artistic or craft products (Fig. 4.5).

5. *Music, Drama, and Dance*

A closely allied program area consists of the performing arts—music, drama, and dance. These represent forms of personal expression that, unlike arts and crafts, do not result in a tangible product. Instead, the practice and performance of a given activity, whether playing an instrument or taking part in a dance or dramatic performance, is the key element in the creative experience.

Music in particular, is a highly popular program element, including both social or artistic/cultural emphases, such as:

choral groups or folk singing	instrumental practice
bands and orchestras	rock-and-roll groups
opera or operetta performance	drum and bugle corps

Similarly, dramatic leisure pursuits are extremely diverse:

children's theater	charades and dramatic games
one-act plays	storytelling
marionettes and puppetry	theater clubs and parties
variety and talent shows	

FIGURE 4.5. Example of Arts and Crafts Programming—Kamloops, Canada.

97

CHAPTER 4
Leisure-Service
Program
Development

KAMLOOPS ARTS AND CRAFTS CLUB

KAC membership: $35 year ($15 seniors). Gift certificates available for memberships or class fees. Contact Wendy 376-4443 or Geri 374-9945

STAINED GLASS

Mixed Level
Thursday 7:00 to 9:30 P.M.
January 27 to March 17, 1994
Lower Lounge, Heritage House
KACC members: $45.00   nonmembers: $50.00
Supplies extra
Instructor: Brenda Davy
Information: Geri 374-9945

DRAFTING FOR OVERSHOT WEAVING

Intermediate and Advanced weavers:
February 12 & 13, 1994
Saturday 9:30 A.M. to 3:30 P.M. (bring a lunch)
Sunday 9:30 A.M. to 12:30 P.M.
Lower Lounge, Heritage House
KACC members: $40.00   nonmembers: $50.00
Supplies included, samples will be woven
Instructor: Joan Cameron
Information: Janet 376-9956

WATERCOLOURS

Beginners: Tuesday 7:00 to 9:30 P.M.
February 1 to March 8, 1994
Lower Lounge, Heritage House
KACC members: $35.00   nonmembers: $40.00
Supplies extra
Instructor: Olga Burr
Information: Anne 374-2403

WATERCOLOURS

Intermediate and Advanced: Wednesday 1:00 to 4:00 P.M.
January 26 to March 16, 1994
Lower Lounge, Heritage House
KACC members: $50.00   nonmembers: $60.00
Supplies extra
Instructor: Dora Richmond
Information: Anne 374-2403

POTTERY

Contact Erna (579-9576) for dates and times

WOODCARVING

Intermediate
Tuesdays 7:00 to 9:30 P.M.
March 15 to April 12, 1994 (4 classes)
Lower Lounge, Heritage House
KACC members: $30.00   nonmembers: $35.00
Plus a small charge for wood and tools
Instructor: Gerry Watson
Information: Nora 579-9521

REGISTRATION

January 13,1994 (Thursday) 9:30 A.M.. to noon and 7:00 to 9:30 P.M., Lower Level, Heritage House. Information: Geri 374-9945.
Mail in registration deadline: January 11, 1994. Mail to: KACC, Box 522, Kamloops, V2C 5L2

SURNAME:_____ GIVEN NAME:_____

ADDRESS:_____ POSTAL CODE: _____ PHONE: _____

COURSE TITLE:_____ FEE:_____

COURSE TITLE:_____ FEE:_____

Please do not mail cash. Cheques Payable to Kamloops Arts & Crafts
Mail to Box 522 Kamloops B.C. V2C 5L2

Dance offers examples of both social and creative pursuits:

ballet   tap dance

modern or experimental dance   jazz dance

ethnic or folk dance   social or ballroom dance

Administrative Values

The performing arts, like arts and crafts, are uniquely suited to serving different age groups and skill levels and meeting varied personal leisure needs. They serve to promote aesthetic creativity, but they also have a strong social element in that they all may be presented within a performing group or club format. Dance in particular has a strong physical fitness component, although it may be performed by individuals with significant disabilities. All types of music, drama, and dance lend themselves both to individual skill development and to performance before audiences.

In addition to involvement as performers, participants may also seek other roles, such as costume designers, lighting technicians, stagehands, publicists, ticket takers, or set designers or builders—thus broadening the range of program participation.

6. Special Events

Initially, special events tended to be thought of primarily as relatively minor program features in playgrounds or community centers, or as holiday or other community celebrations. Today, they include a huge range of activities centered around many different themes, often with large audiences and extensive production features. Examples include:

holiday parties	major sports tournaments
arts and crafts fairs	aquatic displays/exhibitions
Gospel music or jazz festivals	family carnivals
rodeos or Western-theme events	Mardi Gras or "Mummers" parades
ethnic heritage festivals	

As a single example, the annual Children's Festival in Vancouver, British Columbia, involves some sixty-five tent structures, including four large theater tents that seat over 1,500 spectators. Program events that include varied performing arts activities, magic shows, or leading visiting groups, such as the Beijing Children's Opera, attract over 100,000 children, parents, and teachers each year, including many visitors to Vancouver.[4]

In Westchester County, New York, the Department of Parks, Recreation and Conservation sponsors numerous events promoting cultural aspects of different national groups and hosts varied concerts, expositions, shows, and tournaments at its huge County Center auditorium (Fig. 4.6).

Administrative Values

Special events provide highlights to recreation programming by attracting large numbers of spectators or participants to programs that feature activities that are carried on regularly throughout the year.

They promote a spirit of celebration and mingling among different community groups, encouraging them to work together, sharing common interests and

FIGURE 4.6. Listing of special events, Westchester County, N.Y.

99

CHAPTER 4
Leisure-Service
Program
Development

cooperating on various tasks. Often, they may serve as a means of fund-raising, when sponsored by therapeutic recreation or nonprofit youth-serving organizations. Large-scale, colorful events may bring thousands of visitors to a community or region, with substantial income to local businesses that cater to tourism or rely on their attendance. One recreation programmer writes:

Today, the Fort Lauderdale Parks and Recreation Department relies heavily upon sponsors for the ten events and festivals it produces annually. . . . Special events can produce a large profit [from admissions, concessions, and souvenir sales] allowing us to offset costs in other department programming areas that do not generate sufficient revenue.[5]

7. Social Recreation Activities

A somewhat related category of leisure pursuits includes varied informal social recreation activities—defined as the type of program that emphasizes the informal mixing of people in casual, noncompetitive party or club get-togethers.

Social recreation programs include such sessions as:

play days	card parties
scavenger hunts or treasure hunts	picnics and barbecues
potluck or covered-dish suppers	talent shows or fun nights
campfires and marshmallow roasts	

Administrative Values

Social recreation is particularly suited to club activities, neighborhood parties, or similar settings. Ideally, planning and leadership may be carried on by group members themselves, who take responsibility for leading activities, providing refreshments, putting up decorations, and similar tasks.

Two settings where social recreation programs are particularly appropriate are (1) senior centers or Golden Age clubs, where community singing, simple games and dancing often enliven weekly meetings or special birthday or holiday parties for members; and (2) cruise ship evening entertainment programs, that often feature humorous contests, quizzes, midnight deck parties, "welcome aboard" or "debarkation" sessions. In some armed forces bases, which have tended to rely heavily on open bars as settings for relaxation, innovative programmers have initiated a new approach to social recreation, as in the San Diego, California's naval station, where:

> The 32nd Street Yacht Club Enlisted Recreation Center is a unique alcohol- and tobacco-free club serving the young, active-duty sailor. When sailors open the doors (not the hatch), they find a wealth of free services, games, high quality equipment, innovative programming information [that includes pool tables, video games, a lending library, video-making equipment, software and computers, nightly contests, festivals, and weekly tours] and an interactive staff.[6]

8. Cognitive Forms of Play

Another traditional type of leisure pursuits includes quiet activities of a literary, mental, or other cognitive or intellectual nature. Geared to the interest level of different age groups, such activities might include:

book club	poetry club or workshop
current events discussion group	writers' workshop
leisure counseling group	computer hobby group
puzzles	paper and pencil games

Typically, many YMCAs, YWCAs, or YM/YWHAs (Young Men's/Young Women's Hebrew Associations) sponsor numerous classes or clubs devoted to learning fiction and nonfiction writing, business writing, personal memoirs, and similar skills.

Administrative Values

Probably the greatest value of cognitive forms of play as an area of recreation programming is that it serves a distinctly different set of personal needs and motivations from other recreational activities. By contributing to participants' mental development and challenging them intellectually, leisure-service agencies are able to break away from a narrow "fun and games" identity.

9. Life-Adjustment and Personal Skills

More and more, many leisure-service organizations are now offering classes, clinics, or workshops that deal with the kinds of life-adjustment or personal enrichment needs facing many adults today.

While such program elements are often educational in content, they do not address formal educational goals, and are simply more purposeful in their approach than other recreational activities. Among the areas included in this category are home management or interpersonal relationship skills, personal grooming and health care, career development, or other financial or practical concerns. Typical titles of classes or workshops offered by Ys or community recreation departments in their adult programming brochures include (Fig. 4.7):

aerobic exercise and body tone	childbirth education
gourmet cooking	home or auto repair skills
weight reduction	mother-toddler play
women and finance	single parents workshop
introduction to computers	foreign language classes
reversing the aging process	

Administrative Values

Such program elements are usually offered in classlike settings, over periods of six to ten weeks, with fees that usually are moderate, but cover instructional and overhead expenses. Typically, they are directed by part-time, outside specialists who are paid on a per-course basis, provided that sufficient enrollment is achieved for their courses.

FIGURE 4.7. Example of nonprofit agency programming meeting varied age-level personal and social needs. Peninsula Family YMCA, San Mateo, California.

PENINSULA FAMILY YMCA
1877 South Grant St., San Mateo 94402 (415) 286-9622

YOUTH & FAMILY PROGRAMS

Child & Family Programs—Holly Cords   294-2614
  (Indian guides, ChildWatch, birthday party, family events)
Day Camp—Patty Gershaneck   294-2605
  (summer and school breaks, after school San Bruno)
Swim Lessons/Team—Jill Fleming   294-2609
Youth Sports—Steve Martin   294-2624
  (youth basketball, baseball, karate, soccer, etc.)
Teens—Justin Moscoso   294-2617
  (teen leaders, youth & government, teen activities)

ADULT PROGRAMS

Starting a Fitness Program Sign up for an orientation or
  assessment, or call Steve, Ben, Becky, or Kathy below.
Personal Training—Ben Kwock, RN (personal training,
  special medical needs, disabilities)   294-2611
Fitness Appointments Hotline (make/cancel appointments,
  assessment/orientation questions)   294-2682
Aerobics/Group Fitness—Becky Ruppel   294-2610
Aerobics Schedule Hotline   294-2670
Adult Sports—Steve Martin (basketball, volleyball,
  triathlon, biking, hiking)   294-2624
Adult Swim Programs—Jill Fleming   294-2609
Health Education—Kathy McFarland (health classes,
nutrition, weight management, sports injuries)   294-2638
Active Older Adults—Marie Siddons   294-2622, ext. 414

COUNSELING & YOUTH AT RISK

Project FOCYS Youth & Family Counseling   349-7969
  (professional, affordable, sliding-scale fee)
Building Futures Mentors—Kimberly Wheeler 294-2619
  (referrals and adult volunteer mentors)
Youth at Risk Program—Dr. Dale Lete   294-2613

ADMINISTRATIVE/MEMBERSHIP

Executive Director—Beth Salazar   294-2601
Assoc. Exec. Director—Mike Fitzsimmons   294-2602
Membership Director—Mary McNair   294-2603
Membership Bookkeeper—Judy Hartmire   294-2623
Facility Maintenance—Gary Cockrell   294-2607

YMCA Volunteer Hotline   294-2622, ext. 684

10. Social-Service Functions

A final important program category consists of those activities or services designed to address broader social needs of community residents or organization members. Unlike the program elements in the preceding section, which deal with the personal needs of individuals, these have to do with significant health-related, legal, housing, educational, or family concerns of groups. Examples include:

anti-delinquency projects	career or vocational counseling	
discount purchasing plans	substance abuse programs	
health or dental clinics	legal assistance and referral programs	
tutoring or study-hour sessions	nutritional or transportation services	

Administrative Values

Each type of leisure-service agency has its own rationale for sponsoring such services. Nonprofit youth-serving organizations obviously are concerned with the total well-being and development of the boys and girls they serve, which justifies offering such services, along with recreation. Businesses provide such programs as health and fitness activities or stress management and substance abuse counseling in order to reduce employee absenteeism and turnover, and promote job productivity.

Since recreation, park, and leisure-service organizations already work with people of varying age groups and social backgrounds, they are in a logical position to provide such services. In so doing, when they become involved in areas that require special expertise, certification, or other kinds of staff qualifications, they may employ individuals qualified as therapists, social workers, vocational counselors, or rehabilitation specialists. As an alternative approach, they may offer programs jointly with other agencies, within a multiservice center concept.

PRINCIPLES OF PROGRAM DEVELOPMENT

Given this wide variety of possible program elements, ranging from sports and games to human-service functions, how do agency managers and program planners decide *which* activities to offer?

In the past, recreation, park, and leisure-service educators and authors have identified a number of popular approaches or models, which suggest the different ways in which programs are developed. They include the following:

The *traditional* approach, which relies on familiar and popular recreational activities that have been used widely in the past.

The *current-practices* model, emphasizing program elements that are influenced by present-day trends and fads.

The *expressed desires* approach, reflecting the wishes or requests of residents or organization members.

The *authoritarian* model, in which agency managers and planners rely chiefly on their own judgment and interests.

The *cafeteria* approach, which offers participants an extensive menu of varied activities from which to choose.

The *prescriptive* model, employing recreation as a tool for personal intervention or social change.

The *sociopolitical* approach, which responds directly to changing social conditions and the influence of pressure groups.[7]

Particularly for public recreation and park departments that seek to serve a broad constituency of community residents, a number of guiding principles have also been presented in the professional literature. Briefly summarized, these emphasize the need to serve all elements in the community; to provide diversified, socially constructive leisure opportunities; to involve community residents in program planning; to meet personal needs of residents, based on age, gender, disability, and other factors; to schedule activities flexibly, promote them widely, and evaluate them systematically.

These principles are taken into account, as program planners select activities and services that will meet the needs of different age groups and target populations, that are economically feasible in terms of their demands for staffing and facilities, and that are supportive in terms of their agencies' fundamental philosophy and goals.

DEVELOPING THE PROGRAM PLAN: FORMATS AND EMPHASES

At this point, a formal program plan is developed. It provides a comprehensive statement of the agency's operation over the time period lying ahead, including the activities and services to be offered, the groups they will serve, their locations, possible fees and charges, and staffing assignments.

Essentially, the program plan appears in two forms: (1) a public presentation, usually designed as an annual or seasonal brochure that outlines all program activities and services, along with information with respect to schedules, locations, fees, and similar details; and (2) a behind-the-scenes document, often organized with the use of computer software for convenient reference, updating of information, or statistical recording and analysis, which describes the actual internal agency plan for carrying out the program.

Selection of Formats and Program Emphases

The term *format* simply applies to the way in which any particular activity will be presented and experienced. Some of the most common formats in recreation programs include the following:

Instruction. Typically, many agencies present classes over a period of several weeks, or simply brief instruction sessions, that introduce participants to recreation skills.

Competition. The organization and scheduling of individual or team play in sports and games is a popular format; in addition, competition may apply to hobby or craft shows, music or dance performances, and similar activities.

Free play. Unscheduled and unsupervised activity on a playground, in a school yard, or in a picnic ground or beach area is a common recreation format. Similarly, work in an art studio without direct instruction would be a form of free play.

Exhibition or demonstration. Often, instructional programs may have shows or exhibitions as culminating events to attract, inform, and entertain the public.

Still other program formats include the following: *special events* and *parties; clubs* and *special-interest groups; trips* and *outings;* or *leadership training* of skill instructors, officials, coaches, or program volunteers.

A given activity, such as dance or gardening, may be presented for different groups or target populations within several varied formats over the course of a program schedule. Similarly, a particular facility, such as a swimming pool, could be used to house free swimming, instructional classes, pool parties, scuba diving workshops, team competitions, diving exhibitions, and lifeguard training.

Administrative Responsibility for Programs

In a large public leisure-service agency, activities are usually assigned to different administrative divisions, such as those for sports and athletics, aquatics, cultural arts, or senior citizens programs. In another type of structure, responsibility for programming may be assigned to divisions related to facilities, such as beaches and pools, sports fields and stadium, recreation centers, or playgrounds and parks.

Classification by Mission

In some departments, programs may be classified according to their basic missions and expected benefits, which in turn determines their fee-charging status or degree of fiscal support. For example, in the Department of the Navy, Morale, Welfare and Recreation (MWR) activities are classified under three headings:

Category A: Mission Sustaining. This contains activities considered most important for the health and well-being of military personnel; fees are not usually charged for activities in this category. It includes basic entertainment, fitness, library, sports, and shipboard activities.

Category B: Basic Community Support Activities. These are special-interest pursuits that support MWR mission and goals but appeal to a smaller audience, such as amateur radio, arts and crafts, bowling, or theater. These are usually supported by a mix of appropriated (tax) funds, and non-appropriated (derived by participant fees) funds.

Category C: Business Activities. These include more highly specialized pursuits, which are seen as being able to support themselves through the sale of goods and services. They include such elements as amusement machines, bingo, catering services, package stores, rod and gun clubs, scuba diving, and commercial travel services.

Classification by Type and Fee-Charging Policy

In a similar breakdown, the Oklahoma City, Oklahoma, Parks and Recreation Department developed a marketing plan that classified activities as basic, enhanced, and specialized, keyed to three different fee-charging policies (Fig. 4.8).

Classification by Participant Interest Level

In a third approach to activity classification, program elements may be grouped according to the motivation of participants and their degree of skill or interest level (Fig. 4.9). Woodswomen, Inc. (see page 94) uses this approach.

SCHEDULING METHODS

How often should an activity be offered, and for what length of time? In what season of the year, and when during the day or week? Should it be presented on a daily, weekly, monthly, or seasonal basis?

The essential purpose of scheduling is to offer an activity so that it becomes available to the greatest number of participants, achieves the maximum use of facilities, and satisfies agency goals most effectively. With this in mind, schedules must be set that satisfy participant needs and interests, with activities that have continuing mass appeal being offered most frequently, and being given the largest time blocks. Highly popular pastimes, such as sports, aquatics, or arts and crafts should be offered in different formats and often on a *daily* basis while in season; less appealing pursuits may be presented in limited time slots, on a *weekly, monthly,* or *"occasional"* scheduling time frame.

With respect to age groups, school-age children are normally served in programs in the late afternoon or early evening hours, or during school vacation periods. Working adults usually are scheduled during evening periods or weekends, while retired individuals usually attend senior centers during the daytime hours.

Seasonal and Holiday Programming

Many activities are scheduled at specific seasons of the year, based on climatic factors and traditional customs. Often, recreation agencies offer holiday events or special classes at the time of national or local holidays and celebrations. When school systems, for example, take a midwinter break, many commercial agencies, such as private tennis centers, may offer special clinics, short-term classes, or tournaments.

FIGURE 4.8. Classification of program elements.

Basic	Enhanced	Specialized
Benefits all citizens. Totally supported through tax base. Nonfee programs.	Benefits all citizens, with participants receiving most benefit. Partial costs recovered by fees.	Benefits participants only. Self-supporting or mostly self-supporting though fees.
After-school youth centers At-risk youth programs Basic classes for kids Basic horticulture programs Beautification efforts Gyms—regular hours Maintenance Myriad Botanical Gardens (outdoor) Open tennis courts Outdoor recreation Self-taught classes at community centers Senior citizens center programs—regular hours Trails Unreserved picnic facilities at parks and lakes	Adaptive programs Athletic fields (baseball, rugby, soccer, softball) Community center classes Crystal Bridge at Myriad Botanical Gardens Fishing classes and tournaments Garden center Leased facilities Martin Park tours Permitted lake activities (i.e. fishing, boating) Special events (i.e., Easter egg hunt) Special senior classes at community centers Youth athletic leagues	After-school fun clubs Athletic leagues Building rentals Concessions Equipment rentals Golf Myriad Botanical Gardens Gift shop Myriad Botanical Gardens rentals Rose Garden weddings Special events (i.e., Trout fish out) Summer day camp Swimming lessons Swimming pool rentals Tennis centers

Source: Oklahoma City Parks and Recreation Department 1994–1995 Marketing Plan.

FIGURE 4.9. Categories of participant skills and interests.

Which Woodswomen adventure is right for me?

To help you choose the right journey, we offer the six levels described below. Our staff would be happy to talk to you about your personal travel goals and the suitability of any trip for you.

R Relaxers: For those who want to stop and smell the roses while traveling and learning. Though some physical challenge is included, the pace is generally more leisurely.

S Skills Clinics and Trips: For those who want to learn a new skill in a day or weekend. You'll get plenty of support in these active clinics.

L Leadership Trips: The Woodswomen leadership philosophy is offered though weekend workshops and in combination with week-long wilderness trips.

ET Eco-Travel: For those who prefer to be active each day while spending the nights in comfortable B&Bs, inns, cabins, or cottages.

WI Wilderness Journeys: The original Woodswomen trip—an opportunity to learn or expand your outdoor skills while discovering nature, being physically active, and camping in pristine areas.

HA Highly Active: On these physically challenging wilderness trips, get ready for an invigorating adventure that's great for mind and body!

Scheduling in Multiuse Facilities

In community centers or other facilities where many different types of pro-grams may be offered, major time allocations are usually given to those ele-ments with the largest participation or enrollment, and which most closely fulfill the agency's mission.

Typically, a large ice rink complex is likely to have major daytime or early evening time blocks devoted to free skating periods—sometimes for general participation, and sometimes for special age groups. Other time slots will be given to hockey team practices (often in the early morning hours), figure skat-ing practice and instruction, hockey games, or other exhibitions or contests. An example of such scheduling is found in large aquatic and fitness facilities, such as the Douglas Snow Aquatic Centre in North York, Ontario, Canada (Fig. 4.10).

In some cases, scheduling may involve the complex task of assigning sev-eral different groups simultaneously to different facilities. In a large commer-cially operated summer day camp in Southampton, Pennsylvania, for example, over thirty different groups of campers (based on age bracket and gender) must be assigned throughout the day and week to sports, games, crafts, aquatic, dining

FIGURE 4.10. Basic weekly schedule in Douglas Snow Aquatic Centre in North York, Ontario, Canada.
Note: **In addition to these regular time slots, other periods are set aside for synchronized swimming, lifesaving classes and junior lifeguard club, swim team practice, and "adapted" aquatics for persons with disabilities. These activities take place primarily on weekend days.**

	Monday	Tuesday	Wednesday	Thursday	Friday	Saturday	Sunday
Lane Swimming • 50-m pool	7:15 – 8:45 A.M.•	7:15 – 8:45 A.M.•	7:15 – 8:45 A.M.•	7:15 – 8:45 A.M.•	7:15 – 8:45 A.M.•		12:05 – 1:45 P.M.•
• Age 13 years and older • Sauna and whirlpool are open	9:00 – 10:30 P.M.	9:00 – 10:30 P.M.	9:00 – 10:30 P.M. ▲	9:00 – 10:30 A.M.			
Lane/Leisure					9:00– 10:30 P.M.		
Lane Swimming • 18 years and older • Sauna and whirlpool are open	11:45 A.M.– 2:00 P.M.	11:45 A.M.– 2:00 P.M.	11:00 A.M.– 2:00 P.M.	11:45 A.M.– 2:00 P.M.	11:45 A.M. – 2:30 P.M.		
Leisure Swim • Everyone welcome						2:00 – 4:15 P.M.	2:00 – 4:15 P.M.
• Sauna and whirlpool are open					7:05 – 9:00 P.M.		
Senior Swim			10:05 – 11:00 A.M. (pp)		2:30 – 3:30 P.M.		
Preschool Swim			10:05 – 11:30 A.M. (pp)		2:00 – 3:30 P.M. (pp)		

room, social, and other facilities on a schedule that provides balance and variety for all groups. The task is made more complex by the need to provide indoor meeting space for rainy days.

Sequential Scheduling

Another type of scheduling involves the planning of time periods for different stages of a major program activity—as in the case of elimination sports tournaments that progress from local to district, state, or national levels. For example, in the popular Hershey Track and Field program, the following schedule is normally observed:

Local, district, and state/provincial meet dates vary and are determined by the state chairperson.

Local meets are held in the spring and early summer.

District meets are generally a few weeks after the local meets (May or June).

State/province meets are usually held in late June and early July.

North American final is held in Hershey, Pennsylvania, in August.

FIGURE 4.11. Diversified social programs and special events in armed forces recreation.

MWR July Calendar

1997   1997

Sunday	Monday	Tuesday	Wednesday	Thursday	Friday	Saturday
		1 Aerobics 1700 @ Fitness Center every Mon, Wed, & Fri **Fitness Center Classes** Chinese Kick Boxing 1630 Wm's Self Defense 1745 every Tue & Thu	**2** **Hot Pockets Pool Tournament** 1700 Sign-up 1730 Play Begins	**3** Chinese Kick Boxing 1630 Wm's Self Defense 1745 **Tough Break Pool Tournament** 1700 Sign-up 1730 Play Begins	**4** Independence Day **FREEDOMFEST '97** 1600-2100 Fireworks 2100	**5**
6 Mariner Club Free Movie 1900 The Big Squeeze **SILVER SPURS RODEO** 1300-1630	**7** Aerobics 1700 @ Fitness Center every Mon, Wed, & Fri **Camp Adventure (Week 5)**	**8** Chinese Kick Boxing 1630 Wm's Self Defense 1745 **Swim Classes** Level I, II, III and Preschool Call X5196	**9** Aerobics 1700 @ Fitness Center every Mon, Wed, & Fri **Hot Pockets Pool Tournament** 1700 Sign-up 1730 Play Begins	**10** Chinese Kick Boxing 1630 Wm's Self Defense 1745	**11** Aerobics 1700 @ Fitness Center every Mon, Wed, & Fri **PAINTBALL NIGHT Trip** 1800-2300	**12** Take-a-Kid Fishing Weekend Poles & Equipment available at Outdoor Adventure Center
13 Mariner Club Free Movie 1900 "The Firm"	**14** Camp Adventure (Week 6) **Deep Water Aerobics,** NTC Swim Ctr. 1130-1230, MWF, 12 Classes $22 AD, $27 all others **DEFY TRAINING BEGINS**	**15** Chinese Kick Boxing 1630 Wm's Self Defense 1745	**16** Aerobics 1700 @ Fitness Center every Mon, Wed, & Fri **Hot Pockets Pool Tournament** 1700 Sign-up 1730 Play Begins	**17** Chinese Kick Boxing 1630 Wm's Self Defense 1745	**18** Junior Officer Party at Lake Baldwin 1630-1930 **ROCK & BOWL 2200 - 0100**	**19** **WET-N-WILD** 0830-1800
20 Mariner Club Free Movie 1900 "Rocky"	**21** Camp Adventure (Week 7) Mariner Club Free Movie 1900 "The Untouchables"	**22** Chinese Kick Boxing 1630 Wm's Self Defense 1745	**23** Aerobics 1700 @ Fitness Center every Mon, Wed, & Fri **Hot Pockets Pool Tournament** 1700 Sign-up 1730 Play Begins	**24** Chinese Kick Boxing 1630 Wm's Self Defense 1745 **Spades Tournament at** Mariners Club 1700 Sign-up 1730 Play Begins	**25** Aerobics 1700 @ Fitness Center every Mon, Wed, & Fri	**26** **DAYTONA Beach** Overnight Trip
27 Mariner Club Free Movie 1900 "Gotti"	**28** Aerobics 1700 @ Fitness Center every Mon, Wed, & Fri Mariner Club Free Movie 1900 "Sister Act"	**29** Chinese Kick Boxing 1630 Wm's Self Defense 1745 **DEFY PROGRAM BEGINS**	**30** 5K Run Before Bre Gun 0545 at NTC Gym **Finals Hot Pockets Pool Tournament** 1700 Sign-up 1730 Play Begins	**31** Chinese Kick Boxing 1630 Wm's Self Defense 1745	**MWR** For the time of your life! NTC Orlando Main Office Monday - Friday • 0730 - 1600 • Bldg. 2034 • 646-5135	

Scheduling in a broader sense takes place when program participants move through a sequence of different activity formats. Beginning with instructional classes or free play, they may take part in competitive play or special-interest clubs and ultimately move into leadership training programs to work as volunteers or even paid professionals within an area of activity.

PUBLICITY AND PROGRAM REGISTRATION

As the recreation program is set in motion, two important tasks involve *publicity* and *registration*.

Publicity in varied forms is essential to ensure that the public at large, or the organization's membership, is fully aware of the activities and services that are being offered, as well as information regarding their scheduling, location, possible fees or charges, and age limits or required previous experience, or other important program details.

Publicity normally is carried out through printed materials, such as program brochures, mailed schedules, newspaper stories, or other public media. It is part of the broader agency program of public relations, which goes far beyond the promotional or advertising function, to include a two-day process of communication between the leisure-service agency and its stakeholders (see Chapter 8).

Registration is the process of signing up individuals in advance for any form of recreational, park, or leisure-service participation. It guarantees participants a place in the activity, and helps managers know how many persons will enroll or enter any program in advance, so they can plan intelligently to staff and conduct it. Registration gives advance warning of inadequate registration or enrollment, so that an activity may be modified, shifted, or canceled, if necessary. It provides a means of screening individuals who may be seeking participation, or of giving them more detailed information about the activity or service, or guiding them into the appropriate location or level of activity.

Registration Methods

There are several different methods used in registering participants in recreation programs (Fig. 4.12), as follows:

1. *Mail-in registration.* Individuals fill out a form indicating the program that they intend to join or the service they are requesting, and giving appropriate details about themselves, along with a registration fee, if required. This is mailed to the agency by a stipulated deadline.
2. *In-person central registration.* Prior to the beginning of a season or semester of classes, participants register at a central office. In-person contact permits them to gather more information about the program activity.
3. *In-person registration at program location.* This approach permits the participant to have a brief interview with the program director, coach, or other leader, and to gather additional specific information or guidance.

4. *Telephone registration.* Many agencies have initiated automated telephone registration systems for such services as golf course tee-time reservations, campsite advance reservations, and similar uses. Credit-card payments may be used to carry out this procedure, and in many cases an individual may be required to have a county or township pass or resident registration number to facilitate the reservation.

Computers are increasingly being used to carry out registration transactions, since they are useful in giving up-to-date enrollment totals at any given time, confirming courses or events, making admission decisions, or other procedures. In addition, computer technology may be helpful in screening participants for eligibility for a given program, with respect to such factors as age, residence, family, or school status.

FIGURE 4.12. Example of registration form: Kamloops, British Columbia, Canada, Park and Recreation Department.

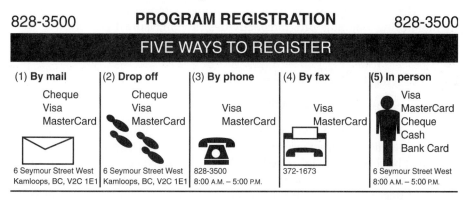

828-3500   **PROGRAM REGISTRATION**   **828-3500**

FIVE WAYS TO REGISTER

(1) **By mail**	(2) **Drop off**	(3) **By phone**	(4) **By fax**	(5) **In person**
Cheque Visa MasterCard	Cheque Visa MasterCard	Visa MasterCard	Visa MasterCard	Visa MasterCard Cheque Cash Bank Card
6 Seymour Street West Kamloops, BC, V2C 1E1	6 Seymour Street West Kamloops, BC, V2C 1E1	828-3500 8:00 A.M. – 5:00 P.M.	372-1673	6 Seymour Street West 8:00 A.M. – 5:00 P.M.

1. Mail In
Fill out the mail-in registration form included in the brouchure. Attach your cheque for the required amount or use your charge card number and mail it to:
Parks and Recreation Services
6 Seymour Street West
Kamloops, BC, V2C 1E1
Your receipt will be mailed to you.

* Note: Post-dated cheques will not be accepted. Cheques are payable to the City of Kamloops.

2. Drop off
Complete the mail-in registration form included in the brochure, attach your cheques or use your charge card number (no cash please) for the required amount and drop it off to:
Parks and Recreation Services
6 Seymour Street West
Kamloops, BC, V2C 1E1
Your receipt will be mailed to you.

* **Note:** Post-dated cheques will not be accepted. Cheques are payable to the City of Kamloops.

3. Phone In (8 A.M. to 5 P.M. working days)
Fill out the mail-in registration form included in the brouchure. You will be required to give your charge card number and expiration date, as well as the information on the registration form. Please have it ready. Your receipt will be mailed to you.

4. Fax
Fill out the mail-in registration form included in the brouchure. Our FAX number is **372-1673.** Your receipt will be mailed to you.

5. In person
Come into the Parks and Recreation office at 6 Seymour Street West. Our friendly staff will process your registration.

DON'T WAIT—Sign UP NOW!
Classes may be cancelled due to insufficent enrollment, so please don't leave your registration too late and be disappointed. A full refund will be given to any participant registered in a class that is cancelled.

PROGRAM IMPLEMENTATION

After the earlier steps of planning, scheduling, publicizing, and registration have been carried out, the program is ready to be put in motion. Program implementation—that is, the actual delivery of leisure services—is generally governed by guidelines, policies, and procedures that have been established by the recreation, park, and leisure-service organization. For example, the National Little League publishes an operating manual that presents a comprehensive set of guidelines covering every element of program operations, such as the eligibility of young players, drafting procedures, scheduling, team practices, safety and disciplinary rules, and other guidelines for coaches and officials.

Supervisory Responsibilities

Based on such operational guidelines, it is the responsibility of agency program supervisors to be certain that all activities are carried out in strict adherence to stated policies and procedures. In so doing, supervisors must be vigilant in monitoring ongoing program activities, making sure that effective risk-management guidelines are observed, and that the goal of "total quality" management and participant satisfaction is consistently achieved.

Need to Support Agency Mission

While emphasis is often given to "numbers"—that is, judging a program's success by its ability to attract large numbers of participants throughout the year—this must be considered only one basis for measuring its performance. Instead, it is critical that the organization's basic philosophy governs all program planning and decision making and that every activity and service be scrutinized in terms of whether it is designed to achieve long- and short-term goals and objectives. Increasingly, benefits-based management approaches, as described in Chapter 3, have been accepted by leisure-service organizations. Public and nonprofit agencies in particular must be able to justify themselves in socially convincing terms if they are to continue to receive financial support through tax-based funding or voluntary giving.

Risk Management and Legal Issues

Throughout program operations, it is imperative that a systematic risk-management plan be in place. As Chapter 9 shows in detail, this involves a variety of responsibilities to maintain a high level of safety and accident prevention, particularly in sports and outdoor recreation activities.

Beyond the need to maintain safety practices, other legal issues may involve problems of sexual harassment or sexual abuse of participants. Discrimination of any kind based on gender, race or ethnicity, or physical or mental disability—beyond rational and clearly defensible policies—cannot be tolerated as programs are carried out. Beyond the need to avoid lawsuits or other legal claims, leisure-service agencies should be proactive in promoting positive values with respect to serving all special populations.

Within each specialized area of leisure service, different sets of rules or policies may apply. For example, in the area of sport management, schools and colleges must observe rules that are laid down by educational authorities or athletic conferences with respect to eligibility of amateur players, scheduling of practice sessions, and similar issues. In the area of therapeutic recreation, numerous guidelines and standards that have been evolved by professional societies and/or accreditation or certification bodies must govern program practices.

Total Quality Management

Finally, an important thrust in recreation programming throughout the late 1980s and 1990s was the need to strive for total quality management and a high level of participant satisfaction. Christopher and Susan Edginton described the concept of total quality program management in the leisure-service field as an approach that requires a commitment to the highest possible standard of program delivery. It emphasizes the need for efficient performance by staff members on every level, along with readiness for innovation, and an information-driven sensitivity to the reaction of program participants.

Total quality programming (TQP) requires, they write, the use of benchmarks, statistical analysis, and continuous measures of achievement. Employees must be empowered and encouraged to develop creative new ideas for leisure programs.[8]

Satisfaction Guarantee: San Mateo Parks and Recreation

The stress on achieving the maximum degree of participant satisfaction is illustrated in a pledge made by the San Mateo, California, Parks and Recreation Department to its constituents. Featured prominently on the contents page of its program brochure, it reads:

> We constantly strive to provide you [the public] with the highest quality recreation programs. If for any reason you are not completely satisfied with a class or activity, please tell us so we can respond to your concerns. In addition to using your feedback to help us improve, for nearly all of our programs, we will arrange one of the following upon your request:
>
> 1. Transfer to another time or activity.
> 2. A full credit for future use for any activity we offer.
> 3. A full refund.
>
> Some of our programs, for example Adult Leagues, Facility Permits, and Tour and Travel, have different, specific policies which apply. Your complete satisfaction with these programs is equally valued, and we will work with you to resolve your concerns and satisfaction in these activities as well.[9]

Participants are urged to contact the San Mateo department at any of its recreation centers, or by letter or telephone, to request a refund or credit or to resolve other difficulties. A number of other leisure-service agencies are adopting such practices, confirming the field's acceptance of marketing and benefits-based management approaches.

SUMMARY

Program planning and implementation represent a key function of recreation, park, and leisure-service managers today. Defined as the provision of activities, services, and facilities to assist the public's pleasurable and constructive use of leisure, programs are drawn from ten different categories of recreational pursuits and related personality-enrichment or social-service activities.

The program planning cycle begins with the development of agency missions, goals, and objectives, and the assessment of participant needs and interests, and ends with the evaluation of program activities. Several different formats through which activities may be presented are examined, along with guidelines for scheduling offerings, registering participants, and carrying out programs.

Emphasis throughout the chapter is placed on ensuring that program activities reflect and support the agency's mission and goals, and that they adhere to strict regulations for risk management and other rules or policy guidelines governing the care of participants, accessibility for different populations, and similar practices. The chapter concludes with a summary of the emphasis on total quality management that many recreation, park, and leisure-service agencies have adopted in recent years.

CLASS DISCUSSION TOPICS AND ASSIGNMENTS

1. Develop a seasonal program plan for a public or nonprofit agency that offers activities drawn from only *one* of the ten activity categories listed in the chapter, such as sports and fitness, outdoor recreation, or performing arts. In this plan, indicate your goals and objectives, the needs-assessment methods used, the specific activities that would be offered, their formats and schedules, and the people they would be designed to serve.
2. Many of the program elements offered by such leisure-service organizations as YM and YWCAs, the armed forces, or company employee-service units deal with life adjustment, personality enrichment, and social-service needs. These are not recreational in the common understanding of the term. What is the rationale for providing such program opportunities?
3. In a free-wheeling, unstructured discussion, talk about recreation program experiences you've had that were most enjoyable or significant. What made these activities so appealing and important?

Before analyzing these cases in class, review the guidelines suggested in Chapter 3 (pp. 76–77).

Case Study 4.1 *Meeting the Marketing Challenge*

YOU ARE SEAN DALY, director of the health and physical recreation center of a large urban YMCA in a neighborhood with varied residential and business areas. Your exercise and physical fitness program has become very popular in recent years with the growth of public interest in fitness.

However, a new, privately owned health spa has just opened a few blocks away. It has a glamorous, high-tech design and all the latest equipment, including a swimming pool, Jacuzzi and whirlpools, flashy decorations, and rock music playing regularly, as well as a bar. You are certain that you will be losing many of your regular clients, who are style-conscious, up-scale yuppies (young urban professionals) and who are impressed by this facility and its "with-it" image and high-powered advertising.

From a marketing perspective, how can you meet this challenge?

QUESTIONS FOR CLASS DISCUSSION AND ANALYSIS

1. *The new commercial health spa is offering attractions with which you cannot compete. What can you offer that they cannot?*

2. *What target markets are open to you that might not be suitable for the new health spa? From a pricing and cost point of view, do you have an advantage?*

3. *Design a campaign intended to hold your present clientele against the challenge offered by this new competitor and to reach groups that you have not targeted in the past. Consider both program elements and ways of involving individuals and groups in the YMCA's fitness program.*

Case Study 4.2   *Military Recreation: Expanding the Human-Service Function*

YOU ARE DAN GARCIA, a civilian recreation specialist at a U.S. Army Air Force base in Europe. The recreation program has generally been successful, with good participation in sports, crafts, social activities, sponsored trips, and similar activities. However, the base has also had a growing problem of substance abuse—involving alcohol and narcotics—particularly among younger enlisted personnel, but also including many officers. It is believed that there is a high degree of tension on the base, with a number of men and women suffering from stress and burnout. Marital difficulties are common, along with family breakup and growing numbers of teenage dependents involved in antisocial activity.

You have been asked by your commanding officer, Captain Jerry Saunders, to develop a plan for reducing these problems through the Morale, Welfare and Recreation operation. You've never had experience in designing or carrying out programs with this type of purpose. How could you go about it? Where would you begin?

QUESTIONS FOR CLASS DISCUSSION AND ANALYSIS

1. *Is Captain Saunders' request a logical one? In what way—although it represents a difficult challenge—would it offer a positive opportunity for you?*

2. *As a starting point, what kinds of involvement might you ask from others on the base, both to get helpful ideas and to ensure support for the program you will be proposing?*

3. *As you review the chapter, what kinds of activities, formats, and services immediately come to mind as possible program elements?*

Case Study 4.3 — *Rocky Times with the Rock Festival*

YOU ARE JANE DALEY, recreation and park director in a small oceanfront community that depends heavily on tourism and vacation-home residents. For several years, you have sponsored a rock festival each Easter week. Generally, community merchants have favored this, since it brings the area publicity, and visiting college students have filled the motels and patronized the restaurants in town.

Increasingly, however, motorcycle gangs have been coming to the festival, creating problems of drinking, drugs, and fighting with local high school boys. Many of these attending also sleep out on the beach, which creates problems of safety and sanitation. The local chamber of commerce is still in favor of continuing the annual rock festival, although the town board is leaning toward discontinuing it.

The police chief feels that his force is too small to supervise the event properly. However, since several members of the force gain substantial income from the overtime hours they put in during the week, he is reluctant to call for an end to the rock festival.

QUESTIONS FOR CLASS DISCUSSION AND ANALYSIS

1. *Weighing the pluses and minuses, is this program worth continuing? As recreation and park director, what do you see as the key arguments on each side?*

2. *Is there any good way to control the misbehavior that has been occurring?* *What other resources could you draw on to manage the program?*

3. *Should the police chief's concern about his officers' added income be a major factor in decision making with respect to the rock festival?*

REFERENCES

1. "Member Success Profile," *Employee Services Management*, September 1991, p. 13.
2. Rossman, J. Robert: *Recreation Programming: Designing Leisure Experiences*, Champaign, Ill., 1995, Sagamore Publishing, pp. 4–5.
3. Ford, Phyllis, and Blanchard, Jim: *Leadership and Administration of Outdoor Pursuits*, 1993, p. 215. State College, Pa., 1993, Venture Publishing.
4. Fladell, Ernie: "Children's Festivals: Where They Come from and How to Grow One of Your Own," *Trends*, 34 (2), 1997, pp. 23–29.
5. Cicora, Ken: "Sponsoring Special Events," *Parks and Recreation*, December 1991, p. 27.
6. Jackson, Kimberly: "MWR Club Sails into the Future," *Parks and Recreation*, October 1993, pp. 50–53.
7. Kraus, Richard: *Recreation Programming: A Benefits-Driven Approach*, Boston, 1997, Allyn & Bacon, pp. 23–31.
8. Edginton, Susan, and Edginton, Christopher: *Youth Programs: Promoting Quality Services*, Champaign, Ill., 1994, Sagamore Publishing.
9. Program Brochure, San Mateo, Calif., *Department of Parks and Recreation*, 1997.

Facilities Development and Maintenance

MWR facilities here [on the island of Guam] are not unlike the rest of the Navy: bowling center, gym fitness center, outdoor fields and courts, picnic areas, youth center, swimming pool, skeet and trap range, nine- and 18-hole golf course, single sailor facility and all the programs and activities that go with them . . . . Patrons are very athletic-minded, and participation sports and fitness programs outnumber the total use of all other programs combined.[1]

White River State Park [in downtown Indianapolis], the culmination of a 20-year dream for community leaders, offers central Indiana residents and visitors a variety of educational experiences, cultural attractions, urban beauty, family entertainment and recreational opportunity. More than just an urban oasis, the park is a key component of the city's continuing revitalization of downtown, and an important link in the city's greenway trails program, which continues to take shape.[2]

INTRODUCTION

We now move to a second important function of recreation, park, and leisure-service managers—the planning, design, construction, maintenance, and operation of areas and facilities.

In the past, recreation facilities were thought of chiefly as outdoor resources such as parks, forests, lakes, beaches, and scenic sites, or the kinds of areas or buildings designed for more intensive or supervised play, such as playgrounds, sports fields, or recreation centers. Today, with the diversification and expansion of the leisure-service field, recreation and park facilities include an enormous range of new, sophisticated kinds of areas and structures. Huge aquatic and fitness centers, elaborate theme parks or water-play parks, family play centers, sports complexes, environmental centers, and varied types of innovative commercially sponsored leisure facilities represent the wave of the present and the future.

Clearly, the management of areas and facilities constitutes a key area of responsibility for leisure-service managers in every type of agency. This chapter therefore presents a detailed description of the development and operation of recreation, park, and leisure-service facilities. It addresses the following understandings and competencies listed as essential in the Baccalaureate Degree standards of the NRPA/AALR Council on Accreditation:

Understanding of the concept and use of leisure resources to facilitate participant involvement (8.19).

Understanding of principles and procedures for planning and designing leisure services, resources, areas, and facilities (8.22/8.23).

Understanding of and ability to implement principles and procedures related to operation and care of resources, areas, and facilities (8.31).

Understanding of ecology and its application to the management and use of resources (7B.02).

Understanding of the principles of land-use planning, including identification, evaluation, development, and management of land and water resources (9B.07).

O B J E C T I V E S

At the conclusion of this chapter, readers should be familiar with the following management concepts and practices:

1. The major types of recreation, park, and leisure-service areas and facilities, including traditional facilities operated by public departments and newer types of facilities developed by other sponsors.
2. The planning process and standards used in facilities development, and approaches used in planning specific types of facilities.
3. Acquisition, planning, and design processes used in facilities development to meet programming needs.
4. Facilities construction and maintenance guidelines and standards, including safety, vandalism-protection, and accessibility factors.
5. Newer trends in facilities planning and development, and in natural resource management, including partnerships among public and private agencies.

FACILITIES: THE MANAGER'S ROLE

Facilities development and operation is an important responsibility of leisure-service managers in American and Canadian communities. Public recreation and park departments in particular operate extensive networks of indoor and outdoor facilities, including playgrounds and parks, community centers of various types, sports complexes, swimming pools and beaches, ice rinks, and numerous other types of specialized leisure-service areas.

Although other staff members may be directly responsible for designing, constructing, or maintaining such facilities, it is the manager who must provide leadership in determining community or membership needs for recreation areas and facilities, and making sure these needs are met. The manager must also be aware of current trends in leisure-service facilities and should be ready to pursue cooperative relationships with other organizations in planning innovative areas and structures.

Obviously, the places where people recreate are critical in terms of providing opportunities for a full range of creative and enjoyable leisure experiences. A barren schoolyard or refuse-filled park offers little to encourage positive forms of recreational participation.

During the early decades of the twentieth century, U.S. and Canadian public recreation and park departments offered a limited range of playgrounds, parks, sports facilities, and community centers. In time, new and varied kinds of places for play began to be developed in order to meet more diversified leisure interests.

Traditional Types of Recreation Facilities

Several major categories of recreation and park facilities are briefly described below, with the kinds of program elements they house. Chiefly, these represent facilities operated by public recreation and park departments, although in many cases nonprofit, commercial, or other types of leisure-service agencies may also manage such areas and facilities.

Playgrounds

Designed primarily for children and youth, these range in size from tiny "tot-lots" to larger play areas that are often attached to schools or indoor recreation centers. Their equipment may be limited to such familiar items as slides, swings, sandboxes, and jungle gyms, or they may also include statuary or structures based on themes of children's play, or areas and materials used for creative play or exploration, as in so-called adventure playgrounds.

Parks

These may include small neighborhood parks, as well as much larger areas or nature reserves, sometimes amounting to hundreds of acres. Larger parks typically offer sports facilities, band shells, riding trails, skating rinks, and other specialized facilities for play.

Recreation Centers

Traditionally these have been buildings with both indoor and outdoor facilities for a variety of sports, social, creative, and other group activities. In addition, these centers may include facilities or areas for youth centers, senior centers, or human-service programs, sometimes shared with other community agencies (see Fig. 5.1).

Sports Facilities

These include fields, courts, or other outdoor areas for popular team and dual or individual sports, such as baseball, softball, soccer, tennis, and golf. Often the facilities are attached to recreation centers, or in some cases they may be freestanding in parks, as sports complexes serving several seasonal activities. Indoor centers often contain spaces for basketball, volleyball, floor hockey, wrestling, or martial arts.

Art Centers

In addition to spaces in general recreation centers for arts and crafts, a growing number of cities have art centers that house studios for classes in various creative activities, as well as exhibition galleries and, in some cases, meeting rooms for lectures, or auditoriums that house music, theater, and dance groups.

FIGURE 5.1. Mobile recreation units. In addition to their fixed-site facilities, some departments offer mobile units designed to assist under-served neighborhoods with linked recreation and education programs, special events and other social services.

City Streets / At Risk Youth Division
2705 N. 15th Avenue, Phoenix, AZ 85007
602-262-7370 • FAX: 602-262-7333

Civic Arenas and Auditoriums

Many cities today sponsor civic auditoriums or exhibition halls, with rooms of various sizes that are useful for music, dance, or theatrical performances, or for community meetings. In some cases, these facilities are built through a combination of public and private funding and management, and house entertainment events, hobby shows, trade shows, conferences, and garden and home shows.

Facilities Serving People with Disabilities

Many communities today operate facilities serving individuals with physical or mental disabilities. In some cases, these facilities constitute special sections of other facilities used by nondisabled persons, to facilitate integrated participation in selected program activities. Today, all new recreation facilities or structures being renovated must be designed in accordance with architectural standards, ensuring access to persons with disabilities.

Other Facilities

Other recreation areas today may include marinas or boat-launching ramps, stadiums, zoos and botanical gardens, various types of museums, historic mansions, skating rinks and ski centers, environmental education centers, riding stables, and other more specialized facilities. In addition, many public agencies own and operate camping sites of various types, ranging from close-by locations for day-camp operations to wilderness camps at a distance.

NEWER TRENDS IN FACILITIES DEVELOPMENT

During the 1980s and 1990s, the widespread acceptance of an entrepreneurial and marketing-based emphasis in many public and voluntary leisure-service organizations created a new pressure to develop facilities and programs that lent themselves to fiscal self-sufficiency. Andrew Cohen points out in *Athletic Business:*

> . . . large multiuse parks are springing up in communities across North America, boasting active and passive outdoor recreation—pool complexes, in-line and ice skating rinks, batting cages, miniature golf courses, basketball, volleyball and tennis courts, skateboard facilities, ball fields, soccer pitches, lakes, woodlands and trail systems for walking and biking.[3]

As an example of the diversity of program elements in many new facilities, the city of Matsqui, British Columbia, Canada, built a huge new recreation center in the early 1990s, at a cost of $4.9 million. In addition to its innovative swimming areas, combining an eight-lane competition pool and a wave pool within the same body of water, it includes a diving tank, 55-meter indoor/outdoor water slide, shallow tots pool, sauna, and various water spray units. Other amenities in the Matsqui aquatic center include a physiotherapy, clinic, surf-side cafe, child-care area, senior center, aerobics room, and a fitness weights room.

A 1993 report by *Athletic Business* showed the range of areas and facilities in indoor recreation centers operated by recreation and park departments in cities throughout the United States (Table 5.1).

TABLE 5.1. Facilities in Indoor Recreation Centers

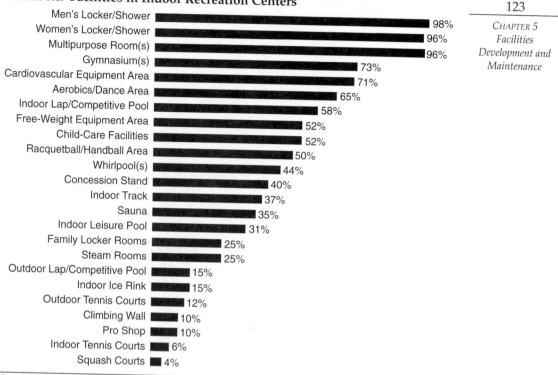

Facility	Percentage
Men's Locker/Shower	98%
Women's Locker/Shower	96%
Multipurpose Room(s)	96%
Gymnasium(s)	73%
Cardiovascular Equipment Area	71%
Aerobics/Dance Area	65%
Indoor Lap/Competitive Pool	58%
Free-Weight Equipment Area	52%
Child-Care Facilities	52%
Racquetball/Handball Area	50%
Whirlpool(s)	44%
Concession Stand	40%
Indoor Track	37%
Sauna	35%
Indoor Leisure Pool	31%
Family Locker Rooms	25%
Steam Rooms	25%
Outdoor Lap/Competitive Pool	15%
Indoor Ice Rink	15%
Outdoor Tennis Courts	12%
Climbing Wall	10%
Pro Shop	10%
Indoor Tennis Courts	6%
Squash Courts	4%

Source: Schmidt, Sue: "Cities on the Move," *Athletic Business*, Oct. 1993.

Commercial Facilities: Theme Parks and Play Centers

Another important thrust in facilities development has been the construction of hundreds of elaborate theme parks, which have become important target destinations in the travel and tourism field (Fig. 5.2). Designed to attract families in particular to clean, wholesome, and imaginative environments that include technologically advanced rides, shows, and other exotic settings, these new amusement centers have varied themes as the basis for their appeal. Some deal with storybook or fairyland ideas, others with cartoon, jungle, or Wild West settings, or trips into the future.

On a less elaborate scale, many locally based commercial sponsors today offer varied types of family-oriented recreation facilities that are designed to appeal to the entire age range. Such facilities may include video game galleries, miniature golf, playground equipment for children, pizza, and other food services, and varied forms of entertainment, along with modified sports areas.

Diversity in Park Systems

To illustrate the variety of outdoor recreation facilities offered by public recreation and park agencies today, the Westchester County, New York, Department of Parks, Recreation and Conservation operates numerous parks,

FIGURE 5.2. Dollywood Theme Park. Map showing location of varied program areas and facilities (restaurants, theaters and showplaces, craftsmen's centers, country fairs, shops and rides) in immensely popular park in Great Smoky Mountain National Park region.

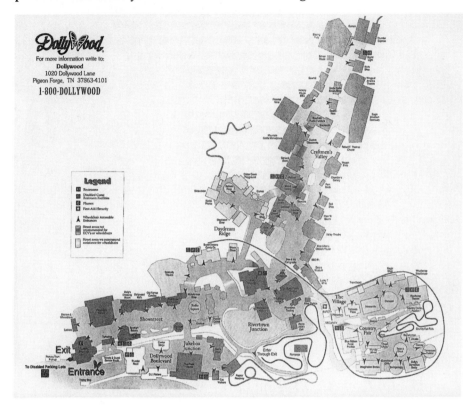

nature reservations, lakes, swimming pools, golf courses, ice rinks, boating facilities, a special music camp, environmental centers, and historical sites (Fig. 5.3).

Different facilities host specially designed program elements. For example, the calendar of events at Washington's Headquarters Museum, an authentic historical site, includes Revolutionary-period crafts of quilting, yarn spinning, chair reeding, basketry, and colonial herb gardening, as well as celebration of holidays or events related to the Revolutionary War.

FACILITIES DEVELOPMENT: THE PLANNING PROCESS

Facilities development involves several distinct phases, including planning, property acquisition, design, construction, and maintenance. Planning may be carried out at several levels ranging from the design and construction of a single building or other facility to the overall analysis and projection of goals and policies for a total recreation, park, or leisure-service organization.

FIGURE 5.3. Map showing location of 44 different Westchester County recreation and park facilities, with section of brochure showing over 22 activities available, keyed to park locations.

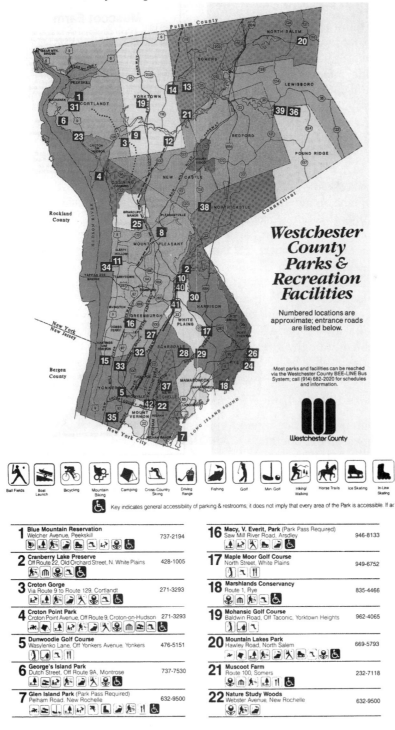

Planning Sequence

The following steps are typically followed in agency-wide planning studies, particularly in public recreation and park organizations.

1. Determine agency's mission and long-range goals, as described in Chapter 3, and revise these, if necessary, based on present and projected demographic, economic, social, and environmental trends.
2. Conduct internal and external environmental scans to develop comprehensive inventory of agency programs, facilities, and their uses, along with other available community resources. Based on these, develop mapping charts that illustrate strengths and weaknesses of present system.
3. Carry out survey of public or organization membership needs and interests, present leisure involvements, and attitudes with respect to possible need for new or expanded open spaces and facilities.
4. Survey available open spaces or sites for potential park or other facility development, along with analysis of their availability, in terms of means and costs of acquisition. Analyze environmental impact concerns.
5. Explore possibilities for partnerships, lease, or property transfer arrangements, along with other legal means of acquisition, as well as potential revenue capability from facilities under consideration, in order to develop a full financial feasibility plan for facilities under consideration.
6. Develop short- and long-range goals and objectives for facility development and management, including specific proposals for areas and structures that are supported by data drawn from previous steps. These are then presented through appropriate channels, making use of department review processes, public hearings, city council reviews, and other steps.

Facility and Open-Space Planning Guides

Recreation and park facility and open-space planning is carried on at every level of government operations: federal, state or provincial, and local. On the federal level, a number of systems for classifying parkland and other outdoor recreation resources have been developed through the years, including a set of categories ranging from primitive, undeveloped wilderness areas to urbanized, heavily used park facilities.

On the local level, open space and recreation facility planning has utilized a number of approaches, including: (1) the application of models based on neighborhood and community leisure needs and (2) the use of standards relating population numbers to acreage or transportation factors.

Neighborhood and Community Planning

Neighborhoods are generally regarded as residential sections of a larger city or town, usually about three-quarters of a mile to a mile square, with fairly homogeneous populations. The term *community* is usually applied to larger residential areas, comparable in size to high school districts, just as neighborhoods are comparable to elementary school districts. Many basic leisure-service facilities are developed according to neighborhood and community needs, including:

(1) neighborhood play lots or tot lots, (2) neighborhood playgrounds, (3) community playfields and parks, and (4) recreation centers of various types designed to meet either level of need for indoor programming. Planning intended to serve neighborhoods or communities may assign such facilities to areas on the basis of population numbers or so that individuals on different age levels will have access to them within a stipulated travel distance.

Open-Space and Facility Standards

A common rule for determining the amount of open space or parkland needed for community recreation has been 10 acres per 1,000 population. Another approach has been the standard that 10 percent of a community's overall acreage should be devoted to parks and open space.

Similar guidelines have been developed with respect to different kinds of parks. Small parks of one acre or less should have a service area with less than a quarter-mile radius to meet the needs of a concentrated population in apartment complexes or townhouse developments, or special age groups such as young children or the elderly. Neighborhood parks, including playgrounds, should consist of fifteen or more acres, with service radius of up to one-half mile, to serve populations of up to 5,000 residents. Community parks, including varied sports, aquatic, or natural areas, should serve several neighborhoods, with a one- to two-mile service radius.

In addition, other standards have defined the number of facilities of different types that should be provided to meet public needs, based on population totals. For example, ice hockey requires an area of 22,000 square feet, including support areas; one such indoor rink should be provided for each 100,000 in population and may be expected to serve people within a one-half to one hour of travel time.

Tennis requires an area of 7,200 square feet for a singles court; one court should be provided for each 2,000 in population and should serve people with a service radius of one-fourth to one-half mile.

Football requires a minimum of 1.5 acres; a football field should be provided for each 20,000 in population and should serve people with a service radius of one-fourth to one-half hour of travel time.[4]

Based on such general standards, a task force of the National Recreation and Park Association developed a model through which communities or other types of leisure sponsors might measure their own needs for recreation open space or developed facilities. It provided a supply-demand method based on the following concepts:

- *Participant rate* (PR): The percentage of a given population that will participate in a specific activity.
- *Participation days* (PD): The average number of times each individual user will participate in a recreation activity during a year.
- *Demand* (D): The number of people who can reasonably be expected to attend or participate

in a particular recreation activity during a year.

- *Design day* (DD): An average weekend day during a peak season of use for a particular activity.
- *Design capacity* (DC): The percentage of participation days that can be expected to occur in a specific activity on a design day.
- *Spatial standards* (SS): Reasonable capacities of recreation facilities or areas by spatial unit at any given time.
- *Turnover rates* (TR): The number of times a recreation activity spatial unit can be used during a single day.
- *Facility need* (FN): The number of spatial units required to accommodate a particular activity.[5]

Making use of these concepts, planners carry out surveys of the population to be served, measuring the demand for each type of activity or facility. The participation rate multiplied by the base population and an estimate of the number of participation days yields the total number of preference days that will occur during a year, leading to the following formula:

$$\frac{\text{Preference} \times \text{Design Capacity}}{\text{Spatial Standard} \times \text{Turnover Rate}} = \text{Facility Need}$$

The facility need should then be measured against the currently available supply of facilities in the community in order to determine the number of new facilities that would be needed to serve the projected demand for participation.

GENERAL PLANNING PRINCIPLES

Realistically, in many crowded or financially disadvantaged communities, such precise standards and sophisticated planning methods may not be feasible. In such cases, recreation and park managers are likely to rely on a general set of planning principles, such as the following.

1. Recreation and park systems should be established to meet varied community needs and should provide equal recreational opportunity to all, as far as possible.
2. Planning should reflect the needs and wishes of all citizens and should involve them in systematic assessment processes.
3. Each recreation facility should be centrally located within the area it is intended to serve and should provide safe and convenient access for all residents.
4. Each facility should be designed individually to ensure that it is adapted to the specific needs of the area it will serve. Beauty, functional efficiency, economy, and safety are important design considerations.
5. Planning decisions must take into account the capability of the recreation and park agency to operate the facility under consideration (see Chapters 9 and 10 for a fuller discussion of fees and charges as a key factor).
6. Communities should have a long-range plan for site acquisition with a regularly updated plan to ensure that properties are acquired while still available.
7. Similarly, there should be a comprehensive plan for effective maintenance of all properties, with a schedule for remodeling or rehabilitation of facilities.
8. Plans for acquiring and developing new facilities must be reviewed in terms of long-term budgetary and staffing factors; it is a mistake to add new facilities if a department is unable to maintain existing facilities satisfactorily.
9. Intergovernmental planning with other public agencies is a must, and possible cooperative projects with governmental and private agencies should be considered for joint acquisition, construction, and operation of facilities.
10. Recreational facilities should be designed and developed to permit the fullest possible use by different groups on a year-round and round-the-clock basis. Planning must consider not only physical sites. and structures but also program operations.

Although traditional planning guidelines have urged that facilities be distributed equally throughout the community being served, this has rarely been achieved in actual practice. However, every effort should be made to meet the special priorities or needs of each neighborhood or district within the larger area in order to serve different groups of residents appropriately.

Comprehensive Master Planning

As indicated, in many communities, counties, or special park districts, master planning may go beyond a simple analysis of leisure facilities and open spaces. Instead, it may be an integral part of total community master planning. In such cases, studies are likely to involve professional consultants or planning firms, in addition to agency staff members, planning specialists within city government, and volunteer groups of citizens (Fig 5.4).

Putnam and Walker describe the role of professional facilitators in a recent master planning study for the management and preservation of Garden of the Gods Park in Colorado Springs, Colorado, one of the most beautiful and popular parks in the United States. With the help of a team of professional

FIGURE 5.4. *Marina Development and Management.* **This marina, Skipper Bud's at Northpoint Marina, on Lake Michigan, is one of numerous boating complexes operated by a Midwestern company, Skipper Marine Development, that conducts project feasibility and marketing studies, marina design and construction, hospitality enhancement, operations management, renovation and maintenance, for public and private agencies in several states.**

consultants, they formed focus groups of citizens and staff members to review user surveys, maps, videos, photographs, and other forms of data, and to develop recommendations with respect to park traffic, nature interpretation, rock climbing, and other aspects of the park's management—with a minimal degree of friction.[6]

Master Planning Reports

When the planning process has been completed, final reports should include both short- and long-range recommendations with respect to the agency's mission, changing priorities, and policies—along with detailed proposals for property acquisition, new or remodeled facilities, and similar needed actions. Accompanying these recommendations, there should be detailed justifications for acquisition and development, supported by analyses of projected costs, anticipated revenues, and action steps to be taken.

Particularly in the case of open spaces that are to be developed, the ecological impact of planned facilities should be carefully reviewed with, if possible, supportive testimony from environmental groups or authorities. The social benefits of recommended changes should be presented, along with other factors, such as physical risk and safety factors and accessibility for persons with disabilities.

FACILITIES PLANNING IN OTHER TYPES OF AGENCIES

Nonprofit organizations such as the YMCA or YWCA usually combine recreation with other educational or social service functions, and their facilities must be designed to serve these purposes. Typically, they tend to operate buildings for varied indoor programs, but have limited outdoor facilities for special recreational use. Funds to support property acquisition or construction are raised not through taxes or bond issues, but usually by means of fund-raising drives in the community.

Other youth-serving organizations, such as Boys and Girls Clubs, also construct and maintain buildings, usually with indoor sports facilities, clubrooms and workshops, and other areas suited to their special purposes. In contrast, Boy and Girl Scout councils have a more varied pattern of facility use. Many councils own their own campgrounds and conference centers, while others make heavy use of camps and other outdoor recreation resources through long-term leases with state and other park agencies. Local troops frequently meet in schools, churches, or other buildings owned by community agencies.

Campus recreation programs generally are held in facilities that are available in the college or university setting: gymnasiums and sports fields, fitness and aquatic complexes, theaters, arenas, or other auditoriums for cultural programs. Employee recreation units often have well-equipped fitness facilities and may also have on-site sports areas, or in some cases, nearby camps for use by employees and family members. Armed forces MWR programs have a wide range of sports areas, aquatic facilities, and indoor structures for social activities, hobbies, and similar pursuits.

In the past, many treatment facilities, such as psychiatric hospitals or physical rehabilitation centers, were designed for varied recreation facilities, such as gymnasiums, auditoriums, art studios, swimming pools, and in some cases, even outdoor sports areas such as golf courses. Due to the impact of deinstitutionalization, which reduced the patient or resident population in many such facilities and managed care, which resulted in much shorter stays in others, such facilities are less frequently found. However, many public recreation and park departments or voluntary agencies today offer specially designed areas or facilities to serve individuals with disabilities.

PROPERTY ACQUISITION FOR FACILITIES DEVELOPMENT

Following the approval of planning report recommendations, the next step in recreation facilities development involves the acquisition of needed properties or open spaces. Obviously, if a leisure-service department or other organization already possesses the property that it plans to develop or build on, it need not go through the steps of acquisition. If it does not, there are a number of alternative ways of obtaining property. In older, impacted cities, for example, it has often been possible to *create* open space through urban renewal programs that involve the demolition of blighted tenement areas or razing of old factory or railroad yard areas. In many cities, parks, playgrounds, plazas, and other recreation areas have been created in this way.

In general, the methods through which municipalities may acquire land for recreation and parks are as follows.

Purchase

Direct purchase of property from its owner is the most common method of land acquisition. Through the right of eminent domain, government may acquire property by means of condemnation, with the court fixing a fair purchase price if the owner is unwilling to sell his or her land directly.

Transfer

Recreation lands may be acquired by transferring or exchanging properties from one government department to another. As suggested earlier, dumps, warehouses, river frontage properties, and even tax-delinquent lands may become available. Although such land may appear inappropriate for recreation development, through landfill and other engineering methods it often can be converted to outstanding recreational and park use.

Other types of marginal properties that may be acquired include the following: (1) railroad rights-of-way for hiking trails; (2) utility rights-of-way for hiking, biking, or horseback riding; (3) flood plains for seasonal use as linear parks, with picnic areas and trails; (4) properties surrounding water supply reservoirs; (5) airport buffer lands; (6) power generation sites, which may provide useful boating, swimming, and fishing close to hydroelectric plants; and (7) areas atop municipal underground parking facilities.

Leasing

Long-term leasing arrangements are sometimes used to make land available for park use. These are best applied between government agencies or departments. If the intention is to use the property for recreation on a permanent basis, the temporary nature of the lease poses a special risk when the arrangement is with a private owner.

As indicated earlier, many nonprofit youth-serving organizations are able to lease public recreation and park areas for long-term use as campgrounds.

Gifts

Many cities and counties have been able to acquire substantial park properties through gifts and bequests from public-spirited citizens. Although this is obviously the least expensive form of land acquisition, such properties should be accepted only when free from narrow use restrictions and suitable in location and topography for recreational use. Organizations like the Nature Conservancy have in some cases been able to promote such gift arrangements, or to carry out fund-raising campaigns to purchase large tracts of wildlands that would otherwise have been sold for commercial development.

Dedication by Subdividers

A growing practice in many suburban communities is to require a land developer or subdivider to set aside a certain percentage of property for recreational and park use. In some cases, this land is deeded to an organization of persons who have bought houses in the development. In others, the land is given directly to the town or other government in which the land has been developed.

John Crompton points out that such "exactions"—local government requirements that subdivision developers or builders must dedicate park land or specified amenities, or pay a fee to be used by the local government unit to acquire and develop park and recreation facilities—have a long history in the United States. He writes:

> The thinking behind this requirement is that since new development generates a need for additional park and recreation amenities, the people responsible for creating that need should bear the cost of providing amenities.
>
> In essence, the public sector is transferring the cost of providing public amenities to the private sector. This approach has become an attractive alternative to conventional methods of financing park and recreation [facilities] to many government officials.[7]

Easements

In some cases, land may be made available for recreation without direct acquisition. This may involve an agreement between government and private property owners that permits specified recreational use of the land. In some cases, flood-control lands or property adjoining highways or airports is made available for recreation on this basis, without the land being transferred to the public recreation and park development. In others, owners of undeveloped land are given a reduced tax rate as compensation for keeping the land as open space rather than developing it.

Property Acquisition by Nonpublic Agencies

Acquisition of recreation and park properties by nongovernmental organizations is generally a simpler process. Therapeutic and industrial agencies usually do not purchase separate properties for recreational purposes, but instead include this function as part of the overall facility development effort. In some cases, companies or associations of employees separately acquire properties for development as camps or sports areas, usually through a regular purchasing procedure. Similarly, voluntary agencies typically buy properties for development, although they may also rely on gifts or, in some urban centers, on rebuilding older structures or unused school buildings that have been made available to them.

In a growing number of cases, property acquisition and facility development are carried out through the cooperative efforts of public agencies and private, commercial recreation operators. For example, in the White River State Park in Indianapolis (see page 118), or the huge Chelsea Piers waterfront complex along New York's Hudson River, varied sponsors manage different facilities within the overall complex—some for profit and some not.

In other cities, public/private cooperation has resulted in unused or underutilized harbor and marine areas being revitalized for boating, fishing, and other water-based recreation through arrangements under which the commercial sponsor provides the bulk of development funding and has a long-term rental agreement to manage the facility.

Similarly, in a number of cities, major sports stadiums have been built cooperatively, with the owners of professional teams paying a portion of the construction cost and holding long-term leases for use and management of the structure—including parking, refreshments concessions, and sky-box rentals. In many communities, public recreation and park departments cooperate with public school systems in the joint construction and use of athletic fields and other facilities.

DESIGN AND CONSTRUCTION PROCESS

Following the acquisition of properties based on planning recommendations, the next step involves the design and construction of the facilities that are to be developed on the site.

The design process usually involves the following steps: (1) selecting and employing a qualified architectural or engineering firm, based on a legal contract that outlines all responsibilities and commitments of the task; (2) providing all relevant information regarding the purpose and function of the facility, as well as input from community groups or other potential users; (3) preparing preliminary drawings; and (4) reviewing and revising successive designs until the plan is acceptable to all concerned.

Within each of these steps, the leisure-service manager should play a significant role. As this chapter has indicated, in most situations an outside architectural or engineering firm is employed to design recreation and park projects, although some municipalities have their own design staffs for routine assignments. Often such planning and design specialists are able to assist in feasibility studies, and in handling controversy and building public consensus in approving the proposed facility design.

Bishop and Layton, for example, describe the work of Design Concepts, a Colorado firm that has worked on over ninety projects, ranging from small playgrounds or sports complexes to large wildland areas and multimillion dollar community parks. The key, they write, is developing a public process in which all the stakeholders

—including the park's neighbors, other potential park users, and town officials—feel that you have listened to their concerns and desires for the park and that these issues have been considered carefully. Through public meetings, design workshops, and other ways of communicating ideas, you can create a list of priorities and possibilities and show why some elements should be included and others not. . . . The final design may be quite different from what some individuals or groups had hoped for, but by that time most participants will have come to understand why.[8]

In some cases, an architectural or engineering firm may be hired through a design competition. Marion Weiss describes the process of holding an international design competition for a new park and community center in the Olympia Fields Park District in Illinois. The competition was widely publicized, with over 500 firms and individuals submitting entries that were judged by an expert jury, based on four criteria: (1) aesthetic and symbolic quality, (2) economic feasibility, (3) functional quality, and (4) historic preservation and conservation.[9]

Recreation and park managers should seek to become as fully involved as possible in each construction project, according to the following guidelines:

1. The recreation and park director should become familiar with all background information related to the facility plan and should be actively involved in all public hearings and planning sessions about it.
2. He or she should meet and discuss the project with all public officials or civic leaders, such as city council members, members of planning boards, or school administrators, who have a stake in it. He or she should be thoroughly familiar with their views and wishes and consider their suggestions seriously.
3. He or she should insist on being involved in the selection of the architectural or engineering firm that is to do the plan, pressing strongly for the selection of a designer who is highly qualified by experience and performance

rather than the lowest bidder or the firm with political connections.
4. He or she should strive to be present at all design and modification conferences to make sure that program needs are considered.
5. When construction begins, he or she should visit the site regularly either with staff members or with the architect on inspection visits. He or she should study the construction process carefully and note all problems. It is important to follow up on these immediately to correct errors that might be much more expensive and difficult to remedy later.
6. He or she should insist, through channels if necessary, that all construction details or standards be carried out or followed exactly as specified. If unforeseen conditions appear, such as possible drainage or soil problems, any changes in the design or construction should be carefully reviewed and agreed upon in writing, along with changes in contracted costs, if necessary.

In smaller communities, the manager is likely to be intimately involved and may work closely with the designer, participating in laying out excavation lines, making decisions regarding materials, and even instituting change orders directly at the construction site. In larger cities, however, the recreation and park manager tends to be less involved, either because his or her own responsibilities are too demanding or because departmental lines are more sharply drawn. Instead, the major responsibility for selecting the architectural firm, approving the design, and following up on the construction process falls to the city or town engineer.

Design Criteria: Questions to Be Asked

Does the facility's design serve the agency's key goals and objectives, and is it geared to meeting changing public needs and interests or new shifts in recreational programming? Will the facility be one that can be efficiently managed, with convenient access and egress, by agency staff members, handle different types of activities going on concurrently, and sturdy in terms of not requiring excessive maintenance or rehabilitation?

Are the projected costs of construction and ongoing operation available within the agency's budget, and are they realistic as demonstrated by similar projects that have been recently completed? If construction bids turn out to be excessive, are there design options at lesser costs?

From an environmental standpoint, has the impact of the planned design been carefully reviewed by experts (individuals or groups) in this field, and have visual, aesthetic, and traffic elements been approved by neighbors and other stakeholders? Have all safety hazards of the facility been analyzed and eliminated in the planning and design stage?

While risk management is discussed in full detail in Chapter 9, several obvious safety design features are illustrated in the following box.

Examples of Safety Design Features

1. Laying out all aquatic areas, whether swimming pools or beach of lakefront areas, to facilitate careful supervision and efficient emergency procedures and (in the case of natural sites) avoid built-in dangers, such as hidden rocks, low diving areas or dangerous currents, or conflict with boating uses;

2. Using safety surfacing in playgrounds under climbing or swinging apparatus and equipment that has a minimum of inherent risk in the play experiences it offers;

3. Laying out contiguous areas so one does not impose possible accidents on the other (for example, a baseball field immediately next to an outdoor area for senior citizens);

4. Using guard rails or similar barriers next to steep inclines or natural hazards, such as those found in some national or state parks;

5. Providing needed safety equipment or approved features in all crafts and construction areas, particularly those using power equipment or tools, electrical units such as kilns, or acids or other possibly dangerous substances.

Another important concern in facilities construction today is making them accessible for children and adults with varied types of disabilities. In both the United States and Canada, public, nonprofit, and commercial recreation organizations must accept the responsibility for providing a full range of leisure opportunities for persons with disabilities. Through programs of modified sports and outdoor recreations, we have come to realize that persons with visual or auditory disabilities, cerebral palsy, orthopedic limitations, and reduced mental functions can take part in and enjoy camping, swimming, various sports, and even such relatively high-risk activities as downhill skiing.

Kennedy and Smith point out that changed public attitudes led to and were strengthened by several pieces of federal legislation in the United States that dealt with the design of recreation facilities. These included the Architectural Barriers Act of 1968 (P. L. 90-480), Section 504 of the Rehabilitation Act of 1973 (P. L. 112), and the 1990 Americans with Disabilities Act. Almost all federal, state, and provincial governments today have made strenuous efforts to remove architectural barriers in older construction and to design new facilities to ensure accessibility for persons with physical disabilities.[10] The National Society for Park Resources, the National Research Council, and numerous organizations concerned with architectural standards have developed guidelines for facilitating access to recreational and park facilities and improving opportunities for successful participation. These include:

1. Design of walks and trails, with minimum widths and grades, appropriate surfaces for wheelchair use, elimination of expansion joints, and appropriate resting and pickup places for disabled and elderly persons;
2. Picnic tables, fishing areas, specially designed nature trails, golf putting areas, and similar facilities that permit use by the blind or those in wheelchairs;
3. Redesign of ramps, doors, vestibules, dressing rooms, swimming pools, toilets, drinking fountains, showers, and similar areas to facilitate use by disabled persons.

Beyond assuring access for disabled persons in all facilities, a growing number of communities have designed and built special facilities for their use. For example, the Phoenix, Arizona, Parks, Recreation and Library Department joined forces with a volunteer organization, the Telephone Pioneers, to develop a $2.5 million recreation park for persons with disabilities and their families. This park, the largest of its kind in the United States, includes a therapy pool and spa designed for wheelchair accessibility, adapted baseball fields, tennis and basketball courts for wheelchair play, a "tactile" play area for children with visual disabilities, other modified areas, and a Braille directory of the total facility. Many facilities today are being designed and built for integrated use by both disabled and nondisabled people to promote mainstreaming of those with disabilities.

DESIGN OF SPECIAL FACILITIES

137

CHAPTER 5
*Facilities
Development and
Maintenance*

Over the past three decades, the design and construction of many different types of recreation and park areas and facilities have become more sophisticated, in terms of meeting participants' needs and guarding against negative environmental effects.

Outdoor Recreation Areas

For example, numerous authorities have developed principles and methods for the planning and design of golf courses, including the need for feasibility studies, effective site selection processes, development costs and financing methods, architect selection, design and contouring features, landscaping, and maintenance.

Increasingly, designers have identified the positive impacts that golf courses can make on the environment. Properly designed courses can, Marty Parkes points out, produce oxygen for the surrounding community, absorb traffic noise, provide open green space, filter rainfall, and help to prevent soil erosion.[11] The U.S. Golf Association, through the work of a team of skilled agronomists working with its Green Section, has promoted extensive research at major land-grant universities to promote these benefits. In some regions, golf courses are being constructed on landfills, abandoned gravel pits, or mining sites as part of total ecological recovery efforts.

In some cases, new technologies have been developed for the design of outdoor recreation complexes. For example, in the early 1980s, the U.S. Forest Service used computers to design ski slopes that would blend with the rugged terrain of the Rocky Mountains. The service found that computers enabled them to design trails that reduced visual impact (scarring of slopes and obtrusive machinery) and resulted in greater safety. Although computers provided maps and detailed visuals that showed slopes complete to the last tree, rock, and gully, they obviously could not make key design decisions. This was the responsibility of knowledgeable designers and ski slope managers.

In other settings, designers have been able to reroute or reconstruct streams, both to restore their ecological well-being and to provide improved river-rafting or canoeing opportunities.

Senior Center Design

With the growth of the elderly population and facilities to serve older men and women, the design of senior centers has become increasingly complex. Intended to house the varied social, recreational, health-related, nutritional, and other programs serving older participants, senior centers may be sponsored by public or voluntary agencies. Although many centers meet on a part-time basis in churches or other community buildings, the trend is toward designing or developing new structures that will provide optimal facilities for the specialized programs needed by senior citizens.

Based on a study of senior center facilities carried out for the National Institute of Senior Centers, a number of key architectural guidelines and checklists for multipurpose centers has been identified. The study found that many centers failed to provide adequate lounge space to meet varied leisure needs and social interests, and that they often lacked proper kitchen and storage space and equipment, along with up-to-date mechanical systems for heating and air-conditioning. Other needed senior center facilities include multipurpose rooms, craft shops, bathrooms, offices, consultation and meeting rooms, and adequate hallways and entry areas.

Beyond these guidelines, many communities have developed multigenerational facilities to serve as many residents as possible, rather than centers designed only for elderly persons.

Youth Centers: Boys and Girls Clubs Guidelines

National organizations such as the Boys and Girls Clubs of America often offer advice and technical assistance to local chapters or agencies with respect to planning and designing facilities. This body in particular has a national task force on building design and has sponsored clinics for its member agencies on building design and construction. The following guidelines are adapted from a statement of "do's and don'ts" for club executives and boards planning a building program:

1. Define exactly what you expect of the new building before you start to design it (i.e., number of members, types of programs, other special uses).
2. Establish how much money can be spent, and do not make any detailed designs until you have obtained cost estimates from a competent builder that will give a general picture of the kind of building you can construct within your budget. It is more effective to start designing under the proper restraints than to try to cut costs from a completely designed building that turned out to be too expensive.
3. The club director should take the lead in designing the structure, with an architect or competent builder's help. An experienced director knows what is needed and what not to have in a club, and it is more effective to let the architect design the building around his or her concepts than to try to modify an architect's design to meet a club's needs.
4. Don't hire an architect unless he or she is willing to minimize the cost of the building within the limits of durability and low maintenance and maximize its useful space. The architect should be the practical engineer type who is an expert on materials of construction, cost-saving techniques, and other practical concerns. A good builder can provide helpful input during the design process.

Fiscal Concerns

Throughout the planning and design process, agency managers, boards, and architects or engineers must be constantly aware of the fiscal factors involved in facility development. For example, William Jansen points out that in initial stages of determining the feasibility of new marina construction, it is necessary to analyze three important elements: (1) the projected cost of the new facility and the sources of its funding; (2) the market for boating slips and slip rental pricing factors; and (3) the possible design options and their relative advantages, disadvantages, and costs.[12]

Jansen stresses the need for marina developers to do a realistic analysis of total project costs, including access roads, utility, installation, site development, and harbor protection structures. There must be a detailed projection of marina revenues to ensure that adequate funds will be generated for debt retirement, operation, repairs, and future improvements.

MAINTENANCE AND OPERATION OF FACILITIES

Once a leisure facility has been completed, it is ready for operation. This includes two elements: (1) *maintenance,* meaning the continuing process of keeping the park, sport field, indoor center, or other facility as clean, safe, attractive, and functional as possible; and (2) *operation,* which includes the assigning of reservations or scheduled group or individual uses of facilities, monitoring usage rates, enforcing risk-management practices, and other agency policies with respect to facilities.

Good maintenance will earn respect for a recreational and park facility, encourage participation, and lengthen the life of a facility and the equipment in it. Poor maintenance practices will do just the opposite. In addition, through regular inspections and prompt repair of broken equipment or dangerous conditions, accidents will be prevented and lawsuits avoided. In the case of facilities that receive heavy, intensive use, such as beaches in tourist areas, regular cleanup operations are essential.[13]

Written Maintenance Plans

Routine maintenance operations are facilitated by the use of written plans that outline all responsibilities for field personnel in simple, clear terms. These should include the following elements:

1. *Maintenance standards*—the minimum acceptable level of maintained condition for an area, facility, or equipment item;
2. *Routine maintenance tasks*—these include tasks such as cleaning, lubricating, painting, litter and trash removal, planting, fertilizing, watering, weeding, and mowing;
3. *Procedures for maintaining*—concise descriptions of how to do the tasks in the most effective and efficient manner possible ;
4. *Frequency*—daily, weekly, monthly, biannually, annually, or other guidelines for when work must be done, including seasonal variations;
5. *Materials, supplies, and tools*—detailed statement of all materials and equipment needed to perform tasks.
6. *Personnel*—minimum number of personnel required to carry out tasks, with identification of technical skills required and standardized statement of time needed to carry out tasks.

Such a written maintenance plan is best presented in a format with several vertical columns and the wording as short and simple as possible. It should include four elements: (1) goals and objectives of the maintenance plan; (2) a detailed inventory of the park and recreation system, resulting in an accurate listing of all the features, facilities, buildings, and equipment at each department-operated site; (3) a list of maintenance tasks and the standards needed for carrying these out; and (4) a format for scheduling maintenance work. As a final step that helps organize the work effectively, it is necessary to develop a form for daily maintenance work and assignments.

Finally, work order request forms should be developed for nonroutine, non-recurring maintenance tasks—specific, isolated jobs that are not part of the regular schedule.

Developing Work Standards: A Systems Approach

Within this overall process, managers should constantly strive to improve maintenance performance while keeping costs at an affordable level. One approach is to develop a system that classifies facilities by type and assigns them different levels of maintenance priority.

For example, a highly visible downtown park might be classified as an "A" area, with the grass cut two or three times a week, trash collected twice a day, and flower planting automatically irrigated and receiving daily attention. In contrast, a low-priority area, such as a utility right-of-way, might be classified as a "C" or "D" area, requiring only a bimonthly trash cleanup and annual grass and weed cutting.

To illustrate such an approach, the San Jose, California, Parks Division uses a maintenance plan that itemizes the individual tasks that must be performed at two frequency levels—one for *optimum* care and the other for *minimum* care, during active and inactive seasons of the year, based on climate and usage volumes (Table 5.2).

Although such systems-based maintenance plans may seem to be overly technical or time-consuming, the reality is that well-documented and carefully detailed standards and work plans provide evidence of the department's efficiency and help to eliminate waste or resist unreasonable demands. For example, the Parks and Recreation Department of Edmonton, Alberta, Canada, has initiated a systems-based maintenance program, called the Parks Maintenance Management System (PMMS), structured to improve planning of work programs, define and document budget allocations, and measure productivity. Through PMMS, work plans are prepared for each task that describe the time and equipment needed (personnel, vehicles, tools, and materials) to provide a specified level of maintenance quality. Cost projections are specified for each element and are used as the basis for monthly and weekly work scheduling.

The widespread use of computers has made it possible to access expenditure accounts, materials inventory control, workload cost tracking, work scheduling, and similar information quickly and conveniently. Realistically, a comprehensive and up-to-date computerized data system is critical to all such maintenance efforts.

TABLE 5.2. **Partial Listing of Frequency and Levels of Care of Tasks Performed by Grounds Maintenance Personnel**

141

Chapter 5
*Facilities
Development and
Maintenance*

Task List	Frequencies*			
	Optimum Care Level		Minimum Care Level	
	On-Season	Off-Season	On-Season	Off-Season
1. Pick up litter	D	D	D	D
2. Clean restrooms/drinking fountains	D	D	D	D
3. Rake tanbark/sand areas	D	D	D	3W
4. Sweep perimeter of building	D	4W	D	3W
5. Set out refuse	3W	2W	2W	2W
6. Irrigate turf	2W	W2	2W	W2
7. Check trees/ties/stakes	D	D	3W	2W
8. Rake bleacher areas	4W	3W	3W	W
9. Irrigate flower beds	D	W2	4W	W2
10. Clean picnic areas	2W	W	W	W2
11. Mow turf areas	W	W	W	W2
12. Remove spent flowers	W	M	W	M
13. Edge ground-cover	M	M2	M	M3
14. Prune/trim hedges	M	M2	M	M2
15. Spray flowers/insect control	M	0	M	0
16. Fertilize flowers	M3	0	M3	0
17. Rake leaves, shrub/turf areas	M4	W	M4	W
18. Mulch shrub areas	M6	M6	M6	M6

Source: Modified from Mills, A. S., Harris, R. W., and Conway, K. L.: "Case Report—San Jose," *Parks and Recreation*, Jan. 1980, p. 89.

*D, daily; W, weekly; 2W, 3W, 4W, two, three, four times weekly; W2, every other week; M, monthly; M2, M3, M4, M6, once every 2, 3, 4, and 6 months. On-season is the 8-month period from March 1 through October. Off-season is the 4-month period from November 1 through February.

Contracting of Maintenance Functions

Another important trend in facilities maintenance has consisted of subcontracting selected functions to private companies. This privatization strategy can yield significant savings since nonpublic operators are often able to deliver services more economically because of their ability to resist bureaucratic or political pressures and expand or contract their workforces on a seasonal basis.

This approach is being applied to such functions as security operations, park maintenance, trash collection, tree trimming, and numerous other special services. In some cases, entire operations, such as golf course or tennis center management, have been turned over to private firms (see page 266). In general, such subcontracting practices should not be viewed as a "last-resort" effort to cut costs, but rather as a legitimate tool to improve performance or agency productivity.

To illustrate the kinds of controls that are used to monitor the contracting of maintenance functions, the Board of Parks and Recreation Commissioners of Kansas City, Missouri, has published a number of project manuals giving the exact format of contract documents and performance specifications within different areas of maintenance. Its manual for grounds maintenance of boulevards and highways, for example, gives details regarding the kinds and strengths of herbicides that must be used to control weeds, including the chemicals used, the spraying procedure, required environmental conditions (rainfall, wind velocity, and minimum daytime temperature), and required results in terms of weed decline thirty days after herbicide application.

Similar performance specifications should be part of all facility maintenance-subcontracting agreements to ensure quality performance and minimize the risk of later lawsuits,

PREVENTIVE MAINTENANCE AND LIFE-CYCLE PLANNING

Within the overall facilities management process, it is essential to develop policies that prevent deterioration and help to maintain the quality of recreation areas and structures. This need is particularly pressing in many parks, forests, or lakes that have been subjected to steadily growing volumes of outdoor recreation enthusiasts—often making use of off-road vehicles or watercraft that contribute to pollution or threaten wildlife and vegetation. Planners in such settings have developed preventive strategies to curb destructive visitor practices and restore environmental health.

In many cases, a key strategy has been to restrict automobile traffic in major national, state, or provincial parks. For example, in Yosemite National Park, more than four million persons a year have visited the park's seven-mile-long valley floor, creating bumper-to-bumper gridlock. In the fall of 1997, the National Park Service announced a radical new plan to turn back the clock:

> . . . tearing up roads and parking lots, tearing down buildings and bridges, and all but banning cars inside the valley by 2001. Day visitors to the park would have to leave their cars behind, boarding shuttle buses heading into the valley. Overnight visitors could drive in to their hotels and campgrounds but would then have to park their cars for the duration of their visit.[14]

Similarly, in New York City's famous Central Park, the overuse of the park's central Great Lawn by millions of softball players, picnickers, sunbathers and walkers required a two-year shutdown of the 45-acre area, and an $18.2 million face-lift using advanced horticultural and engineering expertise. To protect the rich new turf, rules govern play on the lawn's eight fields and restrict their use for two-week periods on a rotating basis.

In terms of protecting developed recreation areas and structures, other recreation and park departments have initiated a "life cycle planning" approach to keep their facilities in sound working order. The Nova Scotia, Canada, Sport and Recreation Commissions defines this approach as a systematic way of

. . . forecasting the maintenance and replacement requirements of the components of a facility over its complete life span [including] developing the resources needed for repair, retrofit and improvement projects . . . . Life cycle planning is used primarily for major indoor facilities—arenas, pools, gymnasiums—but it is equally applicable to outdoor facilities, large and small.[15]

In a late 1990s' report, the Commission pointed out that many of its major facilities had been built during a relatively short period of time in the 1970s. Generally speaking, maintenance of these facilities had been "minimal," the Commission concluded, with a resultant wave of demands for emergency repairs and unanticipated replacement of costly elements. By applying a facility life-cycle model that paralleled human growth and development, from "prenatal" and "childhood" stages when maintenance problems were few, to "adulthood" and "old age," when many facilities required major reconstruction or were no longer functional, it developed several recommendations for facility conservation and improvement. These recommendations called for a full commitment to the life-cycle planning process, along with regular inventories and assessments, and strategies to provide effective maintenance and conservation services that would anticipate and prevent problems leading to facility decline. A key element in this approach is to project future costs of ongoing maintenance and capital improvements, and make budget allocations for them as necessary.

Strategic Maintenance Planning

Many other recreation, park, and leisure service agencies have adopted similar strategic maintenance-planning approaches that include all of the elements required to keep areas and facilities in the optimum condition over time. The Westchester County, New York, Department of Parks, Recreation and Conservation outlined the need for such approaches in a recent policy statement:

> Additions to our facilities in recent years, such as new parks, picnic areas, ball fields, and play equipment, coupled with aging buildings and the lack of a strategic plan to maintain and support these facilities, could lead to serious park management problems. These factors, when considered in conjunction with decreasing maintenance budgets and increased pressure and maintenance responsibilities, provide a daunting challenge.[16]

In order to develop proper control, cost-effective services, and coordinated functions, a strategic maintenance plan was developed that served as a benchmark for evaluation and led to a total review of agency policies and procedures in the Westchester County park system. With such elements as improved cost accounting and a time management system, a work control center and ordered routine of planning and scheduling maintenance functions, the overall strategic maintenance plan was designed to serve as a useful tool in performance evaluation. Through the use of a computerized database, it provided timely and accurate management reporting and tracking of personnel, money, materials, machinery and materials, and automated scheduling of the maintenance of equipment, grounds, and physical plant.

PROGRAM OPERATIONS AND FACILITY MANAGEMENT

Finally, a critical concern of management is to link agency facilities with program operations, so that both functional areas are efficiently coordinated. This means that all elements of facilities management—including event coordinating, engineering, security, maintenance, and housekeeping—must be arranged to permit the successful conduct of programs in many different formats. Several of these operational functions, such as those involving publicity or risk management, are described in detail in Chapters 8 and 9.

Example: Facility Reservation Procedure

The need for facility and program managers to work closely together is shown in a Facility Reservation Procedure Manual developed by the Phoenix, Arizona, Parks, Recreation and Library Department, which defines guidelines for the rental and use of park and recreation facilities. It outlines procedures for the public to reserve certain recreational areas (rooms, gymnasiums, athletic fields, auditoriums, snowmobiles, community center buildings, theaters, art centers, sports complexes, and pools) for exclusive use at a given time by individuals, groups, or organizations.[17]

To accomplish this, reservation applicants are assigned to "user classifications," which determine their level of priority and whether or not they must pay fees for facility rental. For example, "nonfee users" include groups that have formally affiliated with the Phoenix Parks, Recreation and Library Department, groups that are cosponsoring programs or events with the department, recognized youth groups or professional associations, schools, and other city departments.

In contrast, "fee users" include individuals or groups renting facilities for such purposes as meetings, weddings, social events, or reunions on a nonprofit basis, or "commercial users," meaning program sponsors using facilities or areas for profit purposes, or as part of other business functions.

Throughout the facility reservation process, computers provide invaluable assistance in classifying and approving users, scheduling areas and buildings, recording payments, and similar functions.

Other Facility-Use Policies

Facility and program managers must also coordinate their efforts in enforcing department policies that protect areas and structures from damage or misuse of any sort. For example, the Phoenix reservation procedure manual specifies that it is necessary with each facility use by outside groups to conduct pre- and post-walk-through tours to determine damages and/or appropriate clean-up charges. Where necessary, user groups provide appropriate settlement or deposit fees are retained.

In addition to this basic policy, special-activity request forms must be completed by user groups if any of the following activities or arrangements are to be part of programs or events: playing of amplified music; the use of tents or other structures; the sale of food; use of alcoholic beverages; animals present (horse/dog show, pony rides); amusements such as carnival rides brought into park; fireworks; fund-raising activities; sale or solicitation of any goods or services; and political or religious gatherings.

PARTNERSHIPS IN MAINTENANCE AND CAPITAL DEVELOPMENT

In order to maintain recreation and park facilities successfully under growing economic constraints, many public leisure-service agencies have developed partnerships with other community groups that have taken a larger share of responsibility for facility management.

In Long Beach, California, for example, the public Department of Parks, Recreation and Marine redesigned maintenance operations throughout the 1990s so that light maintenance and litter pick-up responsibilities in many areas were assumed by neighborhood associations. It also sponsored Adopt-A-Park, Adopt-A-Beach, Dedicate-A-Tree, and Beach Clean-Up days to leverage community support for clean-up efforts. In Long Beach, youth sports leagues also provide a significant portion of field maintenance, and cooperative agreements with the Conservation Corps and partnerships with county Social Service agencies also provide assistance for general park and beach maintenance.

Such approaches represent strategies that have been adapted by many public and nonprofit leisure-service organizations and are described in fuller detail in Chapter 8 as part of public relations and community development techniques that flourished in the 1990s. Privatization arrangements under which private or commercial organizations make a major funding contribution to the construction of stadiums or other facilities, based on long-term leasing agreements, became increasingly popular as well.

SUMMARY

The design, construction, and maintenance of recreation, park, and leisure-service facilities represents a critical function of managers in this field. The chapter begins by describing the major types of traditional and innovative areas and facilities that are operated by leisure-service agencies.

The facilities management sequence begins with planning that determines the community or other agency needs for open space, developed areas, or structures to house recreation programs. It describes the use of space and facility standards, neighborhood and facility guidelines, and other methods of arriving at short- and long-term recommendations for acquiring and developing sites.

After outlining several familiar methods of acquiring properties, the chapter presents guidelines for designing facilities, including the manager's role in the process and issues related to safety standards and accessibility for special populations. It continues with the construction phase of facility management, including the use of systems-based maintenance methods at different levels of care. Several types of outdoor and indoor recreation areas and facilities are described in more detail, and the chapter concludes with a discussion of preventive maintenance, life-cycle facility planning, and public/private partnerships in facility development and operation.

SUGGESTED INDIVIDUAL OR GROUP CLASS PROJECTS

1. Survey available recreation and park facilities within the community, county, or other local government jurisdiction. If feasible, determine the extent to which they meet the chapter's suggested standards for parks, open space, or specific types of facilities, as well as providing access for persons with disabilities. This project's report might be presented to the class with slides or videotaped illustrations.
2. Develop preliminary designs for facilities intended for any of the following purposes or populations: (a) a senior center; (b) a major activity area, such as aquatic complex or multiuse sports center; (c) a college/university recreation center or youth-serving organization. This project should not be approached from an architectural or technical viewpoint, but rather with chief concern for management functions such as programming, supervision, and similar tasks. If possible, visit existing facilities of the style you selected.
3. Develop a maintenance plan that outlines the most efficient and economical approach to care for a large park or other outdoor facility, *or* that initiates environmental policies to upgrade and protect a similar site.

Note: These projects would be best suited for upper-level undergraduate or graduate classes with students who have had a degree of professional experience. As tasks requiring research and visitations, they would have to be carried out over a period of time, possibly as term projects.

CASE STUDIES FOR CLASS ANALYSIS

147

CHAPTER 5
*Facilities
Development and
Maintenance*

Before analyzing these cases in class, review the guidelines suggested in Chapter 3 (pp. 76–77).

Case Study 5.1 *Boating or Birds: A Philosophical and Environmental Issue*

YOU ARE BRIAN DOLAN, managing director of a county recreation and park department. Your agency operates a small marina and boat-launching site on Bluefield Lake, a popular area for public boating and fishing. Most of the lake's perimeter is privately owned, and there is constant pressure for more access to the water.

The county also owns considerable frontage on Bluefield Creek, a somewhat marshy stream that flows into the lake. You have carried out a planning study that shows it would be feasible to dredge and widen the mouth of the creek to construct a large new extension to the marina with as many as 100 new slips and moorings and additional launching ramps. With the likelihood of supplemental funding from private, state, and federal sources, you are about to submit a proposal to your county board of supervisors for building the marina addition.

Suddenly, objections are heard from several environmental groups. They claim the creek and the marshland surrounding it provide an irreplaceable habitat for wildlife, particularly birds. They are strongly opposed to dredging the area and building the marina addition. The board hearing is tomorrow, and the environmental groups plan to show up in force to fight your proposal.

QUESTIONS FOR CLASS DISCUSSION AND ANALYSIS

1. *As managing director of the recreation and park department, what is your philosophical position with respect to maintaining and protecting the natural environment?*
2. *What are your most potent, practical arguments in favor of the marina proposal?*

3. *What could you have done in terms of strategy to anticipate or forestall the opposition of the environmental groups?*
4. *Now that the environmental issue has been strongly raised, are you prepared to rethink your plan?*

Case Study 5.2 *Community Relations and the Ball Park*

YOU ARE MARY DIBENEDETTO, director of the Marshall County Park and Recreation Department. Your agency has operated a large public park, used chiefly for sports, for a number of years. Known as Jefferson Park, the area has become rundown and overgrown due to inadequate funding for maintenance over a period of years.

Under a new agreement with the South Side Sports League, a county-wide association that sponsors seasonal sports (softball, flag football, and soccer), the league would become responsible for maintaining the park and for scheduling its uses. In the first year, the South Side Sports League cleaned up three ball fields and a track, improved fencing, and rehabilitated a pavilion structure in Jefferson Parks. They began a fund-raising campaign to raise money to put in a night-lighting system, and sports activity in the park increased steadily.

However, a committee of Marshall County residents living close to the park appeared at the department's monthly meeting. They claimed that the league was totally dominating the use of Jefferson Park facilities and was not granting field permits to local youth who had formerly used it for informal play, because they were not affiliated with any approved organization. Beyond this, they were concerned about the traffic, parking, and noise problems that might stem from the proposed night-lighting system.

QUESTIONS FOR DISCUSSION AND ANALYSIS

1. *How could this problem have been avoided or dealt with at an earlier stage of planning with the South Side Sports League?*

2. *How can you balance the priorities of neighborhood residents against those of the larger Marshall County population?*

3. *What are the alternative approaches for dealing with the problem now?*

Case Study 5.3 *State Park Policy: Getting the Bare Facts*

YOU ARE JIM HOLSTEIN, director of a state park system in a southern state. For several years, there has been a problem with skinny-dipping at several of the rivers and lakes in or bordering your parks. Groups of adults have selected sites where they sunbathed and swam in the nude, and the location of these sites gradually became known, attracting other skinny-dipping enthusiasts.

At first you tried to prevent this by legal action, but found it was difficult to enforce the law, which was vague on the issue. Finally you decided to resolve the matter by setting aside two areas along somewhat remote rivers that have fairly secluded beach and swimming sites, letting it be known that persons swimming and sunbathing in the nude there would not be prosecuted, although ordinances would be strictly enforced elsewhere.

Initially, this seemed to work. Growing numbers of nudists began to use the selected locations. However, new problems have developed. Numerous voyeurs are now hiking in to spy on and photograph the nude bathers. Families with children who boat or raft past these beaches are complaining of seeing immoral behavior. Worst of all, there have been several incidents of sexual assaults on isolated nude bathers.

QUESTIONS FOR CLASS DISCUSSION AND ANALYSIS

1. *Was your initial decision to set aside spots for "approved" nude bathing a sound one?*

2. *In establishing these sites, you did not clear the matter with state police officials. Your own state park rangers can give tickets but do not normally have law enforcement authority for criminal acts. What can be done now to provide a safer environment?*

3. *What basic principles regarding the use of state park facilities should be observed? Is it your place to legislate morality, and is this a moral issue? Perhaps you had better do some research to determine exactly what the law is with respect to nudity in such locations and learn what policies are followed elsewhere.*

150

Chapter 5
Facilities
Development and
Maintenance

REFERENCES

1. Divine, Robert: "USA Overseas, Isolated and Remote," *Parks and Recreation,* December 1996, p. 54.
2. Grass, James: "Indiana Park Combines Past and Future," *Parks and Recreation,* January 1997, p. 47.
3. Cohen, Andrew: "Competing Interests," *Athletic Business,* October 1997, p. 33.
4. Lancaster, Roger, ed.: *Recreation, Park and Open Space Standards and Guidelines,* Alexandria, Va., 1983, National Recreation and Park Association, pp. 60–61.
5. *Ibid.,* p. 46.
6. Putnam, Terry, and Walker, Melissa: "Mastering the Master Plan," *Parks and Recreation,* June 1996, pp. 56–60.
7. Crompton, John: "Alternative Approaches to Securing Recreation and Park Amenities through Exactions," *Journal of Park and Recreation Administration,* 15 (1), Spring 1997, p. 16.
8. Bishop, Axel, and Layton, Bobby: "Creating Consensus on Controversial Parks," *Parks and Recreation,* August 1997, p. 40.
9. Weiss, Marion: "American Green: Olympia Fields Park and Community Center," *Parks and Recreation,* August 1995, p. 57.
10. Kennedy, Dan, Smith, Ralph, and Austin, David: *Special Recreation: Opportunities for Persons with Disabilities,* Wm. C. Brown Publishers, Dubuque, Ia., 1991, p. 90.
11. Parkes, Marty: "Golf Courses Benefit the Environment," *Parks and Recreation,* April 1996, p. 85.
12. Jansen, William: "Marina Development in the Public Sector," *Parks and Recreation,* November 1992, p. 46.
13. *Beach Maintenance Report,* Metro Dade County, Fla., Parks and Recreation Department, January 1977.
14. Lelyveld, Nita: "Yosemite: Help for Mother Nature," *Philadelphia Inquirer,* November 16, 1996, p. A-3.
15. *Recreation Facility Development: Life-Cycle Planning,* Sport and Recreation Commission, Nova Scotia, Canada, 1997.
16. *Strategic Maintenance Plan,* Westchester County, N.Y., Department of Parks, Recreation and Conservation, 1998, pp. 1–2.
17. *Field Operations Procedures Manual,* Phoenix, Ariz., Department of Parks, Recreation and Library, October 1995, pp. 2–4.

CHAPTER Six

Creative Fiscal Management

It is this new reality [the need to do "more with less"] that has caused managers to look beyond the traditional financing concepts and strategies that have been used and to supplement them with new imaginative approaches. . . . Managers of sports organizations are required to seek out scarce resources from a wide range of possible sources and to use their marketing and financing skills to ensure scarce resources acquired are allocated in such a way that they yield optimum social and economic benefits. These are exactly the requirements of an entrepreneur.[1]

While some people complain about an admission charge to enjoy land where logging, grazing and mining are still heavily subsidized by the Federal Government, most recreational users seem willing to pay something for using public land, according to preliminary surveys across the country. In national parks, most of which have long charged admission fees, there has been a 5 percent increase in visitors thus far this year [1997] over last, despite a doubling of fees at some of the most popular sites and the introduction of fees at some areas that were previously free.[2]

INTRODUCTION

Fiscal management—that is, the process of planning, gathering, and strategically using money to support recreation, park, and leisure-service agency operations—represents a key responsibility of managers on every level in this field.

In an era in which fiscal cutbacks have affected many public and nonprofit organizations, including armed forces, therapeutic, and employee-service recreation programs, it is essential that managers be thoroughly familiar both with the accepted principles and practices of money management, and with newer and more creative ways of gathering revenues and using them productively. Therefore, this chapter presents guidelines for the preparation and execution of annual budgets, accounting, and auditing procedures, using a variety

151

of fund-raising methods creatively, and developing a comprehensive marketing approach in order to achieve a degree of fiscal self-sufficiency. Also, the following understandings and competencies are listed as essential in the Baccalaureate Degree standards of the NRPA/AALR Council on Accreditation:

> Understanding of and ability to apply both traditional and innovative techniques of financial management, including development of budgets for operating and capital budgets, revenue generation and accountability, pricing of services, cost analysis and financial forecasting (7A.01).

> Knowledge of marketing techniques and strategies (8.28).

> Understanding of the relationship of business, society and the economy, including the role of the entrepreneur (7A.03).

> Understanding of the economic impact of leisure service programs upon the general economy (9A.04).

O B J E C T I V E S

At the conclusion of this chapter, readers should be familiar with the following concepts and practices:

1. The overall process of financial management in both nonprofit and profit-oriented leisure-service organizations, including the legal structure, policies, and procedures that govern its operation.
2. The economic impact of recreation, parks, and leisure-service programs on national life and community well-being.
3. The nature of different types of budgets, including capital and operating, line-item, functional, program, and other types of budgets.
4. Common patterns of budget planning and development, including the process of budget submission to governing authorities.
5. Accounting and auditing principles and procedures, including purchasing procedures, controls over expenditures, and periodic or annual budget reports.
6. Varied sources of funding, including tax allocations, bond issues, gifts and special funding drives, enterprise funds, assistance from community organizations, and fees and charges.
7. Entrepreneurship approaches and innovative marketing methods as they apply to fiscal management and agency policies.
8. Privatization, partnerships, and other creative strategies used in leisure-service agencies today.

THE ROLE OF FISCAL MANAGEMENT

Within every area of leisure-service operations, it is essential for managers to develop skills in handling the fiscal resources that provide the basis for all operations. Certainly, every form of public service, including recreation and park programming, must rely on adequate financial backing and intelligent fiscal decision making. The same principle applies in nonprofit, private membership, commercial, therapeutic, and other types of leisure-service agencies.

The tasks involved in fiscal management fall under two kinds of headings: (1) those functions that have traditionally been defined as appropriate procedures governing every stage of financial operations, which tend to be similar within all public and many nonprofit organizations; and (2) those innovative, creative, and entrepreneurial approaches that managers have evolved in recent years to combat funding cuts and the so-called era of austerity affecting community organizations.

Traditional Approaches

Characterizing the first approach, Hjelte and Shivers described fiscal management as the process including:

> The administration, custody, protection, and control of all revenues received by the recreation system from all sources and properly expending funds for approved purposes. . . . The purpose of fiscal management is to handle and be responsible for all money matters (financial records, accounting, collections, protection, controls, investments, expenditures, conformance to laws and administrative directives, property inventories, debt services, and other items of value).[3]

In all types of recreation, park, and leisure-service organizations, financial operations are governed by laws that control the receiving and expenditure of money. In cities, towns, villages, or county or park district systems, there are detailed regulations that outline the appropriate sources of funding, the procedures for presenting budget plans and having them approved, mechanisms for overseeing purchasing or other payments for utilities or contractual services, auditing and reporting requirements, and similar controls.

Creative Approaches

The second approach to fiscal management deals with the reality that far from being a minor area of public or nonprofit agency service that is fully subsidized by tax funds or charitable contributions, the provision of leisure services has become an immense element in the nation's economy. Beyond this, recreation, parks, and leisure-based programs and facilities have become an important source of revenue, employment, and healthy growth for many community and regions.

Today, the amounts of money spent on varied forms of commercially provided recreation are staggering. Literally hundreds of billions of dollars are given to major professional sports teams through lucrative television contracts, and even mediocre professional athletes routinely earn millions of dollars each year. Equally immense sums are spent on other kinds of entertainment and amusement, hobbies, or leisure-related goods and services.

At the same time, many of our most important forms of organized recreation services are literally starved for fiscal support. Four decades ago, the economist John Kenneth Galbraith wrote in a landmark book, *The Affluent Society,* that while the public is generally willing to spend huge sums *privately* on varied leisure pursuits, it is reluctant to provide adequate support for essential *public* services.[4]

In the period of fiscal constraint during the 1980s and early 1990s, many public recreation and park budgets were cut to the bone—resulting in inner-city playgrounds, parks, and recreation centers that were poorly staffed and maintained, with almost nonexistent programming. Similarly, many nonprofit and cultural arts agencies also suffered major cuts in funding and were forced to slash some programs and even to close some facilities.

Stemming from the need to become more fiscally self-sufficient, many leisure-service organizations moved forcefully into an entrepreneurial, marketing-oriented operational mode. Summing up the trend, John Crompton wrote:

> The role of the public recreation and park manager has changed from that of being an administrator primarily concerned with the allocation of government funding to that of an entrepreneur who operates in the public sector with minimal tax support. He or she is charged with the responsibility of aggressively seeking out resources for the agency and exploiting them to ensure that client groups receive maximum possible satisfaction.[5]

It should be stressed that while entrepreneurs are often referred to as "risk takers," they are not wild or irresponsible gamblers. Instead, they take calculated risks, making maximum use of market intelligence before venturing in new directions.

CHALLENGE TO AGENCY MANAGERS

How skilled and sophisticated must leisure-service managers be today to function successfully within the two areas of fiscal responsibility: (1) maintaining traditionally sound management processes and (2) providing innovative leadership in a highly competitive economic environment?

Realistically, it is *not* necessary for all leisure-service managers to become financial wizards. Provided that they have a basic understanding of the elements of budget making and fiscal management, and that they continue to learn and grow in this field, seeking expert help when necessary, they can operate successfully. Obviously, in larger organizations, particularly profit-seeking commercial recreation businesses, a higher level of financial expertise is helpful. However, in such settings, it is likely that managers will have gained such expertise both through formal education and practical experience as they climbed the career ladder to their present levels of authority. Normally, entry-level personnel are given fairly routine or mechanical tasks having to do with fiscal functions at the outset, and so they gradually gain familiarity with the overall system.

BUDGET OPERATIONS: PRINCIPLES AND METHODS

We now turn to an examination of several of the established functions of traditional fiscal management, beginning with an understanding of the use of budgets.

Meaning and Function of Budgets

The term *budget* comes from the French word *bougette,* meaning "bag" or "wallet." This would suggest that many leisure-service managers think of their budgets primarily as bags full (or partly full) of money, which they use to purchase equipment, hire personnel, or pay charges. However, the word should have a broader meaning. The budget should be thought of as a management plan through which a work program or project is outlined, including the financial details and schedules necessary to achieve predetermined goals. Ellen O'Sullivan defines *budget* as a

> . . . financial plan often including detailed income, work and resource allocation plans for carrying out a program of activities in a specific time period, often a fiscal year.[6]

The well-conceived and effectively presented budget should do the following:

1. Provide a general statement of the financial needs, resources, and plans of the organization, including an outline of all program elements and their costs and allocations for facilities and personnel.
2. Inform taxpayers and government officials (or in other types of organizations, stockholders, boards of trustees, college officials, hospital directors, or company managers) of the amounts of money spent, the sources of revenue, and the costs of achieving departmental goals.
3. Help in promoting standardized and simplified operational procedures by classifying all expenditures and requiring systematic procedures for approving them.

Whereas in the past a budget was often viewed as a one-year financial plan, sound practice now requires that budgeting be a continuous process, with planning, presenting, implementing, and auditing functions going on throughout the year in an ongoing cycle. In addition to the agency's annual budget, which sums up its overall operation, many smaller service units—such as program divisions, park maintenance branches, or individual special events—are likely to have their own budget plans.

Types of Budgets

The most common budget format is the line-item type, in which each category of spending is itemized according to its anticipated expenditure for the fiscal year ahead. Line-item budgets have several subtypes, including *object* classification, *function* classification, *organizational unit* classification, *performance* classification *by fund.*

Object Classification Line-Item Budget

This type of budget classifies all proposed expenditures according to a systematic breakdown of objects paid for by category. Typically, categories would include elements such as personal services, purchase of supplies and equipment, or contractual services. The major object groups in a widely used object classification system are as follows:

1000	Services—personal: involves salaries and wages
2000	Services—contractual: involves work performed, services rendered, or materials supplied on a contractual basis
3000	Commodities: supplies and materials
4000	Current charges: includes rent, insurance, licenses, etc.
5000	Current obligations: fixed expenses such as interest, taxes, loans, etc.
6000	Properties: cost of equipment, buildings, or land
7000	Debt payment

Although object classification budgets offer a convenient means of looking at the major categories in which money is spent, they do not relate expenditures meaningfully enough to programs or to the organizational units or administrative divisions that are assigned funding.

Classification by Function or Agency Unit

In some budget systems, therefore, proposed expenditures are assigned to the specific agency function they will serve, either in general terms that describe agencywide support services (such as parks maintenance, administration, or personnel) *or* the names of specific *department units* that carry out these tasks. This approach to budget planning may also include *program* budgeting, in which the sums assigned to specific branches of program delivery are itemized. For example, in a health and fitness program, such items as fitness testing, staff in-service training, or nutrition and weight-management classes might be assigned separate budget numbers and funding amounts.

Performance Budget

The performance budget represents a combination of object and function classification methods. Expenditures are classified by listing the main expenditures by object or categories of objects to be purchased (including services, materials, or other charges) in the left-hand vertical column and the functions of the departmental operation horizontally across the top of the page. By examining such a budget, it is possible to tell more clearly just *how* money is spent. For example, the budget will show exactly what amounts are allocated for items such as staff salaries, rentals, supplies and equipment, and printing and postage for a specific aspect of the program, such as senior citizens' centers. Increasingly, performance budgets are being used to isolate major units of work, or special programs, and to identify them and describe in detail their operation, purposes and costs.

To illustrate a budget plan that includes both department expenditures and revenues, Table 6.1 shows a budget summary for the Parks and Recreation Department of San Mateo, California. It identifies four kinds of budget figures: the appropriations *proposed* for a given year, the *amounts* adopted by the city council or other authority, the *actual* amounts spent, and the sums *projected* for the fiscal year ahead. It also designates the major program elements (cultural arts, etc.) and their costs; identifies the sources of budget funds, including both the general fund (tax appropriations) and other grants and earned revenues; and provides a breakdown of allocations into separate personnel, operating, and capital budget outlays.

TABLE 6.1. **Budget Summary, San Mateo, California Department of Parks and Recreation**

DEPARTMENT SUMMARY	Actual 1994–95	Adopted 1995–96	Estimated Actual 1995–96	Proposed 1996–97	Projected 1997–98
EXPENDITURES					
By Program					
Cultural arts	407,534	395,962	398,683	425,446	433,964
Community centers	1,349,723	1,425,631	1,415,388	1,397,050	1,428,468
Athletics	346,632	368,860	391,419	406,260	414,385
Aquatics	478,681	507,024	478,762	510,294	519,526
Youth services	291,535	299,747	329,668	400,156	408,153
Technical and administrative service	637,411	586,361	641,704	684,411	699,205
Landscape resources	2,143,162	2,343,914	2,183,978	2,515,348	2,561,054
Golf services	1,109,340	1,259,959	1,243,384	1,315,590	1,329,829
Capital improvements (transfer to fund 9)	343,300	224,500	224,500	368,500	384,000
Total	7,107,318	7,411,958	7,307,486	8,023,055	8,178,584
By Category					
Personnel	4,353,105	4,744,875	4,517,835	4,893,208	4,991,074
Operating	2,342,035	2,383,385	2,554,768	2,577,645	2,629,562
Capital outlay	68,878	59,198	10,383	183,702	173,948
Capital improvements (transfer to fund 9)	343,300	224,500	224,500	368,500	384,000
Total	7,107,318	7,411,958	7,307,486	8,023,055	8,178,584
REVENUES					
Recreation earned revenue			1,819,640	1,760,783	1,777,888
CDBG grant			10,000	10,600	10,812
Less fee waiver assistance			(32,000)	(32,000)	(32,640)
Recreation actual revenue			1,797,640	1,739,383	1,756,060
Parks revenue			18,000	24,917	25,314
General fund			4,023,962	4,574,665	4,683,381
Fund 11 subtotal			5,839,602	6,338,965	6,464,755
Golf revenue			1,675,000	1,818,116	1,928,116
Golf interest income			65,379	67,500	67,500
Use of golf fund balance			(272,495)	(201,526)	(281,787)
Fund 19 subtotal			1,467,884	1,684,090	1,713,829
Total			7,307,486	8,023,055	8,178,584

This reflects the distinction that is commonly made between operating and capital budgets. The *operating budget* is the document that contains detailed statements of all administrative costs in the form of personnel salaries, office rentals, gasoline, typing paper, baseballs, or paintbrushes required to operate the department for the course of one year. In many cities, the fiscal year is identified as July 1 to June 30, although it may be identical to the calendar year or any other legally authorized one-year period. In a few cases, budgets may be set up for a two-year period.

The *capital budget* is a separate document that includes plans and proposed expenditures for carrying out major purchases and construction projects of a substantial and long-term nature. These would include the purchase of heavy snow-removal trucks or parkland or the construction of new golf courses, ice rinks, or recreation buildings. They might include major renovation projects but would not include routine maintenance charges.

Classification by Fund

A final type of budget used by some leisure-service agencies classifies revenues or expenditures in different funds within the organization's overall fiscal structure. These might include the following types:

1. *Special revenue fund*—to account for the proceeds of specific revenue sources (other than special assignments) or to finance specified activities as required by law or administrative regulation;
2. *Debt service fund*—to account for the payment of interest and principal on long-term debt other than special assessment and revenue bonds;
3. *Capital project funds*—to account for the receipt and disbursement of monies used for the acquisition of capital facilities other than those financed by special assessment and by enterprise fund;
4. *Enterprise funds*—to account for the financing of services to the general public where all or most of the costs involved are paid in the form of charges by the users of such services (examples might include golf courses, skating rinks, or sportsmens' centers);
5. *Intragovernmental service funds*—to account for the financing of special activities and services performed by the designated organization unit within a governmental jurisdiction for other organization units within the same governmental jurisdiction.

THE BUDGET PROCESS

The budget process in recreation, park, and leisure-service agencies is normally divided into three stages: (1) preparation; (2) presentation and authorization; and (3) implementation.

Budget Preparation

The preparation of an annual budget is the responsibility of the agency's chief executive and his or her key staff members, usually under the leadership of a financial officer or other staff members entrusted with this task.

As indicated earlier, like the entire fiscal process, budget making must be carried out within a framework of applicable laws, regulations, and court decisions that have been translated into operational policies for government or other organizations. State-enabling laws, for example, and city charters or other special laws have usually assigned taxing powers to municipalities or other local government units, and have specified regulations that govern other management practices, such as employment of staff members, acquisition of properties, or passage of bond issues. Normally, such broad regulations are supplemented by local ordinances or administrative procedures that require an itemized budget of appropriations be placed before the city council, and that may also define the method of presentation, the calendar of presentation, required public hearings, the officials who must be consulted, or similar details.

Such controls do not usually apply in nonpublic organizations. Instead, the laws governing commercial enterprises might require that stockholders of a corporation receive detailed financial statements or prospectuses, as well as all major fiscal plans, before their implementation. In other specialized forms of leisure service, such as employee recreation programs, the armed forces, or therapeutic recreation, budget processes might simply require advanced presentation of fiscal plans (including anticipated revenues and expenditures) for review by agency comptrollers, a finance committee, or other administrators.

The actual task of budget preparation requires gathering a mass of data regarding past and current programs, revenues and expenditures, charges, deficits, and other elements that must be considered in making up the new budget plan. This task is greatly facilitated today by computer software that rapidly accumulates, sorts, accesses, and analyzes data of all kinds.

Varied approaches that are used by fiscal managers to make budget decisions today include *increment/decrement* budgeting, *zero-based* budgeting and *cost-benefit* analysis.

Increment/Decrement Budgeting

This is a budgeting method that consists of adding or subtracting a given percentage of the current budget in making up the new budget proposal, usually based on an administrative decision, or on projected growth or decline in agency operations for the period ahead. Each element in the budget is then subjected more or less uniformly to this percentage-based addition or reduction in funding, although there can be a measure of flexibility in its application.

Zero-Based Budgeting

This method, which came into vogue during the period of severe government agency cutbacks during the late 1970s and 1980s, is an approach requiring that every program element and expenditure be reevaluated annually to determine its relative merit. Not intended as a replacement for traditional budgeting procedures, it forces decisions to be made on points such as these:

1. Is the department overstaffed at its current level?
2. Does the department continue to serve a useful purpose and function in the overall operation of the organization?
3. Should a certain program or programs be curtailed to fund an alternative higher priority program?
4. Are available funds used to promote recreation goals and objectives, or promote an individual's whims?

Thus, rather than simply modifying the previous year's budget, or justifying only the additions or increases, zero-based budgeting requires total justification of every agency function to build a new budget.

Cost-Benefit Analysis

This is a somewhat similar approach that seeks to determine the value of different agency programs or service elements and the priority that should be assigned to them by balancing their fiscal costs against their positive derived outcomes. Cost-benefit analysis can be used to: (1) foster valid comparisons within and between operational facilities and program units; (2) permit the assignment of priorities to specific programs and services; (3) provide targets and guidelines for management decision making and resource allocation; (4) assist in continual evaluation of agency objectives and procedures; (5) provide valuable support data for justifying budget requests; (6) identify high- and low-cost programs and services as related to maintenance, administration, and direct leadership costs per participant-hour of service rendered; and (7) provide essential data for policy formulation and revisions.

Guidelines for Budget Preparation

In most large organizations, formal guidelines are prepared that outline the steps and procedures that must be followed in preparing annual budgets. Within the armed forces, for example, the Bureau of Naval Personnel issues a comprehensive manual that gives step-by-step instructions for using a Microsoft Excel computer program to develop annual budgets for non-appropriated fund (NAF) expenditures.

Normally, as part of all budget plans, specific expenditure items are accompanied by explanatory paragraphs, or "narratives," which explain and justify the recommended items. These may document the need for given expenditures, show whether they represent increases or decreases from past budget items, or summarize their inclusion based on cost-benefit analysis.

Steps of the Budget Hearing Process

In all public recreation and park agencies, and in many nonprofit or other types of leisure-service organizations, the budget preparation and hearing process must follow a fixed sequence of steps during the year. For example, the 1997 Budget Guide of the East Bay, California, Regional Park District outlines the stages that budget development goes through from May through December as follows:

May–June	Preparation and review of financial forecasts
May–August	Capital improvement plan preparation
July	Policy and criteria setting/goals and objectives drafted
August–September	Budget preparation and recommendation
October	Board and Park Advisory Committee review
November–December	Public hearings and adoption

As in other municipal or special-district recreation and park agencies, the budget development process follows a sequence of request proposals being developed at divisional levels, reviewed and revised through other administrative or financial management offices, and ultimately being approved by other committees and submitted to the appropriate officials and boards as a final proposal. In the East Bay Park District, budget development involves the following steps:

> The Executive Committee of the Board of Directors assesses the District's financial condition and reviews the Board's objectives for the new year. The General Manager sets the criteria for developing departmental objectives and budget requests. The departments then submit their requests to the Assistant Controller, Finance, who reviews the requests, discusses them with the Assistant General Managers, and makes a budget recommendation to the General Manager. After reviewing the objectives and the corresponding appropriations, the General Manager submits a preliminary draft budget to the Board Finance Committee and the Park Advisory Committee for their review and recommendations. As soon as these recommendations are received, a proposed budget is drafted and submitted to the Board. Copies are made available to the public, and two public hearings are held. After the public hearings, the Board makes its final recommendations and any revisions. The budget is typically adopted before the beginning of the fiscal year.[7]

Throughout this process, emphasis is placed on making sure that all budget items reflect the legitimate needs of the community and constituency to be served and the goals of the agency. It is a mistake to inflate a budget request deliberately, in the expectation that it will be reduced by a certain percentage to come out with a reasonable budget total. During the course of review by the city's financial analyst, hearings, and other means of examining budgets, each item will be carefully scrutinized and *must* be strongly justified.

BUDGET APPROVAL HEARINGS

The municipal council or other local public legislative body usually schedules a series of public hearings on all of its proposed budget sections to provide the general public with an opportunity to voice pros and cons. Such hearings should be well-publicized and attended.

Public hearings represent a crucial stage if the budget that has taken so much effort in preparation is to be carefully considered and fairly evaluated. Public hearings, whether on a village, town, county, or large city level, can be tense and sometimes extremely difficult. The introduction of pressure groups and political lobbying, the presence of committee chairpersons from the city's legislative body, and clashes between a mayor and a city council or between representatives of different districts of a city all create a potentially challenging atmosphere.

Careful Preparation

The recreation and park executive must be thoroughly familiar with the proposed budget, including each item and its justification. It can be extremely embarrassing for the manager to fail to locate needed background materials or the documentation for items under sharp questioning by an appropriations committee chairperson.

Opening Statement

The manager should make a brief opening statement that describes the prime thrust of the department, its goals, and some past successes. The statement should clarify the new directions and priorities found in the budget and should present a positive and optimistic picture of the work of the department. This statement should be delivered in a relaxed, conversational manner rather than ponderously read.

Response to Questions

Responses to questions raised at the hearing should be short and informative. Just as in a courtroom, do not answer more than is asked and do not wander off into dangerous territory that may open up discussion points not within the area under questioning. Responses should be precise and factual, not philosophical.

Demeanor of Manager

At all times the manager should strive to be affirmative and confident. He or she should not backpedal or vacillate under fire. It is a serious mistake to reply to challenges with such comments as, "Well, I didn't really expect you would pass that item" or "I don't feel I can fight for this program." Such expressions of weakness may imperil the entire budget presentation.

After public budget hearings and behind-the-scenes meetings and revisions—including possible estimates of revenues during the year—additional changes are usually made to the budget proposal. However, barring sudden changes in the municipality's financial position or other unusual circumstances, if the plan is a sound one it will be accepted and authorized for the coming year.

SOURCES OF LEISURE-SERVICE FUNDS

In a 1997 research report published in the *Journal of Park and Recreation Administration*, Gladwell and Sellers summarized the fiscal status and financial trends of public park and recreation departments in medium-sized communities in the southeastern United States. Comparing studies done in the late 1980s and mid-1990s, they reported that the data suggested:

> . . . positive trends in total operating and capital budgets, per capita spending, ratio of spending for parks and recreation to general local expenditures, and employment levels of both full-time permanent staff and temporary part-time staff. Local taxes were the primary revenue source for funding local parks and recreation. User fees and charges were used more frequently as a revenue source for operating expenditures than as a revenue source for capital outlay.[8]

Taxes as Primary Funding Source

Local taxes represent the most common means of financing the ongoing operations of local public recreation and park departments. They fall into four major categories: general, special, millage, and special assessment taxes.

General Taxes

General taxes represent the most common form of tax revenues used to support recreation and parks. They consist of the local real estate or property taxes, which are the chief source of municipal funds or of local school-district financing. These are derived by assessing industrial or residential property within the borders of the municipality at a given rate; this is usually expressed as a percentage ranging from 20 percent to 50 percent of market value. A tax rate is established by the municipality for a given fiscal year. When the assessed value of the property is multiplied by the tax rate, the resulting figure is the tax that must be paid by the property owner.

The general real estate tax normally provides support for services such as police, highways, health, sanitation, recreation and parks, and similar services. Not infrequently, in suburban areas individuals must pay separate taxes to the county, township, or village for different services provided by each of these units of government. Normally, however, all real estate taxes are paid into the general fund of a single government unit, and it is from this source that budget allocations are made to support public services.

Special Taxes

In some cities and more commonly in areas that are served by a special park or recreation and park district, special taxes may be used to support public recreation. Thus, taxes on liquor, amusement admissions, or items such as motorboat fuel may be assigned directly to the support of municipal recreation and park services.

An example of a special tax levied to support construction of a large new recreation facility may be found in a special sales tax approved by the Texas legislature, assessed against the residents of Arlington, Texas, to pay for a new baseball stadium and other park facilities in that city. Based on this precedent, the city of North Richland Hills, Texas, passed an additional sales tax to support a $40 million park-improvement program, including a new 23-acre family aquatic complex.

Millage Taxes

A millage tax represents a specific tax (usually low and therefore expressed in mills) leveled against the assessed value of residential or industrial property. Here, too, the amount derived is assigned directly to a recreation and park fund and used exclusively for that purpose. In some states, such as California, millage taxes are authorized in the state education code and assigned directly to the support of school recreation and other community-related programs.

Special Assessment Taxes

In some municipalities, the custom is to tax only residents who stand to benefit from a particular service for the support of that service. Special assessment taxes are frequently used to support highway and sewer construction programs; in some cases they are also used to support recreation and park developments for residents in separate districts of a community.

Bond Issues

Bonds represent a second major support of municipal recreation and park programs. They are normally applied only to the financial support of major capital development programs. With respect to recreation and park departments, they are used chiefly for the acquisition of land and the development of major facilities such as large parks, swimming pools, stadiums, ice rinks, sportsmen's centers, or golf courses. In some cases a municipality or large recreation and park district may float a substantial bond issue that includes a number of separate recreation and park development projects; in other cases, a bond issue may be intended to support the development of a single major project.

Bonds represent a form of deferred payment by which the cost of any government enterprise can be spread over a period of years rather than applied to a single year's budget. In addition to recreational and park facilities, they are also used to pay for the development of schools, highways, sewer systems, and similar projects. Bonds are normally to be repaid within a ten- to thirty-year period, thus ensuring that those who will use the facilities over this period will pay for them at a reasonable rate.

There are several types of bonds, which vary according to their method of retirement: term bonds, callable bonds, and serial bonds.

Term Bonds

In the term bond, the government agency promises to pay off the entire principal at the end of a given period of time. Normally, it would use the *sinking fund* method, under which an annual sum is put aside each year, with the amount accumulating each year until the full principal has been set aside at the end of the term of the bond.

Callable Bonds

Callable bonds are a special type of bond in which the government has the option of calling in bond issues for payment at a specified time before the end of its term or at any time it chooses. Since bond interest rates tend to fluctuate, it is thus possible for the issuer to call in a bond and reissue it at lower interest rates, depending on market conditions.

Serial Bonds

Under the serial bond method of financing capital outlays, the government pays the bond purchaser a specified portion of the principal, plus interest, each year that the bond issue is in effect. Thus, a percentage of the bond is reduced each year through payments of approximately equal sums. This is similar to the way in which homeowners normally pay off mortgage indebtedness over a period of years.

Other Types of Bonds

Bonds may also be classified according to their method of gathering funds for debt service. *General obligation bonds* are those in which the payment on interest and principal is drawn from the general tax revenues of the municipality. *Assessment bonds* are those in which the money is derived from special assessments on residents benefiting from whatever has been built, such as a golf course, marina, or cultural center.

Government Grants

A third major source of funding for local public recreation and park departments is federal and state grants. For example, during the mid- and late 1970s, a considerable share of funding for local public agencies came from four federal assistance programs: the Land and Water Conservation Fund, the Community Development Block Grant program, the Comprehensive Employment and Training Act program, and General Revenue Sharing funds.

During the early 1980s, many such programs were cut sharply or discontinued entirely. However, there continue to be a number of federal or state grants directed to meeting the needs of special populations, such as the aging or the disabled, or to assist in facility development. For example, Table 6.2 shows grants obtained by the Phoenix, Arizona, Parks, Recreation and Library Department over a recent five-year period to support its At-Risk Youth program. These sources included special funding from the state supreme court, Division for Children, community development block grants, the governor's office, Department of Housing and Urban Development, and the Phoenix Police Department, as well as grants from United Way and the Nestle Corporation.

Other Funding Sources: Foundation Grants

There are several different types of foundations: (1) *special purpose foundations,* created by will or trust instrument to meet a special charitable purpose; (2) *company-sponsored foundations,* tax-exempt nonprofit bodies legally separate from the donor company but with trustee boards that facilitate corporate giving; (3) *community foundations,* composite foundations usually set up as trusts, functioning under some form of community control to serve a given community or area; and (4) *family foundations,* usually established by a living person or family rather than by bequest to serve as a continuing vehicle for gift giving and as a means of reducing taxes.

TABLE 6.2.   Examples of Grants Supporting Human-Service Programming

City of Phoenix
Parks, Recreation and Library Department
At-Risk Youth Division—Grant Programs
1993–1996

Grant & Funding Source	1993/94	1994/95	1995/96	1996/97
Summer Recreation, Arizona Supreme Court	$63,000.00	$49,000.00	$31,000.00	—
Step Program, Urban Parks and Recreation Recovery (UPARR)	$15,000.00	—	—	—
Teens N' Training, JTPA	$70,000.00	$105,000.00	—	—
Total Education Enrichment Network, Comcare	$51,000.00	$53,000.00	$51,000.00	$122,432.00
Nestle's Very Best in Youth Project, Nestle Corp.	$10,000.00	$10,000.00	—	—
Police Activities League-Recreation, AZ Supreme Ct	—	$22,594.00	$17,000.00	$11,384.00
Curfew Diversion Program, CDBG	—	$41,000.00	—	—
Juvenile Diversion Program, AZ Supreme Court	—	$50,000.00	$31,000.00	$25,000.00
City Streets Mobile Unit, AZ Division for Children	$22,500.00	$17,000.00	$11,250.00	—
Youth Sports Program, US HUD	—	$75,000.00	$50,000.00	—
Youth Recreation Programs, AZ Governor's Office	—	$250,000.00	—	—
X-Tattoo: Tattoo Removal Program, United Way	—	—	$13,000.00	—
New Turf Gang and Drop Out Prevention, Comcare	—	—	$132,000.00	$51,177.00
Truancy Diversion, AZ Governor's Office/Children	—	—	$25,000.00	$25,000.00
Domestic Violence, AZ Governor's Office/Women	—	—	$109,000.00	—
WUZZ-UP Teen Cable Program, HUD	—	—	—	$52,000.00
Enterprise Community Truancy Program, HUD	—	—	$100,000.00	$200,000.00
X-Tattoo-Neighborhood 301 Blockwatch, PHX PD	—	—	—	$9,930.00
Police Activities League (Staffing) AZ Supreme Court	—	—	$50,000.00	$38,000.00
Domestic Violence/Violence Prevention, DOJ	—	—	—	$178,000.00
JTPA IIB—SYETP, City of Phoenix Human Services	—	—	—	$98,000.00
Totals per Year	$231,500.00	$672,594.00	$620,250.00	$810,923.00
Total to Date				$2,335,267.00

The leisure-service agency that seeks funding from foundations must approach the task in an intelligent and well-organized way. It is important to develop proposals that will clearly fit the general purpose of a foundation, that they will regard as significant and needed, that will be economical in terms of expected outcomes, and that do not represent already available services.

The following strategies are suggested for recreation and park agencies that seek to develop grant proposals for foundations but may also readily be adapted to other types of fund-raising. They involve several steps.

1. *Establish a foundations committee.* The department should develop an ongoing, capable group of staff members and interested citizens—including business-people, professionals, and other individuals—who are willing to assist in this task. The committee must have a competent chairperson to lead its efforts.
2. *Prepare lists of foundations.* Several excellent sources are available in public libraries. These should be carefully analyzed to identify foundations whose purposes and past pattern of giving seem appropriate to the needs of the recreation and park department.
3. *Develop a proposal concept.* Foundations committee members consider possible approaches or concepts and select those with greatest potential value that might have specific appeal for appropriate foundations. At this point, they may sound out the foundation to determine its possible interest in the project, if personal contacts are feasible at this stage.
4. *Prepare a formal grants proposal.* This should contain five carefully presented elements: a *needs assessment* analysis to justify the proposal, a description of the *project's goals* and *objectives,* a review of the *pertinent literature* or other background information, the proposed *plan of action* or methodology, and the *budget section,* including information on staffing, timetable, and cooperating agencies.
5. *Present the proposal.* The grant proposal should be neatly packaged and sent by mail with an accompanying letter or should be delivered personally if personal contact has been developed.
6. *Follow through.* Shortly after the proposal has been sent—usually within two to three weeks—a meeting should be requested to discuss it. At this point, it is possible to present arguments supporting the proposal, to indicate a willingness to modify it or accept other suggestions of the foundation, and generally to work together to bring the proposal to the point of approval.

Effective strategies for developing grants proposals include the need to consult with community groups, develop partnerships with other agencies for the projects that are proposed, and aim at important social needs. Also, government or nonprofit organizations should be prepared to shoulder a substantial portion of the costs of the project under consideration themselves, and to undertake full responsibility for it at a given point.

Fees and Charges

Fees and charges—often referred to as "revenue sources"—have become an increasingly important source of needed income for most leisure-service agencies.

Types of Fees and Charges.

At an early point, Hines categorized the most common types of fees and charges as follows:

1. *Entrance fees.* Charges made to enter large parks, botanical gardens, zoos, or other developed recreational areas, such as fairgrounds, game preserves, or historical sites;

2. *Admission fees.* Charges for entering buildings offering exhibits or performances, such as grandstands or museums;

3. *Rental fees.* Charges for the exclusive use of property that is not consumed or destroyed and that is returned, such as boats, cabins, canoes, checking facilities, skis, archery equipment, or parking;

4. *User fees.* Charges made for the use of facilities or participation in activities usually carried on simultaneously with others, such as artificial ice rinks, ski lifts, driving ranges, swimming pools, or golf courses;

5. *License and permit fees.* Charges for the right to carry out certain activities, such as hunting, fishing, or camping; vending or exhibition permits;

6. *Special-service fees.* Charges for special or unusual services, such as entry fees for team competition, instruction in organized classes, summer camp enrollment, and workshops or clinics.[9]

In the past, most public recreation and park departments were satisfied to obtain approximately 10 percent of their operating funds from fees, charges, concessions, rentals, and similar sources. By the mid-1980s, many departments were gathering as much as 25 percent or more of their budgets from such revenues, and they expected some elements of their programs to be totally self-sufficient financially.

Figure 6.1 shows how, in one California city, the proportion subsidy through tax allocations for recreation programs declined from approximately 82 percent in 1972–73 to 51 percent in 1992–93. Revenues through fees and charges increased in the athletic program alone from $12,000 in 1972–73 to $250,000 in 1992–93—a twenty-fold expansion. In addition to growing participation, these changes reflected the shift in many municipal recreation and park departments from highly subsidized, low- or no-fee activities, to more formal registered activity that is self-supported.

Pricing Methods

What strategies are used in setting prices for programs and services in leisure-service agencies? Should fees for participation in a health spa operated by a municipal recreation and park department or YMCA be comparable to those charged by a chain of commercial fitness centers? What are the impacts of fees at different levels, in terms of excluding major population groups that cannot afford to pay program charges, or in terms of attracting others who prefer the aura of exclusivity or high quality that a stiff registration fee may convey?

Pricing approaches vary according to the nature of the sponsoring organization and its philosophy and social mandate. Public and voluntary agencies are generally more obligated to consider factors of social need than are private or commercial organizations. However, the latter providers must be aware

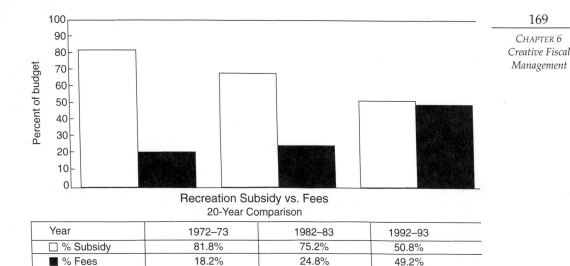

Year	1972–73	1982–83	1992–93
☐ % Subsidy	81.8%	75.2%	50.8%
■ % Fees	18.2%	24.8%	49.2%

Proportion of subsidy steadily drops

FIGURE 6.1. Proportion of subsidy through tax allocations.

Source: San Mateo, Cal. Reengineering Progress Report, Oct. 1994.

that they can price themselves out of business by setting fees that are too high or that they can create ill will through unreasonable pricing tactics. In some cases, pricing policies may be differentiated by client groups; a rental charge may be higher for a profit-oriented organization than a nonprofit group. A public agency may charge higher fees in wealthy neighborhoods than in poorer ones or may waive charges or provide scholarships for disadvantaged participants.[10]

Variable pricing for the same activity within a single agency's program may be based on the desirability of given time slots. For example, in a commercially owned tennis complex, much higher hourly rates will be set for prime hours on weekends than during the week. Thus, prices may be deliberately used to redistribute the participant load, by setting higher fees at peak demand times, such as major holiday weekends at camping or other outdoor recreation attractions, and lower fees at less-attended times.

Similarly, lower prices may be offered for children, elderly persons, groups of individuals, or members of affiliated organizations. Discounts may be given to patrons willing to register for longer periods, accept fewer services, volunteer their time, or assist an agency in other ways. In setting membership fee levels for many recreation programs, public recreation and park agencies may also use residence/nonresidence, age levels, length of period of participation, and family status as pricing factors, as shown in Figure 6.2, the fee scale for a major fitness and aquatic facility in Prince William County, Virginia.

In another example, the Vail, Colorado, Recreation District sets different fees for its summer day camp, based on three categories of residence (Nonresident, Eagle County resident, and Vail Recreation District taxpayers), the period of participation, and "second-child" fee discounts (Fig. 6.3).

DON'T MISS THIS OPPORTUNITY!
RENEW YOUR PASS PLAN NOW!

Pass Plan prices will increase on May 1, 1992

Regular Six-Month Pass

	Through April 30, 1992		May 1, 1992	
Type	Resident	Nonresident	Resident	Nonresident
Adult	$175	$220	$195	$245
Youth (under 18)	$130	$165	$150	$190
Couple	$265	$330	$295	$370
Dependent (3–22)*	$ 50	$ 75	$ 75	$100
Senior	$ 90	$110	$ 90	$110
Senior Couple	$175	$220	$175	$220

Regular One-Year Pass

	Through April 30, 1992		May 1, 1992	
Type	Resident	Nonresident	Resident	Nonresident
Adult	$315	$390	$350	$440
Youth (under 18)	$235	$295	$265	$330
Couple	$475	$585	$525	$655
Dependent (3–22)*	$100	$150	$150	$190
Senior	$160	$195	$160	$195
Senior Couple	$315	$390	$315	$390

* Dependent passes are available with the purchase of an Adult, Couple, Senior, or Senior Couple Pass. If 18–22 years old, the dependent must be a current full-time college student.

No Increase in the Special Pass

Although pass plan renewals will be taken during all hours of operation, the following schedule outlines the times during which additional staff will be available to provide speedy processing.

April 2–23

Tuesdays and Thursdays	6:00–9:00 pm
Sundays	12:00–3:00 pm

April 25–30

Saturday	11:00 am–2:00 pm
Sunday	12:00–3:00 pm
Monday through Thursday	6:00–9:00 pm

For more information call 791-2338, extension 102

FIGURE 6.2. Fee scale, Chinn Aquatics and Fitness Center, Prince William County, Virginia.

In general, the public has accepted the escalation of fees for recreation, park, and leisure-service programs and access, provided that it has been gradual, accompanied by effective public relations explanations of the need for fees, and in many cases linked to annual pass arrangements or family discounts.

Such fee scales make it clear that many public and nonprofit leisure-service agencies charge substantial fees for participation. In the case of outdoor recreation and travel organizations like Woodswomen, Inc. (see p. 107), they may

Facility Member Category		Joining Fee	Monthly Fee
Full Facility Age 18+	(family)	$250.00	$53.00 per adult
	(individual)	$200.00	$53.00
Special Hours* Age 18+	(family)	$200.00	$43.00 per adult
	(individual)	$150.00	$43.00
*weekdays:	8:30 A.M. – 4:00 P.M.	8:00 P.M. – 10:00 P.M.	
*weekends:	anytime		

Facility Member Category		Joining Fee	Monthly Fee
Teens Age 13–17	(parent is a member)	none	$26.00
	(parent not a member)	$75	$26.00
Under Age 13	Free when accompanied by a parent who is a Facility Member.		

Passport Membership		Joining Fee	Monthly Fee
Full Facility Age 18+	(family*)	$300.00	$110.00 (2 adults)
	(individual)	$200.00	$60.00

Membership in the entire YMCA of San Francisco Association.
*2 adults living at the same household.

FIGURE 6.3. **Facility membership fee schedule, Peninsula Family YMCA, San Francisco, California.**

amount to thousands of dollars for specific activities. However, their revenues should *not* be viewed as profit; instead, they help to sustain all program services and often are used to subsidize other recreation activities.

Other Issues

In addition to determining pricing levels related to fees for program participation or admission to facilities, there are several other areas of fiscal policy in which appropriate charges or costs must be determined. These include:

1. Determining appropriate rental charges for the use of publicly owned facilities by community organizations.
2. Conversely, establishing appropriate rental fees that the public department can pay for the facilities of other organizations that it uses for activities.
3. Setting fees for organizations, such as companies or private-membership associations, that register groups of participants in public programs, or that obtain other special recreation services.
4. Determining appropriate rates of return from concessionaires operating in public recreation and park areas, or who are subcontracting the operation of public facilities.

As an example of how fees and charges are determined for the use of facilities, the director of an aquatic center at Oklahoma City Community College points out that renting pool lanes to local swim teams provides substantial income through several months of the year. He writes:

> . . . [W]e charge $5.50 [per lane] an hour, and our gross annual income is approximately $30,000. Additional fees can be charged for use of workout equipment, timing systems exercise equipment, and more. . . . [When hosting competitive swim meets] we currently charge $50 an hour for the lap pool or diving well, or $75 an hour for exclusive use of the entire facility [and other charges for lifeguards, security, and maintenance and janitorial services].[11]

Many public recreation and park departments also gather revenues through the rental of halls, meeting rooms, indoor arenas, picnic areas, and similar facilities to private individuals or groups, for parties, conferences, or other events.

Concessions

A closely related type of revenue source for public recreation, park, and leisure-service agencies involves the use of concessions. Under such arrangements, public recreation and park managers authorize private individuals or businesses to sell merchandise or services in parks, stadiums, or other publicly owned facilities. Concessions are generally granted when the public department cannot provide a service efficiently or economically in comparison to the commercial organization. Some of the areas of service in which concessions are commonly granted are boat rentals, refreshment stands, equipment shops, and instructional services.

While the sale of refreshments might appear to be a relatively minor source of income, in reality it may yield substantial sums. Many motion picture chains depend heavily on theater sales of popcorn, candy, soft drinks, and other refreshments. In baseball stadiums, which have traditionally been the settings for inexpensive family outings, costs have climbed to the point that a typical family visit to Atlanta's Turner field in the late 1990s—including four average-price tickets, parking, two game programs, two souvenir caps, four hot dogs, four soft drinks, and two small beers—cost $129.16.[12]

Gifts and Bequests

A unique source of funding for many leisure-service agencies consists of gifts and bequests from private sources, such as individual donors, family foundations, or business contributors. Some large city parks have been the personal gift of a public-spirited individual or family. Larger estates as well as smaller properties have often been bequeathed to municipalities with the understanding that the land would be used solely for recreation and park purposes.

A recently developed strategy that many colleges and universities have used successfully in gathering alumni support has been urging potential contributors to name their institutions in their wills. Some leisure-service organizations have begun to use this approach; a number of suburban YMCAs now urge their members to make them part of their estate planning through wills, trusts, or insurance policies.

Sale of Merchandise

A growing fund-raising approach for many nonprofit organizations has involved the manufacture and sale of a wide variety of items, which usually are decorated with the logo of the agency involved. This approach has the twofold effect of (1) raising funds directly on profit from the sales and (2) expanding community awareness of the organization by making its image visible in many settings.

The Police Athletic League, for example, manufactures and sells the following articles: sports bags and carrying cases, windbreaker jackets, T-shirts, PAL jewelry, briefcases, playing cards, and numerous other items (Fig. 6.4). As part of the sales message, they suggest:

> These items can be purchased for your exclusive use. You might also consider purchasing items for use as gifts to show you realize the worth of your volunteers, coaches, Board of Directors, and supporters within your own organization.[13]

In a related approach to fund-raising, many public recreation and park departments have published *gift catalogs*. These are portfolios that itemize and illustrate the specific needs of the department in a solicitation of outright donations. The purpose, value, and cost of each item are listed so that recreation and park departments or voluntary organizations can directly encourage private givers to make a contribution geared to their gift-giving capability or in line with their particular needs.

Similarly, the South East Consortium for Special Services, Inc., in Westchester County, New York, publishes a "Share a Dream Catalog," which solicits contributions to finance various agency special projects serving individuals with disabilities.

Grants from Lottery Profits

Another special source of income for leisure-service agencies today may come from the sales of state lotteries, which are generally required to give a portion of their profits to important social-service activities, such as programming for senior citizens.

A useful example is the Province of Saskatchewan in Canada, where several different lottery games, such as *Lotto 6/49*, the *Provincial*, and *Sport Select*, provide funds for hundreds of volunteer groups throughout the province. For example, in a recent year, lottery proceeds amounted to approximately $30 million, which was distributed through Sport, Culture and Recreation Advisory Committees to volunteer organizations and to assist in funding an International Children's Festival, the Saskatchewan Summer Games, and many other events and programs.

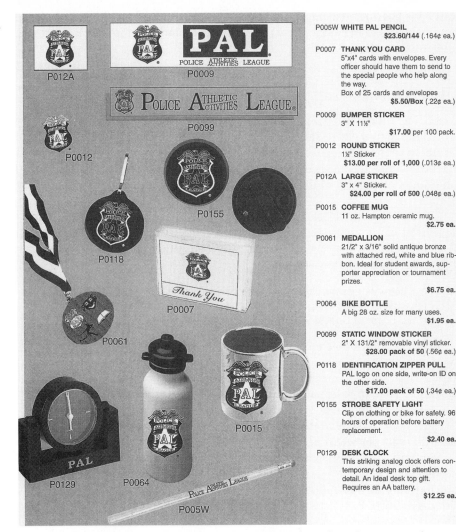

FIGURE 6.4. Example of brochure promoting sales of equipment and promotional accessories: Police Athletic League.

While the use of gambling to finance public and nonprofit recreation activities may seem unusual, it has its parallel in bingo games, which have provided substantial funding through the years to religious institutions and other civic groups. Similarly, many other organizations sponsor Las Vegas Nights or other gambling events, and numerous armed forces bases have slot machines, video poker, and similar forms of gambling.

Commercial Sponsorships

Over the past two decades, many amateur sports organizations and events have gained financial support through the sponsorship of large corporations that have helped build their stadiums or arenas, or sponsored youth-training programs or tournaments.

Typically, the names of major soft-drink companies, insurance companies, banks, airlines, or other huge corporations are attached to teams, and their logos appear on stadiums or uniforms. In cooperation with public recreation and park departments, companies may sponsor marathons, bike races, skating competitions, and similar events—some on a national scale. This sort of mutual assistance is extremely valuable to the public or nonprofit agency serving youth because the commercial concern provides a regional or national framework for events, organizes and publicizes them, and provides substantial prizes and awards.

GENERAL FUND-RAISING STRATEGIES

Many nonprofit community organizations conduct intensive fund-raising drives that incorporate all of the methods just described. These may include a variety of special techniques. Smith, Bucklin Associates, for example, describe *personal solicitations, direct mail, telemarketing,* and the *sponsorship of special events* as tools used by nonprofit organizations to gather contributions. They stress that solicitation packages should contain clear and concise statements about the organization's fund-raising goals, explain why given projects or services are needed, identify the benefits that donors receive, and offer different options for support or participation.[14]

Employee Recreation Revenues

Employee recreation and related personnel services often derive much of their financial support directly from the sponsoring company in the form of funds to build or maintain facilities or salaries for professional staff members. However, many employee recreation programs are also supported fully or in part by annual dues for membership in an employee association or by fees for participating in specific activities. Substantial funding may be derived from cigarette, soft drink, canteen, or other vending machine profits. Increasingly, such programs are relying on their own efforts to provide financial support for their activities, with a self-sufficiency concept governing classes, clubs, sports competition, or travel activities. In addition, many employee services also include discount purchasing plans and similar activities, which may yield a margin of profit.

Campus Recreation

Recreation programs in colleges and universities are generally supported by three different types of sources: (1) the use of institutional funds to assist intramural or student union programs as an important student service; (2) the use of special student activity fees, which are charged on an annual or semester basis, usually at time of registration; and (3) specific fees paid by students, faculty members, or staff to take part in given activities. In addition to these sources, other ways of financing college intramural sports and recreation programs include:

1. *Entry fees and dues*—either charged individually or for teams when entering a league, tournament, or special event;
2. *Admissions fees*—charged to attend or take part in sports nights, carnivals, professional shows or performances, exhibition games, showing of sports films, school dances, or similar events;
3. *Sales*—arrangements made with companies that provide schools with catalogues and items to sell for fund-raising projects, such as magazine subscriptions, cookies, candy, school stationery, or similar products; students may sell these on a voluntary basis or for a percentage of sales income;
4. *Automatic vending machines*—profit from income of vending machines placed in athletic or college union facilities, which sell cigarettes, snacks, soft drinks, or similar products;
5. *One-day special projects*—car washes, paper drives, cake sales, can and bottle recycling collections, volunteering for community service projects, marathons, and similar events.

Military Recreation

As indicated earlier, funding support of armed forces MWR programs is of two types: (1) *appropriated money*, which is allocated by Congress as part of general support of the armed forces, and (2) *nonappropriated money*, which includes revenues derived from post exchange profits, vending machines, military club profits, fees for participation in programs, and similar sources. The proportion of nonappropriated funding has risen steadily since the mid- and late 1970s, and many recreation programs in the armed forces are currently required to have a specified level of self-sufficiency. Indeed, total exchange sales rose in the mid-1980s to over $6 billion, and substantial nonappropriated funds were used to build and renovate commissaries, exchanges, clubs, and other MWR facilities.

Despite this trend, the core of armed forces recreation programs must be supported by appropriated funds that are used both to construct major facilities and to pay for the full-time military and civilian professional personnel who manage these operations. Within this framework, many armed forces recreation programs provide an interesting blend of social-service–oriented activities, such as counseling, abuse-cessation workshops, consumer-education, or similar activities that are normally free of charge and others that are clearly recreational and that have fees for participation.

Therapeutic Recreation

Recreation services to special populations are provided in so many different kinds of settings—nursing homes, special schools for the developmentally disabled, mental health centers, physical rehabilitation or long-term care hospitals, camps for disabled children, or other community-based programs—that no single form of funding is typical of them. Teaff and Van Hyning point out that leisure services in health-care settings like hospitals were traditionally funded from the operation's general revenues. However, in recent years, they write:

> [E]fforts have been made to encourage leisure services to generate their own revenues from services provided directly to patients and clients.[15]

Within this approach, recreation is regarded as an ancillary service charged to Blue Cross or Blue Shield plans, commercial insurance carriers, Medicaid, or other organizations that pay for contracted medical costs. The term *third party* refers to the distinction between the individual receiving the service (first party), the institution providing it (second party), and the organization paying for it (third party). Increasingly, therapeutic recreation specialists in treatment settings are being expected to meet the standards of service and procedural requirements necessary for such reimbursement.

In contrast, community-based special recreation programs for persons with disabilities rely on many of the same kinds of fund-raising strategies as other nonprofit community organizations: membership fees, government and foundation grants, merchandise sales, gift catalogues, direct mail solicitation, telemarketing, special events, and similar methods.

BUDGET EXECUTION: ACCOUNTING AND AUDITING

When a budget plan has been approved, including both projections of moneys to be spent and anticipated revenues from the kinds of sources just described, it must be put into action. A key concern here is that all fiscal practices follow approved procedures, both in general legal terms and with respect to the policies of the agency itself. Exact records must be kept with rigorous accounting and auditing controls, and reports must be issued at stipulated times for review by governing authorities.

To illustrate the practices followed by leisure-service organizations of all kinds, the following statement describes the responsibility of local leagues, as outlined in the *Operating Manual of Little League Baseball:*

> It is the responsibility of a league's Board of Directors to require its treasurer to keep accurate financial records and make adequate financial reports monthly, and a final report once a year at the close of the fiscal period. . . .
>
> It is recommended that the league secure the services of a Public Accountant to set up such books and records and assist the treasurer in the proper recording of transactions and the preparation of financial reports.[16]

The operating manual then goes on to describe a number of the financial procedures that must be followed by all Little League officers. These procedures are generally considered part of the overall process of budget execution.

This is the actual process of administering the disbursements, receipts, and other transactions of the agency that have been approved in its budget. In the cases of public recreation and park departments, the process must conform with state law as it governs the fiscal operation of municipalities within its borders.

Effective Budgetary Controls

An essential element in executing an annual budget is a work program, which outlines tasks to be performed, standards of service and efficiency, and methods to be used. Such a program defines each task, how often it is to be carried out, how long it should take, and what staffing it requires. Thus, it breaks down all departmental functions into measurable units. Since overall costs have already been calculated in the budget, it is possible to measure the cost of each unit of service or activity and thus to control the amount of expenditures within each area of maintenance or program leadership.

With such a work program, an allotment system may be set up to schedule expenditures on a monthly or quarterly basis. This provides a means of control through which all funds are spaced out properly through the year and in which it should not normally be necessary for any expenses to go beyond the allotted amount.

As an example of cost-control procedures within the armed forces, the U.S. Navy outlines exact procedures that must be followed with respect to all spending or revenue-gathering practices. Anne Hemingway describes the role of cost centers on thousands of ships, bases, aircraft squadrons, or other Navy units, which spend millions of dollars annually to support operations:

> Funding normally is issued quarterly in the form of operating targets (OPTARs) which are administrative limits on the use of funds. A cost center OPTAR manager is assigned to account for the cost center's authorized funds. . . . [He/she] typically prepares requisitions, travel orders, certifies invoices, and reconciles all transactions in the cost center's OPTAR log.[17]

FINANCIAL ACCOUNTING

All of the procedures that have been described fit under the broad heading of the "financial accounting system." Accounting is concerned with systematically gathering, recording, and reporting all data related to the fiscal operations of an agency or business organization. It provides an accurate, up-to-date picture of all income and expenditures, payrolls, property inventories and requisitions, and other financial transactions. Basically, it represents the built-in watchdog or monitor that helps safeguard and control the fiscal management process.

Customarily, financial records and reports must be verified by accountants independent of the agency whose financial status and performance is being measured. Different types of organizations have different reporting requirements; these are prescribed by various agencies, such as the American Institute of Certified Public Accountants (AICPA), the Financial Accounting Standards

---

All such processes must not only be carefully checked, monitored, and recorded, but must be able to withstand critical scrutiny—particularly in the case of governmental expenditures. Frequently, examples of wasteful spending by public agencies, such as legendary tales of the Pentagon spending $600 for ashtrays or hammers, are condemned in the national press, and subject agency administrators to severe criticism. In the fall of 1997, the National Park Service was widely ridiculed for building a "two-hole outhouse," described as the Taj Mahal of restrooms, for over $300,000:

The Pennsylvania outhouse . . . in the Delaware Water Gap National Recreation Area, features a slate, gabled roof, cottage-style porches, and a cobblestone foundation that can withstand an earthquake. The baseboards are covered with $78-a-gallon paint and the wildflower seed planted around the foundation cost $720 a pound. There's no running water, just two composting toilets.[18]

Board (FASB), other health and welfare organizations, and also by state legislation and industry trade groups.

Cost Accounting

Cost accounting is the process of recording financial expenditures so that they are keyed to work performed or services rendered. In essence, it is a way of following up on program or performance budgets. It involves keeping separate accounts for each function within a department, such as administration, facilities, or special services. Cost accounting is useful in the following ways:

1. It facilitates and promotes evaluation of departmental efficiency.
2. It can be used to evaluate individual personnel performance.
3. It is valuable in determining the feasibility of constructing facilities with either the agency's own labor force or on a contractual basis using outside firms.
4. It is helpful in determining the proper balance among different phases of departmental operation.

Accrual Accounting

This is a widely used accounting system under which all encumbrances, or charges, against specified accounts are shown on reports of expenditures that are kept up-to-date. In most large municipalities today, computerized systems provide monthly reports showing total amounts authorized in each section of a budget, the amounts spent to date, and the balance remaining. This system is essential to efficient fiscal administration in that it gives an instant, up-to-date picture of all disbursements and obligations and the current status of each section of the budget.

Balance Sheets

These are a form of bookkeeping report showing the assets and liabilities in a given fund or budget. They illustrate the financial status of a department and its ability to finance future expenditures, particularly with respect to capital development or major rehabilitation or refurbishment projects. Balance sheets may be used to show the actual cost of programs by indicating the initial investment in a facility and the annual costs of operating the activities carried on in it. The information provided in the balance sheet is particularly useful in long-range planning of areas and facilities.

Auditing

A related process is auditing, which is concerned with verifying and confirming the validity of fiscal transactions and determining whether they were appropriately carried out and accurately recorded. There are two kinds of audits: (1) *internal*, or concurrent, which involve daily checking by staff members before payments are made and (2) *external*, or post audits, which are generally made by an outside inspector (a separate agency of government or accounting firm) at regular intervals.

Accounting and auditing are important to maintain internal control of funds within a department. Normally, countercheck procedures must be used, so that more than one employee must verify information, sign checks, approve expenditures, or do similar tasks to prevent dishonesty.

Concurrent Auditing

Audits usually show expenditures only after they have been authorized and transactions have been carried out. However, the procedure of concurrent auditing or control auditing takes place either before or during the expenditure of public funds. It represents a preaudit of expected income or disbursements and assists in preventing improper or inappropriate expenditures.

Customarily, municipal departments must issue financial statements or reports at stated intervals during the year, as well as year-end financial reports. Such reports typically describe the overall operations and revenue of a department. They usually present both operational costs and revenues in columnar form. Items presented under *operations* include the appropriation for each object, expenditures to date, outstanding encumbrances, the unemcumbered balance, and the percentage of appropriations not yet spent or committed.

Audits of Work Programs

A related form of financial control is exerted through a formal check, or audit, of specific administrative or program divisions of a department, or of construction or maintenance projects. Here, instead of an overall balance sheet or accrual accounting system, the emphasis is on checking to ensure that the work plan is up-to-date, that items paid for (in the form of materials or services) have actually been delivered, and that all projects are being carried out as efficiently as possible (Fig. 6.5).

Particularly in commercial recreation businesses, other accounting or auditing procedures may include the use of profit-and-loss statements for major elements of the operation, or productivity-ratio analysis to determine the success of personnel or program units.

FISCAL REPORTS

In addition to monthly or other periodic reporting of financial data that most organizations must provide as part of the fiscal management operation, leisure-service agencies also prepare fiscal reports at the end of each year. These are usually designed for two purposes: (1) as part of formal reports of total activity during the year, which are submitted to governing boards, commissions, or other civic officials or authorities; and (2) as part of annual reports, which serve as public relations statements and are addressed to the public at large.

Formal internal reports of the first type usually contain a bulk of information with respect to different categories of assets and liabilities, with both revenues and expenditures broken down in great detail. As such, they would not be intelligible to the public at large, or to most members of a specific organization.

In contrast, annual reports that are intended for broad distribution usually summarize such information concisely, in easy-to-digest form, as shown in Tables 6.3 and 6.4, for two major youth-serving organizations. Similarly, Figure 6.6 shows how a large public recreation and park organization summarizes financial information in simple diagrams for public information purposes.

FIGURE 6.5. **Cash revenue control form for clubs and messes. (From Cost Control for Clubs and Messes (control snack bar), Washington, D.C., 1983, U.S. Navy Recreational Services, Manual F-7.)**

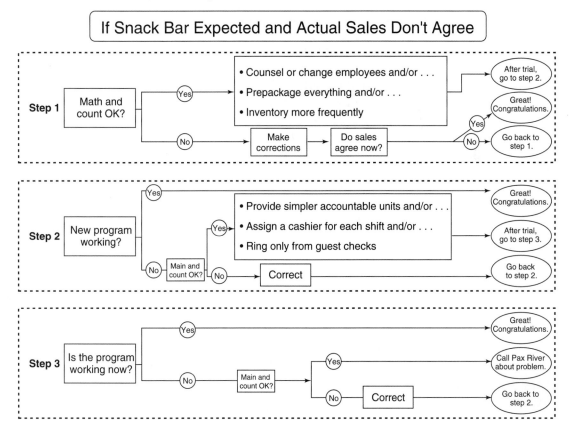

TABLE 6.3. Annual Report of Boy Scouts of America, Summarizing Fiscal Data over Five-Year Period

(In Thousands) Revenues	1996	1995	1994	1993	1992
Registration fees	$29,380	$28,326	$28,249	$28,161	$25,780
National service fees from local councils	4,986	4,944	4,799	4,764	4,616
High-adventure fees	9,886	9,265	8,787	6,886	6,980
Supply operations	21,382	18,513	16,562	18,901	16,693
Magazine publications	843	1,447	3,359	3,423	2,880
Investment income	6,179	5,985	4,869	4,422	3,664
Contributions	534	520	469	671	585
Other	1,697	1,543	1,644	1,115	1,228
	74,887	70,543	68,738	68,343	62,426
Expenses	61,023	62,527	57,330	56,508	57,366
Excess of revenues over expenses	$13,864	$8,016	$11,408	$11,835	$5,060

Note: During this period, the excess of revenues over expenses for the national organization almost tripled.

TABLE 6.4. Annual Report of Boys and Girls Clubs of America
1996 Income C Expenses

Gift Support	Income	Program Services for Clubs	Expenses
Individuals	14.2%	On-site assistance to	
Corporations	23.3%	member clubs and	
Foundations	14.8%	establishment of new clubs	54.2%
Dinners	4.9%	Leadership training	
Trust funds	2.6%	and development of	
Public Grants	9.7%	youth programs	25.2%
Total gift support	69.5%	Total program services	79.4%

Other Revenue		Supporting Services	
Dues from clubs	7.6%	Management and general	15.1%
Investment income	3.2%	Fund-raising	5.5%
Investment transactions	12.5%	Total supporting services	20.6%
Unrealized gains	4.6%		
Miscellaneous	2.6%		
Total other revenue	30.5%	Total expenses	100.0%
Total support and revenue	100.0%		

Note: This summary focuses on providing percentages of revenues and services to clarify the organization's work during the year.

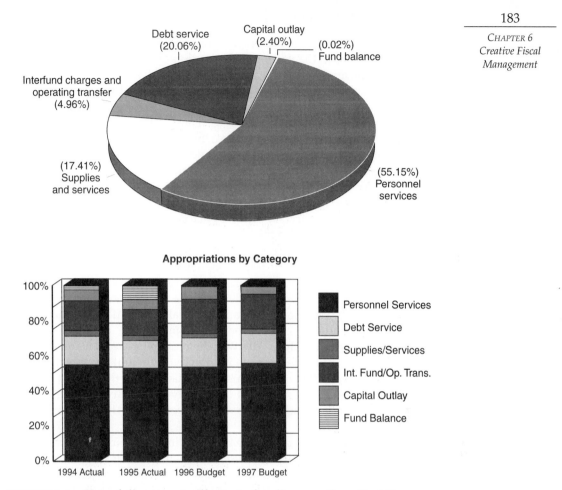

FIGURE 6.6.   Use of diagrams to illustrate funding practices: East Bay,
California Park and Recreation District Planning Report.

*ENTREPRENEURSHIP AND THE
MARKETING APPROACH*

Thus far, this chapter has described traditional practices in budget development
and execution, along with accounting and auditing procedures. It has also given
examples of innovative fund-raising methods used by leisure-service managers.

The term that has been most widely used to describe such innovative fiscal
approaches is *entrepreneurship*. Essentially, being an entrepreneur means that
one is receptive to change, rather than relying conservatively on tried-and-true
management methods and principles.

Entrepreneurial managers are aggressive risk takers, ready to try new ventures—just like successful man and women in the business world who strike
out in untested new directions.

Influence of Marketing Approach

Closely linked to the acceptance of an entrepreneurial model of leisure-service management has been the widespread adoption of the marketing approach in nonprofit organizations of all kinds. The term *marketing* may convey an image of hucksterism or cheap advertising gimmicks. This should not be the case; indeed, the true concept of marketing avoids a "hard sell" orientation that concentrates on "numbers through the door." Instead, it is deeply concerned with consumer needs and wants and seeks to achieve customer satisfaction through a coordinated set of marketing decisions and activities. In simple terms, marketing has been defined as human activity directed toward satisfying needs and wants through exchange processes.

Customarily the marketing process is considered to have four key components: (1) product or service, (2) price, (3) place or distribution, and (4) promotion. Together, these comprise the marketing "mix." Essentially, it represents a systematic approach to planning programs or services that will appeal or be useful to specific audiences or target populations and then delivering these products in the most effective way. Each stage of the marketing process must involve systematic and objective analysis. In the business world, this often requires extensive market research to gather critical information on consumer attitudes, opinions, and reactions to product offerings.

Although the marketing model was developed in the 1950s to serve the business world, it is also relevant to many governmental, nonprofit, educational, health-care, and even religious organizations. In their effort to maximize their revenues and survive within a highly competitive marketplace, all such agencies have expanded their roles, diversifying their programs and services.

Figure 6.7 illustrates several of the key steps in developing marketing action plans for recreation, park, and leisure-service agencies. Four major thrusts have emerged in recent years as part of such marketing efforts: (1) using market segmentation methods to identify promising target groups of consumers and ways of meeting their needs; (2) maximizing revenue potential by developing new, appealing products and services; (3) placing primary emphasis on the highest possible quality in programming; and (4) achieving a high level of customer or stakeholder satisfaction, with expanding the base of participants and retaining those already involved as key objectives.

Market Segmentation

Market segmentation, or "target marketing," as it is sometimes called, is a key programming concept that is based on the principle that it is essential to determine *whose* leisure needs should be served, before deciding *what* activities and services to provide. All decisions with respect to products, pricing, distribution, and promotion depend on a careful analysis of present and potential consumers of recreation, park, and leisure services.

As Chapter 4 shows, such traditional factors as age, gender, family or marital status, racial or ethnic background, and prior recreational experiences have been examined by program planners through the needs assessment process. Marketing segmentation takes this process into more complex fact finding and decision making that deals with the kinds of leisure motivations individuals have, the levels of participation that they seek, the kinds of trade-offs they are prepared to make, in terms of the benefits and costs of given pursuits, and similar elements. It is not limited to analyzing potential *new* participants. Instead, marketing segmentation also involves demographic study of *current* participants, to determine how different program elements attract different user groups, and to measure the level of satisfaction of each group in their activity involvement.

Developing New Products and Services

This strategy is a key element in entrepreneurial leisure-service management. The need to develop new, appealing and unique kinds of program activities and services in order to maximize participation and revenues is found in every aspect of the field.

Within every major category of recreation programming, this sort of diversity and experimentation with new types of services and activity formats is essential to successful marketing and to healthy fiscal growth for leisure-service organizations.

FIGURE 6.7.   Recreation and park marketing strategy.

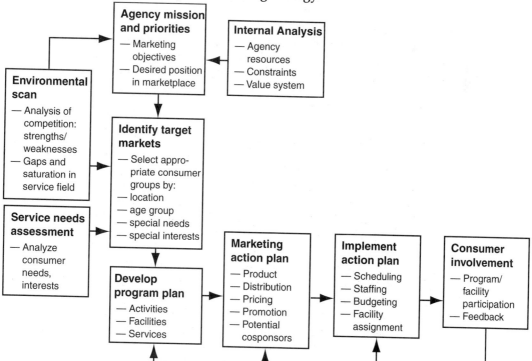

Source: Kraus, Richard and Allen, Lawrence: *Research and Evaluation in Recreation, Parks and Leisure Studies,* Boston, 1997, Allyn and Bacon.

In its Douglas Snow Aquatic Centre, the North York, Ontario, Canada, Parks and Recreation Department offers swimming, diving and water slides, a whirlpool/therapy pool, massage therapy, adult and youth swim classes, competitive swim teams, life-saving instruction and clubs, resuscitation classes, a "pro shop" with swim-related merchandise, fully accessible and adapted facilities, and integrated instruction classes for persons with disabilities. In terms of winter sports, the same department offers a wide range of skiing, snowboarding, and skating program activities designed to meet all interests and age group needs, from basic instruction to high-level competition and leadership training.

Emphasis on Quality

Program diversity is not enough. Instead, at every level of service today, recreation managers must aim at providing facilities and activities that are up-to-date, attractively maintained and directed, efficiently supervised, and highly responsive to participant reactions and suggestions. In the process of registration, program supervision or instruction, gathering and dealing with consumer complaints, follow-up, and systematic evaluation of classes and events, quality must be the keynote.

This emphasis goes beyond simply giving lip service to the principle of maintaining maximum quality. Spector, for example, argues that top management's role is critical:

> Top management must support, even demand, a candid, honest, occasionally brutal evaluation of the way the organization is being run [consisting] of two key components. First, the demand for candid reevaluation must become regular and ongoing [leading to continuous improvement]. Second, top management must put itself through the same paces that it expects of managers throughout the organization. . . . [R]egular diagnosis, analysis, self-examination, and correction become an institutionalized part of the everyday life and fabric of the organization.[19]

Achieving Customer/Stakeholder Satisfaction

This fourth aspect of the marketing approach should normally be the result of the high-quality programming emphasis that has just been described. However, it also involves the need to develop a strong, positive relationship between the agency and its staff and those who are served in the program.

Actually, the relationship begins well before the individual takes part in the agency's programs or makes use of its facilities. Through needs assessments and the use of focus groups, advisory boards, and volunteer involvement, community residents or organization members are given a voice in program planning or overall agency operations. Through prompt and courteous responses to participant suggestions or complaints trust and reliability are established—two important elements in developing positive relationships. This in turn leads to an expanded market and effective promotion.

Clearly, the best advertisement for any form of entertainment or public service is the positive word-of-mouth praise that comes from satisfied and involved consumers or participants. Research has shown that acquiring a new consumer is five times more expensive than keeping an existing one. This, then, must be an essential component in leisure-service marketing strategies—not only *attracting* new participants, but *satisfying* and *keeping* them as active program patrons.

SUMMARY

Fiscal management is a key element in the operating of all leisure-service agencies. It is concerned with the planning and control of money in support of programs, facilities, and other expenditures, and is usually formalized through the presentation and approval of annual budgets that describe projected revenues and expenses in detail.

Several types of budgets are described in this chapter, including line-item budgets, performance budgets, and program budgets. The entire process of budget formulation, review and approval, and execution is described with guidelines for management performance at each stage. Financial accounting and auditing methods are reviewed, along with major sources of funding: (1) taxes of various types; (2) bonds, usually used for capital development; (3) government or foundation grants; (4) fees and charges; and (5) concessions, gifts and bequests, and leasing arrangements.

To achieve a fiscally sound arrangement, leisure-service agencies today must embark on a process of strategic planning within an entrepreneurial framework. This involves a vigorous marketing approach that ensures that programs and services are keyed to public needs or the specific constituency that is being served. It should be stressed that while many of the examples cited in this chapter are drawn from government agencies, they apply equally well to other types of leisure-service organizations.

SUGGESTED CLASS PROJECTS

1. Visit nearby leisure-service agencies to obtain copies of their proposed or approved budgets or financial reports, along with procedural guidelines or manuals controlling purchasing, auditing, accounting, and money-handling activities. Review and compare these in class.
2. With other students, organize a mock budget hearing or bond proposal to be held before a city council or county board of supervisors, with members of the public present. In role playing, criticize or defend specific aspects of the budget or bond proposal.
3. Conduct an informal survey of public and voluntary leisure-service agencies to determine the range of fee structures for recreation programs, membership, or other charges. Determine whether increases in fees or the addition of new charges have affected attendance levels in these agencies, if this has been determined by agency personnel. Determine also whether special arrangements are made to assist those unable to pay certain fees and charges.

4. Select a specific type of community-based service or program for special populations, such as a social club in an urban mental health center, or a day-care center for the elderly. Examine the funding sources of existing agencies of this type, and prepare a fund-raising plan that might draw in new sources of financial support for such organizations.

Before analyzing these cases in class, review the guidelines suggested in Chapter 3 (pp. 76–77).

Case Study 6.1 *Swimming Pool Fees—Who Pays?*

YOU ARE JIM SWENSON, recreation and park director in the village of Hastings. While reviewing your plans for the summer day camp with your advisory board, composed of five elected members and two trustees appointed by the Hastings mayor, the question of summer swimming fees has arisen.

Each year, since the village does not have its own swimming pool, you have had a special bussing arrangement to take day campers or other village children twice weekly to a nearby county pool for six weeks with a charge of $40 per child. You have pointed out to the board that, although Hastings is a comfortable, middle-class community, there are a number of poorer families, and in the past you have not charged children from these families a fee. Two members of the board question this arrangement, feeling that some might take advantage of it. They ask: "How do you decide if a family can or cannot pay the fee? Is there any way of screening families to know if they can afford to pay? Is the policy generally known in Hastings? Are there some families who do not enter the swimming program because they can't afford to pay?"

In the discussion, two recommendations emerged: (1) that any family that indicated it could not afford to pay should be accepted without charge, and that this policy should be made known in the town paper; or (2) that there be a system of screening to judge financial capability, and that the policy be entered in the board's minutes, but not be widely publicized.

QUESTIONS FOR CLASS DISCUSSION AND ANALYSIS

1. *What are the underlying issues behind this situation?*
2. *Discuss the pros and cons of each of the two recommendations that have been presented.*
3. *As village recreation and park director, what is your position? Why?*

Case Study 6.2 — *The Mayor Cracks Down*

YOU ARE BARRY PARSONS, commissioner of a medium-sized municipal recreation and park department. For the past three years, your budget has been frozen, while your maintenance costs have risen, and new facilities have been added, which stretch your capabilities to the limit.

This is an election year, and your mayor, Jeannine Day, is determined not to raise taxes. She has just announced her budget for the following fiscal year. Your department's budget is being frozen for the fourth straight year. You view this as the last straw and call a press conference, which reporters from the two city newspapers and several television and radio stations attend. You announce that, rather than operate a number of inadequate facilities with increasing complaints about poor maintenance and supervision, you are going to have to cut back on your program.

Specifically, you have decided to close a large swimming pool, a golf course, and a nature center and withdraw all personnel from a large park. By doing this, you will be able to provide adequate maintenance for other parks and recreational areas, even with the limited budget. At the same time, you send a memorandum outlining your plan to the mayor and the city council.

Within an hour, Jeannine Day is on the phone. She is furious. Curtly she informs you, "I am not going to take complaints from all the families and neighborhood groups that want these facilities open. Politically, this move is a disaster, and I refuse to be blackmailed by you. You will open these facilities up or you will be fired. Period!"

QUESTIONS FOR CLASS DISCUSSION AND ANALYSIS

1. *Apart from resigning, which you do not want to do because you like your job and your family is comfortably settled in the community, what are your options?*
2. *Was your strategy a wise one? How could the problem have been handled differently?*
3. *If additional funds cannot be found in the budget for your department, what other approaches could you explore to ensure that maintenance and recreation programs are adequately staffed?*

Case Study 6.3 *Third-Party Payments*

YOU ARE DOLORES JACKSON, director of therapeutic recreation in the Activity Therapies Department of the Hutchinson Center for Physical Rehabilitation.

In the past, several adjunctive modalities, such as occupational and physical therapy, have been designed as services receiving third-party reimbursement by Medicaid or Medicare or private hospitalization insurance programs. John Drinan, administrative director of the Hutchinson Center, now asks you to design the recreation programs so that this service can also be filed for special payment for services rendered to patients. If you are to continue to receive administrative support and have your staff remain at its present level, it is clear that you will need to meet the eligibility requirements for third-party payments.

QUESTIONS FOR CLASS DISCUSSION AND ANALYSIS

1. Based on preliminary examination of present guidelines (you will need to do some research to determine these), what steps will you have to take to make the recreation program eligible for reimbursement?

2. Since third-party programs must be designed to meet the needs of individual patients through a medically approved treatment plan, will this affect some of your general recreation programming within the rehabilitation hospital?

3. Present the pros and cons of the plan that John Drinan has asked you to carry out, and develop guidelines, if possible, that might permit you to offer both kinds of programs (those for reimbursement and the general program).

4. If no therapeutic recreation major students are enrolled in the class, you may wish to consult a faculty member in this area or seek other knowledgeable help.

REFERENCES

1. Howard, Dennis, and Crompton, John: *Financing Sports,* Morgantown, W.Va., 1995, p. 9.
2. Egan, Timothy: "Adapting to Fees for Enjoying Public Lands," *New York Times,* August 21, 1977, p. 1.
3. Hjelte, George, and Shivers, Jay: *Public Administration for Recreational Service,* Philadelphia, Pa., 1973, Lea and Febiger, p. 316.
4. Galbraith, John: *The Affluent Society,* Boston, 1958, Houghton Mifflin, pp. 256–57.
5. Crompton, John: *Doing More with Less in the Delivery of Recreation and Park Services,* State College, Pa., 1987, Venture Publishing, p. xi.
6. O'Sullivan, Ellen: *Marketing for Parks, Recreation and Leisure,* State College, Pa., 1991, Venture Publishing, p. 195.
7. East Bay, Calif., Regional Park District, *Planning Report,* 1997.
8. Gladwell, Nancy, and Sellers, James: "Assessment of Fiscal Status and Personnel Trends in Public Parks and Recreation Agencies in Medium-Sized Communities of Southeastern United States," *Journal of Park and Recreation Administration* 15(1), Spring 1997, pp. 1–15.
9. Hines, Thomas: *Budgeting for Public Parks and Recreation,* Washington, D.C., 1968, National Recreation and Park Association Management Aids Bulletin, no. 46, p. 23.
10. Emmett, Janet, Havitz, Mark, and McCarville, Ronald: "A Price Subsidy Policy for Socio-Economically Disadvantaged Recreation Participants," *Journal of Park and Recreation Administration* 14(1), Spring 1996, pp. 63–80.
11. Moler, Chris, and Wood, Bret: "The Financial Impact of Hosting Competitive Swimming," *Parks and Recreation,* November 1997, pp. 71–74.
12. Bragg, Rick: "New Stadium's Price Not Quite out of the Park," *New York Times,* September 2, 1997, p. A-17.
13. National PAL merchandise order form (sales brochure), Coral Beach, Fla., 1997.
14. Smith, Bucklin Associates: *The Complete Guide to Nonprofit Management,* New York, 1994, John Wiley and Sons, pp. 76–79.
15. Teaff, Joseph, and Van Hyning, Thomas: "Leisure Service Financing in U.S. Health-Care Settings," *Journal of Physical Education, Recreation and Dance,* April 1988, p. 25.
16. *Little League Baseball Operating Manual,* Williamsport, Pa., 1997.
17. Hemingway, Anne: "Cost Center Financial Management," *Navy Comptroller,* Washington, D.C., April 1993, Department of Defense, p. 2.
18. Barr, Stephen: "Outhouse Operation at a Penthouse Price," *Houston Chronicle,* October 30, 1997, p. 42.
19. Spector, Bert: *Taking Charge and Letting Go: A Breakthrough Strategy for Creating the Horizontal Company,* New York, 1995, Free Press, p. 27.

Seven

Human Resource Management: Maximizing Staff Performance

In the context of understanding motivation in work organizations . . . what causes a person to report regularly for work each day rather than frequently calling in sick? What causes one person to attack difficult problems head-on, while someone else avoids and procrastinates for long periods? What causes some people to choose to engage in the activities encouraged by the organization, while others seem bent on doing just those things which have been discouraged or prohibited?[1]

HRM [human resource management] is essentially a business-oriented philosophy designed to obtain value from employees, which increases competitive advantage in the marketplace. Instead of seeing employees as cost factors that must be controlled by management, newer approaches to HRM view human resources as assets worthy of investment. In turn, HRM investments are designed to accomplish the strategic plans of the organization.[2]

INTRODUCTION

Closely linked to all other areas of management responsibility in recreation, park, and leisure-service agencies is the function of directing the work of employees on various organizational levels and in a wide variety of job specializations.

Personnel management, or as it is widely termed today, human resource management, may be viewed from two perspectives. First, emphasis may be placed on the traditional functions of recruiting, selecting, training, and supervising personnel within a formal model of bureaucratic policies and procedures. Extending this approach, today many organizations assign a high priority to creative staff development practices, shared decision making, and team planning efforts, and other techniques designed to maximize staff performance and build agency success.

194

Chapter 7
Human Resource
Management:
Maximizing Staff
Performance

This chapter addresses the following understandings and competencies listed as essential in the Baccalaureate Degree standards of the NRPA/AALR Council on Accreditation:

Understanding of and ability to apply personnel management techniques, including job analysis, recruitment, selection, training, motivation, career development and evaluation of staff and volunteers (8.30).

Understanding of the concept of a professional and professional organization as related to leisure services (8.08).

Understanding of ethical principles and professionalism as applied to all professional practices, attitudes and behaviors in leisure services delivery (8.09).

Understanding of and the ability to use various leadership techniques and strategies to enhance the individual's leisure experiences for all populations, including those with special needs (8.18).

Understanding of and ability to utilize diverse interaction and facilitation techniques, including leadership, instructional strategies, counseling techniques, and crisis confrontation and intervention (7C.01).

Understanding of and ability to utilize supervisory techniques (7C.02).

O B J E C T I V E S

At the conclusion of this chapter, readers should be familiar with the following concepts and practices:

1. The scope of employment and types of positions held in recreation, park, and leisure-service agencies.
2. The functions and responsibilities of managers in selecting and supervising employees in public, nonprofit, and other types of organizations.
3. The nature of job classification systems and position descriptions, linked to the process of recruiting, interviewing, and selecting applicants for positions in this field.
4. Methods of orienting new employees and providing preservice training, as well as other later continuing education and staff development processes.
5. Supervisory practices, including coaching and counseling functions, and procedures involving promotion, job transfer, or termination.
6. Job motivation methods, such as reward and award systems, team building, task delegation, and participatory work climate.
7. Career development and professionalization in leisure services within a human resource management framework.

SCOPE OF EMPLOYMENT IN LEISURE SERVICES

During the past several decades, employment in recreation, parks, and leisure services has grown tremendously. In the mid-1990s, government recreation and park employees on all levels totaled 345,000, while those involved in natural resource management numbered 436,000. Employees in travel and tourism roles are estimated at over 4 million, and over 400,000 individuals work in amusement and recreation services, with 1.1 million in such social-service or cultural settings as museums, libraries, or membership organizations.[3] Other positions in private-membership, campus, or therapeutic recreation total in the hundreds of thousands.

How are the millions of men and women who enter or advance in this field each year recruited, trained, supervised, and evaluated?

195

CHAPTER 7
*Human Resource
Management:
Maximizing Staff
Performance*

PERSONNEL PRACTICES IN GOVERNMENT AGENCIES

Any examination of personnel practices within bureaucratic leisure-service agencies must begin with a description of the kinds of jobs that people hold. Customarily, this is done through personnel classification systems and standardized job descriptions. These represent tools that are essential to effective organization. They provide the basis for defining job responsibilities clearly, having comparable salary levels for similar qualifications or job demands, and establishing a career ladder with opportunity for promotion within the system.

Personnel Classification Systems

In public agencies, positions are usually grouped into classes and series within a civil service structure that applies to almost all government employment. The term *class* refers to a group of positions that have roughly comparable responsibilities and qualifications, which may be stated in terms of education, previous experience, and specific knowledge or job skills. Positions on the same class level may be found in different departments and are usually subject to the same policies regarding pay, fringe benefits, promotions, and similar personnel matters.

A *series* represents a form of vertical classification of employees, usually found within a particular department or specialization but with a gradation of skill and qualifications as well as different levels of salary and status. For example, a series of titles within a recreation department might run from recreation trainee or assistant through several grades of recreation leader, ultimately moving up to recreation supervisor or center director.

Classification systems provide an overall structure through which jobs are defined and fitted onto an organization chart and a civil-service plan. Each position is identified as to class or grade and is assigned a salary range, specific work responsibilities, required qualifications (usually meaning education and experience and sometimes including an examination), and personnel benefits such as holidays, vacations, leave, hospitalization, retirement plan, and similar benefits. In general, such personnel systems tend to apply to larger communities or leisure-service agencies, rather than to smaller organizations, which are usually more flexible and informal in their structure.

196

CHAPTER 7
Human Resource
Management:
Maximizing Staff
Performance

Job Categories

Municipal or county recreation and park departments employ a wide variety of workers. For example, civil-service job rolls may include such titles as administrative analyst, architect, building maintenance superintendent, brick mason, camp director, carpenter, cement finisher, city planner, civil engineer, clerk stenographer, and construction project technician.

It would be a mistake to think that all these job categories represent specialized professional employment in recreation and parks. However, every effort should be made to imbue employees who are nonprofessional leisure-service workers with a sense of the mission and purpose of the agency. Through meetings, house publications, and training, they should gain an awareness of the department's work and a sense of pride and loyalty that increases their effectiveness.

Position Levels

James Murphy and his coauthors suggest the following approach to classifying leisure-service positions: (1) *front-line personnel,* such as recreation leaders, therapists, maintenance workers, program volunteers, or others who provide direct leisure services; (2) *middle-level managers,* including recreation and park supervisors, center directors, special-facility managers, and others with a higher degree of responsibility and greater decision-making authority; and (3) *top-level managers,* who are agency directors, park superintendents, chief executive officers in recreation businesses, or key administrators who are responsible for planning, developing policies, structuring organizations, and coordinating the work of other personnel.[4]

Whatever method of job classification is used, thorough and accurate job descriptions must be prepared for each position in a leisure-service agency. These typically include *title, civil-service grade (if governmental), listing of responsibilities and functions, required knowledge and skills, minimum acceptable education and previous experience, and physical or medical standards.*

EXAMPLES OF JOB DESCRIPTIONS AND COMPETENCIES

Several examples of position descriptions or listings of required competencies in different types of leisure-service agencies follow.

The position of Recreation Superintendent is described in a recent job announcement of the Long Beach, California, Department of Parks, Recreation and Marine (Fig. 7.1).

Campus Recreation: University of Alabama

A high-level campus recreation position is illustrated in Fig. 7.2 for the Director of University Recreation at the University of Alabama.

197

CHAPTER 7
Human Resource
Management:
Maximizing Staff
Performance

MANAGEMENT OPPORTUNITY
CITY OF LONG BEACH
"Working Together to Serve"

Posting Date_____

RECREATION SUPERINTENDENT
DEPARTMENT OF PARKS, RECREATION AND MARINE

THE POSITION
The vacant position is one of six Recreation Superintendents supporting two Recreation Bureaus--Community Park Programs and Senior Services and Special Programs. They are responsible for developing, coordinating, implementing, promoting, and administering recreation programs.

EXAMPLES OF DUTIES:
o Responsible for one or more of the following: Community Park Programs, Senior Services, Regional Park Operations and Park Ranger Program, Day Camps, Extended Care Programs, Volunteers, Special Events, Adaptive Recreation, Sports and Aquatics Programs.
o Acts as liaison to advisory boards and community groups.
o Supervises approximately 6 full-time and 26 part-time staff.
o Prepares and monitors annual budgets.
o Develops and monitors performance measures.
o Selects, trains, evaluates, and disciplines staff.
o Prepares and presents written and oral reports for various audiences.
o Responsible for recreation contracts.
o Responsible for developing and maintaining positive public relations and excellent customer service.
o Performs other related duties as required.

ORGANIZATION:
The Parks, Recreation and Marine Department has approximately 460 full-time equivalent budgeted position. The 1996-97 budget for the Department is $37 million. The Department has five Bureaus, including: Business Operations, Community Park Programs, Senior Services and Special Programs, Parks, and Marine, which over see 23 parks, 3 public pools, beaches, marinas, sports fields, and community centers, serving a population of 432,600 citizens.

QUALIFICATIONS:
Graduation from an accredited college or university with a Bachelor's Degree in Recreation, Leisure Studies, Public Administration or closely-related field, and five years of progressively responsible administrative and supervisory experience is required.

Strong administrative skills with a working knowledge of recreational programming is desirable. Candidates need experience in supervising staff with diverse technical skills and directing personnel, budget, and policy development. Strong written, oral and interpersonal communications skills are required.

SALARY:
The salary range for this position is $45,005 - $67,507 per year, depending upon qualifications.

SELECTION PROCEDURES:
Submit a letter of application, comprehensive resume, and names and addresses of three current, confidential references by **NOVEMBER 15, 1996**. Resumes will be reviewed for depth and breadth of experience and for level or relatedness or education. The most qualified candidates will be invited to participate in further selection procedures. If you require an accommodation because of a physical or mental disability in order to participate in any phase of the application process, please advise when submitting your application.

SUBMIT RESUME TO: Ralph S. Cryder, Director
Department of Parks, Recreation and Marine
2760 Studebaker Road
Long Beach, CA 90815-1697
ATTENTION: JONI K. ANDERSON

(The provisions of this bulletin do not constitute an express or implied contract and any announcements contained in this bulletin may be modified or revoked without notice.)

THE IMMIGRATION REFORM AND CONTROL ACT OF 1986 REQUIRES ALL NEW EMPLOYEES TO SUBMIT
VERIFICATION OF IDENTITY AND AUTHORIZATION TO WORK IN THE UNITED STATES AT THE TIME OF HIRE

P 38 19 92

AN EQUAL OPPORTUNITY EMPLOYER

FIGURE 7.1. *Job description:* **Long Beach, CA, Department of Parks, Recreation and Marine.**

198

*CHAPTER 7
Human Resource
Management:
Maximizing Staff
Performance*

Director of University Recreation

The primary goal of this position is to complement the academic mission of the University by affording the University community recreational and fitness services, programs and facilities. Responsibilities in this area are planning; budgeting; decision-making; and program development, evaluation and appraisal.

Responsibilities

Directs and coordinates overall activities of University Recreation:
Student Recreation Center - A 120,000 square foot facility with multi-use floor, running track, racquet, squash and handball courts, aerobics rooms, swimming pool, fitness equipment exercise room, and free weight room with over 500,000 client contacts annually.
Intramural Playfields - A 26 acre multi-use intramural complex for football, soccer, softball, and other outdoor play activity.
Golf Center - An 18-hole facility with full practice facilities, including driving range, two putting areas and a pitching range. Annually 65,000 rounds of golf played.
Riverside Pool - An outdoor swimming complex opened during late Spring, Summer and early Fall for University and community use. Managed cooperatively with the Athletic Department
University Tennis Courts - Outdoor tennis courts for instruction and leisure play.

Leadership and supervision of staff, direct supervision of four department heads charged with day-to-day operations.

Develops, implements and monitors short and long-range planning for University Recreation, consistent with the mission of The University and goals of the Division of Student Affairs.

Directs the development and operation of University Recreation budgets, totaling $2,500,000.

Develops and implements policies and procedures for University Recreation.

Plans and develops new and renovation construction of facilities with Design & Construction office.

Directs the maintenance and repair of $19,000,000 worth of facilities in University Recreation.

Directs overall personnel activities of University Recreation, including decisions regarding personnel actions and strategies, direction in staffing operations, recruitment, hiring, and personnel evaluation.

Maintains the appropriate lines of communication within and without the University regarding University Recreation.

Serves on various Standing Committees within the University Community. Acts as On-Call Dean, a campus liaison during student crisis situations, rotated among Student Affairs leadership.

Qualifications

The Director of University Recreation must have an advanced degree in Educational Administration, Student Personnel, Physical Education, Recreation, Management or a related field. A doctorate in an appropriate field is preferred. Professional progressively responsible management experience in

administration, planning, budgeting and personnel functions of at least seven years is required. Five years must in the recreation field, with responsibilities in managing a broad array of recreation facilities, programs and services. Qualified individuals must have significant experience in developing successful operations with diverse clientele. Demonstrated ability in oral and written communication, research activities, and utilizing new technologies are required. A thorough knowledge of the role of recreation programs and services on a college campus is needed

FIGURE 7.2. *Position notice:* Director of University Recreation, University of Alabama.

Therapeutic Recreation: City and County of
San Francisco

199

CHAPTER 7
Human Resource
Management:
Maximizing Staff
Performance

An upper-level management post in therapeutic recreation in San Francisco is advertised in Fig. 7.3.

FIGURE 7.3. *Position notice:* Therapeutic Activities Director, San Francisco, CA.

CITY AND COUNTY OF SAN FRANCISCO
EMPLOYMENT OPPORTUNITY
The following information describes the civil service classification for which applications are being solicited.
Make sure you read the entire announcement before completing the application form.

CLASS 2557 DIRECTOR OF THERAPEUTIC ACTIVITIES, LHH

Under general administrative direction, directs the inpatient programs of the Activity Therapy Department and Volunteer Services of Laguna Honda Hospital, a large acute and skilled nursing facility which provides treatment and rehabilitation to a wide variety of adult residents in various age groups, some with complex multiple diagnoses; ensures that programs meet established standards; supervises and trains subordinate personnel; coordinates departmental activities with those of other hospital departments; functions as departmental liaison and representative; manages the department's budget; and performs related duties as required. The annual salary range is $45,623 to $55,436.

MINIMUM QUALIFICATIONS:
Four years of management/supervisory experience in a health care setting or non-profit service organization. (College accredited course work, training or certification in therapeutic activities is preferred. Management experience gained in organizations providing services with a long-term care therapeutic focus is desirable. **See Verification Section**).

> **Substitution:** A Master's Degree from an accredited college or university in Gerontology, Therapeutic Activities (including Art, Dance, Music and Recreation), non-profit management or closely related field may be substituted for two years of the management experience requirement.

HOW TO APPLY: Applications can be obtained and filed at Department of Public Health, Human Resource Services, 101 Grove Street, Room 210, San Francisco, CA 94102 or Laguna Honda Hospital, Human Resource Services, 375 Laguna Honda Boulevard, San Francisco CA, 94116 or San Francisco General Hospital, Human Resource Services, 1001 Potrero Avenue, Bldg. 10, 3rd Floor, San Francisco, CA 94110. Interested applicants are encouraged to file immediately. Resumes will not be accepted in lieu of applications. Receipt of applications will be cut-off, suspended or closed when there is a sufficient number of qualified applicants. All such information will be posted at the offices listed above and at the Department of Human Resources at 44 Gough Street, San Francisco, CA 94013. Applications from promotive candidates will be accepted for a minimum of ten (10) calendar days following the issue date of this announcement. Late or incomplete applications will be rejected. Indicate ATTN: 2557 Director Of Therapeutic Activities, LHH when submitting by mail.

VERIFICATION:
1. City employees who meet all the qualifications based solely on employment with the City and County of San Francisco do **NOT** need to provide verification of qualifying experience. City employees who qualify based on a combination of City employment and outside employment do **NOT** need to provide verification of City employment, but MUST verify outside qualifying experience (see 3a. below).
2. City and County employees will receive credit for the duties of the class to which appointed. Credit for experience obtained outside of the employee's class will only be allowed if recorded in accordance with the provisions of Civil Service Commission Rules. This is not subject to appeal.
3. Non-City employees **MUST** verify all qualifying experience as follows:
   a. Written verification of qualifying experience and/or photocopy of certificate or degree MUST BE

Minorities, Women, and Persons with Disabilities are Encouraged to Apply
An Equal Opportunity Employer

JOB DESCRIPTIONS IN OTHER SETTINGS

As in most government agencies, the U.S. National Park Service provides a systematic set of job descriptions for civil-service positions on various levels. For example, it describes the position of park ranger in terms of duties, training, career potential, and qualifications.

Duties of park rangers in the National Park Service include the following: (1) planning and carrying out conservation efforts to protect plant and animal life; (2) planning and conducting programs of public safety, including law enforcement and rescue work, (3) setting up and directing interpretive programs, such as slide shows and tours; (4) coordinating environmental education programs; (5) planning recreation programs; and (6) performing administrative, community relations, and other related tasks.

To qualify for appointment as a park ranger at civil-service grade GS-5, applicants must meet one of the following three basic requirements:

1. Complete a full four-year program in an accredited college or university leading to a bachelor's degree with at least twenty-four semester hours in one or not more than two of the following fields: park and recreation management, field-related natural science, history, archaeology, police science, business administration, behavioral sciences, or closely related subjects.
2. Complete three years of park or conservation experience providing a good general understanding of systems, methods, and administrative practice; have the ability to analyze and solve problems and communicate effectively, and similar skills.
3. Attain appropriate combinations of education and experience as defined in items 1 and 2, with an academic year of study composed of thirty semester hours being considered equivalent to nine months of experience.

Commercial Recreation: Ski Center Managers

In profit-oriented leisure businesses, competency-based hiring tends to prevail. Normally, people who hire employees for such recreation businesses as travel agencies, sports centers, fitness spas, amusement complexes, or theme parks are less concerned with the formal education of candidates than they are with their

---

A Quiet Day at the Park

Formal job descriptions rarely give a full picture of the actual work of leisure-service professionals. Recently, for example, a park ranger at Glacier National Park was assigned to tranquilize and transport a 500-pound grizzly bear from an adjacent Indian reservation to the park itself. In the ensuing struggle, the bear attacked the ranger, causing severe injuries before the ranger killed it with his revolver. *National Wildlife* depicts park rangers as a special breed. As an example of their work during a 9-to-5 hitch, park ranger Butch Farabee at Yosemite National Park pulled a human corpse out of Merced River, changed out of his wet suit to rescue a stranded climber from a sheer cliff, and at nightfall took part in a drug bust. He described it as "one of his easier days."

past employment experience, personality, and ability to do the job. In some cases, they may stipulate college degrees or specific technical course background as important qualifications. Normally, however, commercial employers are not convinced that a degree in recreation and parks is essential for most employees.

As a specific example of qualifications needed by employees in the field of commercial recreation, a research report published at Michigan State University outlined the job specifications and skills needed by ski area managers. Based on a study of over fifty ski centers in a number of states, the following areas were identified as essential, ranked in order of importance:

1. General administration and management techniques
2. Control ticket sales
3. Labor cost control
4. Apply safety regulations and understand liability
5. Determine types of tickets (to be sold)
6. Select lift equipment
7. Personnel management
8. Carry out lift preventative maintenance
9. Accounting
10. Institute ticket and traffic control
11. Public relations
12. Apply safety-checking procedures
13. Design and develop ski hills
14. Utilize the ski school and accident-prevention program
15. Install lifts
16. Marketing
17. Develop ski packages
18. Finance
19. Liability insurance
20. Carry out evacuation and first aid
21. Operate or integrate ski school activities
22. Apply theory of snow grooming and snow textures
23. Operate ground lifts
24. Carry out mechanical maintenance
25. Operate serial lifts
26. Do advertising and promotion
27. Use various types of snow grooming equipment[5]

EMPLOYMENT STANDARDS: DRIVE TOWARD PROFESSIONALISM

Although hiring standards vary among different types of leisure-service agencies, there has been a steady drive toward professionalism over the past several decades. This has included the development of national, statewide, or provincial standards for employment, particularly in public and therapeutic recreation agencies.

Certification and Registration

In a number of states, formal certification procedures for recreation and park employment have been established by legislation, and in such cases the process of screening and approving candidates is a legal one and mandated for employment. The most common pattern, however, has been for state or provincial recreation and park societies to develop plans through which qualified professionals might have their credentials reviewed and approved. In the early 1970s, a National Registration Board was established in the United States through which the National Recreation and Park Association (NRPA) might review and approve the registration plans of various state societies and encourage reciprocal recognition of plans by the different states. In addition, the National Therapeutic Recreation Society (NTRS) developed a national registration system that screened workers in this field.

Several thousand therapeutic recreation workers were registered within this system, making a strong impact on professionalization in this field. In the early 1980s, it was transformed into a certification process with two levels of job titles (professional and paraprofessional) to be administered by the National Council for Therapeutic Recreation Certification, administratively affiliated with the NRPA.

In 1990, a national certification examination was developed by the council, in consultation with the Educational Testing Service in Princeton, New Jersey, and with the assistance of national authorities in this field. Over the next several years, over 15,000 individuals took this test, and research confirmed that it represented a valid measure of professional competence for the approximately 92 percent of candidates who passed it.

Within the broader field of public recreation and park administration, certification has also moved ahead, through a process of credentialing and examination administered through the NRPA. In Canada, a number of provincial societies such as the Parks and Recreation Federation of Ontario have initiated certification procedures; George Nogradi summarizes their value:

> Typically, certification includes assessment of competence through valid and reliable measurement. In addition, certification includes clearly defined standards of practice and code of ethics that prescribe the appropriate conduct for practitioners. . . . In that sense, the certification process is an act of verification, accountability, and control that reflects an agreement between society and a profession about the expectations and roles that are to be performed.[6]

In addition to certification in public recreation and park agencies, a number of other specialized leisure-service fields have developed their own certification systems. As an example, the National Employee Services and Recreation Association (NESRA) has for a number of years authorized certification of recreation and employee services directors in companies throughout the United States. Customarily, such organizations also sponsor professional development institutes for continuing education credits, which are linked to maintaining certification status.

In numerous other areas of recreational participation—particularly those related to sports, aquatics, and outdoor recreation leadership—professional societies established training programs and certification requirements. Customarily, hiring standards of responsible agencies stipulate that candidates meet these requirements as a means of maintaining a high level of service quality and also as a safeguard against lawsuits claiming faulty or negligent leadership and supervision.

203

CHAPTER 7
Human Resource
Management:
Maximizing Staff
Performance

OTHER HIRING SYSTEMS: CIVIL SERVICE

Civil-service requirements for hiring or promoting government employees are ideally based on a combination of education, experience, and examination scores, with military veterans being given preference. However, on the lowest levels of nonprofessional work, such requirements are generally minimal, while on the higher executive levels, appointments are often made by mayors or county executives without regard to civil-service requirements. For the bulk of positions as leaders, program specialists, or other service roles, civil-service hiring is based on examinations and eligibility lists that may be applied on a countywide or statewide basis or through municipal civil-service commissions.

Although their original intention was to provide hiring procedures that ensure a merit-based system of appointments and promotions that would not be subject to political interference, there is widespread discontent with the way civil service has operated in the recreation and park field. Cumbersome hiring procedures make it difficult to hire personnel when needed or when available. The relevance of the examinations themselves is challenged. Too often civil-service officials and examiners are almost totally ignorant of the recreation and park field and the demands made of its practitioners; their examinations reflect this lack of understanding. Fortunately, within the past several years, a number of state recreation and park societies have succeeded in upgrading civil-service requirements and providing input that has helped examinations and other hiring procedures become more relevant to actual professional needs.

RECRUITMENT AND SELECTION OF PERSONNEL

Recruitment, selection, and hiring constitute key elements in the overall personnel management process. Their goal is to employ the best qualified men and women to fill openings in the organization, both on a temporary, part-time, or seasonal basis, and also for full-time positions with a long-term career potential.

Recruitment Methods

Job Description

A written job description should be prepared giving essential information about the responsibilities, salary, personnel benefits, and hiring qualifications and procedures of the position to be filled. It should be concise and attractive, completely accurate, and approved by the department's personnel office or the community's personnel director. If the agency is part of a larger system, such as an armed forces base, its job description must of course conform with the organization's standardized personnel policies.

204

CHAPTER 7
Human Resource
Management:
Maximizing Staff
Performance

Publicizing the Position

Announcement of the job opening should be carried out with the use of newsletters, mailing of brochures, announcements at professional meetings, direct correspondence, or placement of the opening with the personnel-placement service of professional organizations. State or regional recreation and park societies frequently maintain listings of job openings. In some cases, agencies may advertise directly in newspapers or in professional journals.

An example of a hiring recruitment brochure for seasonal programs used by the North York, Ontario, Canada Parks and Recreation Department is shown in Fig. 7.4. Customarily, such brochures are distributed to schools and colleges, or through varied civic organizations, employment agencies, and similar settings. Job notices for higher-level positions normally have much fuller statements of needed competencies, required experience and education, and application procedures.

Consideration of Past Employees

Frequently recruitment may be carried out directly by considering past employees for positions. Many recreation and park departments employ college students during the summer or on a part-time basis during the winter and spring. When they have graduated, they may be considered for full-time employment, with the obvious advantage of having the department familiar with their work and vice versa.

In addition, a number of national leisure-service organizations have developed strong internship programs through which they not only obtain enthusiastic young employees on a seasonal or semester-long basis, but also develop a pool of qualified, college-trained individuals for future employment. For example, the Boys and Girls Clubs of America have developed an extensive program aimed at students majoring in recreation, physical education, social work, or related fields, including both internships and work/study arrangements. College job fairs are often useful in such recruitment efforts.

Selection and Hiring Process

Depending on the organization, the personnel selection process may include any or all of the following procedures: (1) having the candidate fill out a detailed job application form; (2) detailed consideration of the candidate's background, past performance, and references; (3) personal interview with the candidate; (4) a written examination, usually part of a state, county, or municipal civil-service series; (5) a physical examination; (6) a character investigation; and (7) in some cases, a performance test in specific skill areas.

Particularly in larger and more complex agencies, the personnel or human resources department is likely to have a manual covering this function, which outlines in detail all policies and procedures that must be followed in filling job vacancies, hiring new employees, or promoting current staff members. Such manuals or procedural guidelines include the use of application forms and recruitment brochures, adhering to Affirmative Action requirements, the use of interviews and medical examinations, assignment to appropriate grades, and similar details.

HIRING NOW

...for Winter, Spring and Summer Programs.

Enthusiastic youth, adults and senior adults, who desire rewarding part-time work and extra cash are required by the North York Parks and Recreation Department.

During the Winter and Spring, we hire for programs in the following areas:

- **Sports**
- **Fitness**
- **Hobbies and Crafts**
- **Aquatics**
- **Community Recreation Programs**
- **Skating**
- **Skiing**
- **Snack Bars**
- **AND MUCH MORE...**

And while summer may seem ages away, North York Parks and Recreation will soon be hiring for summer positions. This Summer's Place To Be is in:

- **Aquatics**
- **Day Camps**
- **Sports**
- **Community Recreation Programs**
- **Playgrounds**
- **Specialty Camps**
- **AND MUCH MORE...**

Summer job information brochures will be available in early December.

Applications for all positions can be obtained from the Parks and Recreation Department, 5100 Yonge St., 3rd Floor or you can call us at

224-6311

CITY OF NORTH YORK
An Equal Opportunity Employer

FIGURE 7.4.   Seasonal recruitment notice: City of North York, Ontario, Canada.

206

CHAPTER 7
Human Resource
Management:
Maximizing Staff
Performance

Job Application Form

An example of a job application form developed by the Nassau County, N.Y., Department of Recreation and Parks (Fig. 7.5) includes (1) personal details about the applicant, (2) educational background, (3) employment history, (4) personal references, (5) recreational interests and involvement, and (6) listing of specific skills in administrative, supervisory, or leadership areas. This form is used as the basis for interviewers to make hiring recommendations and as a convenient reference source through which department administrators can locate a wide variety of needed skills among staff members.

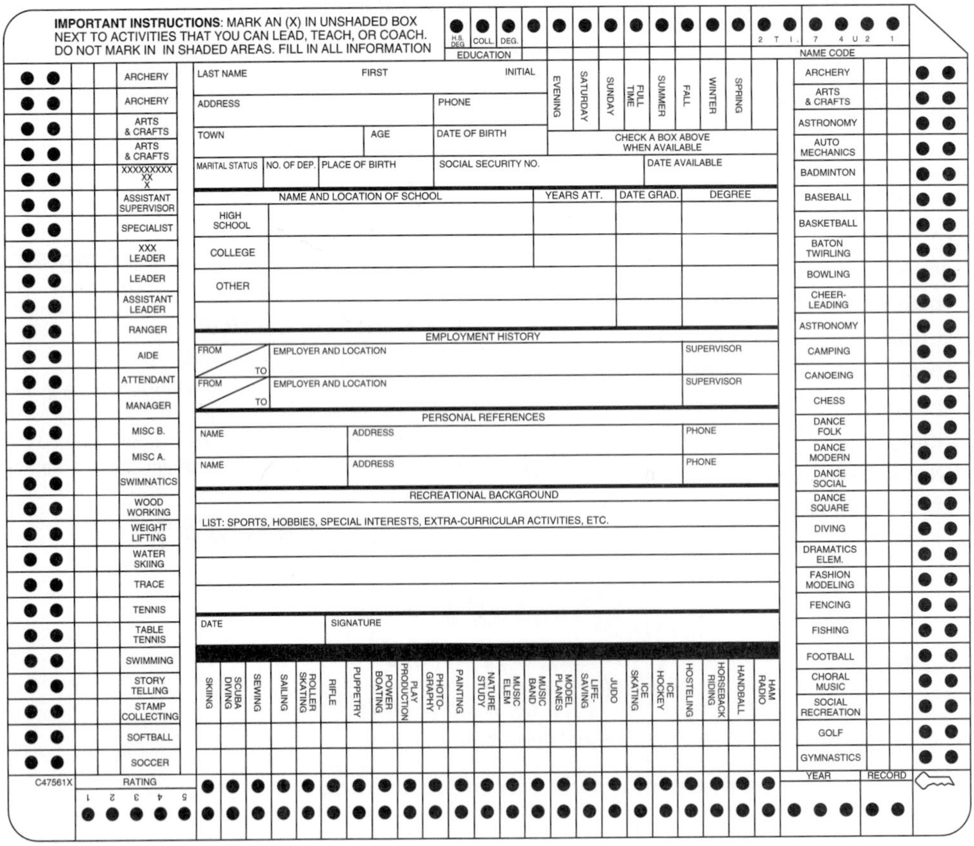

Another form, used by the Long Beach Parks, Recreation and Marine Department, asks questions regarding applicants' experience in such areas as aquatics, sports, or music (Fig. 7.6).

Use of Interviews

Too often, selection methods such as personal interviews are carried out poorly and provide ineffective results. Many individuals who are hired and who then perform at an unsatisfactory level because of poor interpersonal skills or weak motivation could and should have been "spotted" in the interview process.

FIGURE 7.5. **Job application form, Nassau County, NY, Department of Recreation and Parks.**

RECREATION LEADER SPECIALIST
SCREENING CHECKLIST

APPLICANT NAME _____

Applicant: Please assist us in processing your application by completing the following checklist completely and accurately. Thank you!

DIRECTOR/ASSISTANT DIRECTOR
Past experience:
_____# of Years as Director
_____# of Years as Asst. Director

_____# of Years as Teacher
_____Credential only
Well-rounded Background:
List areas of expertise:

AQUATIC SPECIALTY
Required Certifications:
_____First Aid
_____Community CPR
_____Red Cross Lifeguard Training
Desirable Certifications:
_____Water SafetyInstructor
Outdoor Water-related Interests:
_____Swimming
_____Canoeing
_____Kayaking
_____Sailing
_____Sailboarding
Marine Biology Background:
_____Interest
_____Teacher
Previous Youth-related Work
Experiences:
_____# of Years
List:

ADAPTIVE PROGRAM SPECIALTY
(Working with persons with disabilities)
_____# of Years as Teacher
_____# of Years as Teacher Assistant
Other related experiences:_____
_____

MUSIC AND ARTS SPECIALTY
List "T" for teaching experience
List "P" for participant experience

Music   _____ voice
         _____ instrument

Arts   _____ draw/paint
         _____ Ceramics
         _____ Dance
         _____ Drama
Previous Youth-related Work Experiences:
         _____ # of Years
         List:

SPORTS SPECIALTY
List: "T" for teaching experience
      "C" for coaching, "O" for officiating
      "P" for participant experience

_____Baseball/softball
_____Volleyball
_____Basketball
_____Track and Field
_____Soccer
Other: _____
_____
Sports Camp Counselor Experience:
_____# of Years
List:
Previous Youth-related Work Experiences:
_____# of Years
List:

OTHER HIGHLIGHTS NOTED:

FIGURE 7.6.   Job application form, Long Beach, CA.

208

*Chapter 7
Human Resource
Management:
Maximizing Staff
Performance*

Preparatory work should be done before an interview is scheduled. The candidate's references should be carefully checked by either mail or telephone, with the confidentiality of responses assured. The individual's background should be thoroughly examined to determine the appropriateness of his or her experience or education and to identify possible unexplained gaps in employment, too frequent job changes, or other signals of personal or professional instability or difficulty.

The goals of the actual interview are several: (1) to gather fuller information about the relevance of the applicant's experience and education to the position; (2) to assess the applicant's personality an character, including apparent levels of motivation, achievement drive, leadership quality, and personal style; and (3) to evaluate the applicant's overall intelligence, adaptability, and problem-solving or analytical ability. Interviews may range from structured question and answer sessions, in which employers ask exactly the same questions of each candidate, to much more flexible and unstructured sessions in which the candidate is encouraged to "run with the ball."

In general, interviews should be carried out in a comfortable and private setting and should be as pleasant and unpressured as possible. Candidates should be put at ease. The interviewer should permit them to respond fully and should show a sincere interest in all responses. The employer should avoid arguing or disagreeing with the interviewee and should be as positive and objective as possible throughout while remaining fully in control of the session. Questions may be direct, such as eliciting specific information, attitudes, or ideas, or they may be open-ended.

Equal Employment Opportunity

A final important aspect of the screening and selection process involves the need to comply with equal employment opportunity regulations for both moral and legal reasons. In all types of agencies or businesses today, avoiding any form of discrimination based on religion, sex, national origin, race, marital status, age, disability, or character is essential. Questions in these areas may be asked only when there is a clear need to determine a bona fide occupational qualification. Numerous local, state, and federal regulations deal with this problem, and before embarking on the hiring process, employers or department heads should check with their personnel managers, municipal officials, or lawyers regarding

---

In terms of gender-based hiring practices, there has been a striking turnaround with respect to "male-only" or "female-only" policies in many organizations. This has resulted both from the legal pressures just cited, and from the merging of many organizations that formerly served only one sex into agencies serving both, such as the Boys and Girls Clubs or Campfire Boys and Girls, a trend that opened up many new managerial positions for women. Strikingly, even in organizations like the Young Men's Christian Association, which was initially designed for male membership and staffed almost exclusively by men, today memberships include both sexes, and women hold many important positions. As a single example, Fig. 7.7 shows ten key program managers of the YMCA in San Mateo, California. Of this number, seven are women, and three are men.

YMCA Program Managers

209

CHAPTER 7
Human Resource
Management:
Maximizing Staff
Performance

Dale Lete, Ph.D., directs the Youth at Risk Program (YARP) at the YMCA.

YARP has been widely recognized as a model for effective community collaborations.

Patricia Gershaneck is responsible for the success of our popular YMCA Day Camp program, as well as overseeing youth and family programs.

Justin Moscoso has played a leading role in expanding our highly successful teen programs. He has accepted a promotion to the Central YMCA in San Francisco, and will be leaving us July 14.

Holly Cords keeps our busy ChildWatch area running smoothly, directs Indian Guides and birthday parties, and helps plan family events.

Jill Fleming directs our busy aquatics center, which provides lessons and activities for all ages. She is also involved in planning family events at the YMCA.

Mary McNair is membership services director. She is also staff liason for the YMCA Membership Ambassador volunteer program.

Steve Martin brings experience in sports program management to the YMCA. Youth and adult sports are growing rapidly under his direction.

Kimberly Wheeler, MFCCI, (front right) with recent volunteer class of our award winning Building Futures mentor program.

The volunteer mentors receive training in child development and basic counseling skills, and are then matched with a young person age 6-14 who needs a problem solving resource. Call Kimberly at 294-2619.

Newsletter Volunteer: Special thanks to Vinny Vance, of Double V Photography (343-4026) for donating his services to take these staff portraits.

Lynn-Marie Schuette directs our Project FOCYS program, which provides affordable, professional counseling for youth, adults, and families. The reputation of Project FOCYS has made the program a top choice for graduate level interns. See Page 2 for a picture of Project FOCYS staff.

Kathy McFarland was recently promoted to director of health and fitness. She has been instrumental in creating wellness and AOA programs.

Becky Ruppel was recently promoted from Aerobics Director to Administrative Services Director. Congratulations!

FIGURE 7.7.   Program managers, Peninsula Family YMCA, San Francisco.
Source: 1997 program brochure.

these regulations and the procedures that have been designed to satisfy them. (See Chapter 9 for a fuller discussion of legal aspects of hiring practices.)

Similarly, growing numbers of African-American and Hispanic-American professionals have entered this field over the past three decades. However, the number of Hispanic-American leisure-service employees still remains disproportionately low. Research indicates that, although Hispanic-Americans are expected to become the largest minority population in the United States early in the twenty-first century, less than 3 percent of bachelor's degrees in Parks, Recreation, Leisure, and Fitness were taken by individuals with persons with Hispanic or Latino names in the early and mid-1990s.[7]

Selection Process

Depending on the level of the position to be filled, the selection and screening process may be relatively brief or may be complex and drawn out. For example, in a search for an outstanding new superintendent of recreation for the Peoria, Illinois, Park District, more than five months elapsed between the resignation of the previous superintendent and the selection of a new one.

210

CHAPTER 7
Human Resource
Management:
Maximizing Staff
Performance

In some cases, large national organizations or federations of youth-serving agencies have sought to standardize the recruitment and hiring process, to make it more efficient and effective. The Recreational Services Division of the Naval Military Personnel Command, for example, has developed, field-tested, and published a staffing guide to be used in filling Navy Morale, Welfare and Recreation (MWR) Director positions. This guide presents in detailed form the recommended procedures for: (1) announcing the position vacancy through the Navy's Job Opportunity Bulletin; (2) determining appropriate qualifications for the position, including length and type of required prior experience; (3) a ranking/panel process involving a panel of three to five members chaired by a person designated by the activity's Commanding Officer; and (4) the selection process, including review of "best-qualified" individuals, interviews where appropriate, and negotiations with respect to salary, transportation entitlements, and projected entrance-on-duty date. Figure 7.8 illustrates the process and the recommended time-frame for carrying it out.

In many public recreation and park agencies, after full consideration is given to examination scores, interview ratings, performance records, and similar input, candidates are placed on a civil-service eligibility list, with appointments to be made from the three highest-ranking candidates. Appointment may then be made when the opening occurs. In some cases, a candidate may be appointed on a provisional basis because no examination that applies to the position in question has been scheduled. At a later point, he or she would be required to take the examination.

While most nongovernmental leisure-service agencies are less formal or structured in their hiring practices, they often follow essentially the same sequence of advertising positions, preparing job descriptions, and interviewing applicants.

FIGURE 7.8. Recommended hiring process and timetable, in U.S. Navy Morale, Welfare and Recreation Units.

Task	Estimated Time-frame	Action Officer
Vacancy announcement preparation	3 hours—by use of "canned"	Assigned personnelist
Opening/closing date plus receipt of SF 171s	4 weeks	Management
Sending/receiving supervisory evaluations and applicant narratives	10 minutes per applicant	Assigned personnelist
Determining highly *qualified* candidates	Up to 1 week beyond closing date	Assigned personnelist
Panel process	4 to 5 applicants per day	Panel members
Selection (includes interviewers)	1 day maximum	C.O. or his/her designee
TOTAL TIME FROM ADVERTISING TO FILL	APPROX. 6–7 WEEKS	

From *A Staffing Guide for Filling Navy MWR Director Positions,* (Washington, D.C., Naval Military Personnel Command, Personnel Branch, June 1988).

Appointment and Probation

After being hired, candidates normally undergo a three- to six-month probationary period. New employees should be carefully observed and evaluated during this period. If their performance is satisfactory, they are then eligible for permanent employment and may not be discharged except for cause, according to the personnel procedures or union contracts that normally govern such actions.

211

CHAPTER 7
Human Resource
Management:
Maximizing Staff
Performance

ORIENTATION AND IN-SERVICE EDUCATION

The first weeks or months of an employee's job experience should include a thorough introduction to the agency and its personnel and program practices. This might include such elements as a tour of the physical facility or facilities, and exposure to its various divisions and functions, a careful outlining of all responsibilities and procedures, and a period of thorough supervision, with in some cases the individual working directly as an assistant in a center or other facility before begin given more independent responsibility.

A key element in the orientation should be giving the worker a departmental personnel manual that includes detailed descriptions of the legal structure and organization of the department, personnel practices and obligations, guides for leaders in various settings, and a statement of the objectives of the department.

As an illustration of the orientation process, the program for therapeutic recreation field-placement students in the Patient Activities Department of the Clinical Center of the National Institutes of Health in Bethesda, Maryland, includes a general orientation to the department, with visits to each program area, meetings with program area supervisors, and sessions in each of the Clinical Center's ancillary service units—all within the first two weeks of the field placement.

In-Service Education

After the orientation period, there should be a well-organized program of in-service education that heightens employees' understanding of their work, improves their skills, and generally enhances their professional growth.

Areas of Need for In-Service Education

Research studies have identified several important area that should be covered in agency in-service education activities. These include such elements as:

Interpersonal skills, such as goal setting, problem solving, team building, and delegation of authority.

Personal on-the-job factors, such as time management, listening skills, stress management, or public speaking.

212

*CHAPTER 7
Human Resource
Management:
Maximizing Staff
Performance*

Technical job demands, such as equipment operation or product knowledge, word processing, or risk-management principles.

Supervisory skills, such as new-employee orientation, performance appraisals, or the hiring and selection process.

In-service education may take several different forms, both formal and informal. Among the most frequently used are the following approaches.

Individual Conferences with Supervisors.   Workers should be regularly observed and should have the opportunity to meet with their supervisors to discuss their work in a nonthreatening, constructive fashion.

Staff Meetings.   At various levels, staff meetings contribute to in-service training. The staff of a large center or district or even the entire recreation staff of a department may meet monthly to be informed of departmental plans, policies, and similar matters and to take part in problem-solving discussions or project planning. Individual members of the staff may be asked to report on aspects of their work, or committees may be appointed to study special problems and present them to the group. Individuals who have attended professional conferences may be asked to report back to the staff on these meetings.

Special Institutes.   These are short-term training workshops, usually dealing with a special activity within the recreation program, such as theater, arts and crafts, sports, or camping and nature activities. They may also deal with special programs, such as activities for the mentally retarded or the development of golden age clubs. Institutes may last for only a day or two or may extend over a period of several days. Such institutes may be staffed by experts from the department itself or from neighboring departments or professional organizations, or they may be conducted in cooperation with nearby colleges or universities.

In-Service Training Courses.   In-service training courses are comparable to institutes except that they usually are extended over a period of time, with perhaps one morning or early afternoon a week devoted to attendance. In small cities, one such course might also be offered during the winter session. In large cities, several such courses might be offered simultaneously in different districts of the city. The same topics might be covered in each district but on a rotating basis. Normally, in-service training programs are compulsory when scheduled during work hours, although the department administrator may designate them for certain personnel only. In some departments, they may be given as weekend or evening classes and attended voluntarily.

Other In-Service Education Methods.   In addition to the preceding approaches, staff members may be encouraged, given brief leaves, and even assisted financially to attend national or regional conferences in recreation and parks.

They may also be encouraged to attend college or university courses in recreation and parks leadership and administration or to work toward appropriate degrees, with adjustments made in their schedules to make this possible.

A library may be maintained with books and magazines in the recreation field, and staff members should be encouraged to read and make use of these.

Staff members may be encouraged to join professional organizations and participate in their activities, in part because of their value in professional development. Visits may be arranged for staff members to see recreation and park departments in neighboring communities as a form of in-service education.

213

CHAPTER 7
*Human Resource
Management:
Maximizing Staff
Performance*

Training in Other Types of Settings

The content and organization of in-service education programs may vary greatly in different types of agencies, depending on their program priorities and staffing needs.

Boy Scouts of America

For example, the Boy Scouts of America operate with a relatively small core of paid professionals and many thousands of volunteer adult leaders. The national headquarters of the organization therefore develops an extensive training program for leaders with national and regional training events, clearly stated standards and goals, training manuals, and award certificates.

Leadership Training Standards

1. A Cubmaster is trained when he or she has completed the sessions "What Is Cub Scouting? "Program Planning," "Den and Pack Management," and "The Pack Meeting" from *Cub Scout Leader Basic Training*, OR "The Cub Scout Program," "Program Planning," "Pack Administration," "Pack Relationships," and "Webelos Den Program" from *Cub Scout Leader Basic Training Manual*.

2. A Scoutmaster is trained when he has completed the six sessions found in the *Boy Scout Leader Basic Training Manual*.

3. An Explorer Advisor is trained when he or she has completed the three sessions found in the *Explorer Leader Basic Training Manual*, OR attended the group training sessions "What Is Exploring?" "Post Program Planning," and "Post Leader Workshop."

Young Men's Christian Association

The YMCA sponsors an extensive range of courses and certification requirements for its personnel at all levels. Through the year, it schedules many program schools in different geographical locations (see Fig. 7.9), which offer certification classes in the following program categories:

General Program Training	Family
Active Older Adults	Health and Fitness
Aquatics	Sports
Camping	Teen Leadership
Child Care	Youth and Community Development

214

CHAPTER 7
Human Resource
Management:
Maximizing Staff
Performance

1997 Program School Course List

[7] Courses listed will definitely be included in the schedule of the Program School listed at the top of the column.

Requests to add courses will only be considered if the request is made to the Program School director at least seven (7) months prior to the school start date.

Refer to each Program School's brochure for the final list of courses available.

Course	Page	Phoenix, AZ • 1/9-15	Mobile, AL • 1/25-31	New York, NY • 2/26-3/5	Des Moines, IA • 4/3-9	Houston, TX • 4/4-10	Denver, CO • 4/18-26	San Francisco, CA • 5/2-8	Tampa, FL • 5/3-9	Columbus, OH • 5/16-22	Springfield, MA • 5/28-6/3	Baltimore, MD • 5/31-6/6	Long Beach, CA • 6/4-10	Tacoma, WA • 7/25-31
General Program Training	20													
Program Trainer Orientation	20													
Program Trainer Orientation Trainer	20													
Intro. to Property Management	20													
Intro. to Property Management Trainer	20													
Arts and Humanities	21													
"Working With" Series	21													
Working with Children Up to 5	21													
Up to Age 5 Trainer	21													
Working with 5- to 9-Year-Olds	21													
5- to 9-Year-Olds Trainer	22													
Working with 10- to 14-Year-Olds*	22													
10- to 14-Year-Olds Trainer*	22													
Working with 15- to 18-Year-Olds*	22													
15- to 18-Year-Olds Trainer*	23													
Working with Program Volunteers	23													
Program Volunteers Trainer	23													
Working with People with Disabilities	23													
Disabilities Trainer	24													
Working with the Military	24													
Military Trainer	24													
Working with the World	24													
Working with the World Trainer	25													
Core Competency Courses	25													
Building a Career Plan*	25													
Understanding the Mission*	25													
Mission Trainer*	26													
Communication Skills*	26													

* Special scholarships available through Keeping Our Promise Grant. See page 16.

FIGURE 7.9.   YMCA listing of in-service training programs. (Shown is a section of the overall listing, with many additional courses and locations.)

Other courses are offered in areas of management responsibility, including trainer-level certification sessions dealing with such functions as: marketing strategies, program development, facilities management, financial development and budgeting, problem solving and decision making, supervision, and training skills. In addition to such courses, the YMCA sponsors an Executive Development Program that equips senior directors and others to prepare for YMCA branch and corporate executive positions.

215

CHAPTER 7
Human Resource
Management:
Maximizing Staff
Performance

Commercial Recreation: Theme Park Approaches

At theme parks such as the Old Country in Williamsburg, Virginia, and Busch Gardens, job-training programs include such elements as practicing ride operations, operating cash registers, and learning basic food preparation and cleanliness. At appropriate times, the Old Country may hold a practice day for employees' friends and families, which may serve as a dress rehearsal for park employees. As employees gain experience in such tasks as being ride operators, zoo attendants, or food service workers, they may move on to managerial positions as unit or area supervisors. At this stage, they receive additional training in the form of several four-hour sessions or leadership modules, which cover such elements as: (1) the Old Country business philosophy, including leadership styles, supervisor responsibilities, and employee welfare; (2) communication skills; and (3) building employee motivation and a productive working climate.

Sharing Resources

In many cases, smaller agencies or departments that are not able to mount their own in-service education programs because of limited staff numbers and resources have joined with other organizations to cosponsor in-service activities. Several such public departments may cooperate on a countywide level to establish summer leadership-training institutes. Not infrequently, state professional societies develop special courses and workshops for their members in addition to their regular conferences.

ROLE OF NATIONAL ORGANIZATIONS IN CONTINUING EDUCATION

In addition to in-service education provided by leisure-service organizations for their own employees—as in the case of the YMCA, Boy Scouts, or Police Athletic League—major national organizations sponsor a wide range of continuing education courses, workshops and conferences for individuals working within different sectors of the recreation, parks, and leisure-service field. For example, the NRPA sponsors numerous continuing education activities at its national and regional conferences. In addition, it cosponsors varied programs in cooperation with universities, other professional societies, or organizations like the Oglebay, West Virginia, center for continuing education in recreation and parks management (Fig. 7.10).

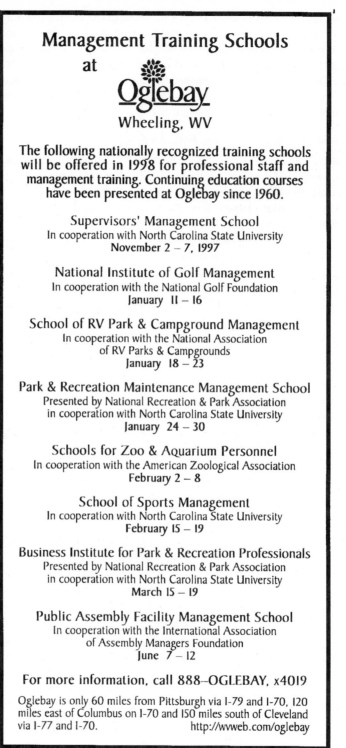

216   FIGURE 7.10.   Continuing education programs: Oglebay, West Virginia.

In the area of youth sports, numerous organizations like the National Youth Sports Coaches Association, the Catholic Youth Organization, or groups representing a particular sport sponsor conferences and workshops designed to upgrade the level of youth sports coaching or league management, improve safety practices, or educate parents and the public at large with respect to appropriate values in this field. Similarly, in armed forces, therapeutic recreation, and other specialized fields, professional societies sponsor numerous institutes and training workshops.

217

*CHAPTER 7
Human Resource
Management:
Maximizing Staff
Performance*

PERSONNEL POLICY MANUALS

As employees continue on the job, an important aspect of personnel management involves the development of sound personnel policies. In many leisure-service agencies that are part of larger systems, such as a recreation and park department within a larger county government structure, these will be influenced heavily by the policies prevailing throughout the overall organization. Thus, in hospital programs, the personnel policies that apply to all employees should automatically be applied to recreation personnel. Similarly, in military recreation programs, all civilian employees (including recreation personnel) will be subject to the same personnel policies.

Public Agency Personnel Manuals

McChesney has written an excellent manual describing personnel policies in recreation and park departments, based on the practices followed in a number of outstanding departments. This manual includes the following major categories of personnel policies:

I. General regulations
   Responsibility
   Adoption
   Revision
II. Classification plan
   Contents
   Maintenance of plan
   Employee review
III. Definitions
   Full-time
   Seasonal
   Salaried
IV. Employment
   Application
   Recruitment and selection
   Appointment
   Probation
   Seasonal
   Evaluation and ratings
   Promotions

Assignment and transfer
Disciplinary actions
Separation and resignation
Reinstatement
V. Hours of work
   Workweek
   Full-time salaried employees
   Full-time hourly employees
   Work schedules
VI. Compensation and related
    benefits
   Salary classification and guides
   Pay periods and time reports
   Deductions
   Holidays
   Overtime
   Vacations
   Insurance
   Retirement
   Credit union

218

CHAPTER 7
Human Resource
Management:
Maximizing Staff
Performance

VII. Absences and leaves
   Absences
   Health or hardship leave
VIII. Travel and vehicle use
   Departmental vehicles
   Private vehicles
IX. In-service training
   Purpose
   Conference attendance
   Staff meetings and conferences
X. Rules of conduct
   Dress and appearance
   Employee cooperation
   Reporting for duty
XI. Relations between employees—
   department—community
   Employee-administrator
   relations
   Employee-community
   relations
   Gifts
   Solicitation of funds
   Management of funds
   Publicity releases
   Employee-patron relations
   Accidents to patrons[8]

In the typical large-city personnel manual, detailed policies are stated with regard to each of these areas of practice. As a single example, typical personnel policies with respect to *disciplinary action* are summarized as follows.

Disciplinary Action

Departmental personnel manuals should clearly specify the required behavior of employees in areas such as dress, smoking or drinking, persistent lateness, acts of dishonesty or pilferage, refusal to perform assigned tasks, violence or verbal abuse of patrons or coworkers, unauthorized absence, use of departmental vehicles, or general attitude. Both informal and formal disciplinary actions should be set forth in the manual. Depending on the nature and degree of the infraction, disciplinary actions should include the following procedures, and should be based on carefully kept supervisory reports:

1. *Reprimands,* either verbal or formal, which are entered in the service record;
2. *Suspensions,* or temporary separations without pay, for specified periods;
3. *Demotions,* involving placing the employee on a lower job classification at a lower rate of pay;
4. *Dismissals,* which are discharges or separations for cause.

Usually such procedures are implemented only in serious cases in which there is clear evidence of the employee's unsatisfactory performance or violation of department requirements. The department should provide opportunity for a hearing or grievance proceedings in the case of such disciplinary actions when the demoted or discharged employee wishes to resist the departmental action. Increasingly, municipal labor unions are playing a role in such proceedings.

Policies in Nonpublic Agencies

Detailed personnel policies like those presented above are most likely to be found in public agencies, having been developed over time through civil service processes or labor union negotiations and agreements that apply to all governmental employees. Large voluntary agencies and therapeutic recreation programs are also likely to have carefully detailed personnel procedures and manuals.

In contrast, many smaller leisure-service programs in private or commercial settings have rudimentary personnel plans. Often, hours of work and leaves are treated flexibly, as are disciplinary actions and evaluation procedures. In many such programs, there are no retirement plans and limited health and welfare benefits.

Ethics in Staff Performance

It is essential that all personnel operate with a high level of personal integrity. In many areas of professional performance, employees come face to face with issues that may significantly affect public welfare and quality of life. Therapeutic recreation specialists often work with patients or clients who are highly vulnerable and who may be harmed by incompetent or immoral practitioners. Public and commercial recreation managers often are in a position to employ substantial numbers of individuals, to make large-scale purchases, or to make other decisions that require impartial and professionally sound judgments. Numerous other groups of leisure-service managers are often faced with responsibilities that require vigilance if the public is to be protected against harm. In fitness programs, for example, serious problems of health may result from inadequate medical screening or supervision of activities.

In all such cases, there is a need for practitioners to operate under a clearly defined code of ethical behavior. Fain writes:

> Struggling to determine what is "right" and what is "wrong" is what distinguishes a group of practitioners and results in the establishment of a profession. . . . However, the [leisure-service] profession has done little to safeguard the public against harm from the incompetence or immoral who . . . do harm.[9]

Obviously, the issue of ethics may be viewed from different perspectives, including both moral and legal guidelines or strictures. Fain goes on to argue that the leisure-service field should develop clearly stated guidelines for ethical behavior in terms of professional and public relationships and that these should be adopted by state societies throughout the nation. Shapiro agrees, pointing out that through its ethical code, a profession's commitment to the welfare of society becomes a matter of public record, thereby insuring for itself the continued confidence of the community.[10]

Recognizing this need, the NRPA formed a task force in 1991 to formulate a code of ethics that would apply to all organization members. It was initially agreed that this code should be short, concise, and backed up by a plan for enforcement. However, in a series of hearings, considerable resistance was expressed to any punitive procedures, and the enforcement element was therefore eliminated from the code. As approved by the NRPA Board of Trustees at the 1994 Congress in Minneapolis, the adopted code contained a number of general statements stressing the need for "integrity," "honesty," and the avoidance of activities seeking personal "gain" or "profit," or in conflict with agency goals.

In a much more extensive statement, the NTRS approved a Code of Ethics in 1990 and a set of Interpretive Guidelines in 1994. This organization's overall code contained an explanatory preamble followed by six detailed sections on

220

CHAPTER 7
Human Resource
Management:
Maximizing Staff
Performance

the obligations of professionals and the profession itself to individuals served, to other individuals and society, to colleagues, to the profession—and to "professional virtue."

Numerous individual organizations have their own codes of ethics; in the case of public agencies, these usually are part of overall codes applying to government employment in general.

SUPERVISION IN LEISURE-SERVICE AGENCIES

Within the older frame of reference of classical management theory, supervisors were expected to play a somewhat authoritarian role, acting as enforcers of the business or other organization's policies, and making sure that workers were fully productive. The *chain-of-command* and *span-of-control* concepts also saw them as links or transmission channels through which the decisions or policies of upper-level management were communicated to line employees and through which employees' views and needs were expressed to company or agency executives.

Supervisory methods tended to be authoritarian, relying on the reward-or-punishment, "carrot-or-stick" approach, and sticking rigidly to procedures outlined in personnel manuals. Even during the human relations era of personnel administration, the practices of democratic, participative management and shared decision making were not shared in many large business or governmental organizations.

Impact of Human Resource Management

However, the growing acceptance of the human resource management (HRM) approach over the past two decades has had a powerful influence on agency personnel practices and supervisory methods.

In the newer approach to human resource management, supervisors tend to play a broader role as *coaches* and *counselors*. Coaching is chiefly concerned with learning and improving on-the-job skills, in which the supervisor passes along his or her experience and knowledge both during the period of orientation and throughout the continuing work experience. Through regular observation and both formal and informal conferences, supervisors assist subordinate employees in upgrading their performance.

Counseling encompasses both encouragement, criticism, and a range of techniques designed to deal with possible problems in the work environment, interpersonal difficulties, or other emotional or social issues that may occur.

As shown in Chapter 2, human resource management represented a new thrust in personnel management, which regarded an organization's employees as an important resource—rather than "cogs" in a machine. According to this approach, it is essential to communicate honestly and fully with employees, to involve them in policy making and problem solving, and to encourage their strong commitment and identification with the organization. Throughout, a carefully thought-out approach to the recruitment, motivation, and management of people is critical.

Normally, this takes place on a one-to-one basis, although it may at times involve groups or clusters of employees. When problems are of a serious, intractable, or deep-rooted nature, or when they involve conflicts of a possible legal nature or major infractions of agency policy, they should be referred to appropriate individuals or offices within the overall organization.

221

Chapter 7
Human Resource
Management:
Maximizing Staff
Performance

When working with individual employees who have demonstrated on-the-job problems, it is essential to deal with the situation's underlying causes. The following guidelines are helpful:

1. Listen patiently to what employees say before making any comment.
2. Refrain from criticizing or offering hasty advice on the problem.
3. Never argue with employees while counseling them.
4. Give undivided attention to employees while they are talking.
5. Look beyond the mere words of what employees say—listen to see if they are revealing something deeper than what appears on the surface.

If the problem is relatively minor, simply helping the employee unburden himself or herself may lead to a solution. Discussing the matter with a helpful and supportive supervisor may suggest commonsense courses of action to take or at least may pinpoint the areas of difficulty and the need to take action. If the problem is more severe or the employee shows a significant level of personal disturbance, the supervisor should recommend a counselor or clinic. At the same time that the counseling effort is friendly and supportive, it must also be realistic in that the employee must come to grips with the consequences of the difficulty he or she is experiencing. For example, if drinking is the problem, the agency's rules and policies must be made explicit, and the employee must recognize that if improvement is not shown, suspension or job termination is a real possibility. If the policy mandates such penalties for employee's behavior, the supervisor must carry them out. The supervisor must recognize that he or she is *not* qualified as a therapist and has a primary obligation to serve the agency, rather than the employee who is having difficulty.

General guidelines for effective supervisory practices within a human resource management framework are outlined in Figure 7.11.

Behavior Modification and Motivational Strategies

As part of the human resource management approach, many business and other organizations have used behavior modification techniques to achieve objectives. The basic premise underlying this approach is that almost all behavior is operant or learned. Therefore, it can be modified or changed by deliberate supervisory action.

Typically, behavior modification is based on the principle that the appropriate use of reinforcers will support desired changes in employee behavior. Reinforcers tend to be of two types: (1) *positive* reinforcers, which add something good, such as a bonus, a "stroke," or a desired change in work assignment, to the employee's life, and (2) *negative* reinforcers, which consist of removing something unpleasant, such as a distasteful task or schedule, from the employee's life. So-called *punishers*, or *deterrents*, may involve low ratings or

The Effective Supervisor

1. Establishes high but attainable expectations for staff in terms of work standards and goals, and makes sure that these are designed to achieve the goals of the department itself.

2. Places staff members in jobs in which their individual abilities are most likely to be fully utilized.

3. Recognizes the universal need for approval, and helps staff members meet this need by (a) bestowing credit and praising accomplishments, (b) showing consideration toward staff members, and (c) acknowledging their share in the total enterprise and their contribution making it a success.

4. Seeks to help staff members become more effective, and removes obstacles to success by providing technical assistance and emotional support.

5. Avoids ego-threatening behavior, and uses the mistakes of subordinates as a basis for counseling and improving performance rather than as an opportunity for threats and punishment.

6. Clearly defines the responsibilities and accountability of staff members and shows confidence in their ability to carry out these tasks.

7. Encourages staff members to participate in policy-planning, decision-making, and program development, not as a "token" gesture but with serious weight being given to their contributions.

8. Exercises leadership when necessary, asserting rank, making decisions, and exerting force to achieve departmental goals.

9. Is an effective link between management and leadership, communicating information helpful to their psychological well-being and morale and to their awareness of total departmental developments.

10. Appraises employee on the basis of objective and measurable performance elements, taking into account differences in the qualities of individual workers and different levels of task difficulty.

11. Does not play favorites, but seeks to reward all workers equally and to provide tangible rewards and status symbols, particularly for high-level performance.

12. Is friendly, sympathetic, and approachable, yet also maintains a sense of dignity based on the rank he or she has been assigned and the authority vested by the department.

FIGURE 7.11.   Guidelines for leisure-service supervisors.

extra work because of poor performance or taking away something good from the employee's environment. Reinforcement techniques are usually far superior to punishment techniques in producing lasting behavioral changes.

Reward Systems

One positive approach to strengthening employee motivation is through the use of rewards and awards. Rewards may take many forms, including the formal recognition of a staff member's superior performance through awards for distinctive service and the accompanying benefit in terms of job promotion. Award banquets, gifts and scrolls, and other ceremonies all provide visibility and positive rewards for high-performing employees.

In some cases—particularly in commercial recreation businesses—cash awards, bonuses, or salary raises provide monetary motivation to employees.

For example, in the U.S. Navy club and revenue-generating programs, a formal system of cash awards for high-level productivity has been used. In other types of agencies, such approaches are generally not feasible.

223

CHAPTER 7
Human Resource
Management:
Maximizing Staff
Performance

Another means of strengthening employee motivation is through job enrichment and flexible scheduling. Recognizing that poor morale may result from monotonous, overly specialized, routine work assignments, many companies in the business world have experimented successfully with more flexible assignments and schedules.

A useful method of making an individual's work more varied consists of rotating it on a regular basis. In the past, many public recreation and park agencies in large cities assigned leaders to the same facility on a full-time, year-round basis. Today few large cities have enough full-time professional leaders to staff all their facilities on a permanent basis. In addition, because of the nature of recreation scheduling and program changes during the year, assigning a person to one location throughout all seasons is neither economical nor logical. Many departments have therefore changed their personnel assignment policies in the following ways:

1. They are rotating assignments at different seasons, so an individual might work at various times in a golden age center, in a youth center, on a playground, or in a camp, depending on where he or she can be most productive at a given time.
2. In addition to their regular assignments, leaders may be assigned to other districtwide or citywide roles, which they can carry on in slack periods during the day or week. For example, a playground director may be given the responsibility of supervising a satellite after-school program during the winter season, may serve as district chairperson for a particular tournament or program, or may be a member of a committee planning a citywide special event.

BUILDING PROFESSIONAL IDENTIFICATION AND HIGH-PERFORMANCE TEAMS

An important thrust in strengthening staff motivation consists of encouraging a strong sense of personal ties both to the profession of recreation, park, and leisure services, and to the individual's agency and work unit or team. To accomplish this, managers should encourage employees to read professional literature, attend professional conferences, become involved in continuing education programs, and strengthen their commitment to the leisure-service field in other ways.

Similarly, it is essential that employees have a sense of pride in their own work units or teams. Moosbruker defines three types of teams: (1) management teams that have significant ongoing responsibility for the organization's operation; (2) task forces designed to achieve a specific goal, after which they disband; and (3) work teams that function in a particular task area over time. A high-performing team, she writes, is:

226

*Chapter 7
Human Resource
Management:
Maximizing Staff
Performance*

Several widely found approaches to problem solving follow:

1. *Authoritarian action.* The manager or supervisor makes a decision alone, with little or no input from subordinates or other personnel. While typical of old-style bureaucratic management systems, this is an undesirable approach in today's human resource management settings.
2. *Avoidance.* Too often, managers may avoid a problem, hoping it will simply disappear or resolve itself over time. Although there is some justification for not making an emergency out of every problem, this ostrichlike approach is not a desirable course of action in most cases, where problems may continue to fester or grow worse.
3. *Analysis by planning specialists.* In some public leisure-service agencies, problems of a serious nature are assigned to special teams of planners, consultants, or experts in systems analysis. Such teams carefully analyze the problem, in some cases making use of computer-based models, and recommend solutions.
4. *Decision by higher authorities.* One approach to dealing with difficult problems is to "pass the buck" by moving them up the chain of command. This may be done either because lower-level employees do not want responsibility for handling more serious problems or because administrators have made clear that they *wish* to be consulted on all such matters.
5. *Group-centered problem solving.* In this approach, the members of the team become involved in a process of group discussion and analysis that examines alternatives and ultimately decides on an appropriate course of action. Such team-oriented approaches to problem solving have become increasingly popular in recent years.

It is generally believed today that the most effective approach to problem solving stresses group participation. With techniques such as group discussion, brainstorming, or role playing, it is possible to get at the root of the problem and understand opposing points of view or alternative solutions.

Brainstorming

For example, brainstorming offers a useful means of identifying possible solutions to difficult problems. It is a process with four basic rules: (1) suspend critical judgment of ideas; (2) emphasize getting a quantity of ideas; (3) free-wheel, by generating upbeat, energetic, and inventive ideas; and (4) cross-fertilize, by "piggy-backing" on the ideas of others.

During the brainstorm process, participants should be encouraged to submit even the wildest or most unusual kinds of solutions or suggestions. At the same time, they should avoid negative or discouraging comments on the ideas that have been put forth. When a good list of ideas has been presented and posted on a board or screen, group members may then analyze them in terms of their feasibility and promise for achieving desired goals in solving the problem.

Whatever method is used, the problem-solving process should rely on a sequence of steps, as shown in Figure 7.12.

227

*Chapter 7
Human Resource
Management:
Maximizing Staff
Performance*

Problem-Solving Process

1. Recognize the problem, including not only its symptoms but also its apparent causes. This may involve varied types of difficulties such as: (a) problems of staff functioning or interpersonal relationships; (b) problems of interdepartmental or interagency relationships; (c) problems of community relationships; (d) problems between staff members and participants; or (e) problems of inadequate finances or other difficulties in the agency's environment.

2. Assign responsibility for solving the problem. This may be the task of a single program leader or supervisor or may be assigned to a small group or task force of staff members, depending on the problem's severity and the resources required. At the same time, the desired objectives of the problem solution should be defined.

3. Investigate the problem and gather all relevant data. This may involve the examination of records, direct observation of a program or facility, interviews with concerned parties, or even formal hearing or other investigative sessions.

4. Identify alternative solutions. Here, several different strategies for solving the problem may be identified and balanced with each other both in their probable degree of success and in the difficulty that might be experienced in implementing them.

5. The solution that appears most logical and most likely to be successful, as well as the most feasible in administration, should be selected and put into action. When this is done, it is usually wise to inform all parties of the decision that has been reached or ideally to have this occur as part of the shared problem-solving effort.

6. When the problem-solving solution has been implemented, it must be carefully monitored and its success evaluated. If it is *not* working, or if new difficulties appear, reviewing the strategy that has been chosen and trying a new solution may be necessary.

FIGURE 7.12.   **Suggested problem-solving process.**

Conflict Resolution

Group-centered techniques are particularly useful in dealing with conflict situations, when two or more staff members, participants, or other stakeholders are in sharp disagreement with each other.

The traditional view of conflict within any governmental or business organization was that it was harmful and should be avoided or prevented at all costs. *Preventing* conflict was a widely shared purpose of administrators. In modern management theory, a somewhat different view prevails. Many experts believe that not only is conflict inevitable but that it is desirable and may be used to constructive ends.

228

CHAPTER 7
Human Resource
Management:
Maximizing Staff
Performance

Obviously, there are a number of different ways of dealing with conflict. One of these is through the authoritarian use of "clout." For example, after one series of heated exchanges regarding the feasibility of a project under consideration, the chairman concluded the discussion by saying, "Now we have everyone's point of view. Those who are not in favor of going ahead with this project may signify by saying 'I resign.'" This may be described as the "win-lose" approach, in which either the power figure or most of the group impose its will without concessions to the others; they *win*, and the others *lose*. Another approach may be described as a "lose-lose" tactic. Here, through compromise or arbitration, neither side attains what it really wants and considers important; thus, both sides lose.

Conflict is resolved most productively when a strong effort is made to involve all members of the group, who are helped by bringing their underlying needs and values out into the open and discussing them in the honest effort to arrive at a consensus. In the "win-win" approach, all participants feel that their thinking has been properly presented and given full consideration by all members of the group. Each member recognizes the rights of other members to have feelings, values, and ideas and strives to respect these rather than fight in a determined way for the alternative that he or she considers to be unilaterally best. Ultimately, through this kind of open confrontation and discussion, decisions can be made that all members recognize are in the best interests of the organization.

A positive problem-solving orientation, which avoids threats, hostility, deception, or the arbitrary exercise of power, will help solve such conflicts in the most constructive way. Techniques such as group discussion, role-reversal psychodrama exercises, (for example, a gang member might play the role of a center director, and vice versa), or the use of third-party mediators are helpful in resolving conflicts.

OTHER ISSUES IN HUMAN RESOURCE MANAGEMENT

Finally, there are three other important issues that leisure-service managers must deal with within the overall function of human resource management: *volunteers, personnel evaluation,* and *labor-relations* concerns.

Use of Volunteers

The sheer volume of volunteer involvement in nonprofit programs and social causes is impressive. A research study by Independent Sector, a group that represents and does research with charitable organizations, found that 93 million Americans volunteer, giving over 20 billion hours a year to services that range from baking cookies for a school fair to serving museums, libraries, and other cultural institutions. In recreation, park, and leisure-service agencies, they fulfill such functions as:

1. Assisting in administrative, promotional, or advisory activities;
2. Working with specific groups or activities, in playgrounds, community centers, and similar facilities, or providing adult direction for teenage or golden age clubs;
3. Mounting special community projects, particularly in areas related to the arts, ecology, or social service, in which special expertise and interest are needed;
4. Providing clerical assistance and helping with mailings, preparation of reports, and similar assignments;
5. Offering special technical assistance (as in the case of residents who are architects, lawyers, or planners) with studies, films, or other projects designed to promote the work of the department;
6. Providing volunteer maintenance of parks, playgrounds, and other resources, including beach cleanups, tree planting, and similar tasks.

229

CHAPTER 7
Human Resource
Management:
Maximizing Staff
Performance

Recruitment of Volunteers

It is usually necessary to seek out volunteers in a systematic way because they rarely tend to appear of their own volition—although some may be recruited individually through word-of-mouth contact or personal involvement in agency programs. The most useful techniques for recruiting volunteers include appealing to organizations with an interest in recreation and community betterment, such as church groups, parent-teacher organizations, or special-interest organizations whose members are interested in promoting their hobby or interests. Hospitals often employ coordinators of volunteer programs, who develop contacts for reaching potential volunteers. In some cases, there may be a community council for social agencies, which services to publicize the need for volunteers and channels volunteers to appropriate agencies for work assignments.

Motivation for Volunteering

In a study of volunteerism in Philadelphia, which included setting up a substantial number of innovative neighborhood projects using volunteers, it was found that those who volunteer typically have certain strong motivations, including the following: desire to serve the community or contribute to neighborhood life; desire to help in programs involving family members; wish to continue in an activity in which they once starred, as in sports; or prevocational value, as in students doing unpaid field work in a field of career interest.

In recruiting and supervising volunteers, it is important that these motivations be recognized and that volunteer workers be given the fullest opportunity to meet their needs satisfactorily.

Training of Volunteers

Volunteers should be carefully screened and trained before being assigned to specific tasks. Those who are unstable, have unrealistic expectations of the volunteer assignment, or lack the potential for making a real contribution should be weeded out by the coordinator or supervisor of volunteers. Next, there should be a series of orientation sessions or meetings designed to familiarize the

230

*CHAPTER 7
Human Resource
Management:
Maximizing Staff
Performance*

volunteers with the objectives and philosophy of the department, departmental rules and policies, principles of recreation leadership, and the specific responsibilities they are expected to assume. If sufficient numbers are involved, special training institutes may be held for the orientation of volunteers.

Supervision of Volunteers

The function of supervising volunteers is similar to that of supervising paid personnel, except that volunteers tend to require closer attention and more technical assistance and advice. Supervisors must help them realize that the department counts on their regular involvement just as it does that of paid employees and that their attendance must be consistent and dependable. If they are given meaningful assignments that challenge their capabilities, their involvement *will* be more consistent than if they are given trivial or mechanical jobs to perform.

Recognition of Volunteers

Finally, it is necessary to make clear to volunteers that their work does make a major contribution to the department. This can be done through simple verbal appreciation, recognition of volunteers in reports and publicity, department meetings in which their work is singled out for praise, special dinners or meetings (sometimes on an annual basis) designed to recognize the work of volunteers and promote fuller volunteer involvement, or awards, plaques, or other tangible expressions of appreciation.

Personnel Evaluation

The *evaluation* or *appraisal* of employee performance is an important part of supervisory responsibility in leisure-service agencies. It is too often neglected or done sporadically by recreation and park managers. It is essential that supervisors regularly rate subordinate employees on criteria such as personality traits, degree of responsibility, enthusiasm, initiative, human relations skills, appearance, specific job-related skills, and overall level of performance during the time period. Such rating scales are most effective when they deal concretely with traits or characteristics that are relevant to the job situation.

Personnel evaluation should be directly shared in a nonthreatening way by supervisors and subordinate employees, with a full discussion of the individual's strengths and weaknesses as well as a specific plan for upgrading performance in the time period ahead. It should be a two-way process, with both individuals sharing their view of the work experience and coming to a mutual agreement about the goals that need to be set.

Because personnel evaluation is an integral part of the total process of agency evaluation, including examination of leisure-service organizational structure, programming, and facilities, it is discussed in more detail in Chapter 10.

Labor-Relations Practices

A final area of concern for leisure-service managers involves the need to work constructively with labor unions that represent agency employees in their membership. Typically, in a number of large cities, recreation, park, and leisure-service personnel are members of municipal employees' unions. The same is true of many recreation personnel who work in hospitals or other health-care settings, or in commercial or nonprofit organizations.

231

CHAPTER 7
Human Resource
Management:
Maximizing Staff
Performance

While the ultimate responsibility for determining policies and practices in this area may not be in the hands of leisure-service managers, but rather assigned to other specialists in labor relations, it represents a continuing concern in many agencies. Beyond this, because many of the responsibilities of human resource specialists—such as hiring, firing, promotional, and affirmative action-related practices—have important legal implications, they are discussed in more detail in Chapter 9, which deals with the entire picture of leisure-service management and the law.

SUMMARY

This chapter provides a picture of the personnel management process that is responsible for productive operations in all types of recreation, park, and leisure-service organizations. In part, this process is based on such traditional personnel functions as developing job descriptions and classification systems, and recruiting, hiring, orienting, and providing in-service education for employees. The preparation of personnel manuals and detailed personnel policies is an important part of the process, as are the supervision of volunteers and the evaluation of employee performance.

Traditionally, such tasks have been carried out according to formal procedures or rules and through official channels that are mandated within the organization's bureaucratic structure. However, growing numbers of leisure-service agencies today have adopted a human resource management approach that is concerned with job enrichment and employee motivation, and has participatory styles of program planning, problem solving, and decision making. The chapter examines these functions, along with conflict resolution and other situations that call for group-centered processes, trust-based staff relationships, and similar interpersonal approaches.

A number of other personnel management tasks, such as systematic evaluation of employees or relationships with labor unions, are dealt with more fully in later chapters.

DISCUSSION TOPICS OR CLASS ASSIGNMENTS

1. As a group project in class, present one or more "mock" hiring interviews, with both interviewers and interviewees assigned specific mode of behavior—such as intimidating, passive, "know-it-all," evasive, competent, etc. Then discuss each presentation and conclude with guidelines for successful interviewing approaches.
2. As a class exercise, prepare a plan for in-service training of personnel in a specific recreation setting. Present the entire plan to the class, and involve fellow students in a number of the activities as a workshop project.

232

CHAPTER 7
*Human Resource
Management:
Maximizing Staff
Performance*

3. Experiment in class with the participative management approach and the delegation of authority by taking full responsibility for a class session on this chapter, dealing with the case studies or other problems faced by supervisors. (The instructor should relinquish all authority for planning or grading class work done during this session.)

4. What is a point of view toward conflicts that reflects current thinking? Identify and discuss several positive approaches to resolving conflicts to improve staff relationships and agency productivity.

Before analyzing these cases in class, review the guidelines suggested in Chapter 3 (pp. 76–77).

Case Study 7.1   *A Supervisor's Right to Suspend*

YOU ARE MARK SCHMIDT, district supervisor of a large municipal recreation and park agency. Within your district, there is one major recreation center. The custodian of this center, John Figgins, has occasionally been reported to be drinking on the job by Mary Cartier, the center manager. You have warned him about it informally but have not put the warnings in his personnel folder since you like John and feel he could overcome the problem.

Late one afternoon you get a call from Mary. John Figgins has been drinking heavily. You hurry over to the center and find John in a drunken stupor in the boiler room. The next day you call him to a meeting in your office at Mary's urgent request. She feels that she can no longer put up with his behavior. You inform him that you are suspending him and bringing his name before the recreation and park board for consideration of possible job termination.

When you confer with the city's personnel director, he informs you that you may have difficulty in making the charges stick since there is no official written record of his past misconduct or your warnings. In addition, the head of the municipal maintenance employees' union has informed the personnel director that John Figgins has diabetes and is prepared to claim that he was having an attack and that his medication caused the apparent drunkenness. The union head indicates that his organization may secure legal assistance claiming that John is being discriminated against because of his disability. In any case, they are prepared to fight the possible firing since they have been looking for a possible test case in this area.

It looks as if you may not be able it impose the suspension or bring him up on charges. Mary Cartier is upset and indicates that she may ask for a job transfer.

QUESTIONS FOR CLASS DISCUSSION AND ANALYSIS

1. *How sound a case do you feel you have for imposing the suspension and bringing John Figgins before the board?*
2. *Exactly what should you have done before this incident to put yourself in* a more solid position for dealing with John's problem?
3. *Apart from warning John or taking strong punitive action, what could you and Mary Cartier have done to deal positively with this situation?*

234

CHAPTER 7
Human Resource
Management:
Maximizing Staff
Performance

Case Study 7.2 *Morale on the Treatment Team*

YOU ARE JANE PORTER, the new director of activity therapies in a large state-sponsored mental health center. You have been successful in having several recreation therapists placed on the treatment team, along with other medical, nursing, social service, and adjunctive therapy personnel.

However, the therapeutic recreation specialists feel that they are not given the same degree of status or respect as the others. Their advice is seldom sought; they are not expected to keep detailed case records or provide input at treatment team meetings. A second problem involves the need to provide regular staff for selected weekend or evening assignments, which are currently handled by part-time personnel. The recreation therapists are reluctant to work at these times, even on a rotating basis. In fact, they cite the examples of other therapists and make it clear that, although there is no formal contract or other stipulation of work schedules, they are not willing to give up their "free" hours to do this job. You have concluded that both their morale and sense of professional commitment are low.

QUESTIONS FOR CLASS DISCUSSION AND ANALYSIS

1. What are the fundamental causes of the difficulties you are facing in working with the recreation therapists?
2. Are the two problems cited in the case study connected in your opinion?
3. What specific steps could you take to deal with the overall problem of morale? How could you improve both situations, and particularly how could you make the evening and weekend work assignment acceptable to staff members? Should you?

235

CHAPTER 7
Human Resource
Management:
Maximizing Staff
Performance

Case Study 7.3 — Subcontracting the Greens— The Union Sees Red

YOU ARE ISAIAH JEFFERSON, facilities manager of the South Wingate Special Park District. Your district operates three golf courses, which have traditionally barely paid for their own operation through greens fees. With the present tight budget, you are unable to maintain the courses adequately or do the rehabilitation that you feel will be required soon. Therefore, after considering exploration, you have decided to subcontract the maintenance of the courses; the job can be done more efficiently and economically, you believe, than you could possibly do it yourself. Two large lawn and garden maintenance companies are interested in the contract and are preparing to bid on it.

If the plan goes through, you do not plan to fire any personnel. Instead, you will transfer them to other locations. However, since several of them are long-term employees and will retire soon, you probably will not replace them and will cut the maintenance staff through attrition.

While the plan makes sense from a fiscal point of view, there is strong labor union resistance to it. The head of the union, Fred Foley, is threatening to fight it in the newspapers and before the park district board and if necessary to call a "job action" to prevent it.

QUESTIONS FOR CLASS DISCUSSION AND ANALYSIS

1. What is the legal basis for this plan? Does the park district have the right to subcontract maintenance functions? What other issues are involved in the decision?
2. Identify the pros and cons of the plan that is being presented to the park board. What positive benefits or negative outcomes can you envision if it is put into motion? How realistic is the view of the maintenance employees' union that it represents a serious threat to their jobs?
3. What steps might have preceded your announcement of the plan to make it more acceptable?

REFERENCES

1. Feldman, Daniel, and Arnold, Hugh: *Managing Individual and Group Behavior in Organizations*, New York, 1983, McGraw-Hill Book Co., p. 107.

2. Frisby, Wendy, and Kikulis, Lisa: "Human Resource Management in Sport," in Parkhouse, Bonnie: *the Management of Sport: Its Foundation and Application*, St. Louis, 1996, National Association for Sport and Physical Education and C. V. Mosby, p. 104.

3. See reports in *Statistical Abstract of the United States*, Washington, D.C., U.S. Department of Commerce, 1997, pp. 410, 416, 779.

4. Murphy, James, Niepoth, E. William, Jamieson, Lynn, and Williams, John: *Leisure Services: Critical Concepts and Applications*, Champaign, Ill., 1991, Sagamore Publishing.

5. Christie-Mill, Robert, and Seid, Bradford: *Job Specifications and Skills Necessary for Ski Area Managers*, Research Report no. 408, East Lansing, Mich., 1980, Michigan State University.

6. Nogradi, George: "The Importance and Impact of Certification for Parks and Recreation Practitioners in Ontario," *Journal of Applied Recreation Research* 19(1), 1994, p. 23.

7. With the growth of participation by minority group members, particularly women, in sport and physical recreation, this becomes a growing concern. See special issue on "Women of Color in Sport," in *Journal of Physical Education, Recreation, and Dance* (September 1995).

8. McChesney, James; *Personnel Policies*, Washington, D.C., 1966, National Recreation and Park Assoc. Management Aids Bulletin no. 66.

9. Fain, Gerald: "To Protect the Public: A Matter of Ethics," *Parks and Recreation*, December 1983, pp. 50–51.

10. Shapiro, Ira: "Ethical Codes and Ethical Code Committees in State Recreation and Park Societies," *Pennsylvania Recreation and Park Society Journal*, Summer 1987, p. 3.

11. Moosbruker, Jane: "Developing High Performing Teams," in Ritvo, Roger, Litwin, Anne, and Butler, Lee: *Managing in the Age of Change*, Burr Ridge, Ill., 1995, NTL Institute and Irwin Professional Publishing, p. 45.

12. Hollister, Kathryn, and Hodgson, Diane: "Diversity Training: Accepting the Challenge," *Parks and Recreation*, July 1996, p. 18.

13. Baker, Octave, in Ritvo, *op. cit.*, p. 171.

14. McLellan, Gina, Shinew, Kimberly, and McCoy, Melanie: "Differences in Needs for Power, Affiliation and Achievement between Male and Female Managers," *Journal of Park and Recreation Administration* 12(1), Spring 1994, pp. 65–78.

Eight

Public and Community Relations: Growing Use of Partnerships

In 1994, through support from the National Recreation Foundation, NRPA [National Recreation and Park Association] began building awareness and support for its programs and missions via a national media relations program coordinated by . . . a Chicago-based public relations firm. At the heart of NRPA's national program is a key message aimed through the media to policymakers and taxpayers: park and recreation services and programs provide cost-effective solutions for some of today's most pressing social problems.[1]

The YWCA's national advertising campaign is designed to inform and educate millions of people about the YWCA and its Mission to empower women and eliminate racism. The multi-million dollar advertising campaign . . . consists of a radio spot, a television announcement, and five printed ads and billboards [to be used throughout the country]. The five ads focus on racial justice, volunteerism, homeless shelter, employment counseling and working for unity.[2]

INTRODUCTION

Public relations represents one of the most important areas of responsibility for recreation, park, and leisure-service managers. Unless they can get their message across to the public, as well as to the specific audience they serve, their efforts will be wasted no matter how attractive a program they offer. It is not just a matter of "selling" a program or of "planning" publicity in a traditional press agentry sense. The task of public relations today is more broadly concerned with achieving public understanding and confidence and involves a two-way communication process.

Closely linked to public relations is the process of community relations, which includes a total effort to work closely with community groups and organizations, to obtain their understanding, support, and assistance, and to join

237

238

*CHAPTER 8
Public and
Community
Relations: Growing
Use of Partnerships*

forces with them in solving mutual problems. Community relations may include varied approaches such as developing neighborhood or center advisory committees or district councils, recruiting volunteers to assist in agency operations, and having synergetic relationships in cosponsored programming or other forms of coordination in community-based leisure service.

This chapter describes and provides guidelines for the management of the full range of such relationships, including partnerships among different types of leisure-service agencies, privatization, and subcontracting arrangements, and the role of recreation and parks in overall community development. It addresses the following understandings and competencies listed as essential in the Baccalaureate Degree standards of the NRPA/AALR Council on Accreditation:

> Understanding of and ability to use diverse community, institutional, natural, and human service resources to promote and enhance the leisure experience (8.11).
>
> Ability to promote, advocate, interpret, and articulate the concerns of leisure service systems for all populations and services (8.14).
>
> Knowledge of marketing techniques and strategies (8.28).
>
> Understanding of and ability to implement public relations and promotion strategies (8.33).
>
> Ability to utilize effectively the tools of communication, including technical writing, speech, and audio-visual techniques (8.34).

O B J E C T I V E S

At the conclusion of this chapter, readers should be familiar with the following concepts and practices:

1. The broad goals of public relations and community relations in recreation, park, and leisure-service organizations.
2. Awareness of the use of printed and electronic media, ranging from newspaper coverage or brochures to television and the Internet, in transmitting publicity and other messages to the public.
3. Specific guidelines for preparing articles, newsletters, and brochures for publicity and public relations campaigns.
4. The use of other types of events, such as tours, open houses festivals, or award ceremonies, to deliver public relations messages.
5. The use of advisory committees, focus groups, councils, or task forces in identifying agency priorities, establishing policies, and solving problems.
6. The extension of public relations into community relations, when leisure-service agencies develop patterns of mutual assistance, coordination, and partnerships in order to achieve important community goals.
7. Guidelines for privatization, subcontracting of agency functions, and other trends involving linkages among different organizations.

Public relations may be defined as a two-way relationship between organizations of various types and the external and internal publics they serve, with the overall purpose of improving public understanding of the agencies' goals and enlisting community support and program involvement.

In terms of a local, governmental recreation and park department, public relations may serve to ensure support that translates into program participation, support on annual budgets, votes on legislation or other initiatives, and volunteer involvement. The specific goals of a public relations program may be listed as follows:

1. To provide accurate information regarding the overall program and offering of the department to the general public to overcome misunderstandings, false impressions, or lack of information about organized recreation;
2. To inform the public specifically about the services, facilities, and programs offered by the department and to encourage their attendance and involvement;
3. To impress the public with the values and benefits achieved by the department and to bring about a sense of satisfaction that the tax dollar is being well spent in this area;
4. To keep the public fully informed of all major plans or policies of the department (this may refer to special new programs, the acquisition or development of facilities, the imposition of fees, or the scheduling of seasonal programs);
5. To bring public attention to a specific project or program at a key time (this may involve a crash effort to publicize a new program or mass event and encourage large-scale participation, or it may consist of a press campaign to give out facts regarding a proposed bond issue for land acquisition);
6. To encourage public involvement in the program in the form of volunteer leadership, serving on councils or advisory groups, or making other contributions.

Many agencies seek to build fuller understanding of the values of recreation and leisure in terms of health and fitness, social relationships, and the overall quality of life. They may stress the economic benefits that recreation brings to a community, the effect of recreation in reducing antisocial behavior, or similar values. In so doing, they may join forces with other organizations

---

Beyond the immediate role of publicity that provides information about the leisure-service agency and promotes participation, public relations is concerned with the overall role that the organization plays in community life. It is closely linked to policy setting, marketing, programming, and other management responsibilities. Its general purpose is to enrich the public's awareness of the recreation, park, and leisure-service field, to dispel misunderstandings, and to create a positive image of the agency itself.

240

CHAPTER 8
Public and
Community
Relations: Growing
Use of Partnerships

or professionals to conduct research, as in the case of a recent study of the economic value of public parks and recreation carried out by the California Park and Recreation Society and the California Association of Recreation and Park Districts.

Public leisure-service departments may sponsor leisure-education workshops for the public at large. For example, the Community Services and Parks Department of the City of Regina, Canada, in cooperation with Saskatchewan Parks, Recreation and Culture Department, has developed extensive handbooks and learning modules designed to educate the public with respect to leisure needs and goals and help them use community leisure resources to the fullest. Similarly, the City of Saskatoon, Saskatchewan, has evolved a leisure-service marketing plan that is essentially a public relations campaign. Its key objectives are listed in Fig. 8.1.

Beyond such efforts, an important public relations function in municipal leisure-service agencies is to present a positive image of the community itself by promoting events and publicizing activities that feature neighborhood vitality, community pride, or other examples of the community's cultural, sports and entertainment attractions, and economic stability.

Responsibility for Public Relations

In a broad sense, public relations is everyone's responsibility in leisure-service agencies. Since the public's perception is heavily influenced by its actual contacts with recreation, park, and leisure-service organizations, the quality and success of programs, the superior appearance and maintenance of facilities, and the efficiency and courtesy with which people are treated by agency employees all lend themselves to a positive image of the organization. Beyond this, the actual planning and execution of publicity and other public relations activities must be assigned to specific staff members, if they are to be successful.

In smaller organizations, with limited programs and staff resources, the agency director or one of his or her immediate subordinates, such as a district supervisor or administrative assistant, is likely to be given responsibility for this function. At the same time, all other staff members may be called upon to assist in public relations efforts. In much larger leisure-service agencies, an entire administrative unit may be assigned to public and community relations functions.

Identifying Audiences for Public Relations

To achieve the kinds of goals that have just been described, leisure-service managers must determine which audiences they are trying to reach. Generally, public relations may involve either a *shotgun* or a *rifle* approach. The shotgun sprays its message over a wide range without trying to identify any single group or tailor a specialized message. In contrast, the rifle is aimed at a specific audience with a message that is uniquely designed for it.

241

CHAPTER 8
*Public and
Community
Relations: Growing
Use of Partnerships*

The City of Saskatoon believes that an aggressive, coordinated and well executed marketing plan is just as vital to optimising the utilization of our leisure service resources as is the quality and usefulness of the services provided.

Therefore the City of Saskatoon, in conjunction with other leisure service providers, intends to develop and execute a leisure service marketing plan with the following key objectives:

a) To maximize awareness to City residents and tourists of all the leisure service opportunities available in our City.

An example of this is the development of or integration with existing/proposed community events calendar widely distributed and published within the City and with tourist information agencies.

b) To create a desire for people to choose leisure services over other alternatives.

This involves creating and promoting the image that participating in the leisure services advocated is the popular thing to do; something that's good for you; something we all should be proud of; etc.

c) To create a friendly, helpful image to the public regarding all front line and support service employees/volunteers.

The City intends to initiate workshops aimed at training front line service staff and volunteers to be City and leisure service ambassadors.

The City will enhance the profile of its leisure service employees (front line and support staff) through such initiatives as special identification apparel or material to make them visible to the public and tourists.

d) To integrate the quality and diversity of our leisure service industry into the City-wide public relations efforts carried out by Visitor and Convention Bureau, Province of Saskatchewan, Economic Development Office, etc.

FIGURE 8.1. Public relations and marketing plan: Saskatoon, Saskatchewan.

External Audiences

There are usually several external audiences that a leisure-service agency's public relations efforts must seek to reach. These include not only the public at large but also specific segments of the public, which may be identified by age category (such as children, youth, or the aging) or by special characteristics (such as persons with disabilities, "singles" populations, or racial or ethnic minority groups). Public relations messages may also be aimed at civic, religious, political, industrial, labor, fraternal, and similar organizations in the community.

In the case of a public relations effort that seeks to influence the public to support a bond referendum or other proposal, the voting population is obviously the target for key messages. If a recreation and park department is initiating a new project aimed at recovering natural resources such as lakes, streams, or wilderness areas that have been abused, it would seek to reach groups or individual citizens concerned with the environment. If its effort is to involve greater numbers of people with disabilities in its programs, the logical target would be the families of individuals with special needs.

242

CHAPTER 8
Public and
Community
Relations: Growing
Use of Partnerships

Internal Audiences

In addition to such "external" audiences, many leisure-service agencies must seek to reach their own "internal" publics or constituencies with public relations messages. For example, on a large military base, armed forces recreation managers must constantly communicate publicity about upcoming programs to uniformed personnel, civilian employees, and dependents. Employee recreation specialists must publicize their offerings to employees on all levels, and program directors of a large YMCA or YWCA must do the same to their membership to promote registration and participation in classes and special events.

CHANNELS FOR PUBLIC RELATIONS

Apart from day-to-day contact in a program-related setting, what channels are used for public relations? In general, they include both *short-term* efforts for immediate publicity effect and *long-term* campaigns to build solid support and positive relationships. For both purposes, the channels include both *informational media* and *interpersonal links.*

Informational media consist of the use of newspapers, magazines, television, radio, the Internet, or similar means of communication. Interpersonal links involve person-to-person connections through advisory committees or councils, task forces, public meetings, or planning sessions, or less formal relationships between professional staff members and leisure consumers.

In planning the use of informational media, certain factors must be taken into consideration: The type and length of the message to be delivered, the purpose of the message, the specific audience to be reached, the time available to prepare and disseminate the message, and the funds available. It is advisable to have both regularly scheduled outlets for public information and specific types of releases or media to publicize events or programs that require separate intensive coverage.

Use of Print Media

Despite the popularity of television and radio, the simplest and most effective means of reaching large numbers of people is through print media, such as newspapers, brochures, and reports. Newspapers, in particular, are an inexpensive outlet for public relations and can provide sustained coverage of a program or activity and immediate and timely means of transmitting information from

---

Brawley points out that the term *mass media* represents a multiplicity of organizations, institutions, and communication outlets, including:

... the mass 'broadcast' media, such as network television and national newspapers, as well as the smaller 'narrowcast' media, such as specialized cable television, magazines, and local newspapers. These media constitute important elements of the all-pervading communications network within which we function today. For example, every day in the United States, 63 million people read one or more of the 1600 different newspapers that are published; 80 percent of the population listens to radio—at work, at home or in their cars; and the television sets that are in 98 percent of all households are tuned in for more than 7 hours.[3]

day to day. In addition, newspaper editors are usually receptive to printing news of popular interest, particularly when it contains elements of human interest.

243

Chapter 8
Public and
Community
Relations: Growing
Use of Partnerships

When a leisure-service manager has news of interest to the local newspaper, one of these basic approaches should be used:

1. Prepare a news release and mail or deliver it to the editor. If possible, address it to the editor by name.
2. Call the newspaper and talk to the appropriate editor or reporter, summarizing the information briefly. The editor or reporter will indicate whether it would be best to have a release prepared or whether the details should be given over the telephone and the story written in the newspaper office. It may be appropriate to send a reporter out to conduct an interview.
3. Arrange a news conference and invite interested reporters and editors. This device should be used sparingly; it is best to save it for really important stories that justify calling such a meeting at a time and place of your own choosing.

Guidelines for Preparing Newspaper Releases

There are several sections of most newspapers that can be used for printing recreation and park releases. These might include general news sections, editorial pages, letters to the editor sections, columns, calendars of public events, or special departments such as sports or women's activities.

A key factor in obtaining newspaper coverage of departmental events or news is maintaining a positive and cooperative relationship with the newspaper editor and staff. This means that whenever newsbreaks occur or interviews are held, information should be given fully and honestly, and reporters should be treated with respect and consideration. Information should never be distorted or exaggerated. When reporters cover stories or events, they should be assisted with transportation, special briefings, or facilities to make their job easier.

Newspaper stories should be prepared with the following guidelines in mind:

1. Newspaper copy should be kept simple, factual, and straightforward and should avoid editorializing. It should consist of short, easy-to-read paragraphs, with the first paragraph (the lead) including all relevant information, such as who, what, when, where, and how.
2. Whenever possible, the release should be limited to one page, with the most important information covered in the early sections and the least important in the later copy, since it is usual editing practice to cut copy or type at the end of a story.
3. In preparing stories, an attempt should be made to feature a prominent or interesting individual or group of people, since readers are generally interested in reading names with whom they may identify or who lend importance to an article.
4. Material should be neatly typed, with adequate margins, headings, and sources given where necessary. The name of the department and the name, address, and telephone number of the person responsible for issuing the release should be printed at the top of the sheet.
5. Copy should be submitted with plenty of lead time to be easily edited and prepared for the printer. It is important to know the deadline of the newspaper to which you are submitting copy and to meet it with a comfortable margin.

244

*Chapter 8
Public and
Community
Relations: Growing
Use of Partnerships*

Magazines

Many of the same guidelines apply to the preparation and placing of articles in magazines. Although it is seldom possible to place articles or releases in national publications unless the story is particularly exciting or unusual, it *is* often possible to have material accepted by local, regional, or state publications. Some large national organizations have their own monthly or quarterly magazines, and other large commercial enterprises have access to the national media either through paid advertising or by virtue of their importance in an economic or cultural sense. Theme park chains, for example, often get coverage of their innovations and programs in the travel or business sections of both newspapers and magazines.

Although most leisure-service agencies cannot pay for expensive advertising inserts in major magazines, there are numerous special publications that reach groups such as municipal officials, recreation and park professionals, planners, or personnel specialists. Other publications are geared to those concerned with rehabilitation, aging, or different population groups. Some magazines are designed to promote tourism and accept articles on interesting events or facilities. Others are concerned with specific interests, such as sports, hobbies, cultural activities, or travel. Generally, magazine articles must be longer and written with greater style or flair than newspaper stories.

Picture stories tend to find a market more easily than written articles without illustrations. It is often helpful to query the editor of a magazine first about his or her interest in a particular story before writing and sending it.

Newsletters and Brochures

Newsletters and brochures are prepared by most departments on an annual or seasonal basis to present attractive descriptions of their programs. They may range from simple mimeographed or photo-offset handouts of a page or two to elaborate four-color brochures. Generally, such brochures include a description of all major locations where programs will be held and a listing of program activities to be offered during a given season.

They should usually include the following:

1. The name of the sponsoring department and its administrator or key staff, the names of board members, and the names of key municipal officials;
2. The major citywide office and telephone numbers and other district or area offices where information or permits may be obtained;
3. A listing and brief description with a map of all major park centers, pools, and similar facilities; in a large community with many facilities, this may appear in a separate directory or guide map;
4. A listing of major activities offered on a citywide basis; this might include separate groups for each age level, special events, leagues and tournaments, courses, or other services;
5. A listing of fees or charges for each activity where applicable;
6. A brief statement of the philosophy or purpose of the department.

Such brochures may be distributed in mailings to organizations, officials, members of committees, or citizens by house-to-house delivery, by having them available at all offices and centers, by distribution through parent-teacher associations, churches, civic clubs, or similar groups, and by mailings to a special list of people who have indicated interest or been involved in previous programs.

245

CHAPTER 8
*Public and
Community
Relations: Growing
Use of Partnerships*

Since such newsletters or brochures represent a major way in which most individuals come in contact with the department and gain an impression of it, they should be colorful, crisp, and attractive. At the same time, making them too thick and elaborate may give the impression of being overly lavish and cause taxpayer criticism.

Some departments print thick and detailed brochures (as an exception to the above recommendation) that have the appearance of a newspaper supplement, particularly to give full information about programs during an upcoming season (e.g., a summer brochure or a fall-winter brochure). In some cases, these may actually be published as an insert in the daily paper or as the major feature in the weekly magazine section of the Sunday newspaper, thus reaching all newspaper readers in the areas.

Other leisure-service organizations publish newsletters periodically as a means of internal publicity. For example, the Morale, Welfare and Recreation (MWR) unit at the Orlando, Florida, Naval Training Center (NTC) publishes *Leisure Edition,* a monthly newsletter that includes promotional information and reports about recreation activities and facilities on the base, as well as other special events or leisure facilities in the Orlando area (Fig. 8.2). In addition, the Orlando NTC distributes numerous colorful fliers promoting specific events, classes, or services on the base.

Many campus recreation departments also publish newsletters to inform students and faculty and staff members of ongoing programs, events, and services. Figure 8.3 shows the cover of *REC Collections,* issued by the Office of Intramural-Recreational Sports at Southern Illinois University, a seasonal newsletter that reports on past programs and services, and publicizes leisure activities in the months ahead.

Other agencies may use brochures to educate the public about their values and goals. For example, the South East Consortium in Westchester County, New York, cites the benefits of its programs for persons with disabilities (Fig. 8.4).

Commercial recreation businesses, such as large theme parks, frequently print colorful and detailed packets of all of their attractions, seasonal events, performances, and other unique features, including news releases, and hotel and food accommodations. For example, the 1998 packet for Dollywood, a unique tourist attraction in Tennessee's Great Smoky Mountains, features a series of major concerts, celebrations, folk events, thrill rides, and activity centers for children and families, with the popular country star, Dolly Parton, depicted throughout.

Television and Radio

These two media provide an important means of reaching the public with spur-of-the-moment news and with direct coverage of actual recreation events. They are useful in reaching all age groups and making a strong public relations

MORALE, WELFARE & RECREATION

LEISURE EDITION

NAVY ORLANDO'S GUIDE TO LEISURE AND RECREATIONAL ACTIVITIES

VOL. 7 ISSUE 7   ORLANDO, FLORIDA   JULY 1997

NTC Commander's Cup Program Brought Back!

The Commander's Cup Program has been established to promote off-duty, voluntary participation of all NTC Orlando personnel in athletics as a means of promoting physical and mental fitness as well as esprit de corps within each command.

FALL SCHEDULE

Football	Racquetball	Badminton	Swimming
Bowling	Softball	Wallyball	Basketball
Soccer	Tennis	Table Tennis	Horseshoes

SPRING SCHEDULE

Bowling	Racquetball	Table Tennis	Tennis
Ultimate	Volleyball	Wallyball	Basketball
Golf	Canoeing	Softball	Swimming

Open to all active duty, family members, reservists, retirees, and DoD employees. A participant must compete on a team within the command of his or her association with the exception of retired participants. Retirees wishing to compete in a Commander's Cup event, must submit their name to the Athletic Director's Office to be added to team rosters most in need of additional players.

In an effort to help equalize the size of the competing commands, some commands will be divided by departments. Each division will be considered as a separate command competing for the Commander's Cup. For example, a player from NTC Support is not eligible to play on the NTC Admin Team. These departments are considered separate commands and such players must play on their own team. The Commander's Cup trophy will be awarded to the commands with the highest point totals at the conclusion of the fall schedule and at the conclusion of the spring schedule.

Athletic Reps and telephone numbers:

1. NTC Admin   PO Bimbo   x4431
   (Security, Supply, Recycling, & Admin.)
2. NTC/Support   PO Parks   x4343
   (TPD, 1st Lt, & PSD)
3. NFAS   Chief Yates   x4696
4. NNPS   MCMC Ashton   x4321
5. NNPTC   PO Wison   x5139
6. DFAS   SGT Teague   x4250
7. NMCRC   SGT Miller   894-3793
8. BMC   PO Lawrence   x5337

For more information on the Commander's Cup program call the **NTC Gym** at 646-5161.

FREEDOMFEST '97

Friday, 4th of July
Lake Baldwin Park
1600 - 2100 • NTC Orlando

Schedule of Events

0900	Softball Tournament •NTC Ball Fields
	Golf Tournament • NTC Golf Course
1500	Splash n Fun Party •Swim Center
	1500 Children Games 10 years & below
	1600 Children Games 11 - 16 years
	1700 Adult Games 17 years & above

The following activities will take place at NTC'S Lake Baldwin Recreation Park.:

1500	Volleyball Tournament
1600	Food, beer, and soda on sale provided by Club Mariner, Great Grinds & Pierside Pizza
	Glacier Bay Frozen Yogurt
	Live Entertainment with **Derek and the Slammers** 1600 -2100
	Wildstorm Entertainment 1600 - 2130
	Horseshoe Tournament
	30 Second Basketball Shootout $1.00
	Caricature Artists $3.00 per drawing
	Character and Celebrity Appearances
	Castle & Dinosaur Moonwalk - Free
	Pony Rides - Free
1630	Face Painting
	Balloon Art
1730	Water Balloon Toss Contest
1800	Glo-light necklaces for sale $2.00
	Watermelon-Eating Contest
1830	Corn-on-the-Cob Eating Contest
	Scavenger Hunt ages 3 - 8 Free
1900	Basketball Shootout Finals
2100	FIREWORKS over Lake Baldwin!

Kick in the Summer at ITT

Suit up, climb in and hang on! The Richard Petty Driving Experience located adjacent to the Magic Kingdom is offering a military discount through 31 August 1997. This unique experience allows you to be a rider or the actual driver of a high performance stock car. In order to obtain the military discount you should pick up a copy of the military discounts flyer at the **ITT Office**.

The Mark Two Dinner Theater offers an entertaining evening that includes a delicious buffet dinner and a professional stage show. Starting 9 July, Mark Two brings "Swingtime Canteen" to their stage. Described as an up-beat, energetic, brassy, entertaining tribute to our boys of World War II by the girls of the Hollywood Canteen, this show is sure to get your feet tapping. Discount tickets for all of Mark Two's performances available at the **ITT Office** for $30.00 each.

Wet 'n Wild continues it's Military Appreciation Days through 15 July. Enjoy all the flumes, pools and rides for just $14.50 per person. Tickets must be purchased at the **ITT Office**.

ITT still has some great seats available for the Orlando Predators vs. the Portland Forest Dragons on 18 July. Our seats are located in the lower bowl of the Orlando Arena. Tickets are $25.00 and $33.00 each.

NFL action is set for the Florida Citrus Bowl on Friday, 22 August as the new Tampa Bay Buccaneers take on the New York Jets with new coach, Bill Parcells. Advance tickets can be purchased at the **ITT Office** for $25.50 and $35.50. These tickets will be limited, so be sure to make your plans early.

Information, Tours and Ticket Office is located in the **Bowling Center** which is in bldg. 114. Call 646-5164 for more info.

FIGURE 8.2.   **Monthly newsletter: Orlando Naval Training Center.**

SPRING 1997   247

CHAPTER 8
Public and
Community
Relations: Growing
Use of Partnerships

REC Collections SIU

Newsletter of the Office of Intramural-Recreational Sports at Southern Illinois University at Carbondale

BRRRRRR!!!!!

WOW, is it cold! The Polar Bear Club (from left to right: Rich Magee, Eric Balch, Craig Duncan, Paul Fawcett, and Bill McMinn) once again took its annual dip in the ice packed waters of Lake-on-the-Campus on January 13. Five of the brave group dared the freezing waters as Carolyn Snyder, Dean of Library Affairs, watched over the frozen bunch.

The annual event promotes the Morris Library Information Fair, which gives patrons of the Rec Center an opportunity to try out some of the latest research technology that Morris Library has to offer.

In this issue:
- Tai Chi Sword
- Intramural Sports
    Wallyball
    Innertube Water Polo
    Table Tennis
- Youth Karate
- Indoor Track Meets
- Sports Medicine
- SRC Pool Renovation
- Open House
- SCUBA Diving
- Snapple Fest

Cover story:
The annual Polar Bear Dip by the OIRS staff.

FIGURE 8.3.   Seasonal program brochure: Southern Illinois University.

impact. Television time, however, is often difficult to obtain. Therefore it is necessary to identify the types of programs that may be likely to use recreation announcements or cover important or interesting citywide events. These include:

1. *News programs.* These may provide direct coverage of events, interviews with personalities, or similar features.
2. *Commentator programs.* These may occasionally deal with recreation topics such as entertaining human-interest features.

248

*CHAPTER 8
Public and
Community
Relations: Growing
Use of Partnerships*

South East Consortium for Special Services Inc.

Heighten Self-Awareness • Sharpen Cognitive Skills • *Improve Balance and Coordination* • Increase Long Term Memory • **DECREASE SOCIAL ISOLATION** *Elevate Emotional Well Being* • REDUCE ANXIETY • Provide Respite • REDUCE STRESS *ENHANCES SELF-CONTROL* • Promote Adjustment to Disability • STRENGTHEN PSYCHOLOGICAL WELL-BEING • **Build Self-Esteem** • *Develop Trust* • Reach Developmental Goals • *Expand Interpersonal* Relationships • *Enhance Communication Skills* • PROMOTE COMMUNITY INTEGRATION • **Increase Life and Leisure Satisfaction** • Enhance Decision Making REDUCE DEPRESSION • *Prevent Decline In Health Status* • Enhance Quality of life • Build Family Unity • Teach Vital Life Skills • Increase Physical Conditioning • **Expand Support Network** • *Learn Acceptable Behaviors* • ENHANCE INDEPENDENT LIVING SKILLS • Increase Self-Reliance • Improve Cardiovascular Functioning • **Foster Creative Expression** • *Maintain Productivity* • *Contribute to Overall Health* • *Enhance Body Image* • *Address Psychosocial Need* • *INCREASE STRENGTH AND ENDURANCE* *Acquire Knowledge and Skills* • Manage Chronic Illness • *TO FEEL GOOD AND HAVE FUN!*

Therapeutic Recreation
THE BENEFITS ARE ENDLESS

FIGURE 8.4. South East Consortium: Listing of program benefits.

3. *Spot announcements, to be used during programs that list community events.* All stations and channels are required to carry a specified amount of public-service programming, and this may be used for recreation announcements.
4. *Interviews and talks.* These are given by department members, participants, or interesting leaders.
5. *Regular departmental programs.* In some cities, a special time is set aside at least once a week for news of the department to be given. Just as there is a sports broadcast or a weather forecast, so may there be a recreation broadcast.

The key factor in securing effective television and radio coverage is the ability to provide timely, interesting, and professionally prepared program materials. If the department prepares its own scripts, they must be done expertly and up to the standards of the network or station. In general, radio time is more available than television time. In attempting to get coverage on the picture medium, it is important to ask questions such as:

Is television the *right medium* for your message?

Do you have something to *show* as well as *tell*?

Can you reach the right *audience* at the right *time*?

Can you properly use *expensive* television time?

Can you *entertain* as you *inform*?

Do you have *time* to spend on a *good* production?

249

CHAPTER 8
Public and
Community
Relations: Growing
Use of Partnerships

Usually it is not difficult to get spot announcements on television and radio. However, more extensive coverage will require developing a contact with the local station director.

Motion Pictures, Cassette Tapes, and Slide Shows

Many leisure-service agencies prepare their own audiovisual materials as a means of reaching community groups, associations, or other special audiences with information about their department. Generally, a motion picture may simply be sent to a requesting group for a specified showing date and thus may reach many civic groups, service clubs, schools, or other organizations during the course of a year.

Local colleges often have courses in filmmaking and will assist in actual coverage, editing, and providing the use of equipment, which would be extremely expensive if rented. It is important to map out the script carefully in advance and to have a thorough review of all plans for the film, although it is possible simply to shoot a random selection of footage over a period of several months and then edit it into an interesting, colorful, and lively film.

As an alternative means of accomplishing the same goals, today's camcorders provide a much less technically demanding means of recording events and preparing visual presentations that can be shown to audiences. Widely used in education today, videotaping uses ordinary television sets for viewing and tends to be well-suited for coverage of ongoing programs.

Slide talks offer a convenient means of reaching an audience with colorful and convincing pictures and accompanying descriptions of a recreation and park department's program. It is a good idea to have a department photographer or a skilled volunteer regularly shoot pictures of special events, facilities, and other features that make good presentations. These may then be easily assembled into an effective slide presentation. If thoroughly familiar with the material shown, the speaker need only put the slides into the correct order and then speak extemporaneously about them.

Since slides are much less expensive as a publicity medium than films, they may be designed to meet special purposes, such as showing to parents' groups to promote a summer camp program and encourage recruitment, promoting interest in doing volunteer work in the department, gaining support for a proposed new facility or bond referendum for land acquisition, or encouraging job applications for summer positions among high school or college students. CD-ROMs offer another means of reaching community audiences.

Speakers

Some leisure-service agencies may assign staff members to make presentations to community groups, clubs, leagues, or other organizations. In some cases, a department actually maintains a speakers' bureau, although this is not

250

CHAPTER 8
Public and
Community
Relations: Growing
Use of Partnerships

common. When it *is* done, it is crucial that the speaker have a fresh and inter-esting message to deliver rather than overfamiliar, tired material. In Canada, some provincial recreation and park societies have also developed public rela-tions campaigns, in which speakers' bureaus are assigned to make presenta-tions emphasizing the benefits of leisure-service programs.

Exhibits and Displays

These provide an opportunity for public recreation and park agencies to inform their communities about their work. Since programs include varied hobbies and activities, displays may include unusual and entertaining presentations to en-tertain and inform the public, such as:

1. *Exhibits.* Art shows, science displays or fairs, photography exhibits, craft exhibits and sales, hobby shows, nature exhibits, and similar presentations can show the products of recreation programs carried on in the department. They may also include illustrated talks or demonstrations of skills, such as glass-blowing or work at the potter's wheel.
2. *Special events.* These may include play days, drama festivals, dance perfor-mances, aquacades, or similar showings. The purpose is not so much to en-tertain an audience as to give a picture of the work of the department.
3. *Displays or demonstrations.* These may be given in varied settings. Central points in shopping malls may be used for demonstrations when large crowds will be there. Schools, libraries, municipal buildings, and hotel or theater lobbies are all places where recreation exhibits or displays may reach large numbers of viewers.

Leisure-service professionals must keep in mind the plethora of media and messages about recreational opportunities with which they must compete. This imposes the need for promotional materials to be of the highest quality possible and geared to reaching appropriate audiences at suitable levels of interest. In program brochures, for example, it is important to present varied activities in as exciting and appealing a way as possible. When part-time guest instructors with outstanding skills or backgrounds are employed, they can be featured in program descriptions, as in the dance class section of San Mateo, California's seasonal brochure (Fig. 8.5).

Annual Reports

Many leisure-service organizations prepare annual reports as part of their over-all public relations program. In a public department, for example, a compre-hensive report may be published each year and officially submitted to the mayor or city manager, city council, recreation and park board, and other municipal authorities. Annual reports may also be designed to reach the public at large. In the latter case, they are likely to be less detailed and more like a brochure in appearance, with photographs and illustrations, colorful layouts, and informal style. Prepared in this way, annual reports serve as useful public relations tools and should be widely distributed to municipal officials, boards and other agencies, while a briefer report is given to the public at large.

Need for Quality and Creativity

251

CHAPTER 8
*Public and
Community
Relations: Growing
Use of Partnerships*

In the past, it was considered acceptable to prepare printed fliers, newspaper stories, cardboard posters, and an occasional radio announcement, all done routinely and with little flair, to herald new programs, special events, or significant developments in recreation and park operations. Although all of these are valid public relations tools, it must be recognized that a much more sophisticated public is now on the receiving end of department communications, and that it is important for all materials to be presented as attractively and professionally as possible.

FIGURE 8.5.   Dance class listings, featuring new instructors: San Mateo, Calif.

Creative Dance: age 5 & 6 years.
In this dynamic class, children will explore creative and physical self-expression. They will discover new aspects of their bodies, minds, and imagination by learning the basic elements of dance and tools for making their own dances. Girls wear any color leotard; boys: T-shirt and shorts. Both: bare legs, bare feet. While Kerstin Dieterich is on maternity leave, her classes will be taught by either Mae Chesney or Jenna Cameron. All classes at Beresford. (Thursday class, 7 meetings; Friday and Saturday classes, 6 meetings.

CD102-114	Th	4:00–4:40 P.M.	$17/21	6/19–7/31	Beres
CD102-112	F	4:00–4:40 P.M.	$15/19	6/20–8/1	Beres
CD102-113	Sa	10:45–11:25 A.M.	$15/19	6/21–8/2	Beres

Making Dances: age 7 years & up.
Develop creativity, self expression, and imagination! Students will learn the art and craft of making dances, with the support of classmates and instructors Mae Chesney (first two classes) and Jenna Cameron (last five classes). Leotard required (any color). Bare feet, ballet shoes, or jazz shoes. (7 meetings.)

CD323-111	Th	4:45–5:45 P.M.	$25/31	6/19–7/31	Beres

Ballet: age 8–12 years.
Try our ballet class taught by our 1996 Snow Queen, Jeannine Vogt! This new class consists of barre, centre floor, and across-the-floor movement. Learn form and technique that will bring out the dancer in you while developing creative expression. Open to new students or those continuing from Creative Ballet. Leotards, tights, or bare legs; pink ballet shoes. (7 meetings.)

CD422-112	M	4:00–5:00 P.M.	$25/31	6/16–7/28	Beres

Check out our new instructor, Danny G. He will be teaching a Hip-Hop class and is also a part of our new summer dance program. "Around the World Adventures."

JAZZ

Hot Summer Jazz: age 9–11 years.
Don't miss this special summertime jazz dance class. Learn jazz warm-ups, jazz technique, and cool new dances that will give you a foundation for creative expression. You will also learn basic concepts of choreography where the whole class will be responsible for the design of a dance. This will be a fun experience for all those participating. Instructor: Daniel Giray. (7 meetings.)

CD880-111	W	4:30–5:30 P.M.	$25/31	6/18–7/30	Beres

Jazz Intensive: age 11–18 years.
Sharpen your jazz dance skills. Learn dance technique and style in this exciting, challenging class. Especially recommended for those planning to audition for the Youth Jazz Performing Troupes in the fall. Instructor: Christi Costa. (7 meetings).

CD882-112	Th	5:00–6:00 P.M.	$25/31	6/19–7/31	Beres

Meet our new instructor, Jenna Cameron, who will be teaching Kinderdance, Creative Dance, and a special class called Making Dances.

Leisure-service agencies should seek out all potential opportunities throughout the year to provide helpful information or services to the public or to encourage press or television coverage. Examples of such opportunities might include:

1. Carrying out a special beautification project at several key entrances to the city with a clear identification of the department of recreation and parks as the city agency responsible for the effort
2. Making special awards with newspaper or other media coverage to:
   a. Most attractive gas stations
   b. Greatest number of new trees planted (on church sites, hospital grounds, etc.)
   c. Outstanding Boy or Girl Scout troop for urban beautification projects
   d. Volunteer leaders with outstanding records
   e. Winners of window box or front lawn garden competitions
3. Sponsoring a special Family Day once a year, when any family group may enter all recreation facilities or programs without charge
4. Using press or television to issue important statements (warnings, suggestions, offers of help, etc.) to the public, such as:
   a. Danger of mushy ice on ponds and lakes in spring
   b. Suggesting and assisting neighborhood recreation events and forming of neighborhood associations
   c. Providing advice, clinics, or contests on home and community gardens

To ensure that such events are properly promoted, at least one staff person should be assigned to this task. He or she should enjoy public relations, and have a knack for it. To help this individual, the department should have a kit of equipment and supplies readily available for public relations purposes. This kit might include: a portable public-address system, still and press-type cameras, a camcorder, poster materials, desktop publishing capability, a portable display complex, and similar materials.

Tours and Open Houses

These forms of interpersonal contact provide a useful way of showing public officials, parents, local residents, service clubs, PTA members, newspaper

---

Every type of leisure-service organization should explore varied possibilities for newsworthy events. For example, the Mercer County, New Jersey, Catholic Youth Organization (CYO) scheduled an unusual fund-raising event, a benefit basketball game between the traveling basketball team of the Philadelphia Eagles professional football team and a team composed of both male and female CYO coaches. The game proved to be a prolific source of public relations through local newspapers and radio and television stations and to yield considerable revenue through advertisers in game program book and ticket sales. Similarly, numerous organizations that serve special populations, such as Camp Confidence—an outstanding year-round camp for the developmentally disabled operated in connection with Brainerd State Hospital in northern Minnesota—sponsor large-scale golf tournaments and other sports events both to raise funds and function as effective public relations ventures.

reporters, state or county authorities, or other interested groups exactly what is going on in a department.

253

CHAPTER 8
Public and
Community
Relations: Growing
Use of Partnerships

Guided tours or open houses are usually scheduled at the time of dedication of a new facility, the beginning of a seasonal program, or other occasion that shows the department in a favorable light. They should be carefully planned, with attention given to the following elements:

1. Preliminary planning of the area or activity to be shown, with a schedule showing what points are to be visited at various times throughout the event;
2. Arrangements for guides, organizing the visitors into groups, rest stops, seating arrangements, briefing sessions, and transportation;
3. Preparation of a mailing list and invitations, mailing, and, if advisable, direct follow-up by television;
4. Preparation of a tour outline, including the itinerary, program, list of those making the tour, schedule, and similar details;
5. Last-minute check of all elements involved in the tour or open house and reminder of all invited participants; pretour publicity in newspapers or other media;
6. After the event, thank-you notes to all involved and follow-up publicity.

Direct Contacts with the Public

Beyond all of the forms of communication and public relations methods that have just been described, it is essential that whenever members of the public have contact with leisure-service agencies, their experience is a positive one. For example, all individuals visiting a department office or telephoning should be treated with promptness, courtesy, and efficiency. Complaints regarding programs or facilities, from whatever source, should be received with serious attention and should be processed through appropriate channels without delay. The suggestions of participants or other residents should be solicited at all times.

Whenever assistance of any kind is given to the department by an individual or organization, this should be promptly acknowledged. All members of the department should conduct themselves with appropriate deportment, dress, and general appearance in their contacts with the public.

Newer Strategies: Using the Internet

Creative recreation, park, and leisure-service managers must constantly be on the alert to recognize and use newer approaches that will make their public relations efforts more successful. One such strategy involves use of the Internet, which has become a major form of communications, entertainment, and marketing over the past several years.

For example, Metro Parks, which serves Summit County, Ohio, and its surrounding region, recently was selected to participate in Time Warner Cable's first high-speed, cable-based computer service, which gives access to the World Wide Web at speeds up to a hundred times faster than conventional modems. Metro Parks' web site offers more than 100 pages of information, and more than 300 high-quality graphic images of the parks. Brent Wood writes:

Metro Parks' new web site has opened this regional park agency to the world of electronic communication and promotion media. Users of the cable system and the customers of the Metro Parks are now just a mouse click away from receiving up-to-date information about their park system and are able to download park maps, monthly newsletters and calendars of events.

Reservation forms, season swim pass applications and other program registrations materials are planned for the future. Users will be able to explore their Metro Parks from the comfort of their own homes.[4]

Similarly, the Westchester County, New York, Department of Parks, Recreation and Conservation has recently installed its own site on the World Wide Web, going on-line with a home page to reach users of the Internet with an extensive menu providing information about the programs and facilities of the county park system. In Westchester County in a recent year:

> . . . over 400 press releases and press advisories were issued to more than 100 daily, weekly and bi-weekly newspapers, radio stations, magazines, newsletters and journals. More than 100 calendar listings were sent out to local cable television stations for their community bulletin boards, and over 50 public service announcements were sent to local radio stations. . . In addition, more than one-half million copies of nearly 100 different flyers and brochures were distributed to parks, 50 libraries, clubs, Ys and associations, and 46 local municipal recreation departments throughout Westchester [with paid commercials running] a total of 434 times on four cable networks throughout the County.[5]

TAILORING PUBLIC RELATIONS TO AGENCY MISSION

Finally, it should be stressed that any leisure-service agency's public relations efforts must be designed to fit the unique character of the organization and the field within which it operates. As a single example within the specialized field of college or university sports management, Appenzeller cites the methods that may be used to promote the image of the athletic program throughout the student body, and with faculty and administration members and trustees. Some of the techniques include:

> Talks with students in assembly and in residence halls,
> Brochures,
> Open houses,
> A sport-art contest on campus,
> Bulletin board displays throughout the campus,
> An Athletic Advisory Council,
> Meet-the-team nights on campus,
> Invitations to sports banquets, and
> Complimentary tickets.[6]

Other useful strategies include sponsoring sports breakfasts and lunches; a Sports Hall of Fame; clinics featuring alumni coaches; letters to parents explaining policies dealing with physical examinations and insurance; and a sports newsletter to faculty, administrators, trustees, and faculty.

255

CHAPTER 8
Public and
Community
Relations: Growing
Use of Partnerships

EVALUATING THE PUBLIC RELATIONS PROGRAM

As part of the total evaluation of a leisure-service agency, it is important to take a hard look at regular intervals at its public relations program. The following questions may be raised in carrying out such an evaluation:

Are there effective and well-produced brochures and pamphlets to inform the public of the program during the course of the year?

Is maximum possible use being made of the public media, such as newspapers, television, and radio?

Is information regarding the program disseminated both regularly and on special occasions to promote or publicize unique situations or events?

Has consideration been given to the use of films, slide talks, speakers, or open houses or tours?

Has the responsibility for public relations been assigned to a competent individual or office within the department, or is it everybody's business?

Are adequate funds provided to carry out this function?

Finally, it is essential that public relations be viewed as a two-way street. It does not just consist of passing out information. It is also a matter of listening to what the community has to say about its offerings and redesigning its program on the basis of this information. Ultimately, the total problem of maintaining an effective community relations program becomes a vital aspect of public relations.

COMMUNITY RELATIONS

The leisure-service agency's community relations program may be seen as an extension of its public relations activities that seeks to create more effective working relationships with community groups and the public at large.

Community relations may operate at several levels: (1) developing and nurturing a wide range of community contacts and informal cooperative efforts; (2) giving fuller emphasis to seeking citizen input and assistance in recreation and park planning and policy making; (3) promoting organized forms of volunteerism by both individuals and community organizations; (4) involving the leisure-service agency in varied forms of advocacy; and (5) making the department a meaningful player in community life.

Community Contacts

As a key strategy leading to personal, professional, and agency success, leisure-service managers should strive to become widely involved in community life through civic groups, service clubs, and similar organizations.

256

CHAPTER 8
Public and
Community
Relations: Growing
Use of Partnerships

Particularly in the case of public recreation, park, and leisure agencies, managers should visit and meet with key individuals in business firms, colleges, hospitals, and other organizations in the area to discuss the philosophy and programs of the recreation and park department, the needs of the city, and other relevant concerns. A manager should *not* ask for direct support at early meetings but should attempt to build a cooperative relationship first before developing the possibility of such ventures. The administrator may offer to assist the company or other institution in improving its own recreation or sports program, including assistance with facilities planning or renovation, advice on activities and special-interest groups, or even the loan of films, books, equipment, or special facilities.

Managers should be prepared to accept speaking and panel assignments frequently and willingly at civic or religious organization meetings in the community and should present a clear and positive picture of their agencies and programs.

The department should prepare and distribute pamphlets giving details of seasonal programs (activities, schedules, dates of registration, locations, and fees) in a thorough, timely, and attractive format. Many residents hang or tack such brochures next to their telephones for ready reference. Some communities use brochures to include general information about public offices and services, including the names and telephone numbers of city officials and departments, special services (such as senior center clubs, health services, or suburban minibus program schedule), and similar materials. Through such efforts, the leisure-service agency will come increasingly to be recognized as an organization that plays an important role in community life, contributing to personal, family, and neighborhood well-being—rather than simply being concerned with "fun and games."

Developing Citizen Input

As earlier chapters on planning methods and program development have made clear, citizen input is an essential part of community relations. This may take several forms. One of the most common is to develop advisory committees that provide information on user needs and preferences, or positions on issues facing the leisure-service agency.

As an extension of advisory committees, many recreation and park departments establish formal councils on three levels: *neighborhood* or *center-based* councils; park and recreation *district* councils, covering larger geographical areas; and *citywide* councils, which frequently involve formal representation from varied civics religious, youth-serving, and other organizations.

In addition to recreation and park boards or commissions, which are usually based on legal authority and have a formal status within the government structure, such councils serve to make citizens' views known to the staffs of public leisure-service agencies, and to develop support for them when needed. In many cases, they also serve side-by-side with civic groups established to care for a single major park or other recreation resource—often with such titles as "Friends of Fairmount Park" or "Central Park Conservancy."

Promoting Organized Volunteerism

257

CHAPTER 8
Public and
Community
Relations: Growing
Use of Partnerships

As Chapter 7 points out, volunteers represent a valuable human resource in many leisure-service agencies. This has long been the case; the recreation movement was borne on the backs of volunteer leaders shortly after the turn of the century and was heavily supported by them through World War II.

In the 1970s and 1980s, as the roles of women in American and Canadian society expanded and grew more diversified, a change occurred that influenced volunteerism in public life. The vast pool of middle-income wives and mothers who had done the telephoning, letter writing, chauffeuring, program leadership, or chaperoning on thousands of volunteer projects began to dry up. Former office workers began polishing their typing and secretarial skills and studying the want ads. Women with college degrees returned for graduate work, and others went back to complete their degrees, usually with a practical eye to job opportunities. Volunteerism was no longer as respectable as it had been, and with the rapid growth of the working woman population, this source of enthusiastic assistance began to dissolve for many social-service agencies.

However, as the era of limits compelled many agencies to cut back on programs and prune their staffs, a new emphasis was placed on smaller, close-to-home operations that could flourish with volunteer help. Volunteers were again being sought—this time through neighborhood organizations and committees that are eager to improve their communities and fight urban blight. More systematic and thorough supervision is being given to volunteers, along with the opportunity to work on truly meaningful projects.

Park and Playground Maintenance

In many cities, neighborhood associations or citywide volunteer organizations have taken responsibility for maintaining parks, playgrounds, or other outdoor recreation facilities. In many other situations, they have carried out major beach or stream clean-up projects, planted street trees, or completed environmental recovery programs.

In Seattle, for example, a unique plan has been developed that delegates routine park maintenance to neighborhood workers hired by a number of neighborhood associations under contract with the city's Park and Recreation Department. Funding is provided from the city's general fund; however, so economical is the approach that some thirty neighborhood parks throughout Seattle are mowed, swept, and trimmed on a "bottom-line" budget that would ordinarily pay for about four full-time park maintenance personnel.

In New York City, a group of neighborhood residents has built and maintained a unique recreational sports field known as the Asphalt Green using the site of an abandoned city-owned asphalt-mixing plant. Constructed and maintained almost entirely with private funds—raised through door-to-door campaigns, benefits, and from foundations—the Asphalt Green provides the only grass playing field on Manhattan's East Side, serving dozens of youth sports leagues. The building has also been remodeled and today houses extensive indoor activities.

258

*CHAPTER 8
Public and
Community
Relations: Growing
Use of Partnerships*

Hundreds of similar examples, large and small, might be cited. In Steilacoom, Washington, the town's Sunnyside Beach was significantly restored, using matching state and town funds and with the assistance of hundreds of community volunteers, including high school and college classes.[7] In Spearfish, South Dakota, a team of volunteers raised thousands of dollars and contributed both amateur and professional labor to rebuild the city's deteriorated playground, an outstanding example of citizens learning to plan and work together.[8]

In other communities, emphasis has been placed on maintaining historic sites, museums, or other heritage-related facilities. In Kansas City, Missouri, for example, in addition to a large-scale Volunteers in Parks program, several different community associations have been formed to serve Heritage Village, a "living history" museum, the New Santa Fe–Watts Mill, (an historic site), the Union Cemetery, and the Northern Miniature Railroad restoration, a popular attraction in Swope Park.

Programming for Persons with Disabilities

In many communities, volunteer citizens' groups join together to provide recreation programs for special populations, such as those with mental, visual, or other physical disabilities. Much of this effort supports such major organizations as Special Olympics or the various wheelchair sports federations. However, it also assists local or regional associations that provide recreation and related social services to persons with disabilities.

Often, recreation and leisure-service professionals help to mobilize other groups in efforts to provide integrated programming in which persons with disabilities are mainstreamed with other people in everyday recreation pursuits.

Carter and Foret emphasize the contribution made by leisure-service professionals in so-called transition networks, which assist persons with disabilities to move from isolated or segregative living environments to more fully integrated lifestyles.[9] For example, the Metropolitan Park District of Toledo, Ohio, has developed a plan called Trail Partners, where nondisabled volunteers accompany wheelchair users and other persons with disabilities on trail outings over difficult terrain.

Similarly, Special Olympics International has initiated an outstanding Partners Club Program, which links special education students (often with mental, social, or other developmental disabilities) with other elementary, junior, or senior high school students who serve as "peer" coaches in training them for athletic competition. As both groups practice and train together, they gain both in physical skills and positive attitudes toward life and each other.[10]

Advocacy in Community Relations

A fourth important way in which leisure-service agencies have an impact on community life is through programs that promote positive social values and behavior.

Such efforts may have two kinds of emphases: (1) educating the public about the important benefits of recreation, park, and leisure-service activities; and (2) using recreation programs as a vehicle for promoting other needed attitudes or behaviors in such areas as personal health and fitness, environmental protection, intergroup relations, or substance abuse.

As an example of the first of these, the National Recreation and Park Association has developed an extensive informational campaign, the *Benefits of Parks and Recreation* training program.[11] Hundreds of professionals and agencies have taken part in full-day workshops in individual communities or at the state level, using videos, resource guides, consultants, and other aids to enrich their ability to document leisure-service values and reach the public with this important message.

259

CHAPTER 8
*Public and
Community
Relations: Growing
Use of Partnerships*

The National Therapeutic Recreation Society has published an invaluable manual, *Impacting Public Policy*, which presents advocacy messages and strategies promoting therapeutic recreation.[12] Recreation and park agencies have developed strong ties with national organizations like the Sierra Club or the Wilderness Society to encourage environmentally sensitive forms of outdoor recreations, and many travel agencies are now sponsoring varied ecotourism outings that support positive ecological practices.

Youth-serving organizations like the Police Athletic League, Little League, or the Boys and Girls Clubs of America have been forceful advocates against drug or alcohol abuse by young people and—in the case of Little League— tobacco chewing, which is often linked to baseball playing but involves a serious health risk.

Examples of Community Development in Recreation and Parks

A number of Canadian cities have made important strides in developing innovative community-development practices—defined as programs intended to achieve economic and social progress for communities through heavy reliance on local resources and indigenous leadership.

Alison Pedlar argues that there is a critical need for recreation and leisure-service professionals to undertake fuller community developments in situations of social or economic distress—particularly for population groups that have become marginal in terms of education, employment, and lifestyle opportunities. People who are socially and economically disadvantaged, she writes:

> . . . are becoming increasingly pushed to the margins of society with less and less access to everyday resources which are . . . generally taken for granted by other members of society. At the same time, there is a general sense of isolation and segmentation of society as people retreat into lifestyle enclaves characterized by consumption [and privatization linked to] a gradual erosion of commitment to the public good.[13]

Such trends, Pedlar continues, make an application of the principles of community development to the leisure-service field more urgent than ever. The City of Calgary Parks and Recreation Department has applied a community-development approach for the past two decades, using a network of community recreation coordinators who provide varied forms of consultation and assistance to over 140 independent community associations and 300 recreation, arts, cultural, and sport organizations in Calgary. In numerous other cities throughout Canada, similar practices have been successful in empowering local people to improve neighborhood life.

260

*CHAPTER 8
Public and
Community
Relations: Growing
Use of Partnerships*

Wayne Stormann points out that in modern society, we tend to use the term *community* too loosely, applying it to any commonality of purpose, activity, identity, or other characteristic shared by groups of people. Instead, he suggests, a true community is marked by feelings of kinship, interdependence, and common purpose, which may in turn be nurtured by self-initiated, spontaneous efforts to improve neighborhood life. As an example, he cites an anthropologist's report on Loisaida, a Puerto Rican section of New York's Lower East Side. In this neighborhood, there were over 100 vacant lots, rubble-strewn dump heaps, breeding grounds for rats and cockroaches, and other health hazards.

Local activists recruited residents to clean up the lots, converting some to "vest-pocket" parks and others to playgrounds utilizing recycled material for equipment. Other lots were turned into community gardens, tended by young and old residents of the neighborhood. Another lot was turned into an outdoor cultural center, *La Plaza Cultural,* where local musicians, poets, and theater groups performed. Still other lots were adopted by nearby schools as teaching centers for lessons in agriculture and ecology.

While these were simple actions, their effects were significant. Stormann concludes:

> As Loisaida demonstrates, genuine community development takes place when the leisure time of people becomes political time. Leisure is invested with communalism and divested of privatism. The empty and dangerous, garbage-infested, unused space became the impetus for an empowering leisure time. [Thus, the effect of this sort of process] is to let recreation spontaneously develop, come "out of" the community; hence, genuine "community re-creation."[14]

PARTNERSHIPS AND COSPONSORED PROGRAMS

A trend of the 1980s and 1990s that seems certain to continue into the twenty-first century involves the full-fledged partnership among different sectors of the recreation, parks, and leisure-service field. The actual nature of the partnership may involve assistance in building or maintaining a facility, funding, or staffing for programs, joint use of a recreation area or facility, or a subcontracting arrangement under which a private or commercial group is given responsibility for managing a recreation operation that had formerly been a governmental responsibility. Selin and Chavez define *partnerships* as:

> . . . the voluntary pooling of resources (labor, money, information, etc.) between two or more parties to accomplish collaborative goals. Partnerships range from situations where two agencies interact briefly around a common problem to those where multiple organizations are represented in an ongoing venture. Partnerships may be highly structured, characterized by legally binding agreements, or they may be quite unstructured verbal agreements between participating parties.[15]

Public Agencies and Community Sports Groups

Public recreation and park departments typically develop strong working relationships with volunteer community sports groups, such as Little League, Biddy Basketball, or other youth-serving organizations in such sports as soccer, hockey, or softball. In many cases, these neighborhood or district organizations take a primary responsibility for organizing leagues on different age levels, providing instructional programs and coaching, and even for purchasing equipment, improving scheduling, and maintaining sports fields or other facilities. Particularly in older cities with severe budgetary problems, nonprofit volunteer groups provide an invaluable source of leadership and political support for public recreation and park departments.

261

CHAPTER 8
Public and
Community
Relations: Growing
Use of Partnerships

Other Examples: Corporate, Military, Universities, Schools

Varied forms of partnerships between public leisure-service agencies and major corporations have developed in recent years. As a leading example, Crompton and Younger describe the Johnson County, Missouri, Park and Recreation District, which developed a successful program of providing recreation for companies in its region. By the mid-1980s, it was serving 15,000 employees of eighty-four different companies, with over 450,000 acts of participation a year. Based on findings of a needs assessment survey, each such program works through a recreation committee formed within the company and has several operational alternatives: (1) activity programs offered at company locations; (2) programs using public facilities leased by the Johnson County Park and Recreation District from local school systems; (3) company programs integrated with those offered to the general public; and (4) classes for employees at private facilities, such as tennis centers, bowling alleys, or ice rinks.[16]

Similarly, the Fairfax County, Virginia, Park Authority established employee fitness programs in three of its eight recreation centers situated close to major industrial parks and corporation offices. Midday sports leagues and carefully monitored fitness services have attracted hundreds of company employees— both on an individual and a contracted basis.[17] Hundreds of other examples may be cited of companies throughout the United States and Canada that have sponsored or cosponsored major tournaments and marathons, sports clinics for youth, or taken responsibility for "adopting" parks.

There are numerous examples of cooperation and full-fledged partnerships between Morale, Welfare and Recreation programs in the armed forces and other community organizations. A common practice has involved the interchange of facilities. For example, Seymour Johnson Air Force Base near Goldsboro, North Carolina, has developed synergetic relationships with many community organizations in its area, resulting in savings for all agencies concerned (Fig. 8.6).

Similarly, the community of Radcliff and its neighboring military installation, Fort Knox, in central Kentucky, developed a positive partnership policy in the mid-1990s, based on their mutual needs. Spencer and Moman point out that due to funding cutbacks, some of Fort Knox's MWR facilities and programs were given the ultimatum of becoming self-supporting or being forced to close down. At the same time, Radcliff needed a convention and meeting facility

> . . . but lacked the finances to build and maintain such a facility. By combining assets, Radcliff can now market and promote the convention facilities located on the military installation. And, by opening their doors to civilian groups, Fort Knox [has gained] greater revenue from increased usage of its facilities.[18]

262

CHAPTER 8
Public and
Community
Relations: Growing
Use of Partnerships

Another example of cooperative relationships or partnerships involves contractual agreement between military bases and university leisure-studies departments to operate summer day camp programs for the children of armed forces personnel. In the early 1990s, the California State University at Chico's Department of Recreation and Parks management agreed to provide a ten-week day camp program for children at three U.S. Navy bases in Japan. Al Jackson describes the program, which was given the Chico mascot's name of Willie Wildcat:

> [It was] designed with a performance plan, four major goals/objectives and eight developmental tasks that were provided by the U.S. Naval Training Unit at Patuxent River, Maryland. . . . The contract required the university to provide 38 student counselors, three camp directors, and two program coordinators as staff for the three camps. The contract required the university to provide a variety of recreational activities daily, divided into ten theme weeks, with one day per week for excursions off-base.[19]

Public school systems have also collaborated with public and nonprofit organizations in cosponsoring recreation programs. Historically, many public school systems were pioneers in providing community recreation programs during the early decades of the twentieth century. While most have given up this responsibility, in many communities school facilities continue to be used to house public recreation activities.

FIGURE 8.6. **Interchange of facilities between Seymour Johnson Air Force Base and community agencies.**

	Seymour Johnson AFB		Community, State, Private Agencies	
	Provides	Uses	Provides	Uses
Pools	●	●	Seyboro Swim Team	Seyboro Swim Team
Golf course	●			High school
Ball fields	●			Junior high school
Gyms		●	Junior high school	
Bleachers	●			Goldsboro P&R Department
Chairs		●	Goldsboro P&R Department	
Toy repair	●			Salvation Army
Water safety		●	Red Cross	
Entertainment	●			Senior citizens
Nature Trails	●			Boy Scouts
Interns		●	Colleges and universities	
Hospital	●			Special Olympics
Hobby shop	●			Wayne Community College
Classes and seminars		●	Wayne Community College	
Big Brothers/Big Sisters	●			Elementary schools
Theater arts			Community Arts Council	
Running track		●	Junior high school	
Recreation center	●			N.C. Recreation and Park Society
Volunteers in education	●			Local School System Society

In San Diego, the city and school district have entered into a contractual agreement for the joint operation of school facilities. School facilities serve as community centers. According to the terms of the contract, the school district makes all playgrounds, classrooms, auditoriums, cafeterias, gymnasiums, storage rooms, and other special facilities available to the municipal recreation department as needed, and recreation facilities are made equally available to the schools.

In a number of Canadian cities, similar policies prevail. The Vancouver, British Columbia, Board of Parks and Recreation, for example, has developed a number of year-round, full-utilization complexes built adjacent to secondary and elementary schools. These include facilities such as indoor swimming pools, community meeting rooms, health and welfare centers, playing fields, teenage lounges, and similar areas.

In other cases, school systems have cooperated with nonprofit youth organizations to work constructively with youth gangs and at-risk youth generally. In New Bedford, Massachusetts, for example, a police substation is housed in a low-income area elementary school, transforming the school into a neighborhood hub featuring after-school programs, a community library, Girl Scout troop, and other youth services. Police Athletic Leagues frequently work closely with school authorities in similar partnership arrangements.[20]

In the therapeutic recreation field, Riveredge Hospital, a private psychiatric hospital in Forest Park, Illinois, has developed a shared services program with the West Suburban Special Recreation Association (WSSRA), a jointly sponsored program of several suburban communities. Beginning in an effort to better serve the hospital's patients in their return to the community, both agencies committed themselves to developing better linkages between community-based programs and clinical treatment centers. The shared services program included several elements: (1) use of varied community facilities for hospital-sponsored programs and vice versa; (2) patients' participating in WSSRA programs, (3) new discharge options, in which Riveredge patients nearing discharge participated in community programs as volunteer recreation aides; and (4) postdischarge integration of patients into community programs.

Increasingly, public recreation and park authorities are cooperating actively with economic development offices, tourist organizations, and other groups to promote outdoor recreation opportunities, entertainment events, historic districts, and other attractions. In a recent example of such partnerships, the New York State Department of Economic Development joined with over fifty ski areas in five regions throughout the state to package and publicize a unique three-day program (including instruction, equipment, and lift tickets) for downhill and cross-country skiing and snowboarding (Fig. 8.7).

Guidelines for Partnership Arrangements

Recognizing that such partnership arrangements may easily result in disputes and conflicts, it is essential that firm guidelines be established that set the ground rules that must be followed. For example, numerous problems may occur when public recreation departments use school facilities. Who should cover

263

CHAPTER 8
Public and
Community
Relations: Growing
Use of Partnerships

264

CHAPTER 8
Public and
Community
Relations: Growing
Use of Partnerships

FIGURE 8.7.   Ski package promotion: public/private partnership.

utilities costs or custodial expenses? What happens when equipment is damaged, or when school areas are not in proper condition when classes begin the next day? The following guidelines are helpful in dealing with such issues:

There should be written policies that clearly indicate the rights and responsibilities of each party, signed by officials representing both groups.

Joint committees should be formed and regular meetings held to monitor the cooperative relationship's operation and modify policies or take action when necessary.

The priority order of availability of facilities for community groups should be clearly established, with rental fees defined and publicized.

Other policies with respect to the types of activities that may or may not be carried on in school settings, regulations with respect to smoking and drinking, costs of utilities and maintenance during community use, and responsibility for cleaning up or repairing damage should also be clearly stated.

265

CHAPTER 8
*Public and
Community
Relations: Growing
Use of Partnerships*

SUBCONTRACTING AND PRIVATIZATION

An important type of partnership today involves subcontracting arrangements in which one leisure-service agency—usually a public recreation and park department—contracts with another organization to operate all or part of a given facility or program. This approach is part of an overall trend in which many traditionally public functions are now being assumed by private profit-oriented firms. One of the most unique examples is in the penal system, where a number of private businesses have won contracts to operate prisons and jails as well as other services within the criminal justice system, such as probation work and policing itself. Private postal service centers are being established across the country, where people can pick up mail from post office-style boxes, buy stamps, and mail packages. Increasingly sanitation and garbage-collection services are being farmed out to private haulers, and over 200 firms now offer dispute-resolving arbitration service in noncritical litigation through "Rent-a-Judge" private courtrooms.

Within the recreation, park, and leisure-service field, one of the strong recommendations of the President's Commission on Americans Outdoors was for fuller cooperation between the private sector and government in providing outdoor recreation opportunities. Privatization represents one of the ways in which that cooperation is occurring today.

Guidelines for Subcontracting

Some of the early, successful examples of subcontracting in recreation and park management were in California. Following the passage of Proposition 13, a statewide tax-reduction measure that forced budget cutbacks in many communities, many California towns explored varied privatization options.

New ventures into subcontracting were undertaken in both small and large communities. For example, when severe budget cuts threatened the survival of the Fair Oaks Recreation and Park District recreation program in Sacramento, two professional staff members formed their own private corporation and submitted a proposal to contract the recreation services from the district. Under the agreement, which was successfully carried out with substantial annual savings, the district provided facilities with maintenance, while the corporation, Leisure Pro, Inc., carried out a full range of programs for different age groups, including sports, fee classes, special events, and day camp programs. The corporation assumed responsibility for the content and quality of programs, publicity, scheduling, and similar functions, while the district maintained control over fee levels and the types of programs offered.

Many other communities have contracted directly with business groups to operate such facilities as golf courses or tennis courts.

For example, the Dallas Park and Recreation Department has operated five large tennis centers throughout the city for a number of years, with each facility containing fifteen to twenty outdoor courts and a full-service pro shop. However, while business was brisk, using permanent city employees to staff the centers was costly and, in the late 1970s, tennis expenditures exceeded revenues three to one. Through the 1980s, the city privatized the tennis center operation with all personnel being hired and paid by the tennis pro, with the city retaining a portion of merchandise sales and half the court fees. With the following policies in place, the tennis center program has covered its direct operating expenses during the 1990s:

> The Park and Recreation Board approves court fees and policies;
>
> The pro/managers operate the facilities and are responsible for other expenses associated with the business, such as labor, marketing, equipment, and office supplies; and
>
> The city is responsible for utilities, court building, and grounds repair and maintenance, and site renovation or expansion costs.[21]

At the same time that they are being privately managed, each tennis center has kept its own identity, with two centers specializing in tournaments and competitive leagues, and the others focusing on junior camps, leagues, and daily reservations.

In some cases, national business chains have taken over management of golf courses for municipal recreation and park departments. A major corporation in this field, the American Golf Corporation (AGC), began in 1973 with three southern California courses and moved into the 1980s with thirteen new courses—four municipal courses in Long Beach, California, five in New York City, and one each in four other cities. When they contracted in 1983 to take over the five New York courses, which were losing over a million dollars a year because of poor maintenance, American Golf Corporation agreed to make over $1.5 million in capital improvements during the first year, along with rent/percentage payments. Within two years, the city was netting about $75,000 annually for each course, compared to a previous loss of $200,000. Today, Jones points out, in the state of New York, which operates twenty-three 18-hole golf courses among its 150 state parks, the public/private partnership has become the preferred vehicle for management.[22]

While such privatization approaches are being widely adopted today, their use involves two important policy issues: (1) the fact that in most cases they are accompanied by significantly higher fee structures, which limit the access of population groups unable to afford their charges; and (2) they represent a threat to many public-service employees who view the transfer of governmental functions to private firms as a challenge to their job stability. Although subcontracting arrangements usually do not involve the direct firing or replacement of existing personnel in a department, they may lead to overall staff attrition or downsizing by nonreplacement of employees. Also, they represent temporary arrangements that may be terminated after relatively short periods, in contrast to the public department itself maintaining a responsibility on a stable, continuing basis.

Concessions

A closely related approach for public leisure-service agencies involves the use of concessions, through which departments authorize private individuals or businesses to sell merchandise or services in parks, stadiums, or other publicly owned facilities. Concessions are generally granted when the public department cannot provide a service efficiently or economically in comparison to the commercial organization. Some of the areas of service in which concessions are commonly granted are boat rentals, refreshment stands, equipment shops, and instructional services.

267

CHAPTER 8
*Public and
Community
Relations: Growing
Use of Partnerships*

The use of concessionaires permits a recreation and park department to provide services, equipment, or refreshments that it might otherwise not be able to offer because of limited staffing. Since concessionaires are private business-people or companies, they are not restricted by civil-service personnel requirements or other municipal bureaucratic regulations. Therefore, they are able to provide the service while charging a reasonable fee and at the same time make a profit on the operation. Customarily, concessionaires pay a percentage of their gross revenue to the department and might also pay an annual fee for the concession privilege.

In all privatization arrangements involving concessions, leases of recreation facilities, or jointly operated programs, it is essential that public-private contracts contain strong safeguards for the municipality or county government, including clauses dealing with appearance of facility, lease length and final ownership, responsibility for utility costs, annual cost of lease, sharing of existing park facilities, sign control, operation standards, use of facility for municipal programs, and similar elements.

CONTRAST BETWEEN COMMUNITY DEVELOPMENT AND PRIVATIZATION

While both of the aspects of community relations that have just been described represent strategies that may be followed by public recreation and park agencies in which they divest themselves of major responsibilities, their effect is markedly different.

The *community development* approach relies on neighborhood residents to take responsibility for initiating or managing recreation programs or facilities, with a major purpose being to create a sense of democratic involvement and empowerment. It stresses the value of recreation, parks, and leisure as a vital aspect in community life, around which people of every background and age can mobilize their efforts—often with the help of public department coordinators or consultants.

In contrast, the *privatization* approach that is found in subcontracting or concessions and lease arrangements essentially means that the public department no longer takes primary responsibility for providing leisure services. Thus, although the private operator is using publicly owned property, recreation has essentially become a commercial, profit-clearing function.

If, as just indicated, rising fees bar substantial numbers of potential participants from healthy forms of leisure involvement that were formerly available to them, the important mission of public recreation, park, and leisure-service agencies is threatened. On the other hand, public leisure-service managers who have adopted privatization strategies may argue that this approach, as part of a

268

*Chapter 8
Public and
Community
Relations: Growing
Use of Partnerships*

total marketing orientation, is the only realistic way in which their agencies can function successfully and provide high-quality leisure opportunities for a major segment of the public.

SUMMARY

This chapter presents guidelines for the conduct of publicity and public relations operations, and gives numerous examples of trends in community relations activities. Its message is that a fragmented or isolated leisure-service field is not functional today. Instead, agencies of all types must coordinate their efforts and cooperate in identifying and meeting public needs for constructive recreation programming.

Most of the examples cited in the chapter deal with public recreation and park departments. However, it is obvious that voluntary, commercial, therapeutic, and other types of leisure-service organizations *must* promote their programs effectively if they are to succeed. Indeed, for many kinds of agencies, such as major companies, recreation itself serves as a useful medium of public relations by providing or subsidizing programs and special events. It should be a key responsibility of managers, who are in a position to see the broader pictures, to promote concepts and initiate policies that will encourage their staff members to develop innovative practices in public and community relations.

Beyond outlining accepted public relations methods in such areas as the use of the print media or using television and radio effectively, the chapter examines partnership practices and presents guidelines for the joint management of programs and facilities. It concludes with a comparison of two related, but sharply contrasting, approaches—the community development model and the growing use of privatization in leisure-service organizations.

DISCUSSION QUESTIONS AND CLASS ASSIGNMENTS

1. Define the terms *public relations* and *community relations*. Indicate their major purposes and the channels through which they are carried on.
2. As an individual or small-group project, plan a major recreational event for a public or nonprofit agency, such as a communitywide celebration. Outline a public relations campaign designed to promote it, including specific examples of television spot announcements, news releases, or other forms of publicity.
3. Develop a script, in outline form, for a videotape designed to show a specific leisure-service agency in a favorable light to various community organizations or possible contributors to its work. As part of this, prepare two or three sample sections of the script in detail, showing both the scenes that will be shot or included, and dialogue or commentary. As an *alternative* assignment, actually videotape several aspects of a selected agency program and prepare commentary for it, without writing an entire script.
4. The chapter contrasts two types of partnership management approaches: *community development* and *privatization* strategies. Describe these two approaches, and show how they differ in purpose and outcomes.

CASE STUDIES FOR CLASS ANALYSIS

269

CHAPTER 8
Public and
Community
Relations: Growing
Use of Partnerships

Before analyzing these cases in class, review the guidelines suggested in Chapter 3 (pp. 76–77).

 **Case Study 8.1** *Sexual Abuse of Children:*
A Critical Concern

YOU ARE MARGARET EVANS, owner-director of a privately operated day camp program. In addition to your adult professional staff, which functions year-round, you hire a number of high school juniors and seniors for expanded programming during the summer months.

You have just heard from the chief of police that your staff members are being accused of sexually abusing the children in the program. Rumors are flying, and a number of parents have also called you angrily, threatening to withdraw their children. The camp is on the brink of disaster.

You go to the police station, where several parents are meeting with the chief. It turns out that one assistant counselor, a high school junior male student, is the focus of all the charges. It is claimed that he made physical overtures to a 12-year-old girl camper while on an overnight camping trip. The police have questioned him and are conferring with the district attorney's office about whether charges should be filed.

QUESTIONS FOR CLASS DISCUSSION AND ANALYSIS

1. *Newspaper and television reporters are pressing you for information about this matter, which has been the only such episode in the fifteen years of the camp's existence. What would be your best action from a public relations point of view?*

2. *Your staff manual explicitly states that counselors will be fired for drinking or drug use on the job and contains rules against counselors driving alone with children in their cars. However, there is no direct statement regarding sexual abuse of children, since such a problem had never occurred. How should you deal with this problem in the future?*

3. *Examining your hiring and supervisory practices, is there anything you could have done to prevent this incident from occurring or to nip it in the bud before it became a serious problem?*

4. *How would you deal with concerned parents at this point?*

270

CHAPTER 8
Public and
Community
Relations: Growing
Use of Partnerships

Case Study 8.2   *Captain Fuller Takes a Hard Line*

YOU ARE MARIA GONZALEZ, civilian recreation director at a naval air station close to a small coastal community, Port Jeffries, with a population of about 7,500.

While Port Jeffries has a parks department with a few small parks, a fishing pier, and several sports fields, it has no indoor recreation facilities or organized leisure programs. Therefore, you have interchanged the use of facilities with the town. They use your pools, gymnasiums, and crafts shops, and you use their sports fields for your intramural programs. You also have welcomed a local Catholic Youth Organization (CYO) to participate in some of your activities for children and youth; several dependents of personnel on your base belong to the CYO, and this seemed like a good thing to do.

A new base commander, Captain Don Fuller, has taken over. He is determined to run a tight ship at the naval air station and cut costs, doing away with all extraneous programs and services. As part of this policy, he has asked you to set up a system of fees, under which all outside groups would be required to pay to use the base facilities. After conferring with Port Jeffries officials and the director of the CYO, you report to Captain Fuller that they would be unable to pay the fees and could no longer use the base facilities. If they were then barred, they would probably no longer let the base's sports programs use their facilities or welcome them to any of their activities.

Captain Fuller is not upset by this. He feels that the air station will have a more efficient and economical recreation program without "outsiders" involved. However, you know that general policy in the armed forces is to encourage cooperative relationships with community residents and organizations.

QUESTIONS FOR CLASS DISCUSSION AND ANALYSIS

1. How can you make your case more strongly to Captain Fuller? If you challenge him or try to get input from "higher ups" in the system, will you risk your own security as a civilian employee?

2. Is there any constructive way you can use community people in this process? From a "dollars and cents" perspective, what is your strongest argument? Develop a plan to deal with the problem.

271

CHAPTER 8
*Public and
Community
Relations: Growing
Use of Partnerships*

Case Study 8.3 *Race and Recreation: A Matter of Conscience*

YOU ARE BILL BARKER, a member of the board of a nonprofit community association within the Springdale Heights area of the city. In the past, there were no African-American or Hispanic-American residents in Springdale Heights because of unspoken policies of real estate offices in the area that regarded this as a racially "closed" community.

Today, there are a few minority group families in Springdale Heights, and the number is growing. However, since your membership system works by having members propose new members, who must be approved by a majority of the members, no African-American or Hispanic-American families have yet been invited to join the association. This means that they cannot use your swimming pool or tennis courts or take part in other social events unless they are specially invited.

A faction of younger white families in Springdale Heights have indicated that they want more racial diversity in the community and in the recreational facilities and programs. They intend to propose minority group members, and if they are unable to gain sufficient support, they intend to initiate a lawsuit designed to remove the tax-exempt status of the association.

QUESTIONS FOR CLASS DISCUSSION AND ANALYSIS

1. *As a member of the community association board who has not taken a stand on this issue in the past, what do you see as the moral issues involved?*

2. *From a legal perspective, research the law to determine the precedents and whether you can be compelled to open the membership in this way.*

3. *When the issue comes before the board, what position do you intend to take? How will you justify it?*

274

CHAPTER 9
Leisure Services
and the Law:
Risk-Management
Concerns

hiring and firing of personnel, access to facilities and programs, the use of properties for recreation and park purposes, policing functions designed to prevent crime or vandalism, and other issues centered about affirmative action, gender, race, disability, or religious practice.

This chapter addresses the following understandings and competencies listed as essential in the Baccalaureate Degree standards of the NRPA/AALR Council on Accreditation:

Knowledge of the legal foundations and responsibilities of leisure-service agencies and of the legislative process and the impact of policy formation on leisure behaviors and service in all levels of government, community organizations, and business enterprise (8.36).

Understanding of legal concepts, including contracts, human rights, property, and torts, as applied to leisure-service agencies (8.37).

Understanding of the principles of risk management planning, and the ability to participate in the development and implementation of a risk management plan (8.38).

Understanding of the use of the law in management of leisure services, including land management, personnel, human rights, financing, and risk management (9A.03).

Understanding of and ability to operationalize legal concepts related to negligence, specifically the conduct and supervision of activity (9C.07).

OBJECTIVES

At the conclusion of this chapter, readers should be familiar with the following concepts, problems, and practices affecting recreation, park, and leisure-service management:

1. The overall framework of legal statutes and court decisions within which leisure-service managers, particularly those in public agencies or commercial businesses, must function.
2. Awareness of the risks of liability claims and lawsuits based on injuries stemming from the use of recreation facilities and programs under circumstances of negligent management or supervision.
3. Specific guidelines for risk-management practices in such areas as outdoor and wilderness recreation, sports, aquatics, amusement park rides, and playground supervision.
4. Methods used to prevent or minimize fiscal losses based on liability claims, including emergency and accident follow-up procedures, participant warnings, waivers, and insurance coverage.
5. Practices used to control or prevent antisocial behavior in parks, pools, and other leisure settings, including criminal activity, drug abuse, sexual molestation, and vandalism.
6. Other types of legal concerns, such as regulations covering property development and environmental issues, labor relations, contractual obligations and torts, copyright infringement, and access to facilities.
7. Issues affecting personnel and participants, with respect to race or ethnicity, gender, disability, religion, and residential status.

LEGAL RESPONSIBILITIES OF
LEISURE-SERVICE MANAGERS

275

CHAPTER 9
Leisure Services
and the Law:
Risk-Management
Concerns

Increasingly, knowledge of the law has become an important job-related requirement for leisure-service managers. What *is* the law, and how does it impact on recreation as a form of community service or business enterprise? A Canadian attorney, David Manning, points out that there are two primary sources of law that affect leisure services in Canada. First, he identifies an "ever increasing, often confusing, and at times, contradictory" body of statutes, regulations, and bylaws that can be broadly labeled "statutory laws":

> These are the laws which are codified and written by the parliaments, legislatures, and municipalities. Secondly, where a situation arises which is not addressed by statutory law, or where that statutory law is to be interpreted, judge-made law is created in the form of judicial decisions. The totality of these decisions form the body of what lawyers refer to as "common law." There is considerable overlap of jurisdiction between federal, provincial, and municipal levels of government. It is not uncommon for legislators at one level to write laws without reference to developments in other levels. It is little wonder that such judge-made common law is confusing and as contradictory as the statutory law which spawns it.[3]

It is within this framework of laws and court decisions that management-level personnel in varied types of recreation, park, and leisure-service organizations must function. Increasingly, managers have become responsible for developing risk-management programs that reduce the likelihood of accidents and injuries that might lead to successful lawsuits and liability claims. Beyond this, recreation and park directors must deal with problems of crime, delinquency, vandalism, and similar concerns affecting their programs and facilities. They must also be aware of general principles that govern contracts between their agencies and other organizations, as well as problems of labor relations and union negotiations, affirmative action practices, issues of possible sexual harassment or child abuse, and similar problems.

While leisure-service managers are not themselves lawyers as a rule, they should become generally familiar with the laws of their states, provinces, or communities as they affect the recreation and park field. Beyond that, in any large government agency or other organization, there are likely to be attorneys or law firms that act as counselors or are on retainer status in such areas. These resources should be used in all contract planning, personnel negotiations, hiring practices, and facility acquisition and development.

LIABILITY AS A MANAGEMENT CONCERN

Liability is one of the most important issues affecting leisure-service managers today. This term is commonly used to describe the situation in which an individual or organization is subject to lawsuit because of failure to carry out certain responsibilities as defined by law or within a contractual agreement. It assumes a set of responsibilities that have been agreed on between two or more entities, such as private individuals, associations, companies, or other parties.

276

*CHAPTER 9
Leisure Services
and the Law:
Risk-Management
Concerns*

The principle holds that any person who fails to live up to his or her responsibilities through negligence or intent must provide compensation to the other party or legal entity.

Types of Liability

There are several different types of liability. In *criminal liability*, government may bring an individual to court because of an alleged criminal act, such as assault or burglary. In *liability based on violation of civil laws*, such as health and safety codes or civil rights laws, government may sue or enjoin an individual or organizations.

The two types of liability of greatest concern in the leisure-service field are *tort liability* and *contractual liability*.

Tort Liability

A tort is a legal wrong committed on a person or property outside of a contractual relationship. The term *tort* comes from the Latin *torquere* and *tortus*, meaning "to twist." A tort may involve either: (1) a direct violation of the legal right of the individual or (2) the infraction of some public duty or responsibility by which the individual suffers special damages.

Intentional torts, such as assaults, fraud, libel, or slander, are classified as criminal and may result in possible imprisonment and/or payments being awarded by the court to the individual who has suffered the tort. Van der Smissen points out that an intentional tort requires the intent to harm, with the act performed being the cause of the injury, and that actual damage occurred.[4] Unintentional torts are caused by negligence and customarily call for the payment of actual damages to the wronged person by the wrongdoer.

Under the law, those subject to lawsuit for negligent action resulting in a tort may include the corporate entity itself, such as a corporation or owner, individual board members or trustees, managerial personnel, and those directly responsible for leadership within a program. In the past, most government agencies and their employees were immune from such claims under the doctrine of "sovereign immunity." This principle held that the state (or local governments as subdivisions of the state) was not liable for injuries resulting from the negligence of its employees or other agents.

Since the early 1960s, a number of state legislatures have abrogated the principle of "sovereign immunity" by enacting statutes that place responsibility for participant safety directly on the agency conducting the program. In California, for example, a clause was added to the state government code that states, "A public entity is liable for an injury proximately caused by an act or omission of an employee of a public entity within the scope of his employment." Similar statutes have been enacted in over thirty states, and although there is considerable variation with respect to the liability of agencies for different types of programs or services, it must be considered that there is no absolute defense against possible lawsuits for injury.

On the federal level, prior to the enactment of the Federal Tort Claims Act (FTCA), agencies of the federal government enjoyed sovereign immunity against liability lawsuits based on negligence—including suits stemming from injuries at federal recreation sites. Under this law, federal agencies are now subject to negligence lawsuits under the law of the jurisdiction where the injury was suffered.

277

CHAPTER 9
Leisure Services
and the Law:
Risk-Management
Concerns

Contractual Liability

In addition to tort liability, which includes negligence injury claims, an important area of concern for recreation and park managers is contractual liability. In simple terms, this refers to legal claims that may be made, leading to a condition of liability based on charges of failure to perform as contracted. Lawsuits are usually concerned with the performance of services or the provision of a given product and seek monetary damages.

Leisure-service agencies may be involved in various contracts with concessionaires, construction or maintenance companies, vending machine operators, utility companies, cosponsoring organizations, transportation carriers, designers and planners, manufacturers and suppliers, and a host of other companies or individuals.

Since contract law is a highly complex field, recreation, park, and leisure-service managers should be careful to seek qualified legal assistance when reviewing or drafting contractual agreements or when there is an issue as to performance under the contract.

Concept of Negligence

Negligence is the key element that must be proved satisfactorily before an individual or organization can be held legally responsible for unintentional torts that have resulted in injury to others. Negligence is generally considered to be an unintentional act of omission or commission, under which an individual fails to do something that a "reasonable" person would do under similar circumstances—or, conversely, doing something that a reasonable and prudent person would *not* do.

Beyond this rather general concept, several more specific elements must be proved before a claim for injury or other loss based on negligence can be won. These include (1) *duty,* defined as an obligation under the law requiring the agency or individual to conform to an approved standard of conduct or behavior to protect others against unreasonable risks; (2) *breach,* defined as failure to conform to the required standards; (3) *proximate cause,* defined as a reasonably or sufficiently close causal connection between the conduct of the agency or individual and the resultant injury or loss to another; and (4) *damages,* defined as actual loss or injury to the interests of another.

Examples of Claims against Leisure-Service Agencies

Because of the very nature of recreational activity, there are many circumstances under which leisure-service organizations may be sued by injured participants or facility users, or their families.

In a relatively high-risk activity, such as skiing, the assumption is that participants must have a reasonable awareness of the risk factor, and the sponsoring agency is not responsible for an injury caused by chance or natural

278

CHAPTER 9
*Leisure Services
and the Law:
Risk-Management
Concerns*

circumstances. However, if the agency has not properly groomed the slope, permitting skiers to become caught in hidden undergrowth and seriously injured, or if it has not provided adequate supervision or has permitted other dangerous circumstances to exist, it may be found guilty of negligence. Obviously, highly dangerous activities require more intensive care and higher standards of supervision than others, subject to the "reasonably prudent" guideline.

In a series of articles regarding the liability of recreation and park agencies for accidents occurring in their facilities or programs, Kozlowski cites examples of cases stemming from playground games such as "crack the whip" or defective conditions in park or playground maintenance.[5] Other cases involve a university's responsibility for preventing a student's alcohol consumption on a field trip, a park management's responsibility for controlling drinking in a park and preventing an ensuing automobile accident, a private beach operator's responsibility for preventing roughhousing that led to an injury, and a city park department's hiring a "career criminal" under the Work Relief Employment Program who, as a maintenance employee, brutally raped a nine-year-old girl.

Other Legal Principles Affecting Liability

In determining the degree of liability of defendants in such cases, a number of other legal principles come into play. These include the following:

> *Contributory negligence.* Conduct by an injured claimant that falls below the standard required for his or her own protection.

> *Comparative negligence.* A legal principle holding that when both the injured person and the defendant are at fault, damages will be apportioned between them according to the degree of responsibility held by each party.

> *Assumption of risk.* The principle in which a person assumes the risk of injury through another party's negligence by voluntarily exposing himself or herself to possible danger.

Several concepts deal with the circumstances under which an individual enters a particular facility, or areas:

1. *trespasser,* a person who enters the property of another without that individual's full knowledge and consent, in which case the property owner has only a slight degree of responsibility for preventing injury;
2. *invitee,* a person who enters another's property with permission and for the mutual benefit of both the property owner and the person entering, in which case a high degree of care is required;
3. *licensee,* a person who enters another person's property, with permission, doing so only for his or her own benefit, in which case "reasonable" care to remove hazards or post warnings is required; and
4. *attractive nuisance,* such as facilities like swimming pools that might reasonably be expected to attract children to enter, and thus require the owner to keep the area in safe condition and take ordinary care to prevent children from trespassing.[6]

The need for effective risk-management planning and supervision has become evident to leisure-service boards and commissions, managers, and staff members on all levels in recent years. As more and more people have visited large national or state parks, forests, and recreation areas, the risk of injury or death from environmental hazards has grown greatly. Falls off cliffs or from horseback, bites from poisonous snakes or attacks from other dangerous animals, exposure to boiling springs or similar hazardous attractions, deaths from freezing, heatstroke, or similar dangers must be guarded against. Controls that will protect participants from their own ignorance of the natural environment or from behavior that *invites* injury or death, such as unsafe boating practices, must be instituted.

In the urban setting, accident prevention, and the development of effective safety practices are equally important. Poorly maintained or dangerous equipment in parks, playgrounds, or athletic complexes, as well as inadequately supervised activities, may lead to serious injury or death.

The need for risk-management planning is critical if agencies are to avoid losses caused by fire, vandalism, or theft of facilities and equipment; claims from persons injured as a result of presumed negligence of the leisure-service agency; costs associated with medical or indemnity payments for injured employees through worker compensation; or reduced public or membership confidence and a damaged image because of avoidable accidents. The potential loss must include the total impact of a serious injury on victims and their families.

Simply developing safety procedures or inspecting equipment is not sufficient. Instead, a comprehensive risk-management plan that systematically attacks each level of the problem is essential. Risk management itself may be defined as an operational approach that is designed to reduce or prevent accidents and injuries or other health hazards, and that seeks to prevent financial loss stemming from them. It includes a set of prevention and control procedures, as well as steps designed to deal with accidents when they do occur, in terms of minimizing their impact on the agency. In practical terms, the prevention and control process begins with the task of identifying potential danger areas and developing accurate reporting and record-keeping systems.

Reporting and Record Keeping

In part, this involves understanding the types of accidents and injuries that may be sustained within any major category of recreational activity. For example, statistics gathered by the Consumer Product Safety Commission report the estimated number of head injuries to children and youth, and the type of playground equipment or vehicle associated with the injuries (Table 9.1).

As the first direct step in an agency's risk-management plan, it is necessary to keep records that maintain an accurate picture of accidents that occur, their locations, and their apparent causes. Frequencies beyond normal or predictable accident rates will become evident and call for corrective action. Furthermore, if control techniques are effective in reducing incidents, record keeping will reveal such improvements.

280

CHAPTER 9
*Leisure Services
and the Law:
Risk-Management
Concerns*

TABLE 9.1. Estimated Head Injuries to Children and Youth Treated in U.S. Emergency Rooms, Linked to Playgrounds and Equipment

Type of Equipment	Estimated Number of Head Injuries	Age of Patient			
		0–4 Years		*5–14 Years*	
		Number	%	Number	%
Playground Equipment	43,372	16,775	75	25,899	76
Slides	9,309	5,012	22	4,297	13
Seesaws	1,523	573	3	950	3
Monkey bars	8,746	2,360	10	8,190	18
Swings	17,565	7,409	33	9,967	29
Trampolines	2,487	259	1	1,958	6
Other	2,407	805	4	1,559	5
Not specified	1,335	357	2	978	3
Children's Vehicles	6,951	5,029	22	1,905	6
Tricycles	1,899	1,629	7	270	1
Wagons	2,228	1,565	7	663	2
Scooters	1,207	507	2	683	2
Wheeled toys	1,617	1,328	6	289	1
Skateboards	4,061	323	1	3,118	9
Roller skates	4,096	361	2	3,168	9

Source: Data provided by Consumer Product Safety Commission (1991).

Facilities Inspection and Hazard Abatement

The next step is to rigorously examine all facilities, areas, and equipment to ensure that it meets appropriate safety or professional standards, is properly maintained, and is in good working order. For example, in a playground, this would include all equipment, such as slides, swings, or climbing equipment, to be certain that it is not hazardous in any way. In a park setting, it might involve all areas involving special risks. Speed limit signs, rock slide warnings, barriers, thin ice warnings, or similar prohibitions should be posted to protect participants against natural hazards. In urban parks and recreation facilities, architectural features such as walks, steps, buildings, and other structures must be inspected regularly. Poor visibility, inadequate barriers or walls, accessible high-voltage transmission lines, inadequate storage facilities for flammable liquids, low clearance, blocked exits, or poorly marked emergency circulation routes are examples of problems that must be identified and corrected.

A classic example of inadequate inspection is the major fire that occurred in the Haunted Castle of a crowded New Jersey amusement park in the mid-1980s, in which eight teenagers were killed. According to newspaper accounts, a foam rubber crash pad attached to a wall caught fire when a youngster lit a cigarette lighter to see where he was in the almost totally darkened facility (a strobe light intended to provide partial illumination was not working). The results were tragic; when firefighters dug through the rubble and charred wood of the ruined "castle," they found the bodies of the eight victims who had been unable to escape through the thick black smoke.

As later investigations and hearings were to reveal, the lack of smoke detectors, sprinklers, alarm signals, or other safety measures undoubtedly contributed to the tragedy. If the Haunted Castle had been classified as a permanent structure, it could not have passed safety code inspections. However, because it consisted of a series of trailers, it was not required by township authorities to undergo such inspections.

281

CHAPTER 9
Leisure Services
and the Law:
Risk-Management
Concerns

Participant Safety Briefing and Preparation

There should be a regular consistent approach to providing all participants with an understanding of the possible risks involved in the activity they are planning to participate in, including risks that may be involved for spectators. They must be helped to understand the nature of unsafe acts and their consequences and the hazards to be avoided. This can be done through posted rules, briefing sessions held in campgrounds, regular supervision and warning by rangers, or similar methods. Strict policies for boating practices, for example, should be enacted and enforced.

Detailed emphatic warnings of the danger of serious injuries in such contact sports as Pop Warner football or high-risk outdoor pursuits should be routinely provided to parents and participants.

Staff Training, Goal Setting, and Supervision

Risk management requires that all staff members be familiar with important safety and accident-prevention principles and be committed to maintaining a safe environment and program. This can best be done if safety and accident prevention are made important items in staff orientation and training and if they are reinforced in meetings, evaluations, and other management procedures.

Staff members should be involved in setting safety goals and objectives, developing reporting and recording systems, and protecting both the public and themselves. It should be noted that employees may run a higher risk of injury than visitors because they are in the recreation setting on a full-time basis and because they must become involved in emergency or lifesaving procedures, such as fire fighting or rescue operations.

Emergency Procedures and Follow-Up

First aid, accident, and other emergency procedures should be clearly identified and made known to all employees. In community centers, fire alarm procedures and building evacuation should be practiced at regular intervals. On playgrounds and in other outdoor recreation areas, there should be precise directions for handling physical injury, sunstroke or heatstroke, drowning, or similar accidents.

In facilities that may hold many participants or spectators, such as theaters, stadiums, dance halls, bowling alleys, or skating rinks, a public-address system to make emergency announcements, an alarm system, telephones to summon

282

CHAPTER 9
Leisure Services
and the Law:
Risk-Management
Concerns

assistance, and other means of communication are desirable. Evacuation or escape routes for visitors and employees and access for vehicles such as fire trucks, ambulances, or tow trucks should also be kept clear.

Staff members should be given instructions regarding appropriate public relations procedures after an accident or other emergency situation. After the New Jersey Haunted Castle fire, the county prosecutor and reporters said they had been "abused, stonewalled and misled" by the amusement park's owners, operators, and representatives. According to newspaper accounts, the park re-opened in a "carnival atmosphere" the day after the fire. Apparently no effort was made to communicate helpfully with the families or provide solace for them. Clearly, emergency procedures in any leisure-service agency should include consideration of appropriate public relations policies after serious accidents or injuries.

First aid supplies and arrangements for transportation should be available in all settings. Today, many departments include cardiopulmonary resuscitation (CPR) and Heimlich maneuver training as part of emergency procedures and first aid training courses.

Insurance, Waivers, and Legal Responsibilities

A final important element in risk-management plans involves the need to have adequate and appropriate insurance coverage, which may be part of an overall insurance policy for a municipality, company, or other organization, or may be designed for coverage of specific high-risk programs.

Many county or municipal governments have blanket liability insurance coverage that protects all departments under a single "umbrella" policy. In other cases, separate departments or agencies believed to have a significant negligence claim risk are empowered to purchase their own policies at appropriate levels of coverage and at premiums they assume within their own budgets.

Since insurance rates vary greatly, it is wise to get a number of quotations before purchasing coverage. It should also be recognized that one or more claims or verdicts against a leisure-service agency may cause a company to raise its premiums sharply or even cancel its coverage, making it all the more necessary to prevent possible claims and protect one's "insurability."

Two examples of insurance coverage of community organizations by public departments are found in Phoenix, Arizona, and Metro-Dade County, Florida. Phoenix has a coordinated Risk Management Policy, based on a self-insured approach. Most activities taking place on the Parks, Recreation and Library Department's property under departmental jurisdiction, including cosponsored programs, do not normally require additional purchase of insurance. Events sponsored by vendors or concessionaires with a higher degree of risk, such as those involving alcohol, a fireworks display, amusement rides, cooking, or police or traffic control, require a Certificate of Insurance prior to departmental approval.

In Metro-Dade County, the Park and Recreation Department has numerous parks at which various private-sector groups sponsor events. Often these groups are unable to acquire insurance independently to protect their events, and must therefore abandon program plans. As a result, the Park and Recreation Department developed Special Events Liability specifications (blanket-type coverage) and solicited bids from insurance firms in the area. A special policy was established at reasonable cost through which local groups could be granted coverage, which permitted them to stage events successfully. This service has been particularly valuable in assisting minority racial and ethnic populations, as well as other fund-raising and cultural organizations, in using the parks.

Many public and commercial recreation agencies require participants to sign liability waivers, under which participants state that they will not hold the department or other organization responsible for accidents that may occur. This is invalid in the case of children, who cannot legally sign away their right to sue, and it is also generally ineffective for other age groups. Instead, van der Smissen suggests that participant acknowledgments that describe the nature of the activity to be engaged in, as well as its potential risks, and in which the participant agrees to obey all established rules and guidelines are a more useful approach. In case of a later lawsuit, the defendant may use such agreements as evidence of contributory negligence if the plaintiff did not follow the agreed-on rules.[7]

283

CHAPTER 9
Leisure Services
and the Law:
Risk-Management
Concerns

SPECIFIC AREAS OF SAFETY CONCERNS

Several specific areas of recreation participation—including playgrounds, active sports programs, outdoor recreation, aquatics, and theme park management—are now examined.

Children's Playgrounds

Each year, over 200,000 children are injured on America's playgrounds, with the bulk of these accidents involving falls. Hudson, Thompson, and Mack point out that playground safety is a complex issue. While the simple answer to solving this problem might be to make surfaces safer, the deeper issue, they write:

> . . . is why did children fall in the first place? Was it because they were on equipment that was too difficult for their developmental abilities and skills? Was it because two children were using the equipment inappropriately without adult supervision? Was it because the equipment was worn and a piece broke, sending the child tumbling to a non-resilient surface?[8]

In 1981, the U.S. Consumer Product Safety Commission (CPSC), with input from the National Recreation and Park Association and the National Bureau of Standards, published *A Handbook for Public Playground Safety*, which presents federal guidelines designed to reduce the number and severity of injuries on public playgrounds.

In the years that followed, improved design and materials made playground equipment safer, and better surfaces below swings, slides, and climbing equipment made falls less serious. Revised CPSC handbooks presented new guidelines and standards to reduce injuries further. Today, the National Playground Safety Institute has become the chief resource for recreation and park agencies in this field, and has been approved by the National Certification

284

CHAPTER 9
Leisure Services
and the Law:
Risk-Management
Concerns

Board of the NRPA to provide certification for playground safety inspectors through seminars, course materials, and testing procedures.

Despite such efforts, however, Steve King reports that a 1995 survey of 900 park departments found that almost 30 percent of departments had never conducted safety audits on their equipment, despite the fact that 46 percent of their play structures were more than ten years old. Beyond this, very few of the audits that were carried out were conducted by certified safety inspectors.[9]

Beyond the need to ensure that equipment itself meets the standards that have been established by such groups, it is essential that the *way* in which children play be carefully supervised to prevent injuries. Many departments have developed detailed guidelines for this purpose (Fig. 9.1).

Youth Sports

Many of the same principles that were presented for playground management also apply to team sports. Beyond these, numerous guidelines for the safe operation of youth sports deal with: (1) the classification of team members by age, height, and weight for appropriate team affiliations, particularly in so-called contact sports; (2) specific rules for play, particularly those aimed at preventing unsafe modes of play, such as "spearing" in football; (3) safety-related conditions for practice, including the use of weight-training and other conditioning exercises, for younger players; and (4) the required use of safety equipment.

Kozlowski summarizes a number of the principles that stem from reported court decisions regarding the general legal duties of those conducting various physical activity programs. He writes:

> As a general rule, individuals responsible for conducting sport, recreation, and physical fitness programs owe the following legal duties to the participant: (1) give adequate instruction in the activity; (2) supply proper and necessary protective equipment; (3) make a reasonable selection or match participants; (4) provide non-negligent supervision of the particular activity; and (5) in the event of injury, take proper post-injury procedures to protect against aggravation of the injury.[10]

Issues of school or college responsibility for training young athletes have been tested in the courts in recent years. For example, the deaths of several young wrestlers linked to strenuous weight-loss regimens and the use of special nutritional substances has led to investigation by the federal government and possible criminal charges in some states.

The responsibility for severe injuries resulting in spinal cord paralysis has been tested in a case in which an injured football player for Texas Christian University was at first granted a lifetime allowance and medical expenses, and then denied them by the courts on the grounds that he was not an employee of the institution.[11]

Health and Fitness Clubs

These are somewhat similar to sports programs in terms of risk-management concerns. Usually such clubs are sponsored by YM/YWCAs, universities, public departments, and commercial businesses, as well as many company-operated programs serving their own employees.

285

CHAPTER 9
*Leisure Services
and the Law:
Risk-Management
Concerns*

Guidelines for playground safety

GENERAL SAFETY

1. Safety is a basic consideration in playground and pool operation and the well-managed recreation facility is a safe place for people to play.

2. Remember that *all* accidents have a cause and might have been prevented. Prevention of accidents is one of the basic rules of first aid training.

3. Be sure that you are a safety-conscious person yourself and that you attempt to instill this attitude in others through your safety program.

4. All staff members at pools or playgrounds should know the procedure for handling cases involving serious accidents or injuries. Discussion of these procedures should take place in one of your first staff meetings.

5. Each playground and pool should have a listing of emergency numbers near their telephone, if they have one. Included should be the Fire and Police Departments and the Central Office. Playgrounds that do not have telephones should have access to two or more telephones within the immediate neighborhood.

6. Know the location of your first aid kit and keep it well stocked. Brush up on your first aid methods.

7. Be sure that all staff members are aware of the areas on a park or playground where accidents generally occur. (Please check list on Guides to Safety to help your program of safety.)

PLAYGROUND SAFETY

1. Check apparatus and equipment daily. If it is not in working condition or is dangerous, place it OUT-OF-ORDER and notify the office immediately.

2. Teach children the correct methods of using the apparatus and insist that they be followed.

3. Prepare, post and enforce simple rules of safety for your playground.

4. Know where accidents are liable to happen and be alert to these areas.

5. Enforce ordinances involving dogs and the riding of bicycles on the playground to the best of your ability.

6. Motor scooters and other types of motorized vehicles are not allowed on parks or playgrounds. Contact police at once if this occurs.

FIGURE 9.1.   Playground safety guidelines. In addition to these general guides, playground manuals usually include specific rules for the use of swings, slides, climbing apparatus, and other pieces of equipment.

There can be serious health hazards connected to exercise machines, weight training, aerobic classes, and other vigorous activities—*if* an individual has not been properly screened medically or if the supervision is not adequate. The knowledge required to conduct a safe fitness program is varied and comprehensive. The American College of Sports Medicine, for example, established a so-called gold standard in fitness certification in 1982, consisting of four days of lectures and examinations

> . . . in basic anatomy and physiology, exercise physiology and kinesiology, identification of coronary risk factors, the physiology of aging, fitness assessment . . . exercise prescription, metabolic calculations, emergency procedures . . . injury prevention, leadership, and methods of determining heart rate and blood pressure.[12]

286

*CHAPTER 9
Leisure Services
and the Law:
Risk-Management
Concerns*

Protecting BC's Children.
SPORT Safe

Creating a Safer Environment
for Sport and Recreation

Harassment and abuse take the fun out of sport and recreation.

You can help prevent it by doing something.
If you suspect an abusive situation, tell someone.

Locally

Talking to someone within your sport or recreation organization, like the coach, manager or club president can often clear up a simple misunderstanding.

Provincially

Contact your provincial sport or recreation organization to voice your concern. Your local organization should be able to give you the telephone number.

Report It

If you suspect child abuse of a physical or sexual nature, report it to your local police and/or local Ministry for Children and Families office, listed in the blue pages of your telephone book.

Helpline for Children - Zenith 1234

If you suspect child abuse, call the operator and ask for Zenith 1234, a 24-hour toll-free service.

Crimestoppers Tips Line 1-888-222-TIPS

You can leave an anonymous tip with a police officer.

Victim Information Line - 1-800-563-0808

Victims can receive more information about services available to them and report crimes through this service set up by the Attorney-General's office.

Youth Against Violence Line - 1-800-680-4264

This confidential voice mail system gives you direct assistance from police officers in your community.

Be Involved
We're all part of the solution.

GP 20614-1

BRITISH COLUMBIA
Ministry of Small Business,
Tourism and Culture

FIGURE 9.2.   An example of policies used to protect children in youth sports programs, in British Columbia, Canada.

Similarly, the YMCA has given thousands of individuals physical fitness training workshops based on a full week of classes and examinations. However, the majority of those employed in fitness centers in the United States and Canada do not possess adequate qualifications, and their programs are therefore subject to liability claims based on unqualified leadership if negligence can be proven.

287

CHAPTER 9
*Leisure Services
and the Law:
Risk-Management
Concerns*

In both sports and fitness programming, a specific health hazard involves excessive heat linked with strenuous exercise, which may cause heat exhaustion, cramps, or strokes.

Outdoor Recreation and Wilderness Activities

There are numerous risk factors involved in such wilderness and adventure recreation activities as river rafting, mountaineering and expeditions, rock climbing, ropes courses, and "initiative" or survival-type activities. Obviously, skilled leadership is a critical factor in helping to prevent serious injuries and death in such pursuits.

As a model for the field, the Wilderness Education Association (WEA) has been training and certifying outdoor leaders in a National Standard Program in cooperation with over twenty affiliated universities in the United States and Canada. In addition to risk management, trail organization, equipment selection and use, first aid and evacuation procedures, sanitation and waste disposal, and campsite selection and ethical fire use are all taught to prospective outdoor leaders.

Specific guidelines have been developed that govern the operation of many outdoor pursuits, including a number that have been brought into indoor settings, such as the use of climbing walls in gymnasiums and fitness centers. For example, Robin Mittelstaedt points out that schools, summer camps, private climbing gyms, health clubs, and colleges today are all building vertical structures to meet the demand for this relatively new pastime. She suggests a number of practices to minimize the risk of injuries in climbing walls, including the following:

Control access to the climbing wall. If possible, lock the facility or climbing area when it is not in use. If it cannot be locked, remove ropes and/or belay devices.

Post rules that must be followed when climbing, belaying, and waiting to climb.

Conduct frequent inspections of climbing wall surfaces and holds [equipment]. Make adjustments, changes, and repairs as necessary.

Provide close supervision of climbing area. The wall supervisor must be in the immediate vicinity, within sight and hearing. He or she should supervise all belayers closely and keep a watchful eye on the climbers.

The manager must document the qualifications of all supervisors, including years of climbing experiences and certifications.[13]

288

*CHAPTER 9
Leisure Services
and the Law:
Risk-Management
Concerns*

Particularly in urban settings, where skateboarding and in-line skating have become extremely popular along park walkways, roads, and other paved areas, numerous accidents and lawsuits have occurred in recent years. In some cases, municipalities or other park authorities have constructed special skateboard parks, skating areas, or mountain bike trails for enthusiasts, while restricting these activities in nondesignated park areas. In other situations, because of the withdrawal of immunity protection for public authorities by the courts, municipalities have closed down these special facilities.

Environmental and Weather Risks

In addition to hazards linked to outdoor recreation participation, there are numerous other possible dangers linked to the settings for outdoor play.

Frequently climatic conditions pose a serious risk. For managers in charge of outdoor recreation and park facilities, it is essential to recognize thunderstorms and lightning as important safety hazards. More than 100 lightning fatalities occur each year, with many of these in park settings. Thunderstorms are more frequent in summer than in winter, with 70 percent of all deaths and injuries occurring in June, July, and August.

Kozlowski cites recent court decisions that hold that there is no legal duty for golf course operators to provide protective shelters or forecasting systems to warn golfers of approaching dangerous weather conditions. However, other decisions conclude that modern technology has made lightning storms more predictable and that golf course managers might be determined negligent for not warning golfers of oncoming conditions.[14]

Staff members should be familiar with appropriate safety procedures to protect both themselves and recreation participants from lightning. For example, at the first sound of thunder, swimming pools should be immediately cleared. First aid training should include guidelines on reviving lightning victims, who may not have been struck directly and killed but who may be in temporary shock and require immediate mouth-to-mouth or cardiopulmonary resuscitation to start their heart and lungs working again.

Flash floods represent another potential danger for wild river rafters or campers and hikers in narrow canyons that may suddenly be filled with raging torrents. Again, care must be taken to warn against such possible hazards.

Transportation Guidelines

Another safety factor that affects both competitive sports and outdoor recreation involves transportation arrangements for teams and groups of participants. Ford and Blanchard point out that few elements of outdoor recreation are more hazardous, hour for hour, than driving. In many programs, they write, there is more risk of serious injury or death on the highways than on the trail or river.[15]

Guidelines to prevent accidents include hiring well-qualified experienced drivers who are skilled in mountain or winter driving and who are thoroughly familiar with safety regulations, and using vehicles suited for this purpose that have been rigorously and regularly inspected and equipped. Rules with respect to driving using alcohol or other stimulants must be rigidly observed, along with other safety measures.

Aquatic Safety

289

CHAPTER 9
Leisure Services
and the Law:
Risk-Management
Concerns

A fourth major area of risk-management concern involves water-based recreation programs in varied settings. With more deaths attributed to drowning than any other cause in major outdoor recreation areas, a high priority must be placed on water safety knowledge and behavior. The National Park Service has assigned staff members to appear on radio and television and visit schools and community organizations to present vital water safety messages. Warnings and information are included in park brochures, and dramatic posters are located in numerous park sites. Some parks prohibit the sale and consumption of alcoholic beverages within their boundaries, since liquor and drugs are major contributing factors in many cases of drowning.

Organizations such as the U.S. Coast Guard, Power Squadron, and the American Red Cross promote boating safety. They urge recreational boaters, for example, to use safe fueling practices, obey the rules of the road, wear flotation gear, carry other needed equipment including compasses and signaling equipment, know distress signals and weather warning signals, and follow guidelines for waterskiing.

Most recreational aquatic programs take place in swimming pools operated by various types of public and private sponsors. The swimming pool manager plays a critical role in maintaining an efficient water safety operation. McNally indicates that the manager's qualifications should include the following:

American Red Cross Basic and Advanced First Aid certification (renewed every three years),

CPR certification (renewed every year),

State pool operators certification (renewal time varies with state),

Knowledge of all programs using the facility,

Knowledge of recreation department aquatic facility emergency procedures.[16]

An essential element in preventing drownings is setting up an effective plan for staffing, maintaining, and monitoring swimming pools. Since personnel at many public swimming pools are college students or teachers working on a part-time or seasonal basis, it is important that they be given a two-day orientation during which each manager and guard should present proof of his or her water safety instructor certification or other required licensing.

Emergency phone numbers and step-by-step procedures should be gone over at this time, and lifeguard procedures and responsibilities should be thoroughly reviewed. Many departments use the orientation period to give CPR training.

Lifeguard Selection and Training

Lifeguards are the key element in preventing accidents and providing rescue and first aid to victims when accidents occur. To avoid being found negligent in the case of a drowning or other serious accident, all recreation agencies with

290

*CHAPTER 9
Leisure Services
and the Law:
Risk-Management
Concerns*

pools must employ qualified aquatic staffs. Supervisors must strongly emphasize the need for guards to be fully observant at all times. Numerous court decisions have found for plaintiffs when lifeguards were shown to have been inattentive while an accident was taking place, by reading, eating or drinking refreshments, chatting with friends, or carrying out other pool duties.

Up-to-date emergency procedures for handling suspected spinal cord injuries (which may arise from diving accidents) and the use of oxygen-delivery resuscitation equipment should be presented. Continual in-service training should ensure that essential job-related skills are practiced and that all needed equipment is readily accessible and in good working order. Finally, rules of conduct for swimming patrons should be conspicuously posted and enforced consistently, both to prevent accidents and to maintain a sanitary and healthy pool environment.

Other Aquatic Elements

There are numerous other specialized areas of aquatic recreation that require special attention. For example, swimming classes or recreation sessions for persons with physical or mental disabilities require extremely careful supervision, including in some cases a staff-to-participant ratio of as high as one-to-one. Increasingly, there is concern about programming for younger children. Many YWCAs, for example, schedule sessions for mothers and babies in which, in some cases, infants learn to "swim" before they can even walk. Organizations in this field, such as the Council for National Cooperation in Aquatics and the American Academy of Pediatrics, now frequently recommend that children below a certain age, such as three years, not take part in organized swimming programs.

A growing area of concern involves water-park risk exposures in the numerous water play complexes that have been developed in recent years, with often turbulent artificial waves, slides, and other facilities that increase the risk of accidents. P. J. Heath lists twenty such risks that water-park managers must deal with, ranging from the need for emergency action plans or adequate signage, to having water-depth markers on coping and deck surfaces and guarding against electrical hazards.[17]

Theme Parks

Many commercially operated theme parks have had severe accidents and costly lawsuits in recent years, as illustrated in the Haunted Castle fire described earlier. With the development of thrill rides such as higher, steeper, and faster roller coasters, a number of parks have had deaths or severe injuries due to falls from such vehicles because of faulty equipment or poor supervisory procedures. One important step in avoiding such accidents is carefully screening and orienting individuals who take such thrill rides.

The Dollywood park complex (see p. 291) provides special guidance for guests with disabilities and deals with issues of wheelchairs, access to facilities, use of service animals such as Seeing Eye dogs, and the use of casts and braces. As part of its risk-management procedures, it has prepared a Ride Access Guide, which identifies eighteen rides and other attractions, their key elements, and the abilities that participants must have to enjoy them safely (Fig. 9.3).

291

Chapter 9
*Leisure Services
and the Law:
Risk-Management
Concerns*

Dollywood RIDE ACCESS GUIDE

Legend:

n/a = Not Applicable

(transfer symbol) This symbol indicates guests who use wheelchairs, must be able to transfer from their wheelchair to a ride vehicle or seat.

(wheelchair symbol) This symbol indicates guests can remain in their wheelchair through the designated ride or attraction.

	Carousel	Balloon Race	Road Rally	Barn Stormer	Twist-n-Shout	Convoy	Tennessee Twister	Bumper Cars	Swingamajig	Wonder Wheel	Thunder Road	Rocking Roadway	Thunder Express	Slidewinder	Flooded Mine	Blazing Fury	Smoky Mtn. River Rapids	Country Fair Falls	Dollywood Express (Train)
Minimum height requirement	n/a		n/a	n/a	39"		39"	42"/46"	42"	n/a	42"		42"	39"	n/a	42"	36"	n/a	n/a
Upper body control	●	●	●	●	●	●		●	●	●			●	●		●	●	●	
Total body control																	●	●	
Accessability (symbol noted below)	➡	➡	➡	➡	➡	➡	➡	➡	➡	➡	➡	➡	➡	➡	n/a	n/a	➡	➡	♿
No Heart Conditions						●		●	●	●			●	●		●	●	●	
Not Pregnant						●		●	●	●			●	●		●	●	●	
No High/Low Blood Pressure						●		●	●	●			●	●		●	●	●	
No back or neck injuries						●		●	●	●			●	●		●	●	●	
Ability to grip firmly by hand						●		●	●	●			●	●		●	●	●	
Not recommended for older adults													●	●		●	●	●	
Elevated Heights									●	●			●			●		●	
Slow even ride						●					●				●				●
Revolving elevated		●	●						●	●									
Revolving	●	●	●	●	●	●			●	●									
Turbulant						●		●	●				●	●		●	●		
Rapid movement						●		●	●	●			●	●		●	●	●	
Dark ride															●	●			
Abrupt drops													●	●		●	●	●	
Loading assistance	●	●	●	●	●	●	●	●	●	●		●	●			●	●	●	●
Special instructions (see below)		●	●						●						●	●	●	●	●
Service animals	n/a	n/a	n/a	n/a	n/a	n/a	n/a	n/a	n/a	n/a	n/a	n/a	n/a	n/a	n/a	n/a	n/a	n/a	●

FIGURE 9.3.   Ride access guide for persons with disabilities,
at Dollywood theme park.

LAW-ENFORCEMENT RESPONSIBILITIES

A related area of legal concern in leisure-service agencies is the need to enforce law and order and protect visitors and facilities from crime and vandalism. This has been a difficult problem, both in impacted urban areas and in large park systems that cover extensive territory.

292

CHAPTER 9
*Leisure Services
and the Law:
Risk-Management
Concerns*

One issue has involved the right to free speech and assembly as it applies to the granting of permits for public "protest" meetings or parades that seek to use park areas. Another problem that has frequently been in the courts has involved the right to sunbathe or swim in the nude in public lakes or beachfronts. Although numerous state and municipal park and recreation departments, and even the National Park Service, have sought to prohibit this practice, judicial decisions have varied, in some cases nullifying local ordinances against nude sunbathing.

Law-enforcement officers within recreation and park areas must be familiar with "search and seizure" procedures, the use of roadblocks, the so-called Miranda warning requirements when suspects are apprehended, and other constitutional principles. It should be stressed that, whereas laws and regulations vary from state to state, the basic principles do not, and all who exercise enforcement powers must be familiar with them. As a general policy, the orientation and training of law-enforcement employees should include these guidelines.

The defacement or destruction of property is only part of the concern of park and leisure-service facility managers today. An immense problem stems from the use of recreational vehicles in outdoor settings that injure the natural environment. As an example, the use of mountain or all-terrain bikes has been extremely destructive to many big-city parks, just as their motorized cousins have damaged wilderness areas in state or federal parks. Beyond such problems, theft, mugging, and other forms of criminal behavior have become increasingly common in recreation and park facilities of every type. Years ago, campers and backpackers felt confident that they could trust their neighbors in the wilderness and could leave their possessions at campsites for long periods of time without risk. Today the situation is quite different; in Yosemite National Park in California, groups of "car clouters" have moved through crowded campsites and trailheads, stealing loot from tents, cars, and recreation vehicles; other parks have experienced similar problems.

In some cases, girls have been sexually assaulted in city pools, and in other situations trespassers have broken into pools at night, assaulting pool guards and robbing and raping others who have entered the pools illegally. As a

Crimes in Urban Parks

Problems in urban parks may range from the relatively trivial to extremely serious crimes. In New York City, golfers on the city's public courses have frequently been subjected to mugging and robbery. On the Pelham Golf Course, for example, a player was robbed while lining up an "approach" shot, costing him $65 and his credit cards. His companion commented, "Something like that disrupts a golfer's concentration." One group of players resorted to traveling around the course in eightsomes and sixteensomes rather than smaller groups. Others have brought guard dogs to the golf course or carried cans of Mace in their golf bags, along with woods and irons.

So-called wilding incidents were noted for the first time when bands of roving youths began to attack and rob fans leaving concerts in Central Park in the early 1980s. It reached its peak when the national media reported the savage mass rape and beating of a woman jogger at night in Central Park by a group of younger and middle teenagers, who seemed to regard the episode as a form of casual "fun." Episodes of gangs terrorizing parks have been noted in numerous other cities as well.

general rule, Kozlowski points out, property owners or facility managers are not held liable for the criminal acts of others in such settings as multiuse trails or open playing fields. However, they may have a duty to provide security where the clear threat of criminal activity is limited to a rather confined area, such as a zoo or amusement park.[18] Similarly, they are likely to be held liable in the case of rapes or other criminal acts against youthful participants on field trips or outings.

Vandalism Control Methods

Obviously, recreation and park agencies are not the only organizations to suffer from such problems. However, because they tend to operate so many separate, isolated facilities that are difficult to patrol and oversee and that are normally open and available to the public, problems of vandalism and crime prevention are particularly acute for them. Punitive or defensive reactions, such as reliance on security guards, surveillance, or police dogs or demands that the police and courts be harsher on violaters who are arrested, rarely succeed in stopping vandalism and park crime.

Instead, there should be a coordinated plan of attack, with three elements: (1) understanding the problem by gathering full information about vandalism and other antisocial acts, (2) reviewing alternative methods of dealing with the problem, and (3) devising and putting a strategy into action.

Understanding the problem involves gathering as complete a picture as possible of current conditions. Focusing specifically on property-directed vandalism, for example, it would be essential to carry out a systematic observation and inspection of recreation and park settings and review vandalism reports and statistics of facility repair and equipment replacement.

All personnel should be required to file damage reports, using a standardized form that details the nature and extent of the damage as well as other pertinent information. This encourages maintenance personnel and supervisors to note vandalism immediately and act on it rather than accept it as inevitable. It should also have the effect of speeding up requests for repair, which in turn helps prevent the buildup of minor damage and the creation of an atmosphere in which facilities are more seriously vandalized.

A second stage of analysis is to examine individual cases selectively throughout a recreation and park system. It will involve a review of condition and damage reports, site observations, and interviews with staff members and possibly participants, nearby residents, and community leaders or businesspeople.

A number of specific approaches may be used to prevent or control vandalism, including the following:

1. Planning and design of facilities geared to minimize damage or misuse;
2. More efficient and prompt maintenance and repair to prevent damaged structures or equipment from remaining in such condition over a period of time, which tends to encourage additional vandalism;
3. Improved staffing and supervision of facilities and fuller programming and scheduling of areas and facilities;
4. A positive program of community relations that will develop support and cooperation in preventing vandalism.

294

CHAPTER 9
*Leisure Services
and the Law:
Risk-Management
Concerns*

To protect signs and boards, which are frequently damaged, it is helpful to use raised or routered lettering, heavy-duty metal signs, tamper-proof fasteners and hardware, stronger posts, and protected bolts. Use of concrete or metal benches and picnic tables, steel-drum garbage receptacles, spring-loaded water faucets, and covered pipes are all helpful.

Use of Rangers and Park Police

The problem of law enforcement in both wilderness areas and urban communities has often been solved with the use of special park police units or ranger forces. For example, the U.S. Park Police, a unit of the National Park Service, functions in urban national parks in Washington, D.C., New York City, San Francisco, and other cities.

> Policing of these areas is accomplished by the use of horse-mounted officers, motorcycles, scooters, helicopters, boats, dogs, and foot patrols. Parks in urban areas require a specially sensitive type of police officer who is able to adapt readily to the needs of the park visitor, and on the other hand, act firmly but with courtesy to those who attempt to violate the law. Officers must easily adapt from dealing with hard-core criminals to assisting people in need.[19]

In national and state parks, rangers or their counterparts under other titles have functions that extend beyond the prevention of criminal activity. Essentially, their task is to protect the natural environment against heedless or deliberate abuse by park visitors and to protect park visitors against the hazards that may exist in wilderness or natural settings.

A new concept of using park rangers has developed in many cities. Young men and women of high school or college age are recruited on a seasonal or part-time basis and are trained to carry out a number of functions involving interpretation, staffing facilities, overseeing park areas, and providing general control and security, short of actual law-enforcement powers. By patrolling wide-ranging outdoor spaces and developing favorable contacts with park users, these young rangers are able to supplement the formal park police or other law-enforcement personnel and perform tasks that do not require armed intervention.

Youth Awareness and Gang Programs

Hundreds of public and nonprofit recreation, park, and leisure-service organizations throughout the United States and Canada have focused on the task of reducing juvenile delinquency and working constructively with youth gangs. In so doing, they recognize that recreation by itself is not a cure-all for preventing youth crime. Since it has many causes, youth crime must be dealt with through a multiservice approach that incorporates counseling and family services, educational tutoring and vocational assistance, substance abuse programs, and numerous other activities.

As a single example of public recreation and park programs for at-risk youth, the Phoenix, Arizona, Department of Parks, Recreation and Library has established a City Streets/At Risk Youth Division that through the 1990s included such programs as:

An innovative Juvenile Curfew Program, in which the department accepted and processed youthful violators of the city's curfew ordinance, providing referral services, counseling with teenagers and their parents, coordinating social services with other agencies, and involving youth in volunteer and community service activities.

An extensive program of job training and development for youth, including varied job internships and the Ranger Cadet program for work in the parks.

Sponsorship of teen councils, a youth advisory board, conferences, newsletters, youth forums, and new teen centers in high-risk areas of the city.

A collaborative sports program with the city's Housing Department, with funding from the U.S. Housing and Urban Development Department, designed to reduce drugs, gangs, and violence, particularly in public-housing areas.[20]

Other municipal leisure-service agencies have developed similar programs, in some cases focusing on gangs with minority-group racial or ethnic identities. The city of Long Beach, California, for example, has established liaison programs with gangs of Hispanic, Southeast Asian, and other minority young people. Other cities have established Midnight Basketball programs to work with older teenagers and young adults, providing constructive sports programs late at night. Still others, responding to research that shows the highest incidence of juvenile delinquency to be in the late afternoon and early evening hours, have strengthened their recreation programs and social services for youth during these hours.

Other Social Control Policies

As part of the overall problem of controlling deviant behavior, many other types of leisure-service sponsors have developed policies dealing with substance abuse, gambling, or sexual behavior.

Increasingly, colleges have found it necessary to establish policies to handle athletes' criminal involvement, including assault, disorderly conduct, drunkenness, drug abuse, or gambling infractions. Similarly, fraternities have been suspended or expelled based on forbidden hazing practices, ethnic or racial discrimination or attacks, group rapes, and similar actions.[21]

Within the armed forces, past policies with respect to the use of alcohol as a totally accepted form of recreation are being rethought. It is recognized that substance abuse in the armed forces represents a major problem—with older service personnel often dependent on alcohol, and younger individuals on marijuana and other drugs—and emphasis is being placed on substance abuse treatment and on nonalcoholic social programming. Similarly, for the first time, as the military grappled with problems of sexual harassment directed at women enlistees, in 1997 the Defense Department enforced a policy of barring the sale of sexually explicit magazines and videotapes on military bases.[22]

296

CHAPTER 9
*Leisure Services
and the Law:
Risk-Management
Concerns*

RECREATION, SPECIAL POPULATIONS, AND THE LAW

The overall issue of maintaining nondiscriminatory policies with respect to serving several different categories of special populations—such as racial or ethnic minorities, women, or persons with disabilities—represents another important concern of leisure-service managers.

Racial and Ethnic Discrimination

Until World War II, there was relatively little concern about serving African Americans or other racial or ethnic minorities in public recreation programs. They were often limited to restricted and inadequate facilities and programs by either law or community custom. Patterns of racial segregation and exclusion prevailed throughout college and professional sports, and many popular youth-serving organizations had strongly enforced racial segregation in their memberships.

Despite initial resistance to civil rights statutes regarding racial desegregation of public recreation facilities such as parks, playgrounds, golf courses, and swimming pools during the 1950s and 1960s, in general there has been a positive transition, and most such facilities are successfully integrated today.

However, it is clear that much racial and gender-based discrimination has continued, particularly in commercial and private settings. For example, two court cases in the Delaware Valley in the spring of 1989 showed that African Americans were systematically excluded from a private swim club—which the court ruled was in fact a "place of public accommodation"—and from a chain of successful health clubs. With respect to the latter, the U.S. Department of Justice found that U.S. Health, Inc., a Maryland-based corporation that operated over forty clubs along the eastern seaboard, had maintained the following practices:

Employees at the Holiday clubs were instructed to discourage black persons from joining; they were reprimanded when they did sell memberships to black persons, and frequently commissions were not paid for such sales.

Persons believed to be black who called Holiday clubs were told that no appointment times were available, although callers believed to be white were promptly scheduled.

Black persons were given brief and superficial tours of the club and little or no effort was made to enroll them. They were often told only about the most expensive membership options, and not of the favorable financing opportunities that were available.

When black persons did join, some were treated rudely by club employees, to discourage them from recommending the club to other black persons.[23]

Following a court hearing, the health club chain signed a consent order agreeing to remedy past injustices and to maintain a full nondiscrimination policy in all future advertising and customer relations. In other documented cases in the mid-1980s, a Buffalo, New York, discotheque was found guilty of violating federal and state civil rights laws in discriminating against minority persons, a Long Island, New York, beach club was also found guilty of discriminating against Jewish families who sought to join it.

Gender-Based Discrimination

In terms of gender-based discrimination, to cite practices in a single city, the Philadelphia Recreation Department and Mayor's Commission on Women conducted a study in the mid-1980s showing that women received less than 11 percent of the permits issued for the use of recreational facilities. In part, this was the result of past policies that gave men the priority for the use of athletic fields and gymnasiums at key hours. Following this, the Recreation Department sought to promote women's sports more fully by forming new teams and leagues and providing more convenient practice and game schedules. Athletic associations that refused to let girls play on boys' baseball teams were refused ball field permits, and the city's Commission on Human Relations joined in efforts to form coeducational youth sports teams. In Canada, the case of a twelve-year-old Toronto girl who wanted to play on a boys' team in the Metropolitan Toronto Hockey League went to the Ontario Supreme Court in an effort to overcome a "separate but equal" policy defined in the province's Human Rights Code. Increasingly, leisure-service managers must deal with such issues.

297

CHAPTER 9
Leisure Services
and the Law:
Risk-Management
Concerns

Over the past three decades, many schools and colleges, park and recreation departments, and other leisure-service agencies have greatly expanded their sports programming to include girls' and women's activities. Lawsuits have compelled organizations such as Little League baseball to admit girls as players. Through continuing legal claims based on Title IX of the Educational Amendments Act of 1972, this trend will clearly continue in the years ahead.

Today, women often continue to be discriminated against, particularly in private-membership organizations such as businesspersons clubs, golf clubs, or similar settings where they may be denied full membership rights or the opportunity to participate on an equal basis.

The issue of whether equal opportunity has been provided within a given school or college athletic program is based on a number of factors. Dougherty and Bonanno define these in terms of whether the interests and abilities of both males and females have been served effectively, and the equity of:

1. the provision and distribution of equipment and supplies
2. the scheduling of instruction, practice, and games
3. the opportunity for quality instruction and coaching
4. the assignment and payment of teachers and coaches
5. the provision of competitive, practice, and locker room facilities
6. the funding provided for all program levels
7. the provision of training and medical care and facilities[24]

Other policies under Title IX allow separate teams for both sexes and, with the exception of contact sports, allow a person to try out for a single-sex sport for those of the opposite gender, if there is no comparable team available for members of his or her sex. Instructional classes, with the exception of those in sex education, are expected to be conducted on a coeducational basis.

Sexual Harassment

An important gender-related concern, with legal ramifications, involves sexual harassment on the job. This may take three forms: (1) pressure to engage in sexual relations, usually directed by a higher-level employee against a subordinate worker, with the threat of firing or demotion if they do not comply; (2) creation

298

CHAPTER 9
*Leisure Services
and the Law:
Risk-Management
Concerns*

of a sexually hostile environment, with unwanted intimacies, jokes, pictures, or other degrading, sexually based actions; and (3) other forms of job discrimination linked to sexual identity.

Although the late 1990s saw a number of efforts to overturn affirmative action policies on the state level, the principle of maintaining equal opportunities based on race and gender still must guide programming and hiring practices in leisure-service agencies today. Linked to this issue, concern about the sexual abuse of children and youth is an important problem today, particularly in the areas of coaching and sports leadership. Most leisure-service agencies today have instituted firm policies to prevent sexual abuse from occurring.

Programming for Persons with Disabilities

With respect to programming for persons with physical or mental disabilities, the Education for the Handicapped Act of 1975 focused national attention on the need to improve educational and other rehabilitative services for persons with disabilities. A number of other federal laws in the United States made it essential that all public and nonprofit organizations serving the public be made accessible to special populations (see pp. 136, 258). In Canada, similar national and provincial laws have enforced such policies strongly.

It is therefore an important responsibility of leisure-service managers to ensure that adequate provision is made for the special recreational needs of persons with disabilities, that architectural or environmental barriers that keep them from participating are eliminated, and that they are served in integrated settings and programs with nondisabled persons whenever possible. This does not mean that all disabled groups can or should be "mainstreamed" in the sense that they are fully integrated with nondisabled populations. Often their degree of disability makes this impractical; they would be unable to carry on the activity successfully, and other participants would strongly resist their involvement. The appropriate solution is to integrate the disabled fully where this can be done and, if not, to develop specially modified, segregated programs.

Realistically, although the politically correct position in this field urges the fullest possible integration or mainstreaming of persons with disabilities, in some cases the families of those with disability—such as individuals with major hearing loss—*prefer* to have them attend special schools. In other cases, integrated participation in camps may be shown to have both positive and negative effects for developmentally disabled children.

A Related Concern: HIV/AIDS

A unique example of problems faced in this area has to do with people suffering from acquired immune deficiency syndrome (AIDS). This fatal disease has spread rapidly throughout the United States and exists at several levels of severity, ranging from those with full-blown AIDS, to those with AIDS-related complex (ARC), to a large group who are HIV-positive but show no signs of illness and may even be unaware of their infections. In many communities, there is a state of near-panic about the disease, resulting in afflicted children being barred from school or those who are ill being restricted from normal health care settings. A number of court decisions have affirmed the right of AIDS patients to work, study, and avail themselves of other community services despite efforts to discriminate against them. Keller, Turner, and Qiu point out that the problem is particularly acute for leisure-service professionals because of widespread ignorance and fear about the transmission of AIDS. However, both professionals and volunteers need to know how to handle blood and other body fluids to prevent exposure to the virus. They write:

299

CHAPTER 9
Leisure Services
and the Law:
Risk-Management
Concerns

> Policies and procedures for recreation and leisure services for dealing with HIV-infected people should be developed before they are needed. What should a recreation employee do if bleeding occurs at a swimming pool, playground or any other recreational setting? How can confidentiality about a participant's HIV status be maintained at the same time that the safety of others is preserved? What should administrators do when they learn that an employee has tested positive for the virus?[25]

Keller, Turner, and Qiu point out that laws on such issues vary from state to state and that it is desirable to develop effective policies on them *before* litigation, rather than after.

From an economic perspective, many commercial recreation organizations today provide specialized leisure opportunities for persons with disabilities. Numerous travel agencies, cruise lines, and other tourism vendors package special vacation trips and other services, particularly for persons with physical disabilities.

Participation by Nonresidents

In a variation of this concern, the issue of exclusion or added charges imposed by communities against nonresidents who seek to use their beaches, pools, or other recreation facilities continues to be the basis of lawsuits, court decisions, and local ordinances.

Whereas in larger cities, individuals are generally permitted to use all facilities (for example, swimming pools, golf courses, museums, or parks) without having to demonstrate residence in the city, this is not the case in smaller communities or suburbs within metropolitan areas. There—particularly for desirable facilities such as parks, lakes, swimming pools, beaches, or athletic areas—the practice has developed in recent years of requiring would-be users to prove their residence, often by use of a special card or laminated "leisure pass."

In a number of large metropolitan districts, civil rights groups have contended that policies excluding nonresidents represent a deliberate effort to keep racial minorities or disadvantaged urban residents out of suburban parks and recreation areas. Kozlowski points out that ordinances may not arbitrarily, oppressively, or unreasonably discriminate against nonresidents; such ordinances would unconstitutionally deny them the equal protection of the law. However, municipal regulations that exclude nonresidents from public recreation facilities are not necessarily unconstitutional. Public safety and health, for example, have been cited as reasonable causes for excluding nonresidents. In addition, court decisions have supported the right of government agencies to impose different fee scales on residents and nonresidents, provided that there is a rational basis for doing so.[26]

Religious Practice as a Legal Issue

Another issue that has emerged as an area of legal controversy for leisure-service organizations in recent years involves varied forms of religious observation and practice. Kozlowski cites a number of examples of lawsuits against recreation, parks, and leisure-service agencies including the following: (1) a suit against the city of Albuquerque to overthrow a ban on showing religious films and holding prayers in its six multiservice senior centers; (2) a suit to prevent the use of prayers by a high school girls basketball team as a structured, formal activity, although the individual, voluntary use of prayers was not enjoined; and (3) a court decision making it unconstitutional for a government agency to provide preferential treatment to a particular sectarian religious group in allowing private displays of a religious symbol—a Jewish menorah—in a city park.[27] Even the right of a local school board to sponsor or permit Halloween parades, parties, or other celebrations has been challenged, based on the holiday's original religious meaning derived from All Hallow's Eve, linked to the Christian feast of All Saints Day.[28]

HUMAN RESOURCE MANAGEMENT AND THE LAW

Public, nonprofit, and commercial recreation enterprises today have become subject to an increasing number of federal and state regulations affecting personnel management, as well as other ordinances or procedural guidelines that are based on existing laws or court decisions regarding personnel. These include varied management concerns such as policies and practices in the area of wages and hours, employee benefits, worker's compensation, safety and health, employees' personal rights, and civil service procedures.

Title VII of the Civil Rights Act of 1964 prohibited federal, state, and local government agencies, as well as unions, employment agencies, and other related groups, from discriminating against employees or potential employees on the basis of race, color, religion, sex, or national origin with respect to hiring, firing, transfer, promotion, salary levels, apprenticeship, or other training programs. Later presidential executive orders extended its regulations against discrimination to federal government contractors and subcontractors and in effect to all organizations receiving federal funds to support their programs.

The Equal Employment Opportunity Act of 1972 amended Title VII by expanding its coverage of governmental agencies and educational institutions and private companies with more than fifteen employees. Based on these laws, government, educational, and other social-service organizations are required to maintain accurate records of their employment actions and practices, to file detailed annual reports dealing with the sex and ethnic background of their employees, and to develop affirmative action plans that list their employment policies and specific objectives designed to promote employment and promotion of minority groups. While there was a public backlash in the late 1990s against certain forms of affirmative action, particularly those establishing racial/ethnic quotas for hiring, college admissions, and similar practices, the essential thrust of the legislation just cited remains intact.

To avoid possible charges of discrimination, managers must be cautious to observe recommended guidelines and procedures, particularly in the hiring process. They typically may *not* ask questions that seek to learn an individual's nationality or family origin, type of military discharge, marital status, number of dependents, arrest or criminal conviction record, religious background, general medical condition or physical disabilities, race or color, or similar information. Although it is possible to gather relevant information in a number of these areas, it is not legal to do so in ways that appear simply to seek out derogatory information or that might provide the basis for discrimination against an individual.

301

CHAPTER 9
Leisure Services
and the Law:
Risk-Management
Concerns

Similarly, firing practices have also become complex from a legal point of view. In many government agencies or other large enterprises that are unionized, employers must show just cause before terminating an individual's employment and must follow required procedures for documenting the person's failure to perform, holding conferences with the person and placing the person "on warning."

Sexual Orientation

An area of personnel management that remains uncertain from a legal perspective involves the sexual orientation of employees. In the armed forces, for example, many servicemen and women with long-term successful records have been discharged following the disclosure of their homosexual lifestyles. In some cases, Boy Scout leaders have been ousted for similar reasons. This issue is of special concern to a number of religious denominations that have developed national policy statements regarding "same-sex" marriages or the ordination of homosexual ministers or other members of the clergy. It also has been publicized in several cases where adult leaders have been accused of the systematic sexual abuse of children and youth—which may occur, of course, in both heterosexual and homosexual contexts.

Labor Relations Practices

Leisure-service managers should also be familiar with other pieces of legislation that affect employment practices. The Federal Labor Standards Act includes minimum wage and maximum hour regulations that must be observed. The National Labor Relations Law and a number of subsequent amendments, including the Taft-Hartley and Landrum-Griffen Acts, provide stipulations with regard to labor union practices. For example, agency or company managers may not interfere with the employees' rights to form or join labor unions or bargain collectively; on the other hand, unions may not coerce or threaten employees to build or maintain their membership.

Managers may have to deal with the powerful unions that often represent government, therapeutic, and commercial employees, particularly in larger recreation, park, and leisure-service organizations. Buechner suggests that the "line official" is at the front when it comes to supervision, handling grievances

302

*Chapter 9
Leisure Services
and the Law:
Risk-Management
Concerns*

and disciplinary action and adhering to other terms of labor agreements. He offers several labor relations "rules of the game" that should be helpful to administrators in working constructively with employees:

Familiarize yourself with the collective bargaining laws of your state and local jurisdiction and keep current on new legislation.

Train your supervisors on how to deal with union complaints and grievances and be sure they are familiar with the terms of the agreement.

Always bargain in good faith, learn to control emotions, and develop patience. Don't give the union cause or opportunity for criticism.

Take disciplinary action as required and provided for under the agreement.[29]

To these guidelines one might add the following advice. It is important to keep in regular touch with the union rather than wait for emergencies. Union members should be kept well-informed about personnel plans and developments and should be involved in major policy discussions, although not in the decision-making process. In confrontations, the recreation and park administrator should insist on courtesy, comfortable surroundings, and orderly procedures. He or she would be wise to listen rather than speak, to acknowledge the sound points of union representatives, to avoid harangues or hot arguments, and finally to withhold *all* decisions until they have been thoroughly reviewed after the meeting.

One area of special conflict that has emerged in recent years in some large cities that have undergone staff cutbacks has been union resistance to volunteer involvement in resource management and maintenance. In Philadelphia, for example, the municipal employees union has challenged the right of large businesses to hire their own maintenance employees to care for gardens or sitting areas in public squares or small parks adjacent to them—in one case resulting in a strong-arm assault on a private maintenance worker. Similarly, union members resisted attempts to privatize elements of the Fairmount Park system through a tree-planting and rehabilitation program supported by a foundation grant. Although the union's concern was that these efforts were a threat to the jobs of regularly employed recreation and park professionals, the reality is that such volunteer or private efforts are being used constructively in many cities today and are essential to the continued healthy operation of their park systems.

In the late 1990s, a somewhat similar challenge arose, as thousands of "workfare" men and women were put to work in public recreation and park systems—often in part-time maintenance tasks—as part of the welfare reform legislation that required individuals to work or attend school to receive public assistance. Many of these individuals do the same work as regular park employees, but earn one-third to one-fifth of their pay and have no job security or benefits. While municipal officials in the late 1990s ruled that welfare recipients in job programs were not employees eligible for unionization, they tried to organize to obtain better pay, grievance procedures, and vacation time. As such, they represent a potential labor relations concern for public recreation and park managers.

Union contracts have posed particular difficulties for recreation and park departments through rigid and inflexible controls over the use of personnel, including possible scheduling at odd hours or on weekends, as well as through limitations on the managers' ability to transfer employees or exert specific forms of discipline or control. However, it should also be noted that, particularly in larger cities, labor unions have been instrumental in markedly upgrading the status and pay of recreation and park employees, improving their working conditions, and giving them a stronger sense of dignity and self-worth.

303

CHAPTER 9
Leisure Services
and the Law:
Risk-Management
Concerns

Each specialized area of leisure-service management may have its own unique problems with respect to staff practices. For example, in many sports programs, youth between the ages of fourteen and sixteen may be hired in such part-time or evening jobs as scorekeepers, concession attendants, batboys or ballgirls. While the U.S. Department of Labor has proposed exceptions to the permissible time standards for such jobs that have been set by federal child labor legislation, this continues to be a controversial area for many recreation and sports managers.[30]

Regulations in Sports Management

Within the overall field of sports management, general legal principles obviously apply, with respect to such areas as possible criminal behavior of athletes, sexual abuse or exploitation of children, nondiscriminatory hiring policies, liability lawsuits based on negligence, and similar concerns.

In addition, however, there are numerous regulations that are imposed by the professional sports leagues themselves or by such governing groups as the National Collegiate Athletic Association that have the force of law in that they can impose sanctions, barring teams or players from participation, or imposing fines and similar penalties. These regulations govern such matters as eligibility for play, owner-player agreements, recruitment by sports agents, the location of sports franchises, "tampering" efforts to attract star players, the sharing of revenues, and similar matters.[31]

Beyond such regulations, sports managers must now recognize that athletes themselves have now begun to sue their coaches or institutions in a number of cases. Citing various abuses having to do with breaches of oral contracts or reneging on promises of scholarships or other negligent or improper acts, such lawsuits represent a new concern for school and college sports officials.[32]

CONTRACT LAW AFFECTING
LEISURE-SERVICE AGENCIES

It was pointed out earlier (see p. 277) that contractual liability represented one of the legal concerns of leisure-service managers. Particularly in view of the trend toward privatization, under which subcontracting, concession, and lease agreements are being used by many public recreation and park agencies, it is helpful to identify guidelines for developing such agreements.

304

CHAPTER 9
*Leisure Services
and the Law:
Risk-Management
Concerns*

Within any given area of performance, it is also essential that important elements of the agreements be spelled out as precisely as possible. For example, in a concessionaire agreement, elements to be covered in a contract would include the length of the arrangement with exact dates on which given actions are to take place; the responsibility of both parties for providing, inspecting, or maintaining equipment; standards of performance; possible charges for costs arising from maintenance or vandalism; nature of advertising or public relations; nature of payments based on flat annual fees, percentage of sales, or net profit; and all other important aspects of the agreement.

Heydt suggests several important principles for the successful management of contracts, designed primarily for local government agencies but also applicable to other types of organizations. These include the following:

> *Read and understand the contract.* One of the basic mistakes contract managers make is their failure to thoroughly read and understand a contract, including all its terms and conditions. A contract is a dynamic document that must be used, not left to collect dust on a shelf.
>
> *Document events, meetings, and conversations.* The history of the contract process, including all meetings, conversations, and modifications, must be carefully recorded, along with a log of performance, so that a proper case for breach of contract and termination may be made, if necessary.
>
> *Head off disputes or performance failures early.* The ability to perceive lack of performance and to take positive steps to either cure the breach or to terminate the contract is critical for the contract manager.
>
> *Ensure requirements of contract are complied with.* Use methods such as critical path tracking or check-off sheets to ensure that contracted tasks are being performed on schedule. There must be timely, satisfactory performance by the contractor during the life of the contract, and payments must be keyed to specific work-completion dates. If there is a breach of the contract and it is not resolved, follow the procedures for properly terminating it.[33]

Numerous other management areas require careful legal investigation and clearance, including the following items.

Leasing Arrangements

Many partnership arrangements between public and private organizations involve leasing arrangements because of the increased costs of acquisition, construction, operation, and maintenance of major facilities today.

The ultimate decision as to whether leasing is an appropriate and feasible action depends on a careful analysis of municipal charters, ordinances and regulations, and state-enabling statutes and court decisions as they apply to a given jurisdiction. Lacking a specific grant of authority from the state, municipalities and counties do not generally have the power to lease their property to private owners or companies.

Fiscal Practices

305

CHAPTER 9
*Leisure Services
and the Law:
Risk-Management
Concerns*

Similarly, other growing fiscal practices of public recreation and park departments may violate existing legal codes. The general legal principle in this area is that local government agencies have no power to engage in business enterprises usually pursued by private or commercial groups, without express legislative authority from the state—or to use tax funds for enterprises that do not promote public purposes.

Among issues that have come before the courts with respect to this principle have been lawsuits related to the right of city-owned recreation complexes to sell alcoholic beverages, operate public ambulance services in competition with private firms, or purchase a large man-made lake to sell hydroelectricity from its power plant and on which to operate a recreational and tourist business. The question of what constitutes rational or justifiable public purposes is constantly being redefined in an era of changing socioeconomic conditions; there is no simple rule of thumb to determine which sorts of "private" enterprises a public agency may undertake.

Another complex legal issue that affects many nonprofit social-service organizations—particularly churches—involves their right to operate gambling enterprises as fund-raising activities. In a number of states, churches and synagogues have sponsored bingo games that were actually conducted by for-profit companies (in some cases with underworld ties), with resultant legal difficulties. In Tennessee, for example, an investigation of bingo led to a state supreme court decision that also invalidated raffles and other fund-raising efforts of scores of legitimate charitable and nonprofit organizations. In all states, it is essential that leisure-service organizations be thoroughly familiar with all laws, and compliant with them, in their fund-raising and other fiscal practices.

Property Uses and Conversions

Numerous court cases have arisen in recent years with respect to the use of private property by the public for recreational purposes, and the conversion of publicly owned lands from wetlands or natural areas to developed recreational facilities.

Robert Lee points out that almost all states have developed recreational-use statutes intended to immunize property owners from liability when people enter their land for such activities as hunting or fishing and are injured or killed, or when their property is damaged or destroyed. However, such statutes are inconsistent with respect to the type or portion of the land that is protected, the recreational activities included (Connecticut, for example, includes hang gliding, sport parachuting, and hot air ballooning), or the maintenance of dangerous sites or attractions. Therefore, private landowners have no guarantee of safety from lawsuits in this regard.[34]

Another major problem exists with respect to the conversion of existing natural areas to recreational facilities. In many cases, plans to drain wetlands, install golf courses or other developed sites, build access roads, or permit commercial concerns to construct resorts and play areas have been successfully fought by environmental organizations.

306

CHAPTER 9
Leisure Services
and the Law:
Risk-Management
Concerns

VARIETY OF LEGAL ISSUES TODAY: GIRL SCOUTS

Finally, it is almost impossible to predict the extreme variety of legal and risk-management challenges that are faced by even such well-established leisure-service organizations as the Girl Scouts of U.S.A.

For example, in the early 1990s, a Pennsylvania girl was turned away from a Girl Scout camp because she had cerebral palsy and needed to use a wheelchair. In response, her family sued the camp under the federal Americans with Disability Act, demanding access. At the same time, a number of Girl Scout Councils restricted their troops from participating in community clean-up days, limiting girls from earning their Keep America Beautiful badge, or curbed door-to-door fund-raising and cookie-sales campaigns because of fears about accidents or attacks that might lead to liability lawsuits.

In 1996, ASCAP (American Society of Composers, Authors and Publishers) sought to impose a stiff royalty charge on all Girl Scout groups for singing songs under its copyright, at campfires, on hikes, or in other scout settings. Only widespread protests resulting in a public relations debacle caused ASCAP to quickly reverse its policy.

Recently, other Scout Councils have resisted claims that some of their programs or facilities were essentially profit-oriented and in competition with commercial businesses—and that their charitable, tax-exempt status should therefore be withdrawn.

Such examples provide only a brief sampling of the kinds of liability and other legal challenges faced by recreation, park, and leisure-service managers today.

SUMMARY

This chapter describes a number of important concerns for managers with respect to issues such as avoiding costly negligence litigation, understanding contractual liability, current limitations on agency fiscal practices and leasing operations, affirmative action and other legal aspects of personnel management, access for special populations, and problems dealing with law-enforcement practices.

Since the practice of law is a sophisticated and complex field with many subspecialties, most leisure-service managers will not develop a high degree of expertise in it. However, they should be aware of the general guidelines affecting their policies and practices in the management functions and should be careful to follow approved procedures or guidelines at all times. Beyond this, they should read articles on legal aspects of recreation and park management in professional periodicals, attend workshops or seminars, and, above all, rely on qualified counsel for advice as new issues or problems appear.

One of the most important functions of leisure-service managers is to ensure that participation in recreation and park facilities and programs is as safe as possible, that natural hazards and program-related accidents are avoided, and that controls over vandalism and other forms of criminal behavior are maintained in the leisure setting.

The logical solution to solving such difficulties is to develop plans for risk management or control of vandalism and crime. The extent and nature of the problem must be assessed, appropriate methods for dealing with it must be selected, and these must be put into action with careful supervision and systematic evaluation. Policies, procedures, and appropriate assignment of personnel play a role in this effort, along with community relations and educational efforts that get at the roots of the difficulty and help remove its causes.

Finally, the chapter stresses the great variety of legal and risk-management problems that leisure-service agencies may face, including social, environmental, law enforcement and other functions or issues. However, carefully thought-out policies and supervision and reliance on sound legal advice can solve most of these difficulties.

307

CHAPTER 9
Leisure Services
and the Law:
Risk-Management
Concerns

SUGGESTED CLASS PROJECTS

1. Select a major type of facility that presents a fairly high risk factor, such as a ski center, rifle and pistol range, riding stable, or swimming pool. Develop in outline form a risk-management plan for this facility, including an assessment of present practices and accident records, needed policies, and a manual for staff training.
2. With other students, conduct a survey of vandalism in several park, playground, or center settings. Prepare and deliver in class a comparative report of the extent and nature of the problem, measures used to prevent or control it, and their apparent degrees of success.
3. Take a specific legal problem area affecting public recreation and park departments, such as: (1) policies leading to the exclusion of nonresidents from programs and facilities; (2) issues regarding personnel management, such as hiring, firing, and promotion; (3) problems or law enforcement; or (4) providing programs for persons with disabilities. Examine the literature on this issue, including reports of specific cases, and outline principles based on your findings that are appropriate for this type of agency. Make these as specific as possible in their application, rather than global in scope.

Before analyzing these cases in class, review the guidelines suggested in Chapter 3 (pp. 76–77).

Case Study 9.1 *Sports Injuries—Reducing the Risk Factor*

YOU ARE SUZANNE BROCK, employee recreation director for a large manufacturing company. In cooperation with the municipal recreation department, you have traditionally cosponsored a major youth football program, ending in a well-attended elimination tournament.

This program has always resulted in good publicity and community relations for your company. However, a number of minor injuries have occurred in the past, and this fall two serious injuries resulted in negligence suits.

The problem is that while you are a cosponsor of this program, you have little control over it. Most of the planning and management is done by the municipal recreation department, and the coaching is done by parents. They are fanatically determined to win and have encouraged or permitted certain risky forms of play such as "spearing," as well as excessive drilling on very hot days, occasionally resulting in heat exhaustion.

You do not want to end your company's participation in this program because it is basically worthwhile and provides excellent publicity. However, you cannot afford further risks of expensive liability claims.

QUESTIONS FOR CLASS DISCUSSION AND ANALYSIS

1. *What is inherently weak in your sponsorship role? How could it be strengthened?*

2. *Draw up a risk-management plan to control the youth football program, reduce the possibility of further serious injuries, and provide fuller protection against lawsuits.*

309

CHAPTER 9
*Leisure Services
and the Law:
Risk-Management
Concerns*

Case Study 9.2 *You're Not a Feminist—But . . .*

YOU ARE DONNA PERRYMAN, a middle-level manager within the operations division of a large theme park. You have had several years' experience in similar programs in smaller commercial recreation settings, working with packaged tour groups and family-oriented programming.

After three years at the park, you feel that you have done well and have received excellent evaluations. However, during this period you have remained at the same job level while several men with less experience have been promoted past you. Although salaries are confidential, through a close friend in the personnel office you find out that you are being paid less than men in comparable positions.

You are not a feminist and take pride in handling your own problems, as well as in being able to compete with men on equal terms. However, this apparent discrimination enrages you. You make an appointment to talk to the company personnel director, Al Bevins. He is pleasant but not helpful. "Several factors go into the promotion process and salary determinations," he says. "Don't quote me, Donna, because I'll deny it and it's your word against mine. But these men support families. You do not, and you have a husband with a good job. That's part of our thinking."

QUESTIONS FOR CLASS DISCUSSION AND ANALYSIS

1. *If you were Donna, recognizing that you cannot prove that Al Bevins admitted the company's discriminatory policy based on gender, how could you make a strong case that the policy did discriminate?*

2. *What is the law in this area? How could it be pursued in legal terms?*

3. *If you chose not to take legal action but to fight the case within the company, what would be your best strategy? How could you avoid compromising your career by fighting too aggressively for your rights? Would this be possible?*

310

CHAPTER 9
*Leisure Services
and the Law:
Risk-Management
Concerns*

Case Study 9.3 — *Controlling the Counselors*

YOU ARE JIM GERASIMOV, the young, newly appointed director of a two-week summer therapeutic recreation camp for children with mental and physical disabilities, in which you have previously served as a counselor.

Don Anderson, director of the nonprofit organization that sponsors the camp, has asked you to be specially vigilant in enforcing the camp's policy against alcohol and drug use on camp grounds. You foresee two difficulties: (1) although you have a master's degree in therapeutic recreation, many of the counselors are close to your age, and some are older; and (2) in the past, some counselors drank beer and smoked marijuana while on night duty, and the policy was enforced only in extreme cases that involved real neglect of responsibility.

For these reasons, you expect that you may have difficulty in preventing drinking or smoking pot, especially with the older counselors who have been at the camp in previous years. What should you do?

QUESTIONS FOR CLASS DISCUSSION AND ANALYSIS

1. *What are the reasons for the policy? What are the risks that might come from violation of the camp's policy against alcohol and marijuana?*

2. *Would the best approach be an authoritarian one—laying down the rule and enforcing it strictly? Or would a group-centered approach to getting the support of counselors be more effective?*

3. *What kind of learning experience will this be for you, as a beginning professional?*

REFERENCES

311

CHAPTER 9
*Leisure Services
and the Law:
Risk-Management
Concerns*

1. Kozlowski, James: "Martial Arts' Participants Do Not Assume Increased Risk of Injury," *Parks and Recreation,* August 1997, p. 30.
2. Dougherty, Neil, and Bonanno, Diane: *Management Principles in Sport and Leisure Services,* Minneapolis, 1985, Burgess Publishing, p. 125.
3. Manning, David: "Legal Considerations in Recreation Administration," *Recreation Canada,* March 1988, pp. 8–9.
4. van der Smissen, Betty, in Parkhouse, Bonnie: *The Management of Sport: Its Foundation and Application,* St. Louis, 1996, National Association for Sport and Physical Education, p. 165.
5. See articles by James Kozlowski in *Parks and Recreation* during the 1980s, in the following issues: September 1983, February 1986, April 1987, and March 1989.
6. Cordes, Kathleen, and Ibrahim, Hilmi: *Applications in Recreation and Leisure, For Today and the Future,* St. Louis, 1996, Times-Mirror/Mosby, pp. 265–66.
7. van der Smissen, Betty: "Where is Legal Liability Heading," *Parks and Recreation,* May 1980, p. 51.
8. Hudson, Susan, Thompson, Donna, and Mack, Mick: "America's Playgrounds: Make Them Safe," *Parks and Recreation,* April 1996, p. 69.
9. King, Steve: "Prevent Playground Injuries with Professional Inspection," *Parks and Recreation,* April 1996, pp. 62–67.
10. Kozlowski, James: "Sports Coach and Physical Activity Instructors Legal Duties of Care in Review," *Parks and Recreation,* January 1996, p. 26.
11. Drape, Joe: "A Question of Responsibility," *New York Times,* October 15, 1997, p. C-1.
12. Nash, Heyward: "Instructor Certification: Making Fitness Programs Safer," *Parks and Recreation,* December 1986, pp. 25–26.
13. Mittelstaedt, Robin: "Climbing Walls Are on the Rise," *Journal of Physical Education, Recreation and Dance,* September 1996, p. 31.
14. Kozlowski, James: Chosen Lightning Protection on Golf Course Must Be Utilized," *Parks and Recreation,* July 1997, p. 46.
15. Ford, Phyllis, and Blanchard, Jim: *Leadership and Administration of Outdoor Pursuits,* State College, Pa., 1993, Venture Publishing, pp. 283–95.
16. McNally, John: "Are Your Pool Personnel Fully Qualified?" *Parks and Recreation,* February 1988, p. 29.
17. Heath, P.J.: "The Top 20 Water Park Risk Exposures," *Parks and Recreation,* July 1995, pp. 66–70.
18. Kozlowski, James: "Limited Liability for Criminal Assaults in Park Facilities," *Parks and Recreation,* May 1996, p. 28.
19. Langston, Robert: "U.S. Park Police Meet Urban Challenge," *Trends,* Fall 1979, p. 25.
20. Wong, Glenn, and McEvoy, Chad: "Crime and Punishment," *Athletic Business,* October 1997, p. 20.
21. "College Expels Fraternity for 'Intolerable' Scavenger Hunt," *Associated Press,* October 20, 1997.
22. Eisler, Benjamin: "Appeals Court Decides Military May Bar Sale of Sex Magazines," *New York Times,* November 22, 1997, p. A-8.
23. Public Notice, of U.S. Department of Justice, and U.S. Health, Inc., in *Philadelphia Inquirer,* May 20, 1989, p. 4-A.
24. Dougherty and Bonanno, *op. cit.* p. 126.
25. Keller, H. Jean, Turner, Norma, and Qiu, Yijin: "The Psychological Implications of AIDS on Leisure Services," *Parks and Recreation,* December 1988, p. 38.
26. Kozlowski, James: "Validity of Non-Resident and Other Discriminatory Regulations in Municipal Recreations," *Parks and Recreation,* March 1982, pp. 28–34.

312

CHAPTER 9
Leisure Services
and the Law:
Risk-Management
Concerns

27. See articles by James Kozlowski in *Parks and Recreation,* September 1996, December 1996, and March 1997.
28. "It Was So Spooky, They Killed It," *Reuters* and *Houston Chronicle,* October 20, 1997, p. 7-A.
29. Buechner, Robert: "Public Employee Unions-Organization," *Management Aids Bulletin no. 81,* Arlington, Va., 1969, National Recreation and Park Association, pp. 39–40.
30. Kozlowski, James: "Recreation Agencies Concerned about Child Labor Laws," *Parks and Recreation,* August 1996, pp. 36–43.
31. Gallant, Harmon: "Labor Relations in Professional Sports," in Parkhouse, *op. cit.,* pp. 119–43.
32. Wong, Glenn, and Sabatino, Scott: "Head to Head," *Athletic Business,* October 1995, pp. 16–17.
33. Heydt, Michael: "Ten Principles for Contract Administration," *Parks and Recreation,* February 1986, pp. 48–51.
34. Lee, Robert: "Recreational Use Statutes and Private Property in the 1990s," *Journal of Park and Recreation Administration,* Fall 1995, pp. 71–83.

Ten

The Controlling Function: Evaluation, Research, and Management Information Systems

At the same time that their departments are attempting to meet demands for more and better services, [social-services managers are] called to account more and more frequently by taxpayers, lawmakers, clients, and their professional peers. What populations are being served? What amount of what service is being provided? What programs are most powerful in bringing about desired changes? Such questions imply that a sound method should exist for evaluating the effectiveness of social services.[1]

The term Management Information System (MIS) refers to the processes and procedures by which raw data are organized into information useful for administrative decision making. Management information systems are commonly computer-based since the repetitive task of tabulating and aggregating large quantities of useful information can be handled most efficiently by data-processing machines. . . .[2]

INTRODUCTION

This chapter deals with the manager's controlling function, based on the need to systematically monitor the leisure-service agency's overall operation, as well as the effectiveness of its individual programs, personnel, facilities, fiscal planning, and similar elements.

When carried on in a carefully designed, systematic way, evaluation represents a form of applied research that may be used not only to document the agency's value, but also to make critical decisions regarding its goals and objectives, policies and procedures. Research is broader in its purpose, intended not only to provide useful information regarding the overall recreation, park, and leisure-service field, but also to develop theoretical understandings of the role of recreation in community life.

Both evaluation and research make use of computers in recording and analyzing data that reflect every aspect of the agency's performance: statistics of

314

CHAPTER 10
The Controlling
Function:
Evaluation, Research,
and Management
Information Systems

participation or budgetary operations, staff performance, environmental impact, risk-management functions, and similar elements. Maintaining a comprehensive databased information system is essential, not only in evaluating the organization's success in meeting its goals and objectives, but also in the ongoing planning and reporting process.

This chapter addresses the following understandings and competencies listed as essential in the Baccalaureate Degree standards of the NRPA/AALR Council on Accreditation:

Understanding of procedures and techniques for assessment of leisure needs (8.21).

Ability to apply methods of assessing recreation activity and leisure needs (9C.04).

Knowledge of the purpose, basic procedures and interpretation of research and evaluation methodology related to leisure services (8.24).

Ability to formulate, plan for implementation, and evaluate extent to which goals and objectives for the leisure service and for groups and individuals within the service have been met (8.27).

Understanding of and ability to apply techniques of program evaluation and policy analysis which measure service effectiveness and the extent to which programmatic and organizational goals and objectives have been achieved (9A.05).

Understanding of the nature and implications of professional standards of practice and external accreditation standards relative to therapeutic recreation service [and to other types of agencies] (9D.05).

O B J E C T I V E S

At the conclusion of this chapter, readers should be familiar with the following concepts and areas of management practice:

1. The meaning of evaluation as an important process used in monitoring an agency's quality and professional performance, and as an aid to management decision making.
2. Several models of evaluation used in leisure-service agencies, including goal-achievement, participant-rating, and standards-based approaches.
3. The application of evaluation methods in determining whether an agency has met professionally established levels of performance, as part of the accreditation process.
4. The relationship of research to evaluation, including research methodologies and several examples of research designed to contribute to management effectiveness in leisure-service agencies.
5. The role of management information systems as a means of monitoring agency performance, including the use of computer software in gathering, organizing, and interpreting data as a means of evaluation and a tool in ongoing decision making.

MEANING AND PURPOSE OF EVALUATION

315

CHAPTER 10
The Controlling
Function:
Evaluation, Research,
and Management
Information Systems

The term *evaluation* may be defined as a systematic process designed to determine the worth or effectiveness of a given field of community service. In every specialized area of recreation, parks, and leisure services today, there is growing awareness of the need to develop meaningful standards and quality controls that can be used to determine the extent to which programs are achieving their stated objectives.

In terms of its application, evaluation may be conducted in any of the following ways:

1. As a periodic function through which an agency carries out a self-study of its total operation every three to five years, as in the case of institutions that apply for renewed certification or accreditation;
2. As a regular function to be carried out at the end of each indoor or outdoor season and after each major activity or program unit;
3. As an ongoing daily process in which leaders and supervisors regularly evaluate program activities and events, staff performance, and other elements;
4. As a critical element in an organization's administrative process that regularly feeds information into its management information system and into varied databases, statistical summaries, and similar records and reports.

Three Models of Evaluation

While it is true that evaluation may be formal or informal, if it is to be used to document the positive outcomes of leisure services or to provide a convincing basis for decision making, it should be based as far as possible on concrete, empirical evidence. With this in mind, three major types of evaluation that rely heavily on systematic data gathering may be identified. These are:

1. Evaluation that is designed to measure the *effectiveness of programs in achieving their stated goals and objectives;*
2. Evaluation that makes use of the level of satisfaction of *program participants* and *staff ratings or feedback* to provide assessments of the agency's operation; and
3. Evaluation that relies on *professionally developed standards, criteria and guidelines for practice,* often used in connection with certification or accreditation procedures.

While evaluation is a way of meeting increased demands for accountability in public and nonprofit organizations, it should not be perceived as a means of automatically justifying a program. Evaluation is essentially a form of applied, practical research, and like other forms of research, it does not seek to "prove" a case. Instead, the evaluator asks a series of questions and gathers evidence as systematically and objectively as possible to determine whether agency goals have been met and appropriate professional standards of practice have been achieved. If evaluation is performed objectively, it may well yield negative rather than positive findings.

316

CHAPTER 10
The Controlling
Function:
Evaluation, Research,
and Management
Information Systems

In addition to these three basic approaches, several alternative ways of carrying out leisure-service evaluation have been identified.

Summative and Formative Evaluation

In the past, evaluation was primarily thought of as *summative*—that is, carried out at the end of a program to measure its success or failure and make recommendations for the future. Today much evaluation is *formative*, with continuous monitoring of a program while it is being planned and implemented.

Preordinate and Process Models

Some evaluation procedures follow a *preordinate* approach, meaning that they have a sequence of data-gathering and analytical steps that have been outlined in advance, with formal standards that serve as a basis for judgment. In contrast, other evaluation studies begin with a *process* in which the agency's staff determine exactly why they need to carry out an evaluation, the kinds of information that will be required, and the best way to gather it. No one approach is correct for all situations, and are often both used in evaluating an agency.

Quantitative and Qualitative Approaches

Like research, evaluation may rely on a heavily *quantitative* approach to recording empirical information—that is, in effect, doing head counts of participation, degrees of satisfaction, revenues and expenditures, qualifications of personnel, and similar elements. In contrast, *qualitative* evaluation would depend more heavily on personal judgment, impressions, anecdotal evidence, appraisals of the group dynamics at work in an agency, and similar elements.

STEPS IN THE EVALUATION PROCESS

Although evaluation may be carried out at many different levels or for different purposes, essentially it involves the following five steps.

1. *Assign responsibility*
To ensure that evaluation efforts are conducted efficiently and coordinated throughout a leisure-service agency, the chief responsibility for planning and carrying out the evaluation process should be assigned to a staff member, committee, or work team that will have this as a continuing function.

2. *Define scope of evaluation*
From year to year, the need for specific evaluations should be identified. Normally, this should include routine follow-ups or assessments of major program elements, events, staff members' performance, and similar subjects.

In addition, there may be periodic appraisals of the overall agency in order to document its performance for accreditation purposes, or as part of a communitywide planning effort.

3. *Identify evaluators*
Who actually carries out evaluation, or makes the kinds of judgments that determine the agency's success and level of quality? Many routine evaluations may be done as part of the work cycle through the year by supervisors, center

directors, or program specialists. However, when a large-scale, major evaluation study is to take place it should be assigned to individuals with special expertise and a level of authority that equips them to do the job.

These individuals who take responsibility for more complex evaluation studies may be either *internal* (that is, individuals who are regularly employed by the organization) or *external* (such as outside consultants). The advantage of internal evaluators is that they are likely to be more familiar with the situation and able to carry out the process more efficiently. In contrast, external evaluators will be more objective or impartial in their judgments and are likely to have more advanced skills of observation and analysis.

4. *Develop instruments and procedures*

As a form of applied research, evaluation should make use of carefully designed and presented instruments, such as rating forms, opinionnaires, surveys, or questionnaires. A leisure-service agency may develop such instruments for routine evaluation functions, using them year after year. For major evaluation efforts, however, guidelines or other instruments developed and published by national professional societies may be used directly, or adapted to an organization's specific needs.

5. *Analysis and conclusions*

When all data gathering has been completed, it is necessary to organize and analyze the evaluation study's findings. Some approaches make use of a quantitative rating method to indicate strengths and weaknesses within different programs or aspects of the agency's performance. A program may be required to achieve a given number of rating points, or score level, to be considered passing for accreditation, or to justify future funding. A profile may be drawn, with the requirement that the agency must meet a minimum standard of performance within each of several categories of service.

Customarily, evaluation findings of this type are summed up in a final report, which is then used in ongoing planning, policy making, or other management processes.

GOAL-ACHIEVEMENT MODEL OF EVALUATION

We now turn to an examination of the three basic approaches to leisure-service agency evaluation.

The first of these, the *goal-achievement model*, seeks to determine whether an organization has succeeded or is succeeding in achieving its stated goals and objectives. As indicated in Chapter 3, goals are of two types: operational and outcomes-directed.

Operational Goals

These may consist of such specific steps as improving registration procedures, initiating a new public relations campaign, raising program enrollments by a given percentage, establishing new programs for special populations, or achieving an improved level of park or playground maintenance.

317

CHAPTER 10
The Controlling
Function:
Evaluation, Research,
and Management
Information Systems

318

CHAPTER 10
The Controlling
Function:
Evaluation, Research,
and Management
Information Systems

Goal-achievement evaluation may measure the agency's success in serving projected number of participants in designated program activities and events—with the implicit assumption that participation in itself is a desirable experience in terms of physical, emotional, or social well-being.

Outcomes-Directed Goals

These focus on the actual outcomes or benefits to be achieved by agency programs. They range from such goals as the reduction of juvenile delinquency or racial tension in a community, to more specific objectives related to teaching specific skills, modifying social behavior of individuals or groups, improving fitness, or measurably lowering the school drop-out rate. (Fig. 10.1)

Recognizing the difficulty in precisely isolating the effects of organized program services, many agencies make use of personal case studies or anecdotal reporting to document the value of their programs. Typically, young people from poor socioeconomic neighborhoods with a high rate of welfare, crime, drug abuse, and gang warfare, who have been involved over a period of time in Police Athletic Leagues or Boys and Girls Club programs, and who have maintained positive lifestyles and gone on to college and successful careers, are often cited as examples of the value of such programs.

While such forms of anecdotal or qualitative findings are not as scientifically acceptable as the kinds of evidence that might be obtained from carefully controlled research studies, often they represent the only realistic way of demonstrating the social values of many recreation programs.

PARTICIPANT AND STAFF RATINGS

A second common approach to evaluation involves the use of ratings by program participants or by staff members.

Using survey forms, questionnaires, or personal interviews, participants may be asked to indicate their level of satisfaction with the overall program, as well as to rate leadership, facilities, fees, schedule, or similar elements. Such forms typically follow a Likert scale format, in which the respondents are not simply asked to reply "yes" or "no" but rather are given a range of possible replies to each question on a four- or five-point scale. They may also be asked to indicate, using an open-ended question format, what they saw as the strengths and weaknesses of the program, and to make suggestions that would improve it.

Two examples of participant rating forms are shown in Fig. 10.2*a*, a simple survey form designed to measure reactions of service personnel to a recreation facility at the Orlando, Florida, Naval Training Center, and in Figure 10.2*b*, a more detailed member survey form used by the Ambler, Pennsylvania, YMCA.

Typically, such participant evaluation forms may be distributed at front desks, in lockers, at the end of class or course sessions, or mailed to agency members or program participants. They may also be used in conjunction with focus groups, discussion sessions held with program participants, or advisory group meetings.

This part of the survey asks you questions about the Fort Worth Youth Sports Soccer Program in which you recently participated. For each of the statements below, circle the response that best describes how much you increased your knowledge, abilities, understanding, etc., due to your participation in the soccer program.

As a result of participating in the Fort Worth Youth Sports Soccer Program, I increased:	Increased A Lot	Increased Some	Increased A Little	No Impact
my ability to talk with other children . . .	A Lot	Some	A Little	None
my athletic ability	A Lot	Some	A Little	None
my knowledge of safe places to play	A Lot	Some	A Little	None
my ability to get along with other family members	A Lot	Some	A Little	None
my respect for coaches and referees	A Lot	Some	A Little	None
my understanding of the importance of teamwork	A Lot	Some	A Little	None
my interest in other recreation activities .	A Lot	Some	A Little	None
my number of friends	A Lot	Some	A Little	None
my ability to control anger	A Lot	Some	A Little	None
my desire to keep playing sports	A Lot	Some	A Little	None
my ability to be creative	A Lot	Some	A Little	None
my knowledge about other community activities	A Lot	Some	A Little	None
my ability to be a good sport	A Lot	Some	A Little	None
my understanding of the importance of doing one's best	A Lot	Some	A Little	None
my ability to play with other children . . .	A Lot	Some	A Little	None
my ability to express ideas more clearly .	A Lot	Some	A Little	None
my respect for the rules	A Lot	Some	A Little	None
my understanding of the importance of staying out of trouble	A Lot	Some	A Little	None
my understanding of the importance of physical fitness	A Lot	Some	A Little	None
my ability to play sports	A Lot	Some	A Little	None

FIGURE 10.1. Section of form used in collaborative project carried on by Department of Parks and Community Services, Fort Worth, Texas, and Dept. of Recreation, Park and Tourism Sciences, Texas A&M University, to evaluate outcomes of Youth Sports Soccer Program. Participants fill out self-evaluation form.

322

CHAPTER 10
The Controlling
Function:
Evaluation, Research,
and Management
Information Systems

to achieve its target income with a variety of revenue-producing activities. Attendance and income were used directly to assess the success of programming in this Y.[3]

Staff Ratings

In combination with participant ratings and attendance/income analysis, many leisure-service organizations routinely ask staff members to evaluate programs they have directed. Their supervisors may also carry out evaluations of activities led by subordinates. Similarly, participants may be asked to fill out evaluation sheets about programs they have taken part in, dealing with such questions as the level of the activity, the adequacy of the facility, the leadership, the fee or charge, the schedule, and similar information.

Some leisure-service agencies have developed a systematic procedure for recording all important information about varied program activities as a mean of determining whether they should be repeated and, if so, with what changes. For examples, the Phoenix, Arizona, Parks, Recreation and Library Department requires that all special events be summed up with a staff report that includes comprehensive information about the program, including problems encountered and recommendations for future programming (Fig. 10.3).

Similarly, in order to systematize staff ratings in other operational areas such as facilities maintenance, many agencies develop instruments designed to measure performance quality as objectively as possible.

STANDARDS MODEL OF EVALUATION

A third major approach to leisure-service agency evaluation involves the use of standards or guidelines that have been developed by national professional organizations as a way of upgrading organization practices, or serving as a basis

FIGURE 10.3. Staff special events report form: Phoenix, Ariz.

1. *Basic facts about the event:* Name, date, time, location, general description, numbers of participants and spectators, and information on volunteers and co-sponsors.
2. *Staffing levels:* Classification of all part-time and full-time staff, who worked on the project, number of hours worked, hourly rates, and total staffing costs (including prep time.)
3. *Supplies and other expenses:* An itemized cost list of program expenses and supplies.
4. *Revenues:* Amount of money collected per participant, and total collected from participants and from any other sources.
5. *Cost per participant:* The net cost per participant and net cost per participating unit (includes participants and spectators).
6. *Program calendar:* A chronological outline of tasks related to planning and implementing the event.
7. *Problems and planned changes:* Description of any problems encountered and any changes recommended if the activity is repeated in the future.
8. *Supporting documentation:* Schedules, financial reports, set-up diagrams, rules, copies of significant correspondence, and any other relevant documents.
9. *Co-sponsorship:* List of cosponsors and what was provided by each, an estimate of dollar value, and contact names and phone numbers.
10. *Promotional material:* Flyers, brochures, press releases, and copies of newspaper articles.

for accreditation or certification decisions. Typically, the standards are created by planning teams composed of educators and practitioners, field-tested, and revised over a period of time before receiving final approval.

In some cases, each standard for effective practice is accompanied by a set of criteria that must be met. In other cases, the standards are followed by explanatory paragraphs, or by suggested evidence-of-compliance statements.

323

CHAPTER 10
The Controlling
Function:
Evaluation, Research,
and Management
Information Systems

ACCREDITATION STANDARDS FOR PUBLIC AGENCIES

In the early 1970s, the National Recreation and Park Association published a manual, *Evaluation and Self-Study of Public Recreation and Park Agencies: A Guide with Standards and Evaluative Criteria.* This instrument was intended to assist local public agencies in examining and upgrading their own operations.

In the mid-1990s, a new manual and visitation procedure was developed to assist local public recreation and park departments in a self-assessment process that might lead to accreditation.[4] Formulated by the National Committee on Accreditation and supported by the American Academy for Park and Recreation Administration and the National Recreation and Park Association, this new manual included 154 standards linked to ten major categories: (1) Agency Authority, Role and Responsibility; (2) Planning: (3) Organization and Administration; (4) Human Resources; (5) Finance; (6) Program and Services Management; (7) Facility and Land Use Management; (8) Safety and Security; (9) Risk Management; and (10) Evaluation and Research. As an example, Fig. 10.4 shows one standard in the Planning category. The manual describes the accreditation process by including procedures for applying for accreditation, the agency's self-assessment process including the standards, and the site visitation team and schedule.

By July 1997, interest in agency accreditation had grown, with approximately forty-five departments either accredited or involved in the process. In addition to these agencies, many other departments are able to use the accreditation standards as informal guidelines for their own management practices.

FIGURE 10.4.   Example of planning standard in the accreditation manual.

2.3.2.2   Master site plan

There should be a master site plan for areas and facilities. As with the comprehensive plan, it should be officially adopted by the appropriate governing body.

Commentary: The Plan sets forth each individual park site or special areas, delineating areas of activity, circulation patterns, building locations, parking areas, and other components for overall development. The plan should include cost estimates for long-range programming. All construction and development should include detailed working drawings and specifications with cost estimates and necessary bidding documents. The plan should reflect the program plan and should have the consultation in the initial planning stage of those who will program, operate, and maintain the area or facility.

324

CHAPTER 10
The Controlling
Function:
Evaluation, Research,
and Management
Information Systems

Accreditation in Professional Preparation

A similar process has been developed by the Council on Accreditation, sponsored by NRPA in cooperation with the American Association for Leisure and Recreation, to evaluate and approve higher education programs offering baccalaureate curricula in recreation, parks, and leisure services.[5] Detailed manuals have been developed that outline the curriculum accreditation process and present standards within nine functional areas: (1) Unit Characteristics, (2) Philosophy and Goals, (3) Administration, (4) Faculty, (5) Students, (6) Instructional Resources, (7) Baccalaureate Degree Standards, (7) Foundation Understandings, (8) Professional Competencies, and (9) Options (Degree Specializations). Examples of the curriculum guides found in the Baccalaureate Degree standards are found in the opening section of chapters throughout this text.

Other standards of practice have been developed in specialized fields such as therapeutic recreation service, sports management, or armed forces recreation. They provide useful examples of guidelines for evaluation that may be used internally by leisure-service agencies, or as the basis for external administrative reviews or formal accreditation or funding procedures.

PERSONNEL EVALUATION

In addition to evaluation of entire agencies and their programs, several specific areas of leisure-service operations also have been the focus of systematic evaluation through the years.

Typically, staff personnel such as recreation leaders, program specialists, or supervisors have been evaluated regularly as part of civil-service codes, union contracts, or other personnel management plans. Such procedures provided essential input with respect to gaining regular job status, promotions, demotions, job transfers, or similar actions, as well as material to be used in supervisory counseling conferences.

To ensure that personnel evaluation was carried out in a systematic and objective way, many leisure-service agencies made use of rating instruments that listed specific personality traits or areas of on-the-job performance. Typically, supervisors were required to rate staff members on a four- or five-point scale dealing with such items as those shown in Fig. 10.5.

In general, such practices reflected the bureaucratic, chain-of-command and span-of-control principles that evolved during the period when classical management theory was most influential. Realistically, they often were ineffective because many supervisors were reluctant to rate subordinate employees harshly—either for fear of disturbing a positive relationship or because it might lead to conflict and tension in the workplace.

Newer Approaches to Personnel Evaluation

Many recreation, park, and leisure-service agencies have adopted new approaches to the evaluation of staff members. Based on contemporary principles of human resource management, these procedures seek to focus on developing positive, trust-based, and two-way-communication relationships that are intended to improve staff performance, rather than simply assign a score to the individual being rated.

Within such a system, evaluation may be based on frequent formal and informal observations of the staff member at work, feedback from program reports, regular supervisory conferences, the reaction of program participants, and similar sources. Instead of the traditional "top-down" approach in which supervisors or division heads rate their subordinate employees in a one-way, authoritarian fashion, some departments have line employees evaluate *their* supervisors (Fig. 10.6).

Other leisure-service agencies have adopted more comprehensive approaches to appraising staff performance and linked it to the overall process of employee career development. For example, in Edmonton, Alberta, Canada, an employee evaluation form is used to evaluate the work of managerial employees. The

325

CHAPTER 10
*The Controlling
Function:
Evaluation, Research,
and Management
Information Systems*

FIGURE 10.5. Nassau County, NY Park and Recreation personnel evaluation form: selected items.

PLEASE PRINT

Employee _____

                         Last Name   First Name

Civil service title _____

Duties (working title) _____

Park or unit _____ Division _____

Period of supervision from _____ to _____

Reason for report _____

1. Job Capability				
☐ Not observed.	☐ Has gaps in fundamental knowledge and skills of his job.	☐ Has a satisfactory knowledge and skill for the routine phases of his job.	☐ Has excellent knowledge and is well skilled on all phases of his job.	☐ Has an exceptional understanding and skill on all phases of his job.

2. Planning Ability				
☐ Not observed.	☐ Relies on others to bring problems to his attention. Often fails to see ahead.	☐ Plans ahead just enough to get by in his present job	☐ Is a careful, effective planner. Anticipates and takes action to solve problems.	☐ Capable of planning beyond requirements of the present job. Sees the big picture.

3. Leadership				
☐ Not observed.	☐ Often weak in command situations. At times unable to exert control.	☐ Normally develops fairly adequate control and teamwork.	☐ Consistently a good leader. Commands respect of his subordinates.	☐ Exceptional skill in directing others to great effort.

4. Executive Judgment					
☐ Not observed.	☐ Decisions and recommendations are sometimes unsound or ineffective.	☐ His judgment is usually sound and reasonable, with occasional errors.	☐ Displays good judgment, resulting from sound evaluation. He is effective.	☐ An exceptionally sound, logical thinker in situations which occur on his job.	☐ Has a knack for arriving at the right decision, even on highly complex matters.

5. Human Relations					
☐ Not observed.	☐ Does not get along well with people. Definitely hinders his effectiveness.	☐ He has difficulty in getting along with his associates.	☐ Gets along with people adequately. Has average skill at maintaining good human relations.	☐ His above average skills in human relations are an asset.	☐ Outstanding skills in human relations increases his effectiveness.

6. Job Accomplishment					
☐ Not observed.	☐ Quality or quantity of his work does not always meet job requirements.	☐ Performance is barely adequate to meet job requirements.	☐ Quality and quantity of his work are very satisfactory.	☐ Performance is above normal expectations for meeting job requirements.	☐ Quality and quantity of his work are clearly superior.

Teamwork Performance Survey

Management Council Position: _____

This survey is conducted to collect feedback on the performance of a member of the Parks and Recreation Department management council. This group is the top level management of parks and recreation. Information from this survey will be used to help the individual and managment council improve work performance.

Information contained on this form is strictly confidential. There is no record of who completed a form and once tabulated the original survey form is discarded. Your candor will help parks and recreation become a better department.

You are asked to respond to a set of questions. The scale is presented on a continuum from strongly agree to strongly disagree. Place your rating based on your opinion concerning agreement with the question.

TEAMWORK VALUES: The following questions concern values and behavior that the Department strives for in team settings. Each individual of a team must participate within certain behavioral boundaries for the group and organization to be successful.

1. This person believes in the established values, mission, goals and objectives of the Department.

☐ Strongly Agree   ☐ Mildly Agree   ☐ Disagree   ☐ Don't know
☐ Agree   ☐ Mildly Disagree   ☐ Strongly Disagree

2. This person shows a willingness to defer their own work when necessary to support others and the greater needs of our customers.

☐ Strongly Agree   ☐ Mildly Agree   ☐ Disagree   ☐ Don't know
☐ Agree   ☐ Mildly Disagree   ☐ Strongly Disagree

3. This person demonstrates a deep sense of personal responsibility and accountability for the quality of our work and the satisfaction of our customers.

☐ Strongly Agree   ☐ Mildly Agree   ☐ Disagree   ☐ Don't know
☐ Agree   ☐ Mildly Disagree   ☐ Strongly Disagree

4. This person understands the importance of their individual role to the success of the team and organization.

☐ Strongly Agree   ☐ Mildly Agree   ☐ Disagree   ☐ Don't know
☐ Agree   ☐ Mildly Disagree   ☐ Strongly Disagree

5. This person practices open and honest communication with other team members.

☐ Strongly Agree   ☐ Mildly Agree   ☐ Disagree   ☐ Don't know
☐ Agree   ☐ Mildly Disagree   ☐ Strongly Disagree

6. This person listens to other team members' ideas and opinions.

☐ Strongly Agree   ☐ Mildly Agree   ☐ Disagree   ☐ Don't know
☐ Agree   ☐ Mildly Disagree   ☐ Strongly Disagree

7. This person understands and demonstrates the role and importance of team skills and teamwork in the performance of the organization.

☐ Strongly Agree   ☐ Mildly Agree   ☐ Disagree   ☐ Don't know
☐ Agree   ☐ Mildly Disagree   ☐ Strongly Disagree

FIGURE 10.6.   Supervisory evaluation form: Arlington, TX, Parks and Recreation Department.

original form has three sections: (1) a description of the individual's primary on-the-job functions and responsibilities and an appraisal of his/her performance in each area; (2) a separate qualitative performance report, dealing with the individual's knowledge, managerial proficiency, personal qualities, and strengths and weaknesses; and (3) development plans, in which the evaluator is asked to indicate actions to be undertaken to improve performance. Sufficient space is allowed for the evaluator to provide detailed additional comments in each section. Fig. 10.7 shows the second and third sections of this form.

In the Edmonton personnel appraisal system, the employee and his or her supervisor discuss the report in detail, and both individuals sign the report. In a separate, confidential statement, the supervisor indicates his or her view of the employee's promotional potential, the type of responsibilities the employee is best suited to handle, and whether the supervisor is prepared to accept the individual for continued employment at this level.

GENERAL GUIDELINES FOR EVALUATION

The essential purpose of agency, program, or personnel evaluation should be clearly understood. It is not simply to provide a rating of the performance of an agency, program, or individual. Instead, its role is to provide an accurate picture of the strengths and weaknesses that have been observed in order to bring about improvement. By indicating which specific standards or goals are not being met, it suggests the steps that must be taken to improve the agency's performance.

Evaluation must be continuous and systematic. It is not just something that happens once or twice a year or only at the end of programs. Programs and activities should be evaluated while they are in process and at their conclusion, and staff members should be regularly observed in action and given feedback that will be helpful to them in improving their performance. Used in this way, evaluation will contribute significantly to an organization's productivity and will improve the quality of service as well as document in objective ways the contribution it is making.

Different instruments or data-gathering procedures may be used according to the type of evaluation being done. Such instruments or procedures seek to gather relevant information in a standardized, objective way. They may be of the following types: (1) closed-ended checklist forms, with essentially "yes" or "no" responses possible; (2) rating scales that have several possible responses to each question according to degree of positive or negative response or other variations; (3) open-ended questionnaires that permit a free or unstructured response; or (4) combinations of any of these.

EVALUATION AS A FORM OF RESEARCH

When properly carried out, with careful selection of subjects and instruments and valid methods of analysis, evaluation should be regarded as a purposeful form of research. Although much research is intended to explore theoretical issues or relationships, research may also be designed to contribute to management effectiveness.

Part B   Qualitative Performance Factors

In the light of the primary functions and responsibilities you have evaluated, describe how you would rate this employee in terms of the following factors:

I.   Knowledge

A.   Professional/technical know-how, on-the-job.

II.   Managerial/supervisory proficiency

A.   Planning (setting objectives, forseeing contingencies, etc.)
B.   Organizing work (making assignments, schedules, establishing priorities, etc.)
C.   Personnel management (finding, placing, directing, motivating, developing staff)
D.   Control (reports, records, expenses, measuring results, etc.)
E.   Communications (written, oral; timeliness, appropriateness, feedback)
F.   Problem solving (investigation, analysis, decision making, business sense, etc.)

III.   Personal qualities (habits)

A.   Appearance (dress, manner, poise, self-assurance)
B.   Energy (drive, ambition)
C.   Adaptability (flexibility, versatility, mobility)
D.   Initiative (ingenuity, self-reliance, self-starting)

IV.   Major strengths: Describe this employee's major assets, strengths, and abilities in the light of his/her relationship to the foregoing and to the requirements of his/her present position:

V.   Areas requiring improvements: Describe the areas requiring improvement in this employee's performance in his/her present position:

Part C   Development Plans

Indicate your plans to bring about improvement in those areas indicated above. For each subject, indicate by priority the type of plan or plans that you intend to employ and the tentative timetable for action. Use the appropriate numbers provided below.

Priority	Subject	Type of Plan(s)	Tentative Timetable	
			Begin: Month, Year	End: Month, Year
1				
2				
3				

Subject

1—Managerial techniques

2—Supervisory techniques

4—Personal facts or habits

5—Communication skills

6—Technical knowledge or subject matter (specify type)

7—Other (specify)

Type of Plan

1—Directed self-development (reading, self-study, etc.)

2—Informal training— (ed. dept. courses)

3—Outside educational programs (seminars, courses)

4—Counseling, coaching

5—On-the-job training

6—No plan at present

Comments

FIGURE 10.7.   Two sections of Edmonton, Alberta, Canada, employee evaluation form.

Obviously, the systematic testing of participants' needs and interests, as discussed in Chapter 4, represents a form of practical research. Similarly, measuring the outcomes of different programs and services, or the relative effectiveness of different leadership methods or fiscal strategies, are all important research functions. When such evaluation procedures meet accepted standards for scientific research, their findings often are published in research journals and are read by other practitioners or scholars in the recreation, park, and leisure services field.

329

CHAPTER 10
The Controlling
Function:
Evaluation, Research,
and Management
Information Systems

Outdoor Recreation and Park Management

Studies in this area cover a wide range of issues. For example, McEwen and Cole have examined the environmental impact of camping in wilderness areas and the effects of different types of campsite management on campground and wilderness maintenance.[6] Scott and Jackson examined factors that limit and strategies that encourage the public's use of urban parks and their relationship to the age and gender of participants.[7] Van Hoff and Verbeeten conducted research into the role of state tourism offices in promoting recreational travel.[8] Crompton, Love, and More documented the importance of recreation, parks, open space, and other leisure opportunities with respect to companies' making relocation decisions.[9]

Studies of Participants and Programs

Many other research studies have examined the motivations and leisure involvement of varied demographic groups, including age, gender, racial/ethnic, and socioeconomic factors. For example, Frisby, Crawford, and Dorer have analyzed the involvement of low-income women in local physical recreation programs.[10] Similarly, Backman and Veldkamp studied the relationship between service quality and user loyalty,[11] and Busser and Carruthers examined the relationship between participants' motivations and constraints and the design and management of recreation programs.[12] Numerous other research studies have reviewed the effect of different fee structures on participation.

The Bureau of Naval Personnel has done systematic research into program user fees throughout its Morale, Welfare and Recreation operations. Prince George's County, Maryland, has carried out community surveys of therapeutic recreation programs and services to gather a comprehensive picture of sponsors, participants, funding, transportation, and similar practices.

Such research studies—and hundreds of other like them—are reported annually at research conferences sponsored by the Society of Park and Recreation Educators at NRPA Congresses and at Canadian provincial research conferences. In addition, they are reported in detail in research journals and other professional publications, such as *Parks and Recreation* or *Recreation Canada*.

Implications for Managers

From a management perspective, recreation, park, and leisure-service professionals on all levels should make a strong effort to be familiar with ongoing research findings, particularly within their own areas of specialization. In this way, they are better able to justify the benefits of their own programs and to make intelligent management decisions based on the findings of current

330

CHAPTER 10
The Controlling
Function:
Evaluation, Research,
and Management
Information Systems

research studies. Simply by becoming knowledgeable, literate spokespersons for the leisure-service field, they enrich public understanding and support and contribute to their own professional advancement.

Importance of Collaborative Research

Beyond this, recreation, park, and leisure-service managers can contribute greatly to the overall development of their field by taking part in collaborative research projects. Realistically, while many managers lack research skills themselves, they often can provide a setting in which competent researchers can carry out valuable studies. Too often, there is a gap between practitioners and academic scholars, which hampers the development of professional theory and practical knowledge. Ross and Young write:

> Collaborative research . . . is an approach that capitalizes upon the shared abilities, ideas, knowledge and resources of both the recreational sport practitioner and the academician. Here, the technical or research-based knowledge of the [scholar/investigator] is joined with the practical, experiential knowledge of the practitioner [thus enhancing] the potential for a successful, satisfying research relationship.[13]

As an outstanding example of such collaborative research efforts, the National Recreation and Park Association initiated a major research study that examined strategies and outcomes of recreation programs designed to serve at-risk youth in American cities. With funding from the National Recreation Foundation, four universities (Clemson, Texas A & M, Arizona State West, and the Pennsylvania State University) initiated a variety of special camps, sports activities, performing arts, and other programs in Cincinnati, Ohio, Fort Worth, Texas, Kansas City, Missouri, and Commerce, California, with striking and statistically based results in terms of delinquency and crime reduction.[14]

Closely linked to evaluation and other research-based processes is the task of monitoring ongoing agency operations throughout the year. This involves the development of detailed accurate information systems that provide timely data and assist agency managers in their controlling and monitoring responsibilities.

Monitoring as a Management Function

Simply defined, monitoring is the process of controlling an agency's operation through direct ongoing observation and documentation of performance. It seeks to ensure that policies and procedures are being carefully observed and that staff members are productively employed.

Depending on the nature of the leisure-service enterprise, the actual goals of the organization will, of course, vary greatly. However, at all times, center directors, program supervisors, and other middle-level managers must monitor the agency's operations to be certain that staff-client relationships are positive, that safety guidelines are followed, and that maintenance, public relations, and all of other aspects of the program are being correctly handled.

The use of daily and weekly reports must be supplemented by other accounting procedures and by personal observation and analysis to ensure their accuracy. In numerous other types of recreation and leisure-service operations, such monitoring must be carried on systematically. In some situations—as in a

331

CHAPTER 10
The Controlling
Function:
Evaluation, Research,
and Management
Information Systems

theme park—the monitoring emphasis may be on the flow of participants through various attractions, rides, and other elements in the park, along with such concerns as cleanliness, safety, and staff performance. In therapeutic recreation, key concerns in monitoring are likely to be the degree to which patients or clients are participating successfully in program activities and the extent to which therapeutic objectives are being achieved.

In a sense, monitoring represents one tool within the broader function of *agency* or *program evaluation*. It provides continuous input, which, when summed up and interpreted, is the basis for making an overall judgment of the agency's quality and effectiveness. Input is of two kinds: (1) quantitative, or statistical; and (2) qualitative, or judgmental. The first kind of input involves the kinds of data that can be summed up numerically, such as program costs and revenues, enrollments and participation, and similar information. For example, Figure 10.8 illustrates the systematic recording of participation statistics (including facility reservations, course enrollments, and competition in adult sports leagues) in San Mateo, California.

FIGURE 10.8. Participation report form: San Mateo, CA.

Recreation Division Quarterly Statistical Report

Section:	Business Services
Fiscal Year:	1996-97
Date of Report:	16-April-97

Quarterly Activity

Escom Course and Membership Transactions / **Net Dollar Value**

Item / Location	1st (Su)	2nd (Fa)	3rd (Wi)	4th (Sp)	Total	Budget	1st (Su)	2nd (Fa)	3rd (Wi)	4th (Sp)	Total	Budget
Athletics/park yard	201	207	303	0	711		3,926	23,062	92,492	0	119,480	
Beresford	4,962	4,953	3,897	0	13,812		174,121	155,658	145,102	0	474,881	
City Hall	3,957	2,158	1,603	0	7,718		162,506	61,741	45,982	0	270,229	
Joinville Pool	2,604	743	518	0	3,865		53,291	28,334	23,348	0	104,973	
Hillsdale Pool	273	0	13	0	286		2,891	0	74	0	2,965	
King Pool	0	0	0	0	0		0	0	0	0	0	
King Center	246	53	80	0	379		7,549	1,596	1,674	0	10,819	
Lakeshore	530	582	320	0	1,432		19,834	16,930	12,798	0	49,562	
Senior Center	238	264	418	0	920		7,278	24,075	88,113	0	119,466	
Shoreview	838	1,032	557	0	2,427		28,802	27,159	19,677	0	75,638	
Total	13,849	9,992	7,709	0	31,550		460,198	338,555	429,259	0	1,228,012	

Scholarship Registrations / **Net Dollar Value**

	1st	2nd	3rd	4th	Total		1st	2nd	3rd	4th	Total	
25% adjustments	12	5	10		27		184	142	155		481	
50% adjustments	47	30	62		139		1,760	897	2,234		4,891	
75% adjustments	188	161	94		443		9,120	5,735	4,599		19,454	
Total Scholarships	247	196	166	0	609		11,064	6,774	6,988	0	24,826	

Facility Reservations Central Center / **Attendance**

	1st	2nd	3rd	4th	Total		1st	2nd	3rd	4th	Total	
Meetings	12	7	4		23		420	297	70		787	
Social events	4	8	7		19		1000	645	485		2,130	
Total Reservations	16	15	11	0	42	0	1420	942	555	0	2,917	0

332

CHAPTER 10
The Controlling
Function:
Evaluation, Research,
and Management
Information Systems

Qualitative data may be drawn from several types of sources. In Arlington, Texas, such input is drawn heavily from participants through the use of:

> . . . direct contact, surveys, comment cards, or focus groups. Problem issues are dealt with immediately. Primary service issues deal with program leadership behavior. PARDner ["PARD" is an acronym in Arlington for Park and Recreation Department] standards and job descriptions outline the performance expected.
>
> Maintenance of parks and facilities is managed by the use of certification check sheets. The check sheets describe the conditions we want present in parks. Trained observers rate actual conditions against the standards. We supplement this method with customer surveys and direct work with user groups. There is one advisory committee that is made up of users of athletic fields. Sport groups are primarily concerned with field maintenance. We meet with them once a month and receive feedback on our service performance.[15]

Such information is invaluable on a systemwide basis, but may also be used to assess operations within separate units of a larger organization. Each such unit's performance may be compared with those of other units, or analyzed in terms of community or neighborhood conditions, economic or environmental factors, or contrasting social needs.

ROLE OF MANAGEMENT INFORMATION SYSTEMS

There is general agreement that we have moved from an industrial era, in which the production of goods and services was at the heart of national life, to an information-centered age. Today, the systematic gathering, analysis, interpretation, and transmission of information is at the heart of all business, governmental, social-service, and other kinds of enterprises. Information may be gathered from both internal and external sources, and the monitoring process just described contributes to the development of comprehensive management information systems (MIS).

The term *management information system* refers to a total database that is gathered, classified, and made available by an agency's staff for management purposes. Its purpose is to maintain an accurate, ongoing record of agency operations to ensure that policies are being correctly followed, that all elements in the organization are working productively, and to facilitate all decision making and strategic planning. Such a database plays an essential role in planning, policy development, decision making, and managerial control of an organization. It makes use of telecommunications channels, networking, varied forms of record keeping and feedback, and appropriate computers and computer software to document and analyze expenditures, procedures, staff assignments, program outcomes, and statistics of participation.

Information that is gathered externally may be useful in determining present and future needs for an agency's services, potential resources or cooperating organizations, the nature of competitive groups, the impact of legislation or economic trends, and similar planning or policy-making needs.

Management information systems may be viewed primarily as collections of data useful to managers within a single agency or department, or to facilitate exchanges of views, facts, trends, and strategies among individuals representing different organizations or professional concerns. Today it would be impractical to conduct such exchanges or to collect and analyze data of any sort without the use of computers.

333

CHAPTER 10
The Controlling
Function:
Evaluation, Research,
and Management
Information Systems

GROWING SOCIETAL ROLE OF COMPUTERS

In describing the functions of computers in recreation, park, and leisure-service agencies today, one must recognize the powerful forces that have transformed our society and economy in recent years. The "megashift" to an informational economy, John Naisbitt pointed out, meant that by the early 1980s over 65 percent of the working population had jobs involving information processing, compared with only 17 percent in 1950. He continued:

> Most Americans spend their time creating, processing, or distributing information. For example, workers in banking, the stock market, and insurance all hold information jobs. . . . Professional workers are almost all information workers—lawyers, teachers, engineers, computer programmers, systems analysts, doctors, architects, accountants, librarians, newspaper reporters, social workers, nurses, and clergy. . . . In our new society, the *strategic* resource is information. Not the only resource, but the most important.[16]

Computers have been a major contributing element in this transformation of society. They have entered our lives at every level, from the most trivial to the most profound functions. In the thirty-odd years since artificial intelligence (AI) began, computers have gone from playing chess games to mimicking human expertise in fields such as assembly-line scheduling, advanced missile guidance systems, or split-second identification and price calculation of items in a supermarket shopping cart. Computers today enable people to shop and pay bills electronically, tap into reference and referral services, and take advantage of popular home computer programs such as games or foreign language instruction. They are now being used in entirely new kinds of formats for both personal and professional purposes. Increasingly, people with similar interests and needs are communicating with each other through so-called computer bulletin-boards, websites on the Internet, or E-mail.

To illustrate the remarkable range of computer applications that have emerged in recent years, it was reported in 1997 that a new software program from Germany allowed one to select from more than 200 sins and automatically match each sin to a repentance, thus substituting a computer and modem for priest and confessional. Cizek suggests the possibilities of this new technology:

The church could capture the sins of its parish or congregation on database. Categories of sins would be established. The clergy could better customize the sermons to address the shortcomings of its particular congregation. While lying might top the list in one church, greed might dominate in another. . . .[17]

While some may find such innovative computer uses to be irrelevant or offensive, they illustrate the degree to which electronic data processing is being used to substitute for formerly person-directed functions.

CHAPTER 10
*The Controlling
Function:
Evaluation, Research,
and Management
Information Systems*

Computer Processes and Components

It is not necessary to understand the scientific basis of computers or their mechanisms to learn how to use them. Instead, it is important to understand the concepts of "hardware" and "software" and how to select and use them. The term *hardware* refers to the computers themselves, which are of two major types: (1) the large mainframe computers that are located in central places in government, business, or university offices, but that have satellite locations where individuals may use them, and (2) smaller microcomputers or word processors for personal, home, or office use. Although it is possible to further subdivide computers into more specialized categories based on cost, size, memory size, input-output speed, and access, the categories presented here are sufficient for a basic understanding of computer hardware.

The microcomputer may be defined as an electronic unit of equipment that stores, manipulates, and presents information rapidly. It is one of five elements that comprise a microcomputing system and may be described as the "brains" or "inner workings" of the system. However, it cannot function without one or more of the following: keyboard, disc drive, monitor, and printer. Beeler describes these as follows:

> A *keyboard* is very similar to a typewriter keyboard. It contains the letters, numbers, characters, and symbols of a typewriter. . . . The keyboard's purpose is to enter information and commands into the microcomputer.

> The *disc drive* transfers information into the microcomputer. A cassette recorder may also be used for this purpose.

> The *monitor* resembles a television set and is used to exhibit information and commands [as a] visual display.

> The *printer* is used to produce a "hard" [printed] copy of the results of microcomputing. Letterhead paper, mailing labels, dittos, roll paper, and typical computer paper may be used. . . .[18]

There are essentially three stages of computerized data processing. The first, called the *input* stage, involves communicating to the computer what it is to do. Input may be in the forms of paper tape, punched cards, magnetic tape, a teletype keyboard, or some other device. The second stage is the *processing* stage, in which the machine analyzes the data or presents it in formats that have been programmed. The third stage is *output,* which is presentation of the product, either on a screen for direct visibility or by computer printout sheets that are fed out with immense speed.

In order to use a computer, it must be programmed—that is, provided with a set of instructions. To do this, computer software has been developed for a variety of specialized uses. The term *software* refers to portable programs, usually on discs, that are inserted into the computer and then provide the formula (or give the directions) through which data are to be analyzed. Typically, software programs such as the Statistical Package for the Social Sciences (SPSS), Statistical Analysis System (SAS), and FORTRAN Library Program are used with mainframe computers. Many other software packages have been developed for use with microcomputers.

Computer Languages

335

CHAPTER 10
The Controlling
Function:
Evaluation, Research,
and Management
Information Systems

A number of user-oriented programming languages have been developed, each for a specific purpose or type of use, which are then translated into language that is intelligible to the machine. These include: BASIC (Beginners All-Purpose Symbolic Instruction Code); COBOL (Common Business Oriented Language), chiefly used for business applications; FORTRAN (Formula Translation); ALGOL (designed primarily for international applications); SCAT and INTERACT, used in monitoring psychological experiments; and numerous others.

So complex is the computer field in the different types of machines, systems, languages, and programs that it often is initially threatening to potential users. Users may fear that they will be displaced by the computer, or will be unable to gain the skills to use them effectively—seeing the computer as a problem-generating machine with the potential for causing stress and anxiety.

However, through the 1980s and 1990s, numerous college and university leisure-service departments initiated courses in computer technology and applications, with the result that most students taking degrees in this overall field had at least a working knowledge of computer methods. Beyond this, various professional societies sponsor computer-use conferences, workshops, or training institutes. For example, the National Recreation and Park Association has sponsored annual computer institutes for faculty members and students since the early 1990s. At a typical conference, held through the Oglebay, West Virginia, Department of Continuing Education, seven leading manufacturers of commercial software designed for recreation and park uses demonstrated their products and offered participants hands-on laboratory experiences in various operating systems environments. Hundreds of computer applications were available in DOS, Novell, UNIX, and Apple Macintosh environments.[19]

As a result of such training opportunities, more and more beginning leisure-service professionals today are computer literate and skilled in applying electronic data processing in varied management functions.

EXPANDED COMPUTER FUNCTIONS IN LEISURE SERVICES

Today, recreation, park, and leisure-service agencies make use of computers in varied management functions, as shown in the following pages.

Needs Assessments and Constituency Surveys

Many leisure-service agencies use computers to examine community recreational needs and interests, or to survey their constituencies, memberships, or target populations. These studies range from marketing studies of theme park visitors to random sampling of community residents or sections of comprehensive community-planning studies.

Constituency studies are conducted in various ways. One approach has been to use computers to analyze the residential location and demographic characteristics of community residents using a particular facility. For example, some recreation and park districts have developed electronic monitoring systems

336

CHAPTER 10
The Controlling
Function:
Evaluation, Research,
and Management
Information Systems

under which each participant who uses a major park or other facility has a plastic registration card that must be slipped into a sensing device at the entrance to the facility. The participant's residence and other relevant information are electronically recorded; with this device it is possible to tell at any time *how* facilities are used (age, neighborhood, or other characteristics of users) or *what* use is made of recreation resources by people from any particular neighborhood.

In some cases, computers have been used to measure not only the specific activity preferences of subjects, but also their leisure attitudes and values. Some researchers, for example, have developed automated leisure-assessment instruments to measure leisure "state of mind," including elements related to perceived freedom, leisure control and playfulness, barriers to leisure involvement, knowledge of leisure opportunities, and leisure preferences. Compared to simple checklists that provide only a rough picture of subjects, such a survey instrument examines attitudes and preferences in much greater depth.

Planning, Scheduling, and Registering Programs

Computers may also be used to analyze preferences with respect to fees and charges, appropriate times for scheduling, and similar factors that affect the scheduling process. They are indispensable today in terms of confirming reservations, assigning the use of facilities, coordinating the work of staff members, and managing all fiscal processes connected to agency programs.

Computer Use in Sports Management

For example, computers have become widely used in scheduling diversified sports events in college and university recreation programs. The intramural sports staff at Brigham Young University, for example, must organize, schedule, and track as many as 500 bowling teams, 700 to 900 basketball teams, and more than 500 flag football teams at different times of the year, along with over fifty-five other sports.

Scheduling several hundred games a week, recording scores, registering forfeits, defaults, team power ratings, and similar data created a statistical nightmare for the coordinating staff until a feasibility study was conducted by the university's computer department, which resulted in the development of a COBOL program and the placement of a computer terminal in the intramural office, with access to an IBM 360 computer. The computer schedules all events and also provides an instantaneous check of each student's eligibility status, identification of officials and evaluation of their performance, and complete history of each team's record. It also produces team game sheets with full game statistics.

Tourism and Travel Reservations

The travel industry has become heavily automated to assure today's consumer a guaranteed "room at the inn." Computer-based reservations provide an instantaneous way of confirming guest arrangements and are also linked in many cases with airline reservation offices, car rental companies, theme parks, and other ententainment centers that are part of a total travel package. Campgrounds, state or federal park systems, and numerous other outdoor recreation facilities and attractions can provide cost-efficient, up-to-the-minute customer service through automated computer networks.

337

CHAPTER 10
The Controlling
Function:
Evaluation, Research,
and Management
Information Systems

In terms of outdoor recreation, visitors to a wilderness or other back-country park site may be helped through computer programs to select hiking trails or other destinations suited to their own interests and capabilities. For example, a software program written in Applesoft BASIC and making use of a 48K Apple IIe microcomputer has been used to assist visitors to the Golden Spike Empire, one of nine tourism promotional regions in Utah. The program contained information on twenty different attractions in the region, ranging from such passive pursuits as sight-seeing or bird-watching, to very active pastimes like hunting or alpine skiing.

Typically, such programs involve a process that takes the park visitor through a sequence of questions, with the computer providing possible choices at each step—either through a "touch-screen" mechanism or with a simple keyboard operation.

Computers in Therapeutic Recreation

Computers have also been used to counsel patients or clients in therapeutic recreation programs. Berryman, Lefebvre, and Peterson developed systems-based methods of identifying patient or client needs and capabilities and designing individualized treatment plans. Similarly, Compton and Price developed the Linear Model for Individual Treatment in Recreation (LMIT), a detailed model for planning, implementing, and evaluating program services for individual clients. Although widespread use has not yet been made of computers in such programs, this is likely to occur in the years ahead.[20]

In addition, computers themselves are becoming part of the programs provided in some therapeutic recreation settings. Computer and video games may have considerable appeal for clients, and applications in education, rehabilitative home and work environments are useful for therapeutic recreation professionals working within a holistic framework.

Program Registration and Scheduling

Several companies have designed software specifically for use in registering, scheduling, and monitoring recreation, park, and leisure-service programs. One widely used program is CLASS (Computerized Leisure Activities System), manufactured by ESCOM, Inc., in Vancouver, Canada. This software gathers information about individuals and families that participate in agency programs. It creates class or program rosters, maintains family databases, records and analyzes revenue information, and assists in target marketing functions.

There are numerous other computer systems designed for use in leisure-service registration and related functions. Ross and Wolter analyzed six of the leading software programs in this field, in terms of the specific functions they provide and such elements as good customer service, transaction tracking capability, and ease of use by the staff. In a 1997 article for *Athletic Business*, they provided descriptive information with respect to over 125 characteristics

338

CHAPTER 10
The Controlling
Function:
Evaluation, Research,
and Management
Information Systems

In Arlington, Texas, the Parks and Recreation Department uses CLASS to process all service information: registrations, facility reservations, and usages, and a breakdown of 61,000 of the city's 122,000 households. Each household is given an identification number, and participation linked to it is sorted by geographical area, gender, age, and program interests. Overall participation data are compared each quarter with statistics from the previous year, in terms of citywide totals, service areas, and specific programs and facilities:

We compare the demographics of our program participants with the characteristics of the population in the service area. From this we can recognize gaps in service coverage. The CLASS system gives us the ability to examine service responses down to the neighborhood level. Market share can be calculated on any of the demographic variables kept by the system. Comparison to prior periods lets us know whether we are improving in delivery.[21]

CLASS also is used to calculate the retention success of programs, as individuals continue or drop out of specific activities. Its facility-usage function examines attendance or reservation levels by time and day of week, helping program planners design an optimum mix of services and revenues for any given time period.

and functions of these software programs (Fig. 10.9). in addition to the *client* and *program/activity records* shown here, the Ross/Wolter analysis includes *on-screen viewing, receipts, reports* and *printing,* and linkage with other *agency support systems.*[22]

Computer processes are widely used to show trends in spending, employee-hour assignments, and equipment condition and usage. They make it possible to integrate varied management functions conveniently, in the sense that they combine analysis of programming, facilities operations, fiscal practices, and personnel performance—thus yielding critical insights to assist managerial decision making (Fig. 10.10).

Personnel Performance

As indicated, computer software programs permit efficient and economical tracking of employee assignments, project status, and costs of all recreation and park program and maintenance functions. Edward Szillat points out that computers assist in improving employee time management, reducing clerical efforts, restricting time abuses, and bringing efficiency to human resource functioning. He writes:

Employee time management systems coordinate all facets of labor time scheduling; time clock entry; daily, weekly, and pay-period reporting. . . . Work schedules may be predetermined for up to more than one year in advance by day, week, month, or year. Advance scheduling simultaneously provides labor cost forecasts and warns of potential labor resource shortages. . . . Employee tasks, job, and location changes may be pre-scheduled or updated throughout the day as they occur, including interface and update to other integrated computer applications such as Maintenance Management and Work Order Scheduling.[23]

	A.E. Klawitter & Associates (800) 666-4AEK	Aspen Information Systems (281) 320-0343	HTE-Programmed for Success Inc. (800) 488-7374	Overtime Software Inc. (800) 467-0493	Sierra Digital Inc. (888) REC-WARE	Vermont Systems Inc. (800) 377-7427
PRODUCT NAME	AEK Recreation Registration	Visual ClubMate	Activity Registration	Registration Wizard	RecWare Activity Registration	RecTrac!
VERSION NUMBER	5	1.0	3.7	2.0	2.7	8.1
PRICE Single-user version Multi-user LAN version	$2,100 $2,300	$1,995 1st workstation, $250 add'l workstation	$4,500 $7,500	$350 1st workstation, $200 add'l workstation	$1,495 $1,995	$2,245 varies according to # of users
PLATFORM Unix, LANtastic	Windows, NT, Novell, Unix, Vax/Vms, DOS	Win95, NT	DOS	Windows 3.1 95 & NT, Novell	Windows/ Macintosh	Novell, DOS, Windows NT
LANGUAGE WRITTEN BY	Thoroughbred	Visual FoxPro V5/C++, SQL	FoxPro	Access	FoxPro	Progress
SOURCE CODE AVAILABLE	Yes	No	No	Additional fee	Yes	Yes
MULTI-USER/LAN NETWORK	Yes	Yes	Yes	Yes	Yes	Yes
HARDWARE REQUIREMENTS						
Disk space required for application Rec processor speed Recommended RAM higher	1GB 486 or higher 16MB or higher	50MB Pentium/100mhz 16MB/32MB NT	10MB 386 or higher 3MB or higher	20MB 486/33mhz 16MB	10MB 486/33mhz 8MB	30MB 486 or higher 4MB o
CLIENT RECORDS						
How many client records can be maintained in the system?	Unlimited	Unlimited	Unlimited	Unlimited	Unlimited	999,999,999
Does program: Create a client file by household? Calculate client age and check against class requirements?	Yes Yes	Yes Yes	Yes Yes	Yes Yes	Yes Yes	Yes Yes
Maintain client history of classes and check against any prerequisites for registration?	Yes	Yes	Yes/No	Yes/No	Yes	Yes
Maintain client history of liability waiver/release completion?	Yes	Yes	No	Yes	Yes	Yes
Maintain client history file with comments/notes?	Yes	Yes	No	Yes	Yes	Yes
Maintain client history file with medical data records?	Yes	Yes	No	Yes	Yes	Yes
PROGRAM/ACTIVITY RECORDS						
Does program define recreation activities by: Season? User defined categories (i.e. sports)? Level of proficiency (i.e. advanced)? Day/time? Location of program offering? Are class/activity start and end	Yes Yes Yes Yes Yes	No Yes Yes Yes Yes	Yes Yes Yes Yes Yes	Yes Yes Yes Yes Yes	Yes Yes Yes Yes Yes	Yes Yes Yes Yes Yes

RECREATION REGISTRATION SOFTWARE CHART

FIGURE 10.9. Excerpted sections of comparative analysis of six recreation software programs (Ross/Wolter).

Member Database

- Member data includes name, address, birthday, membership dates, home and work telephone numbers, and more
- Access member data by name or number, via bar codes, or keyboard
- Indicators include retired, suspended, gender, lost card frequency, handicap index, locker number, club/cart storage number, and user codes
- Determine default greens fees by membership type for time of day and day of week
- Automatically track membership dues balance, miscellaneous receivables, installment billing, number of year-to-date plays, and date/time of last play
- Restrict member payment type as applicable
- Prorate dues automatically by day or month (if desired)
- Share member data between multiusers at one or more courses
- Validate transactions against data integrity parameters
- Eight POS log-in styles by clerk (Quick, Full, Full With Inventory, Combo, Non-Member, Multi-Golfer on One Receipt, Snack Bar, Open Ticket Dining)
- Print check endorsements after POS receipt (if desired)

Point-of-Sale Cash Register

- Integrate computer, programmable keyboards, up to two cash drawers per POS unit, one or more receipt printers, report printer, optional pole displays and bar code readers
- Up to 9,999 user-defined transaction codes (sale of greens fees, membership dues, gift certificates, rentals, food, inventory items, punch-card visits, etc.)
- Automatically post transactions to user-defined general ledger codes
- Discount at four levels: global inventory sale, golfer type, transaction code, or individual inventory item
- Standard or tiered greens fee pricing (up to five time ranges within six date ranges)
- Process transactions for members, temporary players and non-member daily players

General Features

- Accommodates up to 99 golf courses
- Ten holidays with automatic holiday greens fee pricing
- Restrict play by day of week, time of day, and within minimum time period for same golfer
- Track gift certificate balances for members and non-members
- Weekday/weekend equivalent greens fees for dues analysis

FIGURE 10.10. **Golf operations. Many computer software packages are designed to serve management functions in specific areas of recreation and park activity. For example, Vermont Systems, Inc. markets RecTrac software for golf course management. In addition to functions shown above, features include clubhouse operations, course maintenance, accident reporting, income management, and league or tournament scheduling.**

At the same time that human resource management can be made more efficient through electronic data processing, check-in/check-out procedures, and other workstation controls, managers must be aware that employees cannot be reduced to the status of impersonal cogs in a machine, as in classical bureaucratic approaches. Instead, issues of work assignments, staff relationships, motivation and career planning must be dealt with through direct observation, coaching and counseling by supervisors, within a trust-based, humanistic framework.

Department Reports and Publications: Design Functions

A growing use of computers in leisure-service agencies involves so-called desktop publishing—their use in creating forms, brochures, posters, reports, and other promotional publications. As a simple example, a professional modern dance company, the José Limón Company, uses IBM PCs in combination with a WordPerfect program, a Lotus 1-2-3 spreadsheet program, and a database program, SSI, to create biographies, letters, contracts, and program copy for theaters as well as numerous other tasks concerned with touring, fund-raising, and publicity.

Computers have been used to design ski slopes and other outdoor recreation facilities, to create artistic designs ranging from posters to exposition displays, and to solve varied technical problems. Clip-art programs help to create images of animals, currency, demographics, fiscal summaries, and numerous other graphic features as part of preparing visually appealing layouts for brochures, reports, or other promotional or public relations uses.

341

CHAPTER 10
The Controlling
Function:
Evaluation, Research,
and Management
Information Systems

REALISTIC LIMITATIONS OF COMPUTERS

As this chapter has shown, electronic data processing has become an essential tool in all leisure-service operations, and especially in the development of a comprehensive, accurate, and readily accessible management information system. At the same time, some authorities have commented critically that computers are used for rather mechanical and limited functions—and that every effort should be made to use them more creatively in building imaginative new models of professional service. Indeed, the thrust toward seeing computers almost as living things, subject to viruses and actually capable of artificial intelligence, has led some professionals to see them as having a near-miraculous potential for simulating life and creating brilliant new strategies. However, although computers have remarkable capabilities, they are literally useless without human intervention and control. They can never make independent judgments, but must be programmed to make decisions according to predetermined criteria.

Beyond this, computers cannot recognize or deal meaningfully with human values, emotions, or interpersonal conditions. To the extent that recreation and park management is rooted in constructive human relations processes, electronic data processing—and, indeed, all forms of evaluation, planning, and research—must be regarded as tools and not masters. Thus, although they represent immensely valuable tools for today's leisure-service managers, computers must be employed with a realistic awareness of their actual capabilities and limitations.

Accepting this reality, computers make an immense contribution today to the related functions of evaluation, research, and management information processing.

SUMMARY

This chapter is concerned primarily with the process of evaluation as an important means of improving the performance of leisure-service agencies. It defines evaluation, and shows the need for assessing the quality of recreation organizations and determining their success in achieving their goals. Three models of agency evaluation are presented, including (1) goal-achievement; (2) participant and staff rating; and (3) standards-and-criteria approaches.

The chapter presents several examples of evaluation forms and strategies, and outlines the stages and methods used by different leisure-service organizations. After offering guidelines for evaluation of personnel, it examines the use

342

CHAPTER 10
*The Controlling
Function:
Evaluation, Research,
and Management
Information Systems*

of research as an important management tool. It broadens the concern with evaluation to the overall function of monitoring agency performance, and shows the role of management information systems. Linked to the tasks of gathering, analyzing, and interpreting various kinds of data, it shows how computers are being used increasingly in all areas of program planning and implementation, personnel management, and fiscal operations—along with specific applications in fields such as sports management or travel and tourism agencies.

The chapter concludes with a discussion of computer software programs designed for recreation, park, and leisure-service applications, and with a caution about the limitations of computers.

STUDY QUESTIONS AND CLASS PROJECTS

1. Define and compare the meaning of the following three terms: *evaluation, research,* and *monitoring.* What do they have in common, and how do they differ?
2. Break up into small groups to develop appropriate instruments to use in evaluating different types of community agencies, such as senior centers, youth sports leagues, arts and crafts centers, or environmental centers. As an alternative assignment, prepare forms to be used in evaluating personnel performance in two or three specialized fields of service.
3. Invite as a guest speaker a leisure-service manager who uses computers extensively in varied agency operations. Have this individual conduct a class workshop in computer applications related to budget and fiscal management, program registration and scheduling, or facilities.
4. Describe a hypothetical college recreation, park, and leisure-studies department, and outline the elements that would go into a total management information system drawn from this department. What kinds of information would be included, how would it be obtained and analyzed to provide a meaningful picture of the curriculum and guidelines for upgrading its quality and performance?

CHAPTER 10
*The Controlling
Function:
Evaluation, Research,
and Management
Information Systems*

Before analyzing these cases in class, review the guidelines suggested in Chapter 3 (pp. 76–77).

Case Study 10.1 — *Staff Appraisals: Rebellion in the Ranks*

YOU ARE MARY MARCUS, director and program supervisor of a youth center in a crowded area of a Midwestern city. When you took over the center several months ago, you were informed that part of your job would be to submit semiannual evaluation reports on all center staff employees—full and part-time.

Last week, you filled out evaluation forms on all personnel, based on your observation of them at work. While you gave positive ratings to most individuals, your reports on three activity leaders were negative. They had often been late for work, lacking in motivation, and sloppy in carrying out assigned tasks. As required, you gave copies of your evaluations to them to sign. Immediately, it was apparent that they resented your negative evaluations. They behaved in a hostile way toward you, and you have learned that they have begun to spread nasty rumors accusing you of financial mismanagement. As a result, the overall center staff seems to be dividing into two factions—those favorable to you, and those against.

QUESTIONS FOR CLASS DISCUSSION AND ANALYSIS

1. *Did you make a mistake in giving an honest but critical evaluation of these three employees' work? Should you simply have glossed over their negative performance, or even given them a positive report?*

2. *Based on examples given in this chapter, how could you have carried out the personnel appraisal process more effectively?*

3. *Recognizing that a problem situation has developed with these three staff members and their friends, what should you do now?*

344

CHAPTER 10
The Controlling
Function:
Evaluation, Research,
and Management
Information Systems

Case Study 10.2

Proving the Benefits of Employee Recreation

YOU ARE JO CASTAGNO AND BART SMITHERS, codirectors of a successful employee recreation and related-services program for a large Eastern manufacturing company.

With increased economic competition, the company executive officers feel they must cut down on operational expenses, including the subsidies that they give to the employee recreation association. Tentatively, they have decided to eliminate the full-time paid staff—including yourselves—and provide only facilities for self-directed activity. You both are convinced that your operation, which includes a fitness center, sports leagues, charter travel program, and special events through the year, is a valuable one for the company.

You meet with the officers of the employee recreation association to devise a plan for convincing the company officers of the value of your program. Apart from petitions or sending a delegation to the top administrators, what strategy would be effective? All agree that the most powerful argument would be convincing proof of the program's benefit in dollars-and-cents terms.

QUESTIONS FOR CLASS DISCUSSION AND ANALYSIS

1. What specific benefits do you believe your program achieves? Can you define these in quantifiable terms that can be measured?

2. Are there clues in the literature of specific outcomes of employee recreation, in terms of job productivity, reduced health costs, or improved personnel attendance, recruitment, and retention statistics?

3. Could you design an action plan to demonstrate your program's worth? How much time do you need to come up with valid findings?

345

CHAPTER 10
The Controlling
Function:
Evaluation, Research,
and Management
Information Systems

Case Study 10.3 *Program Evaluation Reports: Fact or Fiction*

YOU ARE KEITH MATSUMOTO, the deputy director of a statewide nonprofit organization serving disabled children and youth with sports, social, and other human-service programs.

One of your responsibilities is compiling an annual report of programs and participation, based on statistical data submitted by local area program directors. In one metropolitan area, reports have been submitted of special events, trip activities, counseling sessions, and other services that you believe, based on your casual observation, to be wildly inflated. To confirm your suspicions, you telephone several parents and other volunteers in the area and learn that the numbers submitted to you are totally fictitious. The area directors have simply given you false information to make their program look good and to justify a request for expanded funding.

You recognize now, as you hadn't before, that evaluation often represents a severe threat to employees whose work is being judged. As a result, the temptation to submit false reports exaggerating their program's success is all too great.

QUESTIONS FOR CLASS DISCUSSION AND ANALYSIS

1. *As the deputy director of the agency, what is your obligation, with respect to informing the executive director and advisory board of this situation?*

2. *How could the evaluation process have been made more effective to forestall this kind of false reporting?*

3. *What are the underlying causes of this problem? Suggest a plan for dealing with the causes on a statewide level in the future.*

REFERENCES

CHAPTER 10
*The Controlling
Function:
Evaluation, Research,
and Management
Information Systems*

1. Elkin, Robert, and Vorwaller, Darrel: in Ramanathan, Kavasseri, and Hegstaf, Larry: *Readings in Management Control in Nonprofit Organizations,* New York, 1982, John Wiley and Sons, p. 112.

2. Perlman, Daniel: cited in Kraus, Richard, and Allen, Lawrence: *Research and Evaluation in Recreation, Parks and Leisure Studies,* Scottsdale, Ariz., 1997, Gorsuch Scarisbrick, Publishers, p. 318.

3. Kraus and Allen. *Ibid.,* p. 276.

4. See *Agency Accreditation Visitation Procedures,* National Recreation and Park Association and American Academy for Park and Recreation Administration, 1996, 2d ed.

5. Mobley, Tony: "Accreditation Becomes of Age," *Trends* 3(3) 1993, pp. 21–25.

6. McEwen, Douglas, and Cole, David: "Campsite Impact in Wilderness Areas," *Parks and Recreation,* February 1997, pp. 24–31.

7. Scott, David, and Jackson, Edgar: "Factors That Limit and Strategies That Might Encourage People's Use of Public Parks," *Journal of Park and Recreation Administration* 14(1), Spring 1996, pp. 1–17.

8. Van Hoof, Hubert, and Verbeeten, Marja: "Tourism Research Inquiries: The Response of the State Office of Tourism," *Journal of Travel Research,* Spring 1997, pp. 75–77.

9. Crompton, John, Love, Lisa, and More, Thomas: "An Empirical Study of the Role of Recreation, Parks and Open Space in Companies (Re)Location Decisions," *Journal of Park and Recreation Administration* 15(1), Spring 1997, pp. 37–58.

10. Frisby, Wendy, Crawford, Susan, and Dorer, Therese: "Reflections on Participatory Action Research: The Case of Low-Income Women Accessing Local Public Physical Activity Services," *Journal of Sport Management,* 1997, pp. 8–28.

11. Backman, Sheila, and Veldkamp, Chris: "Examination of the Relationship between Service Quality and User Loyalty," *Journal of Park and Recreation Administration* 13(2), Summer 1995, pp. 29–41.

12. Busser, James, and Carruthers, Cynthia: "Design and Management of Recreation Programs and Services," *Parks and Recreation,* February 1996, pp. 22–29.

13. Ross, Craig, and Young, Sarah: "Research: The Key to the Future of Recreational Sports Management," *Parks and Recreation,* August 1997, pp. 25–26.

14. Witt, Peter, and Crompton, John: "The At-Risk Youth Recreation Project," *Parks and Recreation,* January 1997, pp. 54–61.

15. *Texas Quality Award,* Arlington, Tex. Department of Parks and Recreation, 1997, p. 27.

16. Naisbitt, John: *Megatrends: Ten New Directions Transforming Our Lives,* New York, 1984, Warner Books, pp. 4–5.

17. Cizek, Calvin: "In the Age of Computers—Confession and Repentance Via Modem," *Philadelphia Inquirer,* January 26, 1997, p. E-5.

18. Beeler, Cheryl: "Taking the Byte out of Micro Computers," *Parks and Recreation,* November 1984, p. 29.

19. "1994 Computer Use Institute Breaks Records," *Parks and Recreation,* June 1994, p. 36.

20. Kraus, Richard, and Shank, John: *Therapeutic Recreation Service: Principles and Practices,* Dubuque, Iowa, 1992, Wm. C. Brown, Publishers, p. 170.

21. *Texas Quality Award, op. cit.*

22. Ross, Craig, and Wolter, Stephen: "Registration Information," *Athletic Business,* October 1997, pp. 59–62.

23. Szillat, Edward: "Employee Time Management," *Parks and Recreation,* June 1995, pp. 31–33.

Eleven

The Creative Manager:
Facing the Future

There is evidence to support a direct link between creative thinking and organizational efficiency and effectiveness. Creativity also helps to improve the solutions to persistent organizational problems and has a broader role to play in an organization, since it helps to encourage profitable innovations, rekindles employee motivation and improves personal skills and team performance. . . . A continuous flow of ideas for new products and services, and for improving work processes, provides the platform upon which an organization can develop its competitive advantage.[1]

Leaders and managers of governments, public agencies of all sorts, nonprofit organizations, and communities face difficult challenges in the years ahead. Upheaval and change surround them. Consider, for example, several events and trends of the past two decades: demographic changes, shifts in values, increased interest-group activism, the privatization of public services . . . shifts in federal and state responsibilities and funding priorities, a volatile global economy, and the increased importance of the nonprofit sector. Organizations that want to survive and prosper must respond to these changes.[2]

INTRODUCTION

Having examined several critical functions of leisure-service management in depth, we now return to its most important concern—the men and women who hold key administrative and supervisory posts in recreation, park, and leisure-service agencies. What does it take to be an effective leader and provide inspiration and direction to one's organization—be it a government department, business, hospital, nonprofit agency, or private membership association?

This chapter examines the role of effective leisure-service managers, in terms of their leadership style, personal traits, philosophical values, and professional commitment. It emphasizes the important element of creativity as a key component of successful agency leadership, linked to the growing emphasis on strategic planning and agency reengineering. While the NRPA/AALR Accreditation standards focus on professional competencies rather than management traits, this chapter does address the following Accreditation standards:

Understanding of the concept of a profession and professional organization as related to leisure services (8.08).

Understanding of ethical principles and professionalism as applied to all professional practices, attitudes and behaviors in leisure services delivery (8.09).

Ability to promote, advocate, interpret, and articulate the concerns of leisure services systems for all populations and services (8.14).

Understanding of social psychology and ability to apply its principles (7C.03).

Understanding of the management role, including organizational behavior and relationships, politics of organizations, strategic planning, policy development and implementation, decision-making, cooperative problem-solving and managing conflict (7A.02).

O B J E C T I V E S

At the conclusion of this chapter, readers should be familiar with the following aspects of effective leisure-service management:

1. A clear understanding of the important personal traits possessed by managers in varied types of businesses, governmental, nonprofit, and other organizations.
2. Theories of group leadership, including problem solving and decision making, team building, policy development, and other approaches that build consensus and contribute to a high level of motivation and work accomplishment.
3. The nature of personal creativity and the importance of establishing an organizational climate that encourages creative innovation and professional practice.
4. Managers' role in helping other employees in their career advancement and identification with the overall leisure-service profession.
5. Pressures stemming from so-called practical politics, and the need to work effectively with varied community organizations with differing agendas and priorities.
6. Linked to the preceding objective, the ability to promote positive policies with respect to racial/ethnic, gender, disability, and other potentially divisive concerns, based on a sound philosophy of leisure's role in a democratic, multicultural society.
7. The need for leisure-service managers to manage their own time and energies most efficiently.
8. The ability to explore creative new directions and lead other staff members in a process of structural reengineering, in order to meet oncoming challenges in an era of rapid change.

Probably the most important function that managers in any type of organization must serve today involves the need to lead and inspire others. Chester Barnard, a noted authority on management in the 1930s, argued that the executive's role was to harness the social forces in the organization, to shape and guide values. He described good managers as "value shapers concerned with the informal social properties of organization [in contrast to] mere manipulators of formal rewards and systems, who dealt only with the narrower concept of short-term efficiency."[3]

Beyond this fundamental responsibility, leisure-service managers must inspire and motivate staff members to work at their highest level of capability. They must provide leadership in policy development, program innovation, fiscal operations, public relations, and cooperative involvement with other public and private agencies. Finally, they must strive to meet the demographic, environmental, and social challenges that will become increasingly urgent during the oncoming decades of the twenty-first century. As later sections of this chapter will show, such needs will compel many recreation and park organizations to undergo radical changes and reengineering transformation in the years ahead, and will have a major impact on the role of the leisure-service profession as a whole.

KEY LEADERSHIP RESPONSIBILITIES

Summing up, effective leisure-service managers must be able to provide vigorous and confident leadership with respect to the following kinds of organizational tasks:

1. Developing a strong and consistently expressed and enforced set of values and purpose, both with staff members and with the public at large;
2. Maintaining positive working relationships with other community organizations, or with other branches of the overall system (governmental, federation, or large institution) in which they work;
3. Acting as effective spokespersons for recreation and leisure in community life, for environmental values in terms of the use of natural resources, or for other important societal needs;
4. Promoting a high level of morale and commitment on the part of all staff members;
5. Facilitating communication of management philosophy, concerns, and priorities in a two-way exchange between upper-level executives or boards, and lower-level personnel;
6. Selecting, training, and assigning new staff members, and planning work flow, processes, and procedures; and
7. Developing appropriate performance objectives and work standards, and incorporating new technologies or program innovations into agency operations.
8. Responding to changing social conditions and community or organizational priorities through policy development and agency restructuring.

350

CHAPTER 11
The Creative
Manager:
Facing the Future

NEEDED PERSONAL QUALITIES

Numerous lists have been developed of the essential traits of individuals who are successful in various kinds of organizations and enterprises. One of the important qualities is intelligence—not simply the possession of knowledge or reasoning ability, but also what has been called "emotional intelligence," the ability to understand and control one's own emotions and respond positively to the feelings of others.

The ability to communicate well with others and to influence their thinking and gain their support is also necessary. Linked to this is the drive toward power and influence, not in the sense of wanting to be a powerful autocrat, but rather a readiness to accept responsibility and enjoy taking on difficult challenges.

Particularly in public recreation and park departments, with visibility an important concern, it is helpful for managers to be vigorous, active, and colorful and be able to project a positive and strong image for their departments. Under pressure, they must demonstrate courage, resourcefulness, intuition, and—above all—consideration. Staff and line personnel will perform at a superior level if they are following a strong and thoughtful leader. This is particularly true in moderate-size and large departments where intimate, day-to-day contacts are impossible. Charisma, a difficult-to-describe aura that surrounds exciting leaders and public figures, is simply a combination of these leadership qualities in one dynamic personage.

For new managers in particular, Arthur Freedman lists the following qualities and skills as essential:

Risk taking and assertiveness;

Counseling underperforming subordinates, and designing professional development experiences for them;

Managing conflict constructively and overcoming resistance to planned organizational change;

Controlling one's own anxieties and self-doubt, increasing tolerance for ambiguity and uncertainty, and curbing one's impatience;

Creating motivating work environments.[4]

Linked to these important qualities, within the recreation, park, and leisure-service field it is essential that managers have a sound personal philosophy of the value of recreation and leisure, along with a democratic appreciation of people of every background, and sensitivity to environmental concerns. They should also have four essential traits needed for successful agency leadership:

Human resource management authorities agree that good managers are people-centered, caring, and believe in a cooperative "win-win" leadership style, rather than a power-centered "dog-eat-dog" approach. They have a willingness to risk and to learn from errors. High-achieving managers show a high level of trust and are optimistic about their subordinates' performance, while low-achievers tend to be critical and pessimistic about subordinates.

strong self-management skills, deeply rooted ethical values, the quality of personal creativity, and the ability to build highly motivated teams of employees within their organizations.

SELF-MANAGEMENT SKILLS

One employee relations coordinator in a large Southwestern health care organization describes his typical work day as follows:

> I usually begin work at 7:00 A.M. before the rest of my department gets to the office. I have at least an hour to figure out where I'm headed and to set goals for the day. By about 8:00 A.M., I'm working on various aspects of our employee recreation and employee recognition programs. Our office also works on various institutional projects such as Houston Livestock & Rodeo, United Way, U.S. Savings Bond drive, National Hospital Week, Christmas activities, etc. In addition, we make reservations for tennis courts and institutional facilities like our picnic ground or our employee lounge. Because we work on so many different projects at one time, it is sometimes difficult to focus in on one program.
>
> When my day in the office ends, the recreational program begins. Softball and volleyball start about 5:30 P.M. and end anywhere between 7–11 P.M. I also set up golf and tennis tournaments twice a year on the weekends. Obviously, my job is not a typical 8–5 job.[5]

Not all leisure-service managers have such crowded schedules. However, many do. Too often, managers are harassed, under constant demands, and torn among conflicting priorities. They may use their time in a variety of nonessential ways, and may be plagued by overburdensome paperwork, frequent interruptions, and inadequate scheduling systems. Many managers are their own "slave-drivers," suffering from self-inflicted pressures and anxiety.

David Erickson suggests helpful guidelines for effective time management and increasing productivity:

Log how you spend your time—identifying both significant tasks and "time wasters."

Set specific, realistic objectives and write down goals in order of priority, reserving blocks of time for most important tasks.

Unclutter your desk of everything but work in progress, and keep fewer files with broader categories.

If a recreation, park, and leisure-service manager is poorly organized in terms of developing a logical set of priorities and maintaining a sensible and disciplined daily or weekly work schedule, his or her agency will also likely be inefficiently directed. However, if the manager has developed a number of sensible self-management habits, such problems can be minimized. The business management authority, Peter Drucker, suggests several key principles:

Effective managers know where their time goes, and work systematically at assigning priorities to the most important tasks. They focus on achieving results—rather than simply carrying out assorted tasks. They set priorities and focus on making good decisions, based on taking the right steps in the right sequence. To make too many decisions fast means to make the wrong decisions; what is needed are few, but fundamental, decisions.[6]

Use a daily planning calendar to plan your day, and minimize interruptions as far as possible.

Schedule meetings close to lunch or quitting time—which tends to prevent their running on unnecessarily—and reconsider staying at the office after work hours.

Learn to say "no," take occasional breaks to revive your energy, and have fun, to improve productivity.[7]

ETHICAL VALUES AND PRACTICES

Another important quality of effective managers is that they possess a sound base of ethical values, which are consistently reflected in their decisions and management practices. The kinds of ethical codes discussed earlier (see p. 219), in fields such as tourism services, sports management, or therapeutic recreation service, provide helpful direction to managers in a host of decision-making or crisis situations. In tourism, for example, Hultsman and Hermann emphasize the need to meet widely accepted industry standards and practices, such as guidelines for truth in advertising, to promote consumer confidence, and to enhance the manager's effectiveness.[8]

In the realm of college and professional sports management and fitness programming, ethical concerns play an important role. Scott Branvold writes that the belief that sport is a haven for fair play and justice is largely a romanticized ideal. He continues:

> College athletic programs are being investigated with monotonous regularity, and famous professional athletes routinely appear on magazine covers—for their deeds and exploits *off* the field rather than *on* it. Olympic athletes are banned from competition for drug use, and fitness clubs make outlandish advertising claims while using staffs of high-pressure salespeople with little or no fitness training.[9]

Similarly, Malloy and Zakus cite a Canadian government report concluding that the Canadian sport community generally lacks ethical leadership at all levels of the sport delivery system, with one administrator arguing that "sport has been taken over by TV, political expediency, and money. There are no ethics."[10]

In the diversified field of therapeutic recreation service, the standards of practice that have been developed and published by professional societies outline specific guidelines that should be followed by practitioners in varied types of settings. Those who framed the guidelines identified three ethical concerns that were particularly sensitive in terms of staff-client relationships: respect for those served, telling the truth, and confidentiality. Miriam Lahey points out that many of the ethical problems in therapeutic recreation service stem from the nature of institutional life in treatment settings, such as:

. . . lack of privacy, powerlessness, regimentation, coercion into compliance, and behavior control. Cases relating more directly to therapeutic recreation service included such issues as residents' lack of choice in activities, competing claims of different client groups, and use of recreational activities as rewards or punishments.[11]

While the pressure on high-level college and professional sports executives and coaches is tremendous, those who direct sports programs in community-based recreational leagues or other amateur settings should be able to withstand the tendency to place winning on a pedestal above all other goals.

In other areas of specialized leisure service, such as public, nonprofit, and armed forces recreation, it is important for managers not only to live up to the letter of the law, in strictly legal terms, but also to impose a high standard of moral judgment in all internal and external agency operations.

IMPORTANCE OF CREATIVITY

Another critical quality that successful managers possess is creativity. Particularly in a governmental, social, or business environment that is undergoing rapid cultural and demographic change, organizations of all kinds need to be able to respond to new challenges rapidly and creatively if they are to survive and flourish.

Rather than be limited by past traditional practices or by a conservative outlook that is afraid to risk failure, managers should be free to seek new and different solutions, and to lead their organizations in potentially groundbreaking directions. An important element in such responses is the ability of managers to think and act in imaginative and innovative ways.

Research has shown that possessing creative ability is an essential asset for any leader. Tony Proctor writes:

> Creative leaders hunt actively for new problems and are especially successful in handling new challenges that demand solutions outside the routine of orthodox strategies. They often possess significant vision and are able to inspire others by their creative talents. Creativity is an important human resource and all organizations [should] make use of this resource by devising settings in which creative talents are permitted to thrive.[12]

Creative thinking, which lies at the heart of creative management, involves two kinds of thought processes: *divergent* and *convergent*. Divergent thinking involves beginning with a specific problem or management concern, and generating various perspectives on it—without being limited by rules, "practical" constraints, or past policies. Convergent thinking is used to screen and narrow down the possible perspectives or solutions to a problem, in order to identify the most promising course of action.

Too often, creativity has been thought of as a rare quality, found chiefly in great artists or scientific geniuses. The reality is that all people possess varying degrees of creativity, and that it represents an important ingredient in on-the-job performance—particularly in situations requiring ingenious solutions to problems.

Establishing a Climate to Encourage Creativity

While creativity is usually regarded as an individual's personal trait, it is often heavily influenced by the culture and climate of the organization in which he or she works. Taken together, these terms refer to the shared values, social structures, and goals of organizations, along with the policies, practices, and work-related behaviors that provide a setting for management decision making. The manager's creative role is therefore part of a two-way process, in which the organization's climate and culture affect his or her ability to perform innovatively, but in which he or she is able to promote creative contributions on the part of other staff members.

In an analysis of the factors that promote creativity, de Alencar and Bruno-Faria identified ten important conditions, including the following:

Challenges—Challenging tasks or missions that require the expression of the creative potential;

Colleagues' support—Dialogue and reliance among the work group; interpersonal relationships which favor and stimulate new ideas;

Freedom and autonomy—Freedom to decide how to perform the tasks, with autonomy to make decisions when necessary;

Organizational structure—Limited number of hierarchies, flexible norms, power decentralization;

Organizational support—Recognition and support to the creative work in the organization; availability of mechanisms to develop new ideas.[13]

Limitations on Creative Action

In contrast, environmental obstacles to creative performance include such factors as managers who are not receptive to new ideas or who are distant from their subordinates; lack of training or needed equipment or material resources; an organizational culture that does not encourage risk taking; and task overload, time pressures, and repetitive and overly routine work assignments.

Realistically, although managers may be able to develop highly creative solutions or courses of action to solve agency problems, they may not always be able to put them into effect. Even when they are at a high administrative level, managers may be subject to the authority of other individuals or groups that may veto their plans. For example, a recreation and park superintendent in a large city must normally be responsible to a mayor, city manager, or city council, and political pressures may constrain his or her freedom to act independently.

Within a large, national youth federation, policies established by a national advisory council or by national officers may prevent the director of a local or regional unit from acting freely. In other settings, such as the armed forces or company personnel departments, similar constraints may prevail. Often they result from the legal authority or mandate that governs an agency, or the formal structure within which managers must operate. It is essential, therefore, to understand that within the *informal* structure—the real way in which, day by day, individuals relate to each other and carry out their work—the manager's leadership style may be critical in helping staff members achieve their highest possible level of productive performance.

EFFECTIVE LEADERSHIP STYLES

355

CHAPTER 11
The Creative
Manager:
Facing the Future

As Chapter 7 points out, the leadership style that has been most widely advocated in the human resource management literature in recent years has emphasized a high degree of participatory or shared decision making, along with policies that empower employees on all levels through delegation of significant responsibilities.

Through the years, social psychologists have explored different leadership approaches in work, recreation, and social settings. At first, they identified two primary styles: *autocratic* or authoritarian, and *laissez-faire,* or permissive. These were viewed as two extremes of a continuum, as shown in a widely used model of management styles in decision making (Fig. 11.1). Later researchers added a third style—*democratic* or *participatory*—concluding that in most situations this approach was more effective in motivating group members and achieving a high level of group morale and productivity.[14]

Situational Leadership

Other authorities argue that leadership styles vary greatly from setting to setting and that it is not appropriate to categorize them as "either-or." Instead, the demands of a particular situation call for specific skills or leadership tactics.

FIGURE 11.1.   Continuum of management styles in decision making.[15]

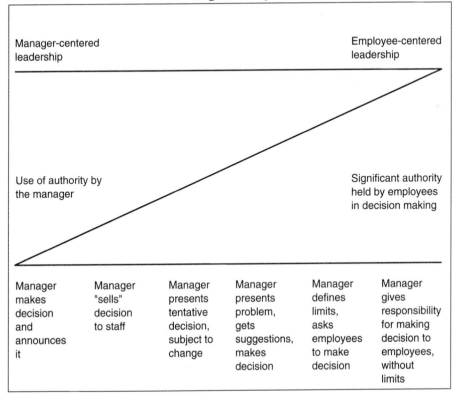

Manager-centered leadership					Employee-centered leadership
Use of authority by the manager					Significant authority held by employees in decision making
Manager makes decision and announces it	Manager "sells" decision to staff	Manager presents tentative decision, subject to change	Manager presents problem, gets suggestions, makes decision	Manager defines limits, asks employees to make decision	Manager gives responsibility for making decision to employees, without limits

Many leaders focus primarily on task-accomplishment, while other are chiefly concerned with providing socioemotional support. Still others employ varying combinations of directive and supportive behavior, with the demands of the work situation influencing the best choice of leadership styles.

In recent years, the context of leadership has changed in many large business, governmental, or social agencies. McGill and Slocum argue that whatever the setting, today followers are more sophisticated, tasks more complex, and the effects of decisions to allocate priorities or reengineer organizations more critical. They continue:

> Consistent with this new context, new models of leadership have emerged—models that are "non-positional," team based, or empowering. These new models call for new leader behaviors. Leaders who act as coaches, stewards, servants, or partners are seen as dramatically different from the leaders of old who used the power of their position and/or their persona to exert their influence.[16]

Working with New Team Structures

As part of such new approaches or organizational leadership, traditional lines of responsibility are often bypassed to create new and more flexible team arrangements. Typically, in matrix approaches to job roles (see page 000), individual and group functions may shift as different assignments are undertaken. Murphy and coauthors write:

> For example, if there is a special arts event and an employee is assigned responsibility for it, she may coordinate the work of other staff members. When another event takes place, she may not have any authority. Those in the matrix usually have certain basic tasks, but their level of involvement and responsibility may vary by work assignment.[17]

In many organizations today, relatively independent work teams are formed as part of this new approach to flexible work assignments. Such teams tend to have a high degree of autonomy in carrying out their functions. Often they develop their own internal leadership. Particularly as individuals are brought together with different skills and levels of authority or job titles, it is essential for them to develop mutual trust and openness, shared values, and goals, and cooperation in problem solving and decision making.

As an example of work team approaches in public leisure-service agencies, the Arlington, Texas, Parks and Recreation Department relies heavily on both temporary and continuing work units in various areas of agency functioning. For example, each staff member has a specifically designed job involving both his or her work assignment and geographical location. Individuals are assigned to work teams, which are responsible for a defined area of agency functioning, based on these factors. There are three levels in the organization: direct service provider, business unit manager, and top administration:

The business unit concept allows each manager to pursue operations as if it were [his/her] own business. A direct line of accountability exists between the manager and the results of the business unit. . . . The units are managed with a high degree of participation between employees and the manager. Annual surveys track the attitudes of employees toward their supervisory system. Problem-solving is done within units, with team formation based on those in the process and with the most knowledge to contribute.[18]

bers are able to take responsibility for their work, monitor their own performance, alter their performance strategies as needed to solve problems, and
adapt to changing conditions. This approach to organizational structure is believed to enhance the organization's success because it puts employees who are
closest to the "firing line" of direct service in charge of their own operations,
and strengthens their commitment to the overall enterprise.

Empowerment of Staff Members

The ultimate goal of such team-building approaches is to encourage empowerment in the agency's workforce. This term describes the process through which
staff members are helped to become more confident and cooperative risk takers
with a strong sense of commitment to the organization and its goals. Quinn and
Spreitzer describe four characteristics most empowered people tend to share:

Empowered people have a sense of *self-determination* (this means that they
are free to choose how to do their work; they are not micro-managed).

Empowered people have a sense of *meaning* (they feel that their work is important to them; they care about what they are doing).

Empowered people have a sense of *competence* (this means that they are
confident about their ability to do their work well; they know they can
perform).

Finally, empowered people have a sense of *impact* (this means that people
believe they can have influence on their work unit; others listen to their
ideas).[19]

CAREER DEVELOPMENT AS MANAGEMENT CONCERN

An important element in the manager's leadership style involves his or her concern about the career goals and progress of subordinate employees. Obviously,
career development is heavily affected by agency hiring, transfer, and promotion policies, and by the criteria used in measuring the work of staff members as
a basis for making personnel decisions.

However, it also depends on the manager's counseling role in helping employees develop positive
career goals, recognize their own strengths and
weaknesses, and evolve constructive plans for job
advancement or change. In part, this process is a
function of professional societies that assist their
members in their career planning. For example, the
National Therapeutic Recreation Society offers
numerous workshops and conferences designed to
promote professional growth and publishes handbooks focusing on career development. In the
field of sport management, organizations like the
National Association for Sport and Physical Education carry out similar functions, and numerous
textbooks and research journals analyze career opportunities and provide guidance to those entering
this field.

Beyond such aids, the challenge for leisure-service managers is to strengthen the long-range commitment of their employees by encouraging them to be *career*-oriented, rather than just day-by-day, *job*-oriented. Farren and Young write:

> Managers must be prepared to function as mentors and coaches in the process of career development. By participating in the career planning of employees, organizations can provide a long-range perspective that will enable workers to seize control of their futures, with a resulting increase in productivity and creativity. Workers who are focused on the future can forge partnerships with their employers by aligning their career goals with the strategic aims of the organization.[20]

When this happens, "job-hopping," rapid turnover, or poor work habits tend to be reduced, and managers have an easier task in working with employees who are enthusiastic and self-motivated. Specific ways in which managers can help facilitate their subordinates' career development include the following: (1) reviewing and discussing promotional and career opportunities with them; (2) assisting subordinates in professional development planning; (3) providing internal training opportunities and valuable job assignments; and (4) encouraging involvement in external seminars, courses, or other continuing education experiences and involvements.

Encouraging membership in professional organizations and societies, whether on a national, regional, or state or provincial level, is an important part of employees' career development. Many references to such organizations in both the United States and Canada are found throughout this text.

THE MANAGER AS MANAGER— THE BUCK STOPS HERE

While the participatory management style emphasized in this chapter and throughout this text represents both the wave of the present and the future, in terms of achieving maximum staff motivation and output, it *can* be carried too far, if the manager abdicates his or her responsibility for making key decisions or exerting strong leadership when necessary. Chris Bergonzi points out that many well-intentioned managers, seeking to create an "enlightened," democratic workplace, have become relentlessly collaborative to the point of paralysis. He writes:

> No decision is too small to involve everyone—call a meeting, talk it over, take a vote, ask for feedback, reevaluate. Decisions often never get made, or they get made poorly, or too late, because collaboration is being confused with democracy, and in the process managers are losing sight of their ultimate obligation to all concerned to make a decision.[21]

Apart from the confusion or inefficiency that may result from participatory management that is carried to an extreme, the reality is that the ultimate success of organizations is the responsibility of managers. In the words of former President Harry Truman, "the buck stops here." In the long run, then, managers must sometimes make difficult or unpopular decisions or take action opposed by subordinate employees. In a systematic study of successful business executives, Phil Leggiere reports that the social skills displayed by these leading managers often have a hard, strategic edge:

> They read people and social situations very well, and use that ability to orchestrate support of their goals. They are adroit consensus builders, savvy negotiators and superb motivators. Interestingly, they strive to avoid complexity and instead articulate a clear, simple focus that tends to make others perceive them as decisive. Though they are not in love with change for its own sake, they are flexible if they perceive flexibility as a means to an end, which tends to make other perceive them as risk-taking and visionary.[22]

Meeting the Challenge of "Practical Politics"

In many cases, leisure-service managers are confronted by conflict situations involving sharply opposed community groups or value systems. These managers must be able to meet the challenge set by practical politics, either in a governmental situation or in the voluntary, therapeutic, or other type of agency in which they hold responsibility. The term *practical politics* may be interpreted in various ways. To some, it refers to the need to deal with political officials, neighborhood organizations, legislators, or state and federal departments in constructive and professionally sound ways to gain support for the department. To others, it suggests that the department head sacrifices professional ideals to the demands or pressures of harassed politicians.

If they are too expedient, "practical politics" players are likely to be losers in the long run. Recreation and park managers who yield to political pressures at every turn, hire strictly on the basis of party affiliation, and give top priority to those neighborhoods and residents who vote "right" are not true professionals. They cannot provide a full measure of service to the overall community, tend to be regarded as politically partisan, and are subject to swift dismissal when elections bring a turnover in party power.

In other types of leisure-service agencies, although political parties may not be involved, other factional pressures or interpersonal conflicts may create problems for managers. Board members or trustees may seek to influence hiring decisions or other business relationships in favor of their friends or relatives. As previous chapters have shown, hiring standards in recreation and parks are often ambiguous or lack strong professional criteria. To improve the work of their departments and strengthen professionalism within the recreation and park field, managers, both as individuals and through their professional societies, must give full support to processes such as certification, registration, and accreditation that will ensure a higher caliber of individuals at work in the field.

To be respected and maintain their credibility, recreation and park managers must consistently meet commitments and back up statements, promises, or threats, whether made in public or private; act in predictable rather than irrational or "on-again, off-again" ways; follow a legitimate and carefully articulated philosophy of recreation and public service; and encourage the airing and sharing of dissent.

The Manager as Activist/Advocate

Beyond these guidelines for personal action, Sessoms urges recreation, park, and leisure-service professionals to participate more fully in the *determination* of public policies that affect their field. He suggests that, traditionally, they have responded to, rather than influenced, the public's decisions regarding its recreational needs and interests and the kinds of systems needed to meet these. Sessoms argues:

> Public policy decisions are made by elected and appointed officials who re-spond to political process, but their decisions include the input of recreation professionals. . . .
>
> The role of activist, facilitator and advocate should not be entered into lightly. It requires sensitivity to the political process, a willingness to stand on principle, and the belief in the importance of the recreation experience and the necessity of the recreation delivery service system.[23]

Such areas of public concern as protecting the environment, providing op-portunities for persons with disabilities, or combating violence and substance abuse among the young provide obvious opportunities for leisure-service man-agers to play a significant activist/advocate role in community life.

LEISURE SERVICES IN THE TWENTY-FIRST CENTURY

All of the needed qualities and skills of effective leisure-service management that have been presented in this chapter will be put to the test in the years immediately ahead. As Chapter 1 points out, the twenty-first century will be marked by numerous social, economic, and environmental changes that will pose both challenges and opportunities for recreation, park, and leisure-service professionals.

What will these changes be?

First, it should be clearly understood that forecasting is *not* an exact sci-ence, and no authority can predict with absolute certainty the changes that are likely to occur in the opening decades of the new century. Cummings and Busser point out that forecasting consists of making informed judgments about the future and making use of varied sources of data and methods of analysis. These include the views of experts, survey findings, extension of past trends, regression analysis, and complex combinations of other analytical and statisti-cal techniques.[24]

Utilizing such methods, social scientists specializing in "futurology" have made predictions about the world to come, such as:

1. The emergence of an "interactive society," in which the sophisticated elec-tronic processing of information becomes a primary tool in business, gov-ernment affairs, entertainment and other aspects of daily life;
2. The creation of other forms of new technology which will transform health care, communication, farming and manufacturing, education and energy production;

3. The globalization of the business world, with a consequent breakdown of barriers among nations, and competition for new markets and products;
4. Increased emphasis on a high level of education required for many areas of employment; linked to this, a growing gap between the rich and poor within and among nations;
5. As part of growing cultural diversity, feminization of many institutions with resulting shifting of value structures, and emergence of a "mosaic" society in which past racial/ethnic minorities become the majority;
6. Environmental issues gaining international prominence and becoming a major governmental concern; and
7. Blurring of work and leisure functions, with more home-based employment, resulting in more isolation and need for fuller social and community involvement.[25]

TRENDS AFFECTING LEISURE-SERVICE ORGANIZATIONS

In addition to these predictions, other trends that will directly affect leisure services are likely to include the following:

The steadily increasing aging population, the impact of electronic forms of play, the commodification of sport and the growing fascination with "extreme" physical recreation activities;

Increased privatization of public services, along with expanded use of partnerships among various types of agencies, including business, nonprofit, private and educational organizations;

Growing variety and sophistication in recreation programming with shifts in emphasis that directly respond to demographic changes, such as Club Méditerranée's new focus on family groups—as opposed to earlier, "swinging," young adult clientele;

Greater emphasis on two contrasting service models—the marketing, entrepreneurial approach and the socially oriented, human-service model—with the benefits-based approach used to incorporate both thrusts;

Greater efforts to bridge the gap between leisure "haves" and "have-nots," both in terms of those with greater or lesser amounts of free time, and those with varying economic capability to enjoy recreation;

Growing concern about promoting family stability and offering alternatives to morally questionable leisure pursuits—including substance abuse, gambling dependency or commercialized and exploitative sex—will also offer challenges to leisure-service managers in the future;

Stronger efforts to link the recreation and park profession with environmental organizations, with promotion of such programming thrusts as "eco-tourism;"

Increased emphasis on meeting the needs of over 45 million persons with disability, in both separate and integrated settings—along with promotion of recreation and leisure as an important source of personal wellness; and

Finally, the need to achieve fuller public awareness of the value of recreation, parks and leisure services as a key contributor to community well-being, along with respect for it as an increasingly unified field of professional service.[26]

Underlying many of these trends and challenges is the reality that organized recreation, park, and leisure services must offer more than fun and games—particularly in public, nonprofit, military, and therapeutic settings. Instead, they must strive to provide significant programs and services that improve personal and community health and well-being. Carter, Keller, and Beck stress that in so doing, leisure-service managers should form alliances with other community service organizations. They write:

> If we refocus our mission and leadership to address common social issues, we can ally professionally with other community change agents. These alliances result in safety nets that ensure service continuity to increasingly limited resources. We must take a stand along with those health and human services agencies in our communities to contribute to the betterment of our citizens and enhancement of [overall] community welfare.[27]

Accompanying such challenges will be the continuing need to upgrade "best practices" and institute "quality management," customer- or participant-centered organizational approaches. Hultsman and Colley argue that recreation and park management in the twenty-first century will call for changing patterns of leadership and organizational philosophy, with professionals on all levels adopting new roles and on-the-job strategies. Leaders and managers, they write, will become customer advocates, facilitators of internal processes, strategic thinkers, breakers of barriers, coach/mentors for employees, and role models for those employees ascending career ladders. At the same time, Hultsman and Colley continue:

> . . . employees will take on roles as team players, problem solvers, decision makers, skilled professionals, organizational resources for superiors, and trainer/mentors for subordinates and new employees.
>   Successful organizations will be fast to respond to trends and evolving customer needs, flexible in the way they perform and adapt to change, flatter in terms of organizational structure, and obsessed with continuous improvement. Organizational success in the 21st Century will depend on increases in mission performance, operating performance, and mission performance.[28]

STRATEGIC PLANNING AND REENGINEERING

Of all the important qualities that will be needed by recreation, park, and leisure-service managers in meeting the challenges of the twenty-first century, one of the most critical will be the ability to provide leadership in the processes of strategic planning and reengineering.

As described in Chapter 2, strategic planning consists of more than simply outlining a detailed sequence of actions that needed to be taken. Instead, Smith, Bucklin Associates point out, a good strategic plan determines the direction for the organization, providing managers and the entire work team with the guidelines to:

Establish the organization's mission, goals and program of internal and external activities;

Allocate human and financial resources and links with other agencies, to accomplish these activities;

Assess whether goals and objectives are being met; and

Systematically evaluate programs, staff, and resources, and provide a basis for establishing new priorities, policies and projects.[29]

Seen in this light, strategic planning is essential for organizations striving to flourish in a rapidly changing environment. The process itself requires a fundamental change both in the structure and the operational philosophy and style of organizations, as shown in Figure 11.2.

Often, strategic planning results in organizations' developing new priorities and images for themselves, as illustrated in Figure 11.3, which shows the new emphasis of the Boy Scouts of America on serving diverse populations—including females.

Resistance to Change

It must be recognized that radical changes in the way any agency does business will not always be welcomed—and indeed may be actively resisted. When faced by the need to develop new missions and goals, to make fundamental changes in operational practices, or to learn new skills, many individuals are likely to have the following kinds of reactions. They may lose confidence in the organization and its management, becoming suspicious and looking for hidden motives. They may resent new or expanded workloads, or having to adjust to new agency policies. As a result, they may become overly cautious and cynical, unwilling to take risks, and feeling pessimistic or uncertain about the future. Overall, if not properly developed and introduced, strategic planning may have serious negative effects on staff morale and performance.

FIGURE 11.2. Traditional and strategic planning contrasts.[30]

Traditional	Strategic
1. Emphasis on stability and efficiency	Dynamic and change-oriented; willing to risk failure
2. Creates blueprint for future decisions	Vision of future guides today's decisions
3. Reactive	Proactive
4. Inaction in face of ambiguity	Action-oriented, even in face of ambiguity
5. Internal focus	External focus
6. Relies on tried and tested	Emphasizes innovation and creativity
7. Fixed, lock-step process	Ongoing, changing process
8. Facts and quantitative measurement emphasized	Less tangible and qualitative factors emphasized

FIGURE 11.3.   Cover of Strategic Planning Report, Boy Scouts of America.

For such reasons, the initial step in developing a strategic planning process involves examining the agency's present *culture*—that is, its expectations, language, motivations, norms, relationships, and daily practices, summed up in the phrase, "the way we do things here." Achieving such an understanding will enable managers and staff members to develop a realistic set of expectations for the planning process and the extent to which it can or should involve radical, abrupt changes.

Steps in Strategic Planning Process

John Bryson identifies ten important steps in strategic planning for public and nonprofit organizations:

1. Initiate and agree upon a strategic planning process;
2. Identify organizational mandates;
3. Clarify organizational mission and values;
4. Assess the organization's external and internal environments to identify strengths, weaknesses, opportunities, and threats;
5. Identify the strategic issues facing the organization;
6. Formulate strategies to manage these issues;
7. Review and adopt the strategic plan or plans;
8. Reestablish an effective organizational vision;
9. Develop an effective implementation process; and
10. Reassess strategies and the strategic planning process.[31]

Implementation of the Plan

It is important that strategic planning be visionary—but also realistic—and that it results in concrete recommendations that *can* be carried out, and that achieve the agency's goals. To accomplish this, it should be accompanied by an operational plan for its implementation, which includes the following:

Specific tactics and tasks. Detailed statements of what should be done, both internally and externally, to achieve the organization's strategic objectives.

Time lines. Flow charts or other schedules that specify the dates when each element of the strategic plan should be carried out or completed.

Assigned responsibilities. Clear statements of which individuals or project teams will be assigned responsibility for carrying out each task.

Required resources. The elements that will be needed, including fiscal resources, staff time and capability, interagency support, public cooperation, or other elements required to carry out each task.

Anticipated outcomes and evaluation measures. The positive outcomes to be achieved by the plan, and the techniques or criteria that will be used to measure its success.[32]

Examples of Strategic Planning

A number of major recreation, park, and leisure-service organizations have conducted strategic planning studies over the past decades, some of them dealing with projected changes during the 1990s, and others extending into the twenty-first century. For example, the U.S. Bureau of Land Management developed a set of priorities for the year 2000, which included such strategies as upgrading visitor information and interpretation services, monitoring environmental protection, improving access to scattered or fragmented public land, developing partnerships with volunteer groups, and working effectively with tourism organizations and the travel industry.

The U.S. Forest Service initiated a National Recreation Strategy that involved major corporations in special projects promoting recreational forest uses. Typically, McDonald's, the huge fast-food chain, assisted managers of the Lassen National Forest in Northern California in providing camping programs for seriously ill children, through its Golden Arches Association.

In Canada, the major federal outdoor resource agency, Parks Canada, developed a National Business Plan for the years from 1995 to 2000 to reorganize its internal structure and develop fuller revenue-yielding services, including a new operational efficiencies and experimentation with "employee takeovers." Similarly, in the mid-1990s, the Canadian Parks/Recreation Association initiated a new strategic management plan to build strong, effective partnerships, emphasize a benefits-based approach, provide stronger public and policy influence, and create new membership structures and governance models.

Numerous public recreation and park agencies have developed strategic planning studies on the local level. In Long Beach, California, for example, a 1997 strategic plan laid out new priorities for short- and long-range outdoor resource development, recreational services, and department operations. In another California community, San Mateo, a mid-1990s' reengineering progress report outlined a set of new management strategies designed to upgrade agency technological equipment and procedures, "customer convenience" practices, and program offerings and participation.

Similarly, national youth-serving and other nonprofit leisure-service organizations have developed comprehensive strategic plans designed to strengthen their operations at the brink of the twenty-first century. In some cases, such plans have involved major shifts in program missions, or in agency structures. In the *1995–1999 Strategic Plan* of the Boy Scouts of America, national and regional offices were consolidated for greater efficiency, new Electronic Publishing, Relationships and Supply Divisions set in motion, other policies defined to promote endowment growth of local councils and enhance Boy Scout public relations—along with a reaffirmed emphasis on an Urban Emphasis program designed to target the special needs of minority urban youth.

The Need to Reengineer

The term *reengineering* is frequently applied to the process that follows such strategic planning studies. In simple terms, it refers to the transformation of agencies needed to carry out the changes that have been identified.

In many cases, reengineering will require not only new roles, staff relationships, or operational procedures but also new values and forms of commitment that will be necessary if planning goals are to be achieved. The effective teams described earlier in this chapter, along with empowerment of staff members, creative problem-solving processes, and other changes can only be realized if all members in the organization have a part in planning and decision making and accept its outcomes.

In some cases, reengineering may be needed to deal with radical shifts in an organization's role and source of support—as in the entire Morale, Welfare and Recreation system in the armed forces during the mid- and late 1990s as a result of military downsizing.

Example of Restructuring:
Vancouver Parks and Recreation

As an example of the radical restructuring that has taken place in many leisure-service agencies, the organization of the Vancouver, British Columbia, Canada Parks and Recreation Department has shifted from a relatively simple structure concerned primarily with divisions responsible for zoos, works and buildings, grounds construction and maintenance, supervised recreation, and similar functions to a much more sophisticated administrative plan.

In the present Vancouver organizational structure (see p. 28), emphasis is placed on such major thrusts as "planning and development," "environment and operations," "administrative and revenue services," "corporate services," "systems and research," and "human resource" operations. Clearly, such new agency divisions reflect a major transformation of the department, designed to meet changing community needs and opportunities as creatively and systematically as possible.

If managers are to be successful in such situations, they must be able not only to envision creative new strategies but also to gain support for them within their organizations and the environment in which they exist. They must be able to deal intelligently with organizational and environmental constraints, in order to overcome entrenched thinking and confront inertia and resistance.

Cynthia Hardy describes the skills that business leaders must have to galvanize an organization and its members into action:

> What exactly do these skills comprise? They involve being able to manage people and understanding organizational politics. They incorporate team building, leadership, and spanning organizational and departmental boundaries. Managers, in addition to having analytic skills, must also possess interpersonal and leadership skills; be able to integrate across functions; adopt a global perspective; be capable of managing technology; and have a sense of social responsibility.[33]

As recreation, park, and leisure-service managers and managers-to-be move into the twenty-first century, such personal and professional qualities will be more and more in demand within all types of agencies in the United States and Canada. In acquiring them, individuals on every level should recognize that management skills and leadership traits are *not* inborn, but can be developed throughout one's career—from one's first part-time, volunteer, or seasonal job, to the point of retirement.

SUMMARY

Managers in all types of leisure-service organizations have important roles to play in promoting and guiding their agencies' ongoing operations, in terms of policy development, fiscal and personnel management, and other vital functions. This chapter describes these leadership responsibilities and the interpersonal skills and qualities needed to carry them out successfully. It discusses principles of effective time management, the role of ethical values and practices, and the ability to think and act creatively. While emphasizing the importance of maintaining a democratic, participative framework for planning and decision making, this chapter stresses the need for managers to *be* managers in terms of operating within a political climate and making hard decisions when necessary. Other important priorities include the need to empower staff members, assist them in career development, and build effective teams.

The chapter concludes with a discussion of the major social, demographic, economic, and environmental changes that are predicted to lie ahead. The role of strategic planning and reengineering of agency structures and practices in meeting these oncoming challenges is presented. The reader should note that, while no case studies are offered, the following study questions and class exercises provide the opportunity to relate the principles found in this final chapter to real situations.

STUDY QUESTIONS AND CLASS EXERCISES

1. Identify an effective manager you have known and complete a personality profile on this individual, emphasizing his or her qualities that led to on-the-job effectiveness or professional success. Share these profiles in class discussion and identify the key elements that appear most frequently.
2. Examine your own life, including study and work involvements, from an "effective self-management" perspective. Recognizing that you face the same challenges that agency managers do in planning, organizing, motivating, and controlling your time and work output, identify your strengths and weaknesses, and define specific objectives or guidelines that will help you become more effective.
3. This chapter presents several important challenges that will face leisure-service managers in the years ahead. These relate to the need for innovative programming, functioning within a political environment, and promoting public understanding of recreation as a vital community service. How might you prepare yourself for dealing with such problems as a leisure-service manager?
4. The chapter discusses strategic planning and reengineering as currently popular management approaches. Define these terms, and give examples of how they might be applied in an educational or leisure-service organization you are familiar with.

REFERENCES

1. Proctor, Tony: *The Essence of Management Creativity,* New York, 1995, Prentice-Hall, p. 2.
2. Bryson, John: *Strategic Planning for Public and Nonprofit Organizations,* San Francisco, 1995, Jossey-Bass Publishers, p. 3.
3. Peters, Thomas, J., and Waterman, Robert H., Jr.: *In Search of Excellence: Lessons from American's Best-Run Companies,* New York, 1982, Warner Books, p. 6.
4. Freedman, Arthur, in Ritvo, Roger, Litwin, Anne, and Butler, Lee: *Managing in the Age of Change,* Burr Ridge, Ill., 1995, NTL Institute and Irwin Professional Publishing, p. 11.

5. "Member Success Profile—Pud Bellek," in *Employee Service Management*, September 1991, pp. 12–13.

6. Drucker, Peter: *The Executive in Action*, New York, 1996, Harper Business, pp. 547–48.

7. Erickson, David: "How to Get Nine Hours of Work into an Eight-Hour Day," *Parks and Recreation*, September 1996, p. 22.

8. Hultsman, John, and Hermann, Carol: "Ethics for Leisure Professionals and the Leisure Profession," *Journal of Applied Recreation Research* 20(2), 1995, pp. 125–40.

9. Branvold, Scott, in Parkhouse, Bonnie: *The Management of Sport: Its Foundation and Application*, St. Louis, 1996, National Association for Sport and Physical Education and C.V. Mosby, p. 150.

10. Malloy, David, and Zakus, Dwight: "Ethical Decision-Making in Sport Administration: A Theoretical Inquiry into Substance and Form," *Journal of Sport Management*, 1995, p. 36.

11. Lahey, Miriam: "The Emerging Ethics Agenda in Therapeutic Recreation," *Journal of Applied Recreation Research* 20(2), 1995, pp. 109–24.

12. Proctor, *op. cit.*, p. 2.

13. de Alencar, Eunice Soriano, and Bruno-Faria, Maria: "Characteristics of an Organizational Environment Which Stimulates and Inhibits Creativity," *Journal of Creative Behavior* 31(4), 4th Quarter 1997, pp. 273–74.

14. Jordan, Debra: *Leadership in Leisure Services: Making a Difference*, State College, Pa., 1996, Venture Publishing, for fuller discussion of leadership theory.

15. Diagram modified from Tannenbaum, R., and Schmitt, W.H.: *Harvard Business Review*, March/April 1958, p. 9.

16. McGill, Michael, and Slocum, John: "A *Little* Leadership, Please?" *Organizational Dynamics*, Winter 1998, p. 40.

17. Murphy, James, Niepoth, E. William, Jamieson, Lynn, and Williams, John: *Leisure Systems: Critical Concepts and Applications*, Champaign, Ill., 1991, Sagamore Publishing.

18. "High Performance Work Systems," in *Texas Quality Award*, Arlington, Tex., 1997, p. 21.

19. Quinn, Robert, and Spreitzer, Gretchen: "The Road to Empowerment: Seven Questions Every Leader Should Consider," *Organizational Dynamics*, Autumn, 1997, p. 41.

20. Farren, Caela, and Young, Marc: "The Manager's Role in Career Development: Linking Employee Aspirations and Organizational Aims," in Ritvo, Roger, et al., *op. cit.*, p. 99.

21. Bergonzi, Chris: "Autocrats Anonymous," *Continental Magazine*, November 1997, p. 26.

22. Leggiere, Phil: "Executive Edge: Sweating the Soft Stuff," *Continental Magazine*, November 1997, p. 45.

23. Sessoms, H. Douglas: "The Recreational Experience: Public Awareness and Public Policy," *Journal of Physical Education, Recreation and Dance/Leisure Today*, October 1986, p. 17.

24. Cummings, Leslie, and Busser, James: "Forecasting in Recreation and Park Management: Need, Substance and Reasonableness," *Journal of Park and Recreation Administration* 12(1), Spring 1994, pp. 35–50.

25. Benveniste, Guy: *The Twenty-First Century Organization*, San Francisco, 1994, Jossey-Bass Publishers, pp. xv–xviii.

26. See Mobley, Tony, and Toalson, Robert, eds.: *Parks and Recreation in the 21st Century*, Arlington, Va., 1992, National Symposium Committee and NRPA, pp. 11–21, for fuller discussion of key professional trends.

27. Carter, Marcia, Keller, M. Jean, and Beck, Teresa: "A Vision for Today: Recreation and Leisure Services," *Parks and Recreation*, November 1996, p. 49.

28. Hultsman, John, and Colley, James: "Park and Recreation Management for the 21st Century," *Journal of Park and Recreation Administration* 13(2), Summer 1995, p. 6.

29. Smith, Bucklin Associates: *The Complete Guide to Nonprofit Management*, New York, 1994, John Wiley and Sons, p. 2.

30. Adapted from Schwartz, Michael, and Burelle, Timothy, in Smith, Bucklin, *ibid.*, p. 3.

31. Bryson, John, *op. cit.*, p. 23.

32. Smith, Bucklin, *op. cit.*, pp. 25–26.

33. Hardy, Cynthia: *Managing Strategic Action*, Thousand Oaks, Calif., 1994, Sage Publications, p. 1.

Bibliography

Anderson, Alan: *Effective Personnel Management*, Oxford, England, 1994, Blackwell Publishing.

Appenzeller, Herb: *Managing Sports and Risk Management Strategies*, Durham, N.C., 1993, Carolina Academic Press.

Austin, David: *Therapeutic Recreation: Processes and Techniques*, Champaign, Ill., 1996, Sagamore Publishing.

Baier, John L., and Strong, Thomas S., editors: *Technology in Student Affairs*, State College, Pa., 1994, ACPA Media Board, Pennsylvania State University.

Bainbridge, Collin, *Designing for Change: A Practical Guide to Business Transformation*, New York, 1996, John Wiley and Sons.

Bannon, Joseph J., and Busser, James A.: *Problem Solving in Recreation and Parks*, Champaign, Ill., 1992, Sagamore Publishing.

Beaumont, P. B.: *Human Resource Management*, Thousand Oaks, Calif., 1993, Sage Publications.

Benveniste, Guy: *The Twenty-First Century Organization*, San Francisco, 1994, Jossey-Bass Publishers.

Bryson, John M.: *Strategic Planning for Public and Nonprofit Organizations*, San Francisco, 1995, Jossey-Bass Publishers.

Bullaro, John J., and Edginton, Christopher R.: *Commercial Leisure Services: Managing for Profit, Service, and Personal Satisfaction*, New York, 1986, Macmillan Co.

Bullock, Charles C., and Mahon, Michael J.; *Introduction to Recreation Services for People with Disabilities*, Champaign, Ill., 1997, Sagamore Publishing.

Camp, Robert C.: *Benchmarking, the Search for Industry Best Practices That Lead to Superior Performance*, Milwaukee, Wis., 1989, Quality Press.

Christiansen, Monty I.: *Park Planning Handbook*, New York, 1977, John Wiley and Sons.

Cordes, Kathleen A., and Ibrahim, Hilmi M.: *Applications in Recreation and Leisure: For Today and the Future*, St. Louis, 1996, C.V. Mosby.

Craig-Smith, Stephen J., and Fagence, Michael, editors, *Recreation and Tourism as a Catalyst for Urban Waterfront Development*, Westport, Conn., 1995, Praeger.

Crossley, John C., and Jamieson, Lynn M.: *Introduction to Commercial and Entrepreneurial Recreation*, Champaign, Ill., 1993, Sagamore Publishing.

Dougherty, Neil J., and Bonanno, Diane: *Management Principles in Sport and Leisure Services*, Minneapolis, Minn., 1985, Burgess Publishing.

Douglass, Robert W.: *Forest Recreation*, Prospect Heights, Ill., 1993, Waveland Press.

Drucker, Peter F.: *Managing for the Future: The 1990s and Beyond*, New York, 1992, Truman Talley Books/Dutton.

Drucker, Peter F.: *The Executive in Action*, New York, 1996, Harper Business.

Durham, Kenneth, and Kennedy, Bruce: *The New High-Tech Manager: Six Rules for Success in Changing Times*, Boston, 1997, Artech House.

Dustin, Daniel L., McAvoy, Leo H., and Schultz, John H.: *Stewards of Access: Custodians of Choice*, Champaign, Ill., 1995, Sagamore Publishing.

Edginton, Christopher R., Compton, David M., and Hanson, Carole J.: *Recreation and Leisure Programming: A Guide for the Professional*, Dubuque, Iowa, 1989, Wm. C. Brown Publishers.

Edginton, Christopher R., Jordan Debra, DeGraaf, Donald, and Edginton, Susan: *Leisure and Life Satisfaction: Foundational Perspectives*, Dubuque, Iowa, 1995, Brown and Benchmark.

Edginton, Susan R., and Edginton, Christopher R.: *Youth Programs: Promoting Quality Services*, Champaign, Ill., 1994, Sagamore Publishing.

Ford, Phyllis M., and Blanchard, Jim: *Leadership and Administration of Outdoor Pursuits*, State College, Pa., 1993, Venture Publishing.

Godbey, Geoffrey: *Leisure and Leisure Services in the 21st Century*, State College, Pa., 1997, Venture Publishing.

Halaby, William E.: *The New Management, Democracy and Enterprise Are Transforming Organizations*, San Francisco, 1996, Berrett-Koehler Publishers.

Hardy, Cynthia: *Managing Strategic Action*, Thousand Oaks, Calif., 1994, Sage Publications.

Henderson, Karla H.: *Evaluating Leisure Services: Making Enlightened Decisions*, State College, Pa., 1995, Venture Publishing.

Howard, Dennis R., and Crompton, John L.: *Financing, Managing and Marketing Recreation and Park Resources*, Dubuque, Iowa, 1985, Wm. C. Brown Publishers.

Howard, Dennis R., and Crompton, John L.: *Financing Sports*, Morgantown, W.Va., 1995, Fitness Information Technology.

Hultsman, John, Cottrell, Richard, and Hultsman, Wendy: *Planning Parks for People*, State College, Pa., 1998, Venture Publishing.

Jordan, Debra J.: *Leadership in Leisure Services: Making a Difference*, State College, Pa., 1996, Venture Publishing.

Jubenville, Alan, and Twight, Ben W.: *Outdoor Recreation Management: Theory and Application*, State College, Pa., 1993, Venture Publishing.

Kelly, John R.: *Recreation Business*, New York, 1985, John Wiley and Sons.

Kraus, Richard: *Recreation and Leisure in Modern Society*, Sudbury, Mass., 1997, Jones and Bartlett, Publishers.

Kraus, Richard: *Recreation Programming: A Benefits-Driven Approach*, Needham Heights, Mass., 1997, Allyn and Bacon.

Kraus, Richard: *Leisure in a Changing America: Trends and Issues for the 21st Century*, Needham Heights, Mass., 2000, Allyn & Bacon.

Kraus, Richard, and Allen, Lawrence: *Research and Evaluation in Recreation, Parks and Leisure Studies*, Needham Heights, Mass., 1997, Allyn and Bacon.

Liebfried, Kathleen, and McNair, C.J.: *Benchmarking: A Tool for Continuous Improvement*, New York, 1992, Harper Business.

McKenna, Eugene, and Beech, Nic: *The Essence of Human Resource Management*, New York, 1995, Prentice Hall.

McKenney, James, Copeland, Duncan, and Mason, Richard: *Waves of Change: Business Evolution through Information Technology*, Boston, 1995, Harvard Business School Press.

McKinney, William R.: *Introduction to Parks, Recreation and Leisure Administration*, Champaign, Ill., 1998, Sagamore Publishing.

McLean, Daniel, Bannon, Joseph, and Gray, Hardy: *Leisure Resources: Its Comprehensive Planning,* Champaign, Ill., 1999, Sagamore Publishing.

Mobley, Tony, and Toalson, Robert, editors: *Parks and Recreation in the 21st Century,* Arlington, Va., 1992, National Recreation and Park Association.

Murphy, James F., Niepoth, E. William, Jamieson, Lynn M., and Williams, John G.: *Leisure Systems: Critical Concepts and Applications,* Champaign, Ill., 1991, Sagamore Publishing.

O'Sullivan, Ellen, and Spangler, Kathy: *Experience Marketing: Strategies for the New Millennium,* State College, Pa., 1998, Venture Publishing.

Pappas, Alceste T.: *Reeingeering Your Nonprofit Organization: A Guide to Strategic Transformation,* New York, 1996, John Wiley and Sons.

Parkhouse, Bonnie L.; editor: *The Management of Sport: Its Foundation and Application,* St. Louis, 1996, Mosby.

Pasmore, William A.: *Creating Strategic Change: Designing the Flexible, High-Performing Organization,* New York, 1994, John Wiley and Sons.

Proctor, Tony: *The Essence of Management Creativity,* New York, 1995, Prentice Hall.

Ritvo, Roger, Litwin, Anne, and Butler, Lee: *Managing in the Age of Change,* Burr Ridge, Ill., 1995, NTL Institute and Irwin Professional Publishing.

Rossman, J. Robert: *Recreation Programming: Designing Leisure Experiences,* Champaign, Ill., 1995, Sagamore Publishing.

Rubright, Robert, and MacDonald, Dan: *Marketing Health and Human Services,* Rockville, Md., Aspen Systems Corp.

Schleien, Stuart J., Ray, M. Tipton, and Green, Frederick P.: *Community Recreation and People with Disabilities,* Baltimore, Md., 1997, Paul Brookes Publishing.

Smith, Bucklin Associates: *The Complete Guide to Nonprofit Management,* New York, 1994, John Wiley and Sons.

Toalson, Robert F., and Hechenberger, Patricia S.: *Developing Community Support For Parks and Recreation,* Champaign, Ill., 1985, American Academy for Park and Recreation Administration.

Tribe, John: *Economics of Leisure and Tourism,* Oxford, England, 1995, Butterworth-Heinemann, Ltd.

Tyson, Kirk: *Competition in the 21st Century,* Delray Beach, Fla., 1997, St. Lucie Press.

van Lier, Hubert N., and Taylor, Pat D., editors: *New Challenges in Recreation and Tourism Planning,* London, 1993, Elsevier Press.

Virga, Patricia, editor: *The NMA Handbook for Managers,* Englewood Cliffs, N.J., 1987, National Management Association and Prentice-Hall, Inc.

Index